HOOSIERS
and the
AMERICAN STORY

JAMES H. MADISON *and*
LEE ANN SANDWEISS

WITH
STUDENT GUIDE ACTIVITIES
BY
JANE HEDEEN

Hoosiers and the American Story was made possible
by the generous support of Lilly Endowment, Inc.

INDIANA HISTORICAL SOCIETY PRESS | INDIANAPOLIS | 2014

© 2014 Indiana Historical Society Press
Reprinted, 2015

This book is a publication of the
Indiana Historical Society Press
Eugene and Marilyn Glick Indiana History Center
450 West Ohio Street
Indianapolis, Indiana 46202-3269 USA
www.indianahistory.org

Educators, Schools, and Libraries:
Telephone orders 1-317-233-4549
Fax orders 1-317-234-0427
Online orders http://education@indianahistory.org

General Orders:
Telephone orders 1-800-447-1830
Fax orders 1-317-234-0562
Online orders http://shop.indianahistory.org

The paper in this publication meets the minimum requirements of American National Standard
for Information Sciences—Permanence of Paper for Printed Library Materials, ANSI Z39.48-1984

Library of Congress Cataloging in Publication Data

Madison, James H.
Hoosiers and the American story / James H. Madison and Lee Ann Sandweiss ; with student guide activities by Jane Hedeen.
    pages cm
Includes bibliographical references and index.
ISBN 978-0-87195-363-6 (cloth : alk. paper)
1. Indiana—History—Juvenile literature. I. Sandweiss, Lee Ann. II. Hedeen, Jane. III. Title.
F526.3.M34 2014
977.2—dc23
                    2014022825

PHOTO BY ELENA RIPPEL

Students from North Central High School and Carmel High School at the National History Day Indiana Central District Contest on March 15, 2014. National History Day challenges students to do the work of historians by choosing topics related to an annual theme and then researching, analyzing, and presenting their work to judges. Projects take the form of exhibits, documentaries, websites, papers, and performances. Participating students overwhelmingly report a preference for NHD over traditional classroom activities because it improves their research skills and strengthens their interest in history. **Opposite:** Noah Sandweiss wrote this poem for an assignment in his fourth grade social studies class in Bloomington, Indiana, in 2006. Fourth graders throughout Indiana study the state's early history and work on projects, such as this poem.

INDIANA

by Noah Sandweiss, grade 4, 2006

I am Indiana.
I wonder how my people will act in the future.
I hear gunshots.
I want America to be peaceful.
I am the nineteenth state.

I pretend I am myself two hundred years ago.
I feel my limestone will be dug out.
I touch my neighbor Illinois' soft cornfields.
I worry my nature will be gone.
I cry for the natives who were moved west.
I am in the Midwest.

I understand I'm not how I used to be.
I say I'm proud to be the Crossroads of America.
I dream of governors in the future.
I try to remember La Salle.
I hope the next president will be from me.
I am a state with ninety-two counties.

CONTENTS

Some Places to Discover Indiana History

Discover more places to visit at http://www.indianahistory.org.

FOREWORD
The Indiana Historical Society and Indiana's Bicentennial

The bicentennial of Indiana statehood in 2016 presents a golden opportunity to engage Hoosiers in our collective past. The Indiana Historical Society—the state's oldest heritage organization, founded in 1830—launched a wide range of exciting bicentennial initiatives to make the history of Indiana personal and real. The efforts include the Indiana Bicentennial Train, bringing a traveling exhibit called "The Next Indiana" to sixteen communities around the state from 2013 through 2016. Exhibits in the IHS headquarters at the Eugene and Marilyn Glick Indiana History Center featuring interactive guest experiences focus on some of the key narratives of state history, such as the formation of the state's 1816 constitution in Corydon, the founding of Eli Lilly and Company, the national impact of Ball Brothers canning jars during the Great Depression and World War II, the L. S. Ayres Company as a cauldron of innovation, and the art and artistry of Hoosier painter T. C. Steele.

The Indiana Historical Society will also make available to schools and teachers a new technological application of our Destination Indiana time travel gallery. Through Destination Indiana, teachers and students can choose the topic, time, or place they would like to explore and journey to their destinations on their computers, tablets, or smart phones. Students can also create their own journeys to submit to the growing database of "places" to visit.

The IHS Press is publishing a number of new volumes that explore our state's history, covering many key topics such as a history of Indiana basketball and poignant biographies of two hundred Hoosiers—men and women who greatly affected the state—in a book skillfully edited by Linda C. Gugin and James E. St. Clair. Of all the books the Indiana Historical Society is introducing, this book, *Hoosiers and the American Story* by James H. Madison and Lee Ann Sandweiss may have the biggest impact.

Hoosiers and the American Story will have many applications but has been created to be used in classrooms in grades 8 through 12 as a supplement to American history textbooks. It provides Indiana examples for the great sweeping topics of American history from the European colonization and battle for empires, westward expansion, the Civil War, industrialization, immigration, agricultural development, age of the automobile, and the fight for equal rights.

That American history happened in their own backyards is a good thing for young Hoosiers to know as they take their place as citizens who must be engaged in the political process and make wise decisions now that will affect their future. As they grapple for solutions to today's challenges, understanding the historical background to enduring issues will play a vital part in choosing the best course. The Indiana Historical Society believes that understanding our connections to the past develops an affinity for place that organically generates citizen engagement.

Beyond the initial target audiences, *Hoosiers and the American Story* will also appeal to adults who want a well-written, highly insightful overview of Indiana, which is beautifully illustrated by historical photographs, art, maps, and documents from the Indiana Historical Society's collections and other important repositories of state, local, and national history. The use and value of this book should serve well beyond the last fireworks of the 2016 Bicentennial. For this, we thank its authors, Lilly Endowment, Inc., and the Care Institute Group, Inc., for enabling us to do our very best work in the service of the people of Indiana.

Best wishes,

John A. Herbst
President and CEO
Indiana Historical Society
July 2014

PREFACE
How to Get the Most from This Book

The stories in this book are written to stimulate conversation and debate. Each chapter begins with an overview that highlights main themes in American history and points to the Indiana stories that follow. The four stories in each chapter are case studies. Some are about individuals who have shaped our state in interesting ways: Tecumseh, William Conner, Albion Fellows Bacon, Eli Lilly, Madam C. J. Walker, Oscar Robertson, and others.

Many of the case studies include stories of everyday people and their experiences: African American pioneers before the Civil War, the soldiers of the Iron Brigade who stood their ground at the Battle of Gettysburg, the immigrants who built churches, stores, and neighborhoods in South Bend and Jasper, the factory workers who made steel in Gary and automobile parts in Anderson and Marion, the city people who moved to new suburbs such as Carmel and Newburgh, and those high school kids who played basketball, from Milan to Muncie.

Not all the stories are happy ones. Indiana's Ku Klux Klan of the 1920s, for example, raises troubling questions that cannot be swept under the rug. The Klan is just one case among many that has divided Hoosiers over issues of race, ethnicity, religion, and patriotism. Troubling, too, are those Hoosier voices that insisted that Native Americans should be removed or that women should not have the right to vote or that immigrants could not be true Americans.

Moving beyond This Book in the Twenty-First Century

Two hundred years is a long time. There is not nearly enough room in these pages to tell all of Indiana's stories, nor is this meant to be a reference book. The end of each chapter lists other sources, including books, primary materials, articles, and websites. The Indiana Historical Society's website provides much more information connected to this book at http://www.indianahistory.org. The basic starting point for further reading is James H. Madison's, *Hoosiers: A New History of Indiana*, published in 2014 by Indiana University Press and Indiana Historical Society Press.

Each reader will bring a different mindset to these stories. That is why the activities sections at the end of each chapter are so important. They ask readers to think more deeply, urging them toward the joy of understanding the past and connecting it to our present.

To learn even more from this book, look at the history around you. Walk around your county courthouse square, such as the one in Terre Haute or Shelbyville; visit a historic home, such as Benjamin Harrison's in Indianapolis or James Lanier's in Madison; canoe down a stream, such as Sugar Creek, as Native Americans did less than two hundred years ago; spend time at a local historical society, such as the History Center in Fort Wayne; talk to an older person; read an old newspaper; research your family's history; enter the state's History Day competition. Experiences such as these take you to places where history comes alive and *you* become the historian.

ACKNOWLEDGMENTS
Our Thanks

Hoosiers and the American Story is the work of many hands. The co-authors, James H. Madison and Lee Ann Sandweiss, worked together to research and write each chapter. Nearly every Monday morning they met at a Bloomington coffee shop to discuss their week's writing. Those conversations brought them the joy of discovering appealing ways to tell some of Indiana's most significant stories. Sandweiss is grateful to the following individuals who made it possible for her to meet the book's chapter deadlines: her husband Professor Eric Sandweiss, her sons Ethan and Noah Sandweiss, Nessie Sandweiss, Christina Snyder, Betsi Grabe, Rebecca Spang, David Polly, Nancy Hiller, and Jim Madison. Madison wishes to add his thanks to the many students and teachers who have helped him learn about Indiana history.

Chapters were sent to the Indiana Historical Society (IHS) Press where managing editor M. Teresa Baer led the IHS team, consisting of education professionals, historians, editors, and graduate student interns. Jane Hedeen, former IHS education program coordinator, created the activities sections of each chapter, which comprise the student guide portion of the book. Outside reviewers of each chapter included John Herbst, IHS president and CEO; William Bartelt, IHS trustee, author, and former high school teacher; Kyle McKoy, vice president, IHS Education and Exhibits; Steve Cox, vice president, IHS Press; and Ray Boomhower, senior editor, IHS Press. Graduate student interns, Elena Rippel and Callie McCune, from Indiana University, Indianapolis, gathered images, wrote captions, and checked facts and sources. Baer and contract editor Chelsea Sutton pulled together all changes from the review team and edited the book. Sutton also created the glossary. Paula Corpuz, retired director of the IHS Press, created the index for the book.

Stacy Simmer, IHS's senior graphic designer, created the beautiful design for the book. Becky Schlomann, IHS bicentennial programs coordinator; Matthew Durrett, coordinator, educational outreach and National History Day in Indiana; and the IHS Education and Community Engagement (ECE) Department, directed by Cynthia Capers, created the web pages that accompany this book at http://www.indianahistory.org.

John Herbst conceived the idea for the book. It was his dream to create a supplemental textbook about Indiana history and civics for the secondary level, and he made it a priority for IHS to create the book, the web pages that accompany it, and the teachers' workshops as a bicentennial project for the IHS.

Contributing from the planning stage were several of Indiana's expert high school social studies teachers: Jon Carl, F. J. Reitz High School, Evansville; Susan Tomlinson, Franklin Central High School, Indianapolis; David Wheeler, North Central High School, Indianapolis; and Troy Guthrie, Morristown Middle School/High School. They and a committee including Herbst, the authors, Baer, and IHS's ECE Department determined the overall content and structure of the book. Under this committee's guidance, the book became useful for eighth grade social studies classes and fourth grade social studies teachers as well as the target audience—high school students.

Far from least, the entire team for *Hoosiers and the American Story* gratefully acknowledges the generosity of the Lilly Endowment for financial support in creating and printing this book, creating the web pages, and hosting the teacher workshops to show teachers how to use this book to fulfill state and federal guidelines. The philanthropy of the Lilly Endowment, Inc., is among the best of Indiana's traditions.

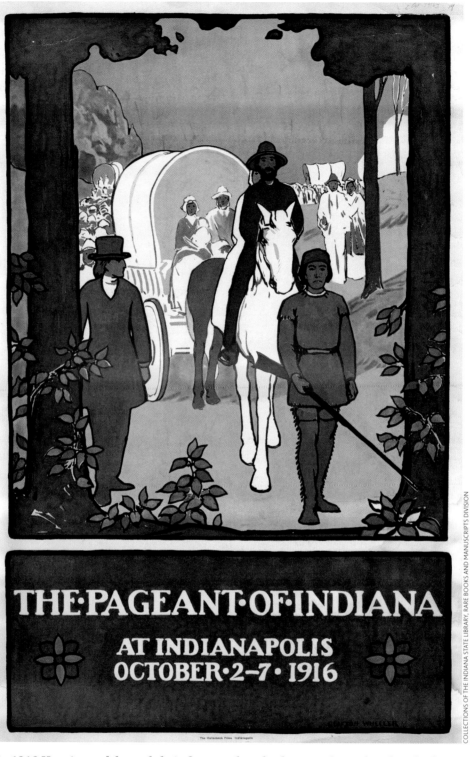

THE·PAGEANT·OF·INDIANA

AT INDIANAPOLIS
OCTOBER·2–7·1916

In 1916 Hoosiers celebrated their first one hundred years of statehood with plays, parades, and other events. This poster appeared for the statewide "Pageant of Indiana," a performance of scenes from Indiana history. The emphasis was on pioneers during the centennial celebration. Over the following century ideas about the Hoosier experience grew to include many new subjects and perspectives. *Hoosiers and the American Story* shares these new ideas in celebration of Indiana's bicentennial.

INTRODUCTION
Hoosier Americans

Indiana is a world all unto itself.

— *Theodore Dreiser,* A Hoosier Holiday *(1916)*

Like meeting a new person, a book needs an introduction. After looking at the pretty cover, why would you want to spend more time with this book? The simplest answer is that in these pages are fascinating stories about Americans who call themselves Hoosiers. Not only have Hoosiers been around for two centuries, their experiences connect deeply to our own present and future.

Indiana is a special place. It may not be a world unto itself, as writer Theodore Dreiser claimed a century ago. But even in our globalized and homogenized twenty-first century, the state and its people claim distinction when they call themselves Hoosiers.

What Is a Hoosier?

Many people have proposed theories to the question, "What is a Hoosier?" James Whitcomb Riley, the famous Hoosier poet, told the story of a brawl in a pioneer tavern that included eye gouging, hair pulling, and biting. Afterward, a bystander reached down to the sawdust-covered floor and picked up a mangled piece of flesh. "Whose ear?" he supposedly called out.

Riley doubtless got a laugh from his listeners. The truth is, no one really knows what the word means.

The authors of this book rather like it that way—the mystery surrounding one of the most well-known nicknames for the people of a state in the nation.

The word "Hoosier" has been in common usage for a long time. In 1835 Sarah Harvey, a new settler in Richmond, wrote to family members in Pennsylvania explaining, "Old settlers in Indiana are called 'Hooshers' and the cabins they first live in 'Hooshers' nests.'" Attesting to her statement at the time was a poem circulating widely in print titled "The Hoosher's Nest."

Hoosiers retained the nickname into the twenty-first century, when state records showed 2,600 businesses using it in their title. It's a brand Hoosiers are proud to have.

Hoosiers and Americans

Hoosiers are Americans, of course, but not quite like people in New York, California, or Texas. We have our own history and our own stories.

This book places Hoosiers at the center of the American story. High school textbooks often short-change Indiana. For example, when American history textbooks discuss canal building in the 1830s, they generally feature New York's Erie Canal. This book

The Hoosier Store was a general merchandise store in downtown Richmond, Indiana. By the time this photo was taken, ca. 1855, the term "Hoosier" was already well-known.

focuses on Indiana's canals. When textbooks explore World War II they tell about home fronts in California or Michigan. This book presents stories of Hoosiers in wartime factories in Gary, Evansville, and Indianapolis.

The stories in this book have themes similar to those in American history textbooks. They spotlight, for example, the struggles for democracy—such as the fight against slavery or the women's suffrage movement—but Indiana's stories have twists and details that are distinctively Hoosier .

Hoosiers built their own traditions over two centuries. Often they have wanted to keep those traditions and to change slowly. As this book shows, they tended to value individual freedom and to prefer small government.

Two Centuries of Change

Despite the Hoosiers' love of tradition, the stories in this book are about change. Change has always been the order of the day. Nothing has ever stayed the same, not even basketball. For instance, a century ago no one imagined that a girl could shoot a jump shot—or a boy for that matter.

In order to understand how the state has changed, we need to know those generations before our own—to realize that Abraham Lincoln with less than a year of formal schooling worked hard to learn reading and math skills in pioneer Indiana; to discover the reasons there are fewer good jobs in Indiana's factories today than fifty years ago; to know why corn grown on Indiana's farms is not like the corn grown by Native Americans or pioneers. We need to learn where we came from because we are all connected to that history, and understanding our history will help us take wiser and more productive steps into the future.

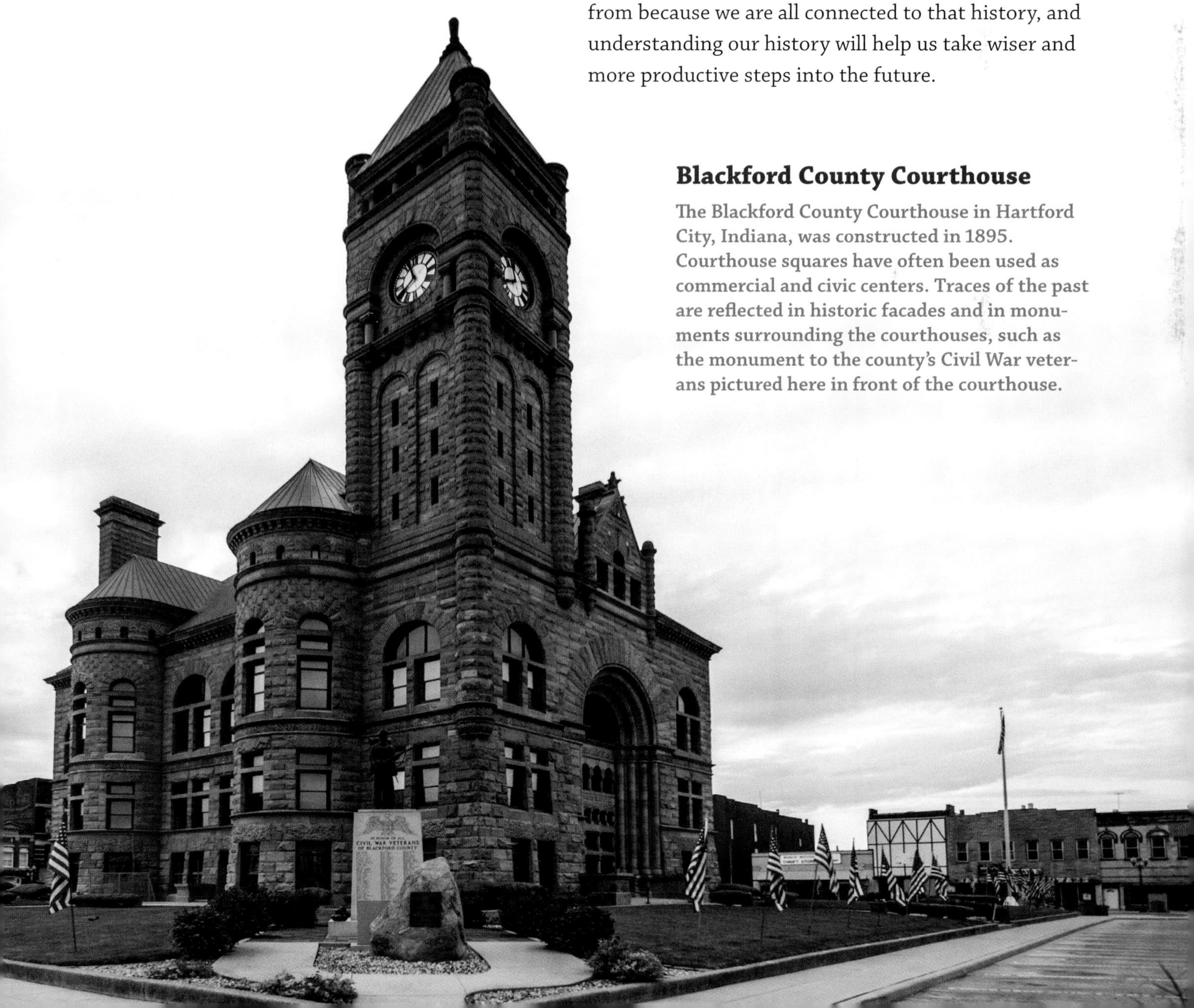

Blackford County Courthouse

The Blackford County Courthouse in Hartford City, Indiana, was constructed in 1895. Courthouse squares have often been used as commercial and civic centers. Traces of the past are reflected in historic facades and in monuments surrounding the courthouses, such as the monument to the county's Civil War veterans pictured here in front of the courthouse.

Indiana Wilderness

Landscapes such as this limestone cliff in western Indiana would have been familiar to the original inhabitants of Indiana—the Indians and the prehistoric people before them. Many such cliffs can be seen today in Turkey Run State Park in Parke County, Indiana.

1

Native Americans in American History

"These knives will be more useful to you in killing Beavers and in cutting your meat than are the pieces of stone that you use."

— Claude Charles Le Roy, in first record of trade between the Miami People and French explorer Nicolas Perrot, 1665–66

Indiana's First Humans

Scientists believe that the first humans to settle in North America probably migrated across a land bridge from the area currently called Siberia along the Bering Strait to the land known today as Alaska. This migration occurred near the end of the Ice Age, between 30,000 and 15,000 years ago. Generations later, some descendants of these first North American immigrants settled in what became Indiana, a land that provided abundant animal life, including mastodons, lush forests, and rivers teeming with fish. Eventually the early people grew crops. The rich soil and long, hot summers were ideal for growing corn, which became a staple of their diet. Even today, vast cornfields checker the Indiana landscape.

Like the first white settlers in Indiana who followed centuries later, the early people were *river-centric*—they lived and traveled along rivers. The Wabash River was one of the most important rivers to these early inhabitants. The Wabash begins in western Ohio and flows west and southwest through Indiana. As the native peoples paddled their canoes from the south to the northeast on the Wabash toward Lake Erie, they had to stop and carry their canoes approximately

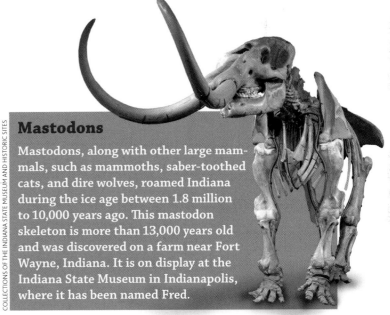

COLLECTIONS OF THE INDIANA STATE MUSEUM AND HISTORIC SITES

Mastodons

Mastodons, along with other large mammals, such as mammoths, saber-toothed cats, and dire wolves, roamed Indiana during the ice age between 1.8 million to 10,000 years ago. This mastodon skeleton is more than 13,000 years old and was discovered on a farm near Fort Wayne, Indiana. It is on display at the Indiana State Museum in Indianapolis, where it has been named Fred.

nine miles over swampland in order to connect with the Saint Mary's River, which connected to the Maumee River. The Maumee, which begins in present-day Fort Wayne, flows east/northeast into Lake Erie. The nine-mile stretch between the Wabash and the Saint Mary's was known as the Wabash–Maumee Portage, a portage being a land passage connecting two bodies of water. This portage became one of the most important locations in early Indiana. It was here that the largest Miami Indian village of Kekionga was located, a site that Americans would capture and rename Fort Wayne. The Wabash also carried Native Americans south to

Physiographic Map of Indiana

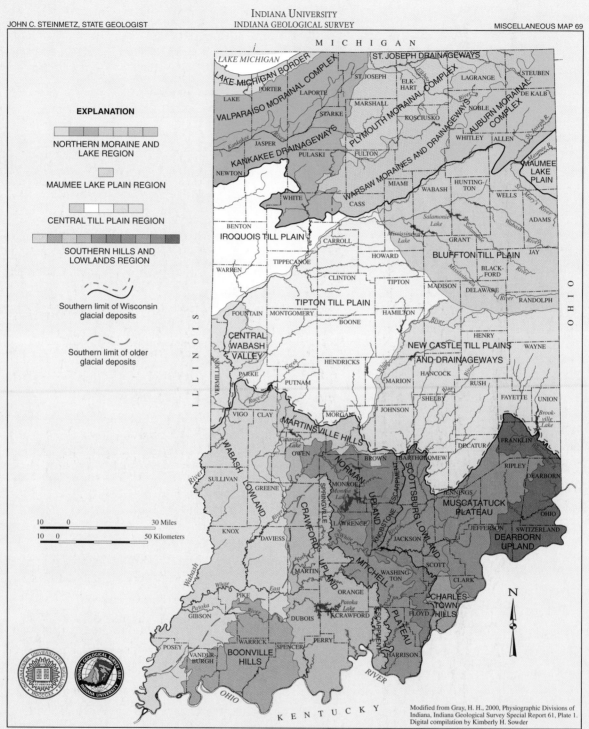

EXPLANATION

NORTHERN MORAINE AND LAKE REGION

MAUMEE LAKE PLAIN REGION

CENTRAL TILL PLAIN REGION

SOUTHERN HILLS AND LOWLANDS REGION

Southern limit of Wisconsin glacial deposits

Southern limit of older glacial deposits

Modified from Gray, H. H., 2000, Physiographic Divisions of Indiana, Indiana Geological Survey Special Report 61, Plate 1. Digital compilation by Kimberly H. Sowder

MAP OF INDIANA SHOWING PHYSIOGRAPHIC DIVISIONS
By Henry H. Gray
2001

Indiana's physical geography is a testament to the legacy of glaciers, which eroded and shaped the land during the ice age. The blue areas of the map indicate a till plain, which is characterized by a flat or gently rolling landscape that was flattened as glaciers melted. This region is well-suited for agriculture because glacial sediment enhanced the soil. The green areas of the map illustrate that some of the melting ice sheets created lakes and also left behind masses of rocks and sediments in ridge-like formations, called moraines, at the edges of the glacial lakes. The last glacier did not reach the bottom third of Indiana, leaving the southern region's steep hills and valleys intact.

the Ohio River, which in turn connected to the Mississippi River and ran all the way to the Gulf of Mexico. In northwest Indiana another important river, the Saint Joseph, provided access to Lake Michigan through land that is now in southwestern Michigan.

Using this early transportation network, early inhabitants established settlements along the river banks. One of the largest settlements was Angel Mounds on the Ohio River near present-day Evansville. Angel Mounds consisted of a village and several large mounds used for ceremonial purposes, surrounded by a log stockade fence. In the twentieth century archaeologists began to study pottery, tools, and other artifacts found at the site.

Another important early settlement that also featured mounds was on the White River near present-day Anderson. Today, visitors to Mounds State Park can see ten prehistoric earthworks constructed between 200 BC and 200 AD by two distinct cultures of people, named the Adena and Hopewell by modern-day archaeologists. Many of the region's mounds were destroyed when the land was cleared for agriculture. The mounds in today's park were preserved by the Bronnenberg family, who settled the land in the 1800s. The restored Bronnenberg house is in the park and open to visitors.

The Europeans Arrive

Although the Spanish had been exploring the North American continent in the early 1500s, it was nearly two hundred years later that the first Europeans arrived in what would become Indiana. These Europeans were French. Some were Catholic missionaries, hoping to convert the Indians to Christianity, but most of the French were interested in trading with the Indians. Among the first Frenchmen in Indiana was René-Robert Cavelier de La Salle, who entered Indiana in 1679 on the Saint Joseph River near present-day South Bend. During the ensuing century, Indians trapped animals and gathered furs to exchange with French traders for European-made metal axes, hoes, guns, glass beads, and cloth. The French sent large quantities of furs across the Atlantic Ocean to European customers. Wabash Valley beaver and fox furs became the height of fashion on the streets of Paris.

The Indians, too, benefited from this trade. Native Americans replaced their stone, bone, or wood tools for more durable ones made of metal; they added cloth to the materials, such as leather and fur, that they used for clothing; they also traded for metal pots to replace their less durable clay or bark containers. But there were huge costs to trading with the French. The Indians were unaccustomed to the alcohol Europeans introduced, so drunkenness became a problem. Diseases such as smallpox and measles were also unintended consequences of the trade. These diseases proved deadly to the Indians who had not before experienced them and so had not acquired the immunities to recover from them.

The French and Indian cultures were different, but the two peoples found ways to live together to their mutual advantage. Because the French were in the territory for trade and not to colonize Indian land, there were far fewer French than Indians. The French had little choice but to negotiate and live peacefully among the Indians. Intermarriage among the French male traders and Indian women became quite common. The offspring of these marriages were called *métis*, meaning

Angel Mounds

Near present-day Evansville, Indiana, is the site of one of the largest settlements of prehistoric Indians, who lived in Indiana from approximately 1000 to 1450 AD. Archaeologists have been excavating Angel Mounds since 1939, and have found a multitude of artifacts, including stone tools, pottery, and a carved stone figurine.

mixed blood. The *métis* became important because they had a foot in both cultures and spoke both the French and Indian languages. Not surprising, then, some *métis* negotiated trade agreements and became important leaders in the region.

In order to protect their trade interests from other Europeans and to establish control of the Wabash River, the French built three forts: Fort Miami (at Kekionga, present-day Fort Wayne), Fort Ouiatanon (near present-day Lafayette), and Fort Vincennes (on the Wabash River in southern Indiana). Vincennes would become the most important French settlement. However, while the French were building their empire in the Great Lakes region, the British were settling the East Coast. By the mid-1700s, British colonials were moving west, crossing the Appalachian Mountains, and encroaching on land claimed by the Indians and their French allies. Clashes erupted. Rather than seeing the French forts as intimidating defense positions, the British redcoats saw them as prizes to be taken.

The French and Indian War, also called the Seven Years' War, began in 1754. Ultimately, the British and their colonial allies (including a youthful George Washington) defeated the French and their Indian allies. When the Treaty of Paris was signed in 1763, all lands east of the Mississippi River, including the Wabash Valley, became part of the British Empire. The French left and so did the relatively harmonious relationship the Indians had enjoyed with the white man for more than one hundred years.

The New Americans and the Native Americans

The Indians soon realized that the British were less interested in the fur trade and more interested in acquiring land. With the French out of the way, three groups struggled for control: Native Americans, British, and American colonists. After the American Revolution, the fledgling United States was intent on expanding its boundaries. In order for that to happen, the Indians had to relinquish their land, and they refused to do so willingly. A series of military battles between the United States government and the Indians ensued; hostilities continued into the nineteenth century. The policies of the new U.S. government would prove increasingly harmful to tribes of the Northwest Territory, the land north of the Ohio River, east of the Mississippi, and west of the former British colonies, which included the land that would become Indiana. As a result, by the end of the first decade of the 1800s, Indians were no longer the majority population in Indiana, "the Land of the Indians."

1.1

Major Native American Groups in Indiana, 1700s–1830s

"This place is situated on the edge of a great plain, at the extremity of which on the western side is a village of Miamis, Mascontens and Oiatinon gathered together."

— *Father Louis Hennepin, on LaSalle's expedition, 1679*

Centuries before statehood, Indiana was the "Crossroads of America," as many tribes of native people passed through the land to destinations elsewhere. However, in the 1600s tribes living in the area were driven north and west by Iroquois raiding parties from the East. When it was safe once more, after one hundred years of warfare, some Indian groups moved south and east into lands that would become Indiana. The southern shores of Lake Michigan, the Ohio River, and the area around the Wabash–Maumee Portage, where the Maumee, Saint Mary's, and other rivers came together, were the busiest regions. Just as their ancestors, native people in Indiana at this time lived along rivers. They were also *preliterate*; that is, although they had distinct and complex cultures, they did not record their customs or history in their own languages. Most of what we know about them is from archaeological evidence and early accounts written by European traders and settlers. As a result, historians are aware of the likelihood of cultural bias, or interpretations from only one perspective—the American perspective—in written accounts. Therefore, to better understand early Indiana history, ask yourself as you read if the information is presented from an Indian or American point of view.

The Miami and Potawatomi

In the seventeenth and early eighteenth centuries, most of the inhabitants of the North American continent were Indians. During this time, many Potawatomi and Miami Indians moved into the territory that would become Indiana, becoming its most prominent

residents. Other tribes also migrated into the area, including the Shawnee and Kickapoo; and some natives passed through for only short periods, such as the Delaware. The Potawatomi concentrated north of the Wabash River and along Lake Michigan. The Wea band of the Miami located their villages on the banks of the middle Wabash, between the Tippecanoe and Vermilion Rivers, near what would become Lafayette. A band of Miami that had been living in what would become Detroit, Michigan, migrated to the portage between the Maumee and Wabash Rivers. This location, named Kekionga, is where the Americans later built Fort Wayne. Kekionga was the most important Miami village, a center for trade with the French and English

The Indians in Indiana

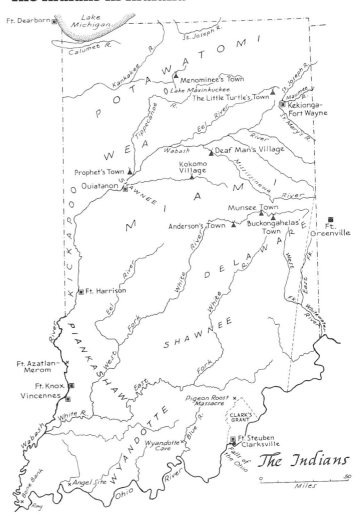

DWIGHT W. HOOVER, *A PICTORIAL HISTORY OF INDIANA* (BLOOMINGTON: INDIANA UNIVERSITY PRESS, 1980), 44.

This map of "The Indians in Indiana," drawn by Clark Ray, shows the approximate location of Native American tribes and villages at the beginning of Indiana's territorial period, ca. 1800.

and the meeting ground for the Miami tribal council. This Miami base would become the center for a combination of northwest tribes, often called the Miami Confederacy. Eventually it would also be the objective of several American military expeditions.

Life in Rhythm with the Seasons

The Miami and Potawatomi lived in sync with the seasons. There were times of planting, harvest, abundance, and scarcity. The tribes grew many crops, including melons, squash, pumpkins, beans, and corn. Corn, or maize, was a staple of their diet as well as an item of reverence used in ceremonies. Both groups traded corn to the French and other Native Americans. They also gathered berries, nuts, and roots, and collected maple syrup. They fished the streams and lakes and hunted deer, bison, bear, and small game.

Work was divided along gender lines. Men hunted, trapped, and traded, while women planted and tended crops, cooked, made clothing, and cared for the children. Boys and girls quickly learned their roles through daily chores and play. Boys learned the role of a warrior. Some Miami men, however, dressed as women and took on female roles—a cultural behavior that astonished French observers.

Native men and women decorated their bodies with ornaments and tattoos. Their religions included elaborate rituals, belief in life after death, and a world of good and evil, along with a stoic acceptance of hardship. The tribes had many social activities. Sports were popular, including lacrosse, which the Potawatomi played with great skill. Harvest festivals and other celebrations included dance and music.

The Miami and Potawatomi lived in villages of houses, called wigwams. Wigwams were built of poles covered with bark or mats woven from cattail. Individuals lived with their extended families, several generations forming a single unit. Each of these units, a group of related nuclear families, formed a clan.

When the French arrived they found it difficult to determine which leader in a tribe had the most authority, because the authority of a chief depended more on personal influence than on specific position. The Potawatomi's power structure was relatively relaxed.

For example, in times of war a prominent chief often led several villages, but seldom could one chief speak for all Potawatomi. By contrast, the Miami had a fairly structured leadership system, which included a principal chief and a grand council of village, band, and clan chiefs who met at Kekionga.

The Delaware and Shawnee Tribes

Also significant were the Delaware and Shawnee Indians, who arrived in Indiana after the Miami and Potawatomi. The Delaware came from northwest Pennsylvania and what would become southeastern Ohio and settled in the central part of the Indiana Territory, along the White River, by 1810. They had been displaced in Ohio by an increasing number of white colonists who were moving west. This was a pattern that would be repeated over and over. The Delaware had abducted Frances Slocum, a five-year-old white girl in 1778 in Pennsylvania and then brought her to Indiana. Slocum is an important figure and will be discussed later in this chapter.

Whereas the Delaware were being pushed west by colonists, the Shawnee, like the Miami, were returning to lands in Indiana by 1760. They had built villages along the Ohio River Valley in the southern part of what would be Ohio, and they began establishing villages in southern Indiana as well. In 1808 two Shawnee brothers, Tecumseh and Tenskwatawa, also known as the Prophet, founded Prophetstown, near the junction of the Tippecanoe and

Chief Little Turtle

Miami war chief Little Turtle spoke out against American expansion into Native American lands. But after the Indians were defeated at Fallen Timbers, Little Turtle submitted to American demands and promoted a strategy of cooperation between Indians and Americans.

Potawatomi Camp Scene

In August 1837 artist George Winter visited an encampment of Potawatomi by Crooked Creek, eleven miles west of Logansport, Indiana. While there, he drew two sketches of his observations that this painting is based on. However, the sketches include a tent (since it was a camp), whereas the painting features a pole house such as the ones Potawatomi and Miami Indians built in their villages at that time.

Wabash Rivers. Like Frances Slocum, the Shawnee brothers were important figures in history, and their stories will be explored later in this chapter.

Similar to the Miami and Potawatomi, the Delaware and Shawnee grew crops and hunted and gathered food. They lived in large, bark, multi-family summer dwellings in the summer, and in single-family dome wigwams in the winter.

Indian Resistance to American Expansion

Before the French lost the French and Indian War, also known as the Seven Years' War, to the British and their colonists in 1763, North American Indians had lived side-by-side and traded with the French on relatively peaceful terms. They had no reason to expect life to be dramatically different under the British. Big changes were coming, however. Within twenty years, the lands east of the Mississippi River, wrested from the French by the British, would be taken from the British by rebellious American colonists in the American Revolution. American settlers wanted free or cheap land to farm and to build towns and roads, connecting the newly won "West" to the East, where the original colonies were now American states.

The Indians did not share the British–American concept of land ownership. As far as they were concerned, the land was still theirs to hunt and farm. Therefore, they did not acknowledge that the Northwest Territory, in which Indiana's lands resided, became part of the new nation after the American Revolution. Because they were not part of its negotiation, the Indians ignored the Treaty of 1783, which established borders for the new country. The Indians and Americans were immediately at cross-purposes.

The Miami, Potawatomi, Delaware, Shawnee, and other natives soon learned that the Americans' intentions were different than those of the French. The Americans or "long knives," as the Indians called them because of the bayonets at the end of their rifles, were not interested in compromise. They wanted land and to impose an American way of life in the land they claimed. Years of bloody conflict ensued. Both sides won and lost significant battles. In 1790 and 1791, Miami war chief Little Turtle led a confederation of natives, including Miami and Shawnee, in victorious battles against American forces in Ohio country. The latter battle, known as Saint Clair's Defeat, was one of the worst defeats ever sustained by the U.S. military in conflicts with Native Americans.

In 1794 American General Anthony Wayne defeated the Miami in a bloody and decisive battle. Fought in a grove of fallen trees near the Maumee River, the Battle of Fallen Timbers and the resulting Treaty of Greenville marked the turning point in favor of the Americans. The treaty stipulated that the Indians sign over to the United States a vast territory that included two-thirds of Ohio, a narrow strip of southeastern

Indiana, the Wabash–Maumee Portage, and the villages of Ouiatanon and Vincennes. In return for these lands, the United States presented the Indians with goods valued at $20,000 and promised annual payments ranging from $500 to $1,000 to the various tribes. The system of providing goods and money to the tribes was intended to make the Indians dependent on the Americans in order to reduce tribal power. The strategy was largely effective. Chief Little Turtle stated that the treaty would "insure the permanent happiness of the Indians, and their Father, the Americans." Little Turtle was realistic as well as optimistic. He knew that the Americans were calling the shots now, but he believed that if the Indians stopped fighting with them, conditions for his people would gradually improve. He resigned himself to adopt American ways and encouraged his people to do the same.

However, numerous Native Americans did not accept the Americans' terms or way of life. One historian described the decade following the Treaty of Greenville as "simply disastrous for the Indians on the Wabash." Smallpox and flu epidemics as well as increasing use of alcohol took their toll. The Americans held the real power, and the Indians grew increasingly dependent on a people who in reality did very little for them and cared for them even less. All aspects of Indian culture suffered—from hunting to religious rituals.

Out of this upheaval, in which the Native Americans experienced demoralizing military defeat and the ravages of disease and alcohol, a powerful Shawnee spiritual leader, Tenskwatawa, or the Prophet, arose. Together with his warrior brother, Tecumseh, who had fought alongside Little Turtle, they spearheaded a formidable challenge to the Americans governing Indiana.

1.2

The Prophet and Tecumseh

The Prophet (1775–1836)

"You must not dress like the White Man or wear hats like them. . . . When you are clothed, it must be in skins or leather of your own Dressing."

— *Tenskwatawa, 1805*

Early life

The Shawnee born Lalawethika was an unlikely leader. As a boy with heroic older brothers, Lalawethika stood out because he failed at almost everything he attempted. He even wounded his right eye with his own arrow. Although he fought at the Battle of Fallen Timbers, he was nowhere near as brave as his brother, the great warrior Tecumseh. Lalawethika turned to alcohol as a young man, which only increased his problems and diminished his self-esteem.

When he was in his late twenties, Lalawethika decided to become a medicine man and apprenticed himself to a tribal healer who later died. When his tribe was stricken with a serious disease, Lalawethika tried everything he had learned to save his people, but much of his medicine did not work. Depressed and humiliated, Lalawethika drank so much alcohol that he lost consciousness. His tribe believed him to be dead. However, while his body was being prepared for burial, Lalawethika woke up and told how he had taken a journey to the spirit world where he had a powerful vision. He said the vision showed two worlds—one was a world of blessings for those who lived as the Master of Life intended, and the other was a world of pain and suffering for those who sinned and defied the old ways. From that day forth, Lalawethika's lips did

Tenskwatawa, the Prophet

The Prophet's portrait was painted by James Otto Lewis for Governor Lewis Cass of the Michigan Territory in 1832. Lewis later went on to paint portraits of several prominent Indian chiefs, tribal meetings, and landscapes, which were published in *The Aboriginal Port Folio* in Philadelphia, Pennsylvania, ca. 1836.

not touch alcohol. He changed his name to Tenskwatawa, which means "Open Door," and vowed to lead his people to the land of many blessings by reclaiming the old traditions.

The Prophet's Teachings

Tenskwatawa, commonly known as the Prophet, began his crusade in the summer of 1805 and soon gained a following as he told and retold the story of his vision. Although Tenskwatawa would always have

Prophetstown

In 1808 Tenskwatawa (the Prophet) and Tecumseh founded a village along the Tippecanoe River just north of present-day Lafayette, Indiana. Named Prophetstown after the visionary Shawnee leader, the settlement was a base for the Prophet's religious movement, which attracted Indians who were resisting American settlement. As Prophetstown was open to followers from all tribal backgrounds, an estimated fourteen tribes were represented in its confederation. However, most came from the Shawnee, Delaware, and Potawatomi tribes. The Indian town existed only four years before it was burned down following the Battle of Tippecanoe in 1811. Prophetstown State Park, pictured here, is located near the confluence of the Wabash and Tippecanoe Rivers, approximately a mile from where the battle occurred. The structure for a recreated wigwam appears in the foreground.

skeptics, an incident the following summer sealed his reputation as a prophet. He predicted an eclipse. When the eclipse occurred, blocking out the sunlight, his followers believed he had made the sun go black. This action quickly removed many natives' doubts and the Prophet's following grew.

Living on the banks of White River, the Prophet sparked a spiritual revival among his followers. His new religion transcended traditional rivalries and united Indians from many tribes and villages. He convinced many Shawnee, Miami, and Delaware to turn from the bad habits of the white man and return to Indian traditions. He preached abstention from alcohol, no marriages between Indians and whites, and a return to traditional gender roles with women as farmers and men as hunters and warriors.

The Prophet taught that the Americans were evil, untrustworthy, and the source of hardship for the Indians. He scorned American leaders such as President Thomas Jefferson and William Henry Harrison, governor of the Indiana Territory. He also rejected "wicked chiefs," such as Little Turtle, who the Prophet thought had sold out to the Americans. He was suspicious of Indians of mixed blood who he perceived as playing both sides of the fence.

Some of the Prophet's teachings were extreme, and he dealt brutally with those who fell into his disfavor. He warned his followers to beware of those who practiced witchcraft. Anyone closely associated with the Americans or opposed to the Prophet's teachings was suspected of witchcraft and targeted for elimination. Indians who had converted to Christianity were frequently accused. Joshua, a Moravian Christian Indian, was one such victim. Joshua had held onto his Christian faith despite his daughters having been murdered in a massacre. In 1806 he was living in a Moravian village in eastern Indiana when he was seized by some of the Prophet's followers. The Prophet himself arrived at the village and declared Joshua guilty. Joshua was tomahawked twice before being burned at the stake.

Another victim of the Prophet's witch hunts was an elderly Wyandot chief called Leatherlips. He was accused of being a witch because he did not support the Prophet and was a friend of the Americans. In June 1810 the Prophet sent six warriors to execute the old man. Leatherlips was charged with causing sickness among members of his tribe. After a brief mockery of a trial, Leatherlips was tomahawked and quickly buried. The Prophet used his religious doctrine to strengthen his political power; only those he perceived as his enemies were accused of witchcraft and executed.

For more than three years Governor Harrison watched with concern the growing number of Indians in Prophetstown, the village the Prophet founded with his brother Tecumseh. As a result, in fall 1811 tensions reached a boiling point. Harrison led an army of about one thousand troops near Prophetstown and prepared to fight. Unlike Tecumseh, the Prophet was not a great military leader, and Tecumseh was away at the time. The Prophet made the first move by attacking Harrison's army before dawn. But, the Indians were outnumbered and were short on ammunition. In the

battle, which would be known as the Battle of Tippecanoe, Harrison's troops forced the Indians to retreat and then burned Prophetstown to the ground. After that, the Prophet lost most of his influence. When Tecumseh returned, he led the Indian resistance through military rather than religious methods. The Prophet fled to Canada during the War of 1812 in which Tecumseh was killed. In 1824 the Prophet returned to the United States and went west with Shawnees who were removed to Kansas. He died twelve years later.

Tecumseh (ca. 1768–1813)

"Brothers—If you do not unite with us, they will first destroy us, and then you will fall an easy prey to them. They have destroyed many nations of red men because they were not united, because they were not friends to each other."

— *Tecumseh to the Osage, 1811*

Early Life

Tecumseh, or "Shooting Star," stood in sharp contrast to his younger brother Tenskwatawa. He was a natural born warrior who fought in his first battle as a youth. He was born to a Shawnee family that had moved from Virginia to land that would become Ohio, pushed by British colonists who would soon rebel and claim America as their own. Tecumseh's father died in battle against the Americans along the Ohio River in 1774. As the Revolution was fought in the backwoods in ensuing years, Tecumseh's mother and a sister moved west to Missouri with many other Shawnee people. Tecumseh and his other siblings stayed behind to be raised by their oldest sister and her husband. Tecumseh yearned to become a great warrior like his father and brother Chiksika. Growing up, he played war games, and Chiksika taught him how to hunt and become a warrior.

Warrior and Spokesman

By the time he was fifteen, Tecumseh had found his purpose—to stop the white man's invasion of Indian land. He traveled extensively and fought many battles before founding Prophetstown with his brother Tenskwatawa, the Prophet. While the Prophet preached, Tecumseh traveled vast distances to different tribes, encouraging them to join the confederation he was building to resist the Americans.

Tall with regal bearing, Tecumseh could hold his own with any white leader. He was intelligent and an excellent orator. William Henry Harrison, governor of the Indiana Territory, had great respect for Tecumseh, even though they were on opposing sides of the land ownership issue. Harrison's job was to acquire as much Indian land for white settlement as he could as quickly as possible. Tecumseh insisted that the land was given to the Indians by the Great Spirit. The land, he stated, belonged to all tribes and not to individual Americans. Harrison considered Tecumseh an "uncommon genius" who had been dealt a bad hand by fate. Recognizing his adversary's many gifts, Harrison said that given different circumstances Tecumseh "would perhaps be the founder of an empire that would rival in glory that of Mexico or Peru."

An experienced mediator, Harrison negotiated a number of treaties with Indian leaders, always to the Americans' advantage. However, bargaining with Tecumseh proved to be more difficult than negotiating with other tribal leaders. The two men met face-to-face three times before the Battle of Tippecanoe in 1811. Each meeting was more heated than the one before.

In August 1810 Tecumseh, wearing traditional deerskin clothing, met with Harrison at Grouseland, the governor's mansion in Vincennes. He brought a large band of warriors with him to intimidate Harrison and the other whites. When Tecumseh was offered a chair, he refused to sit on it. Instead he sat on the ground stating that Indians belonged with "the bosom of their mother." The talks were tense and nothing was accomplished. At one point Tecumseh lost his temper. Although he later apologized, it was clear that hostilities would continue between the Indians and Americans.

Tecumseh and Harrison met for the last time in the summer of 1811. Again, they reached no agreement. After the meeting, Tecumseh left Indiana to encourage southern tribes to join his confederacy. On November 6, 1811, Harrison, knowing Tecumseh was gone, moved his army of around one thousand men near Prophetstown and prepared

for a fight. Without the benefit of Tecumseh's military leadership, the Indians had to retreat, and Harrison set fire to Prophetstown.

The Battle of Tippecanoe, as it came to be called, did not break Native American resistance as Harrison had hoped. Instead, even more warriors joined Tecumseh's cause. As Americans had raided their villages in the past, Indians now raided frontier settlements. When the War of 1812 erupted between the United States and Great Britain, the latter wanting to win back its colonies, Tecumseh and most of the allied Indians joined the British to fight the Americans. On October 5, 1813, Tecumseh died at the Battle of the Thames near present-day Chatham, Ontario. Indian resistance to American expansion to the Mississippi River died with Tecumseh. After the war ended favorably for the United States, the Indians east of the Mississippi were eventually forced to sign over most of their remaining land to the Americans.

Tecumseh

No authentic portrait of Tecumseh exists. This wood engraving was created by Benson Lossing in 1863, based on an 1808 sketch of Tecumseh by fur trader Pierre le Dru. Lossing assumed that Tecumseh was part of the British army and drew him in a general's uniform.

COLLECTIONS OF THE TORONTO (CANADA) PUBLIC LIBRARY

1.3

Frances Slocum/Maconaquah (1773–1847)

Though bearing some resemblance to her family—yet her cheek bones seemed to have the Indian characteristics . . . face broad, nose somewhat bulby, mouth indicating some degree of severity.

— George Winter, from his journal, 1839

The Slocum Family

Jonathan and Ruth Slocum were Quakers who originally lived in Rhode Island. In 1777 their large family, which included a daughter named Frances and eight other children, braved rugged terrain and the danger of Indian attack in a covered wagon to settle in the Wyoming Valley near present-day Wilkes-Barre, Pennsylvania. As Quakers and therefore pacifists, the Slocums had hoped to distance themselves from the violence of the Revolutionary War in the more settled areas of the East Coast. Around the same time, Americans had forced Delaware Indians from the Wyoming Valley, and the Delaware frequently attacked white settlers. Instead of fleeing like many other settlers, Jonathan Slocum decided to stay because he thought the Indians would recognize him as a peaceful man and leave his family alone.

Frances Taken Captive

Frances Slocum was around five years old in November 1778 when Delaware raiders attacked her family's cabin. Jonathan was not present when the attack occurred, but Ruth and all but two of her children managed to flee to the nearby woods. Frances and one of her brothers, who was handicapped, did not make it out of the cabin. The Indians found them. Leaving Frances's brother behind, the Indians threw Frances over one of their horses and rode off. For the rest of her life, Ruth was haunted by the sight of her little red-haired daughter helplessly reaching out for her. A few months later, Indians returned and killed Jonathan and Ruth's father.

Frances Slocum/Maconaquah

In fall 1839 artist George Winter traveled to Deaf Man's Village on the Mississinewa River in Indiana to paint the portrait of Frances Slocum (Maconaquah), which her brother, Joseph Slocum of Pennsylvania, had commissioned. The portrait, "Lost Sister of Wyoming," is probably one of Winter's best known works.

Ruth never lost hope that Frances was alive. On her deathbed, twenty-eight years after her daughter's abduction, Ruth made her children promise that they would never abandon the search for their lost sister. For almost another three decades, they wrote letters, offered rewards, spoke with traders and agents, and traveled as far as Ohio and Michigan to pursue every possible lead. The trail to Frances remained cold.

Frances Found

In 1835, fifty-seven years after Frances was taken captive, Colonel George Ewing, a well-known trader in the Wabash Valley, was traveling on horseback from Fort Wayne to Logansport. He decided to stop for the night at an Indian settlement known as Deaf

Deaf Man's Village

This watercolor of Frances Slocum/Maconaquah's home along the Mississinewa, known as Deaf Man's Village, was painted by George Winter after his visit there in 1839. The village was named for Maconaquah's husband, Shapoconah, who lost his hearing during the War of 1812.

Man's Village on the Mississinewa River, just south of Peru and the Wabash. Ewing took shelter at a large log cabin, which had been the home of Miami chief, Shapoconah, before his death. Ewing spoke the Miami language and had been a long-time friend of Shapoconah.

One night Shapoconah's widow, Maconaquah, told Ewing the fascinating story of her early life. Ewing's suspicion that Maconaquah was not really an Indian was confirmed. She revealed that she was in fact white and had been taken from her family by Indians when she was very young. She told Ewing that she remembered that her family's name was Slocum and that they had lived somewhere along the Susquehanna River.

Ewing wrote letters to newspapers and post-masters in Lancaster, Pennsylvania, hoping to locate Maconaquah's white family. Eventually, a newspaper story attracted the attention of a minister in the Wyoming Valley who knew of the Slocum family's search for Frances. He contacted Joseph Slocum, Frances's brother. Joseph wrote to another sister and brother who were living in Ohio to tell them the news. The Slocum siblings, now all quite elderly, traveled to Indiana, hoping against hope that this woman might be their lost sister.

When Maconaquah encountered her siblings, she was understandably cautious. She had lived among Indians for more than a half century, and she knew that the white man often wanted to remove Indians from their homes. Eventually, her brothers and sister convinced her that she could trust them and that they were, indeed, part of her long-lost family.

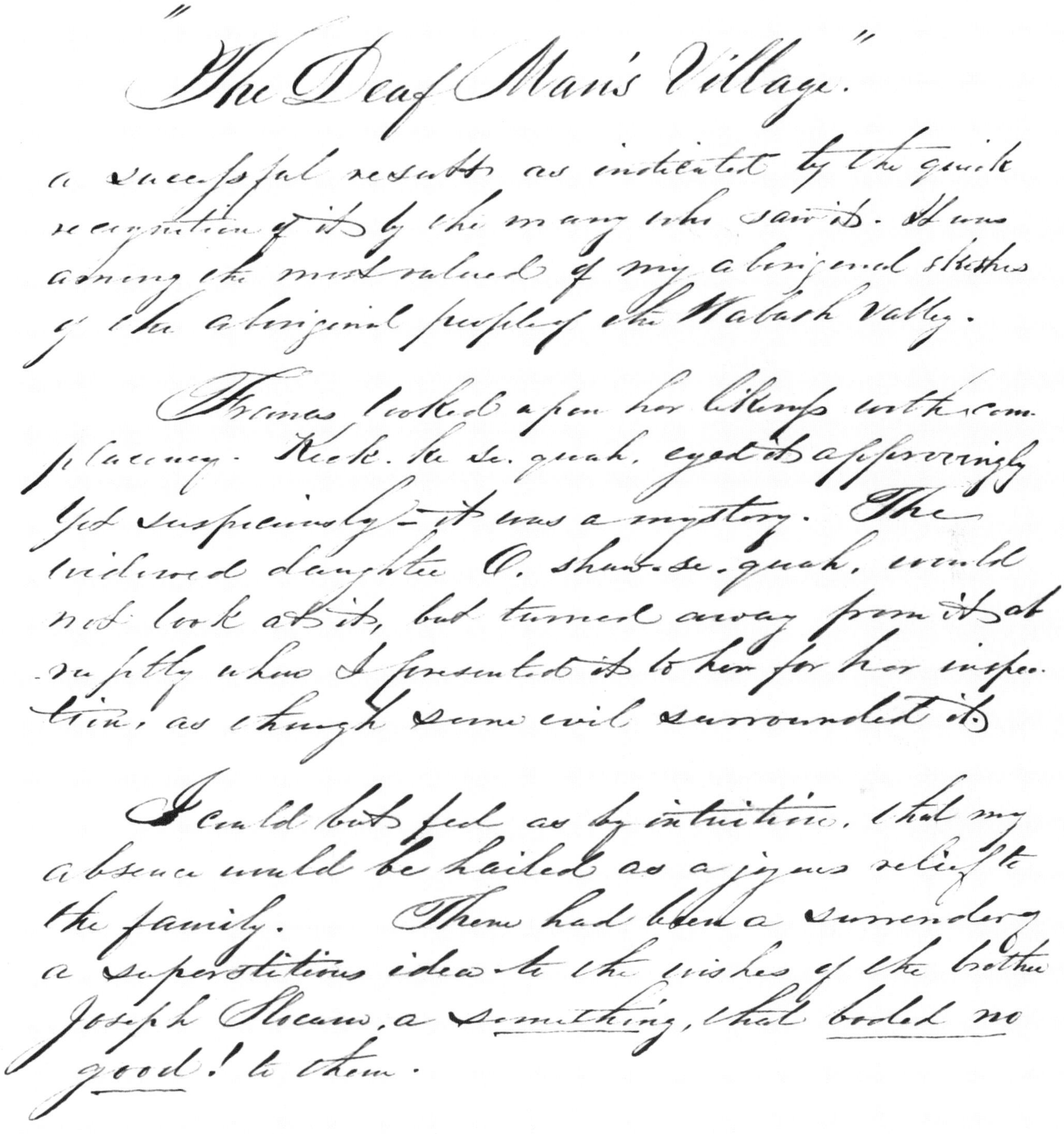
"The Deaf Man's Village."

a successful results as indicated by the quick recognition of it by the many who saw it. It was among the most valued of my aboriginal sketches of the aboriginal people of the Wabash Valley.

Frances looked upon her likeness with complacency. Kick-ke-se-quah, eyed it approvingly yet suspiciously—it was a mystery. The widowed daughter O-shaw-se-quah, would not look at it, but turned away from it abruptly when I presented it to her for her inspection, as though some evil surrounded it.

I could but feel as by intuition, that my absence would be hailed as a joyous relief to the family. There had been a surrender of a superstitious idea to the wishes of the brother Joseph Slocum, a <u>something</u>, that <u>boded no good</u>! to them.

Excerpt from George Winter's Journal

This excerpt from the journal George Winter kept during his journey to Deaf Man's Village in 1839 states in part:

Frances looked upon her likeness [portrait] *with complacency. Kick-ke-se-quah eyed it approvingly, yet suspiciously—it was a mystery. The widowed daughter, O-shaw-se-quah would not look at it, but turned away from it abruptly when I presented it to her for her inspection, and thought some evil surrounded it.*

I could but feel as by intuition, that my absence would be hailed as a joyous relief to the family. There had been a surrender of a superstitious idea to the wishes of the brother Joseph Slocum, a <u>something</u> that <u>boded no good</u>! to them.

Maconaquah's siblings positively identified her by her left forefinger, which had been smashed by a hammer when she was very young and had no fingernail. They communicated with Maconaquah through an interpreter because she knew only the Miami language, having forgotten virtually all English.

Maconaquah's Life among the Delaware and Miami

After almost six decades of separation, the Slocum siblings had a lot of catching up to do. Maconaquah told them about her life after she had been whisked away from them so many years ago. They learned that the Delaware warriors who seized her had later traded her to a childless Delaware chief and his wife who gave her the name Sheletawash, after their deceased daughter. She said that the couple always treated her like a daughter since their own daughter had died. Maconaquah's first marriage to a Delaware brave named Tuck Horse was brief because he did not treat her well, and she returned to her Delaware parents. Subsequently, she was presented as a wife to a Miami brave named Shepoconah, who later became a chief. When Frances joined the Miami people, she took the name Maconaquah, meaning Little Bear Woman. She had four children with Shapoconah—two sons who died when they were very young and two girls who were young women when the Slocums met them. The daughters, Kekenakushwa and Ozahshinquah, had children of their own. Maconaquah was a grandmother.

Maconaquah's siblings tried to convince her to return to the Slocum homestead in Pennsylvania, but she refused. She said that she had always lived with the Indians and she wanted to live out her life with them. However, she agreed to sit to have her portrait painted so they could take it back to Pennsylvania with them.

Maconaquah through an Artist's Eyes

George Winter was an Englishman who came to the United States in 1830. After studying art in New York, Winter moved to Ohio and opened a portrait studio. An adventurer at heart, Winter headed west in 1837 to document the removal of the Potawatomi and ended up near Logansport, Indiana. His detailed sketches of the daily lives of the Indians and of their removal provide a rare glimpse into this little-documented time in Indiana history. Today, Winter is best known for the portrait he painted of Maconaquah in 1839, which had been commissioned by Maconaquah's siblings soon after they reunited with her. Winter communicated with Maconaquah through an African American interpreter who lived with the Miami and knew their language. In his journal Winter writes that she was short in stature and finely dressed. In fact, Winter states that he could tell that Maconaquah's family was quite well off based on their housing and amount of livestock. He also notes that she was a "patient sitter, and wholly abandoned herself to my professional requirements." Winter reported that Maconaquah and her family politely tolerated his presence: "I could but feel as by intuition, that my absence would be hailed as a joyous relief to the family."

Maconaquah's Legacy

In 1840 the U.S. government signed a treaty that required the Miami to leave the Wabash River area by 1845. Maconaquah's family petitioned Congress, requesting that she and her immediate Miami family and their descendants be exempt from removal. Congress granted the request in 1845. Two years later, Maconaquah, often referred to as the "White Rose of the Miamis," died at the advanced age of seventy-four.

Maconaquah is an important figure in Indiana history because she was a rare individual who fully assimilated into Indian culture and was accepted as one of them. She essentially became a Miami, and yet she agreed to meet with her siblings and to sit for her portrait. Winter's paintings and drawings of Maconaquah and her daughters as well as those of Deaf Man's Village where they lived, together with the notes he and her siblings wrote regarding Maconaquah constitute a rare glimpse into the lives and perspectives of the Miami.

Today, Hoosiers can visit Maconaquah's grave in Wabash County in a cemetery that bears her name. In addition, there is a thirty-mile-long Frances Slocum Trail that runs from Peru to Marion, Indiana, and a state recreation area near Peru named for her.

1.4

The Potawatomi Trail of Death

"Your fire has gone out. Your wigwams are cold. . . .
You cannot live in a country where white men multiply as
rapidly as black birds, and as numerous as pidgeons."

— *Indian Agent Abel C. Pepper to the Potawatomi, 1837*

Indian Removal Policy

Indian claims to land were the biggest obstacles to American expansion. After the War of 1812 the U.S. government was determined to remove that obstacle. Initially, the government's policy leaned toward assimilation of Indians, that is, absorbing them into American culture so that they gradually let go of their own ways, particularly in terms of religion and individual rather than tribal ownership. In time, however, Indian removal became the preferred method of expansion. Indian tribes that had been living in the Old Northwest, including present-day Ohio, Indiana, Illinois, Michigan, and Wisconsin, were to be moved west of the Mississippi River. White men were not yet settling those faraway lands.

In the *Emigrant's Guide to the Western and Southwestern States and Territories*, published in 1818, author William Darby praises the richness of Indiana's soil and notes that nearly "two-thirds of its territorial surface is yet in the hands of the Indians, a temporary evil, that a short time will remedy." Hoosiers wanted their government to take action to remove the Indians so they could go about the business of settling it themselves. After the War of 1812, the Native Americans could offer little resistance.

When Indiana became a state in 1816, the Miami and the Potawatomi were the most numerous remaining tribes. Hoosier settlers had to depend on the federal government to make the decisions regarding Indian policy because it was considered a federal issue not a state issue. The Bureau of Indian Affairs, a department under the Secretary of War, had agents in regional offices to enforce federal policy. In Indiana the federal Indian agent was initially located at Fort Wayne and then Logansport.

At first, the government's strategy urged Indians to go into debt so they would be forced to cede their land to pay off their debts. Indian traders were skeptical of the strategy because their primary income came from trading goods with the Indians. Eventually, however, the traders came around to the idea of Indian removal and eagerly helped the process along. Playing both sides of the fence, many of these individuals took advantage of their long-standing relationships with the Indians and their government connections to be first to obtain Indian land once it was available. Then some of these same individuals assisted in Indian removal to the West. A number of these men amassed fortunes buying and selling large tracts of Indian land and became some of the state's most influential citizens. Some of these traders are still well-known today: William Conner, who will be extensively discussed in the next chapter, was an Indian trader and became an integral part of negotiations between Indians and Americans; George Ewing, who "discovered" Frances Slocum; and General John Tipton, a veteran of the Battle of Tippecanoe who became one of Indiana's early U.S. senators.

In 1830 Congress sealed the fate of Native Americans by passing the Indian Removal Act, giving President Andrew Jackson the green light to forcibly move Indians westward. Many Hoosiers were glad that Jackson wasted no time in getting the job done, because they were eager to develop their new state without the obstacle the Indians presented. Jackson and others rationalized that removal would be good for the Indians, because it would remove them from the negative effects of white culture, mostly alcohol, and allow them to adapt to American culture at their own speed. However, there was one big problem—the Indians did not want to leave their land.

The Plight of the Potawatomi

The Indiana Potawatomi signed nine treaties in 1836, ceding their remaining reservations in Indiana to the United States. The U.S. government paid them

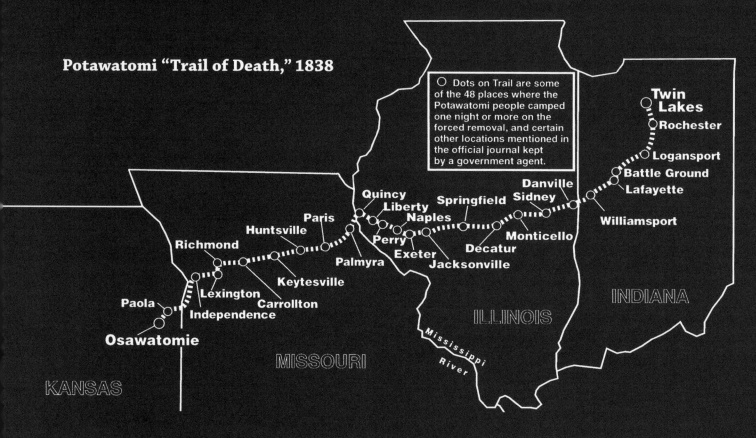

Potawatomi "Trail of Death," 1838

○ Dots on Trail are some of the 48 places where the Potawatomi people camped one night or more on the forced removal, and certain other locations mentioned in the official journal kept by a government agent.

On September 4, 1838, more than 850 Potawatomi were gathered at gunpoint by mounted Indiana militia and forcibly marched more than 600 miles—from their northern Indiana homes to Osawatomie, Kansas. Around forty people, mostly children, died on this two-month march. This map shows campsites on their journey west, as recorded by official U.S. government agents. (This map was adapted from resources compiled by the Fulton County Historical Society and the Potawatomi Trail of Death Association, Rochester, Indiana, including map by Potawatomi Tom Hamilton, "Potawatomi 'Trail of Death' March: Sept.–Nov. 1838," 2004.)

one dollar an acre for their land and gave them two years from the signing of the treaty to move west of the Mississippi. The Treaty of the Yellow River, concluded on August 5, 1836, was by far the most controversial treaty. Three of the chiefs that signed it gave up most of the land on the parcel that included Chief Menominee's reservation a few miles north of Rochester, Indiana. Conspicuously, Menominee's signature is absent from the treaty.

When he learned about these treaties, Menominee was enraged. He called the treaties frauds and refused to move. Menominee told the agents charged with removing his people: "[The President] does not know that you made my young chiefs drunk and got their consent and pretended to get mine. He does not know that I have refused to sell my land, and still refuse. He would not drive me from my home and the graves of

my tribe, and my children, who have gone to the Great Spirit, nor allow you to tell me your braves will take me, tied like a dog." With the support of Catholic missionaries in the region, Menominee, who had converted to Catholicism, petitioned the government to let his people stay on their land. The government refused.

The Potawatomi Trail of Death Begins

August 5, 1838, was the deadline for the Potawatomi to vacate their land. Some Potawatomi had already left the area, but Menominee and others had not. Anticipating the Indians' departure, white squatters started to arrive at Menominee's village and violence erupted. Indiana Governor David Wallace ordered General John Tipton, the former Indian agent, and an armed state militia to move in and arrest Menominee and a few other leaders and begin Potawatomi removal.

After forcing evacuation of the village, Tipton and his men set fire to it to discourage the Potawatomi from returning.

Menominee and two other rebellious chiefs were confined to the village's log church while the Potawatomi were rounded up for the march. On September 4, 1838, the exodus to Kansas, which came to be known as the Potawatomi Trail of Death, began with more than 850 Potawatomi under armed guard. The rebellious chiefs were confined to a cage-like wagon with bars. Father Benjamin Petit, a Jesuit priest who accompanied the Potawatomi, described the order in which they marched:

> The United States flag, carried by a dragoon; then one of the principal officers, next the staff baggage carts, then the carriage, which during the whole trip was kept for the use of the Indian chiefs; then one or two chiefs on horseback led a line of 250 or 300 horses ridden by men, women, children in single file, after the manner of savages. On the flanks of the line at equal distance from each other were the dragoons and volunteers [soldiers], hastening the stragglers, often with severe gestures and bitter words. After this cavalry came a file of forty baggage wagons filled with luggage and Indians. The sick were lying in them, rudely jolted, under a canvas which, far from protecting them from the dust and heat, only deprived them of air, for they were as if buried under this burning canopy—several died thus.

Although the government had wanted the Potawatomi out of Indiana for a long time, they put very little thought into how the journey should be conducted. The weather was hot and dry, there was not enough fresh water, and food was scarce. A baby died on the second day—the first of many deaths to follow.

Witnesses to the Removal

Two European witnesses left detailed accounts that provide a glimpse of Potawatomi life prior to removal and insight into the Trail of Death. English artist George Winter, who later painted Frances Slocum's portrait, arrived in the Wabash Valley just as

removal plans were forming in 1837. His sketches and paintings show the Potawatomi going about their daily lives. From his diary we learn that several individuals were left behind at Twin Lakes as the evacuation began because they were too sick or elderly to undertake the journey. Winter also sketched the Potawatomi at a religious service at their second encampment near Logansport, Indiana, and sketched them leaving this place in single file as well. In his journal Winter wrote that the Potawatomi were driven "out of the land at the point of the bayonet! It was truly a melancholy spectacle, that awoke a deep feeling of sympathy for their unhappy fate."

Father Petit was born in France and had left a promising law career to become a Jesuit missionary in Indiana. He arrived at Menominee's reservation a year before the removal and was full of enthusiasm. He came to regard the Potawatomi as his children; as the threat of removal became more imminent, Petit was determined to accompany them when they were forced to go. He wrote that he would not allow "these Christians souls" to die far from their homes "without the aid of the sacraments of which they partook with such love." In a letter to General Tipton, Petit expressed his outrage, "[I]t is impossible for me, and for many, to conceive how such events may take place in this country of liberty."

Chief Menominee

Chief Menominee was a principal chief of the Indiana Potawatomi when the tribe was forcibly removed from its lands in 1838. He died less than three years after reaching Kansas. In 1909 the State of Indiana erected this statue in memory of the chief at the point where the Potawatomi "Trail of Death" began in Twin Lakes, Indiana.

Father Benjamin Petit's Journal, 1837

Father Benjamin Marie Petit was a Catholic missionary stationed in Indiana in 1837. As he accompanied the Potawatomi on the Trail of Death in 1838, he kept a journal and wrote frequent letters. Below is an excerpt from Petit's journal, which he used as both an account book and as a way to track his activities. (Journal translation quoted from Irving McKee, *The Trail of Death: Letters of Benjamin Marie Petit* [Indianapolis: Indiana Historical Society, 1941], 128)

Dates	Places	Receipts	Expenditures	Activities and reference Notes
August 5	chichié outipé		.50	traveling.—I performed 14 baptisms, 2 marriages, very numerous confessions, many sick. I am a little tired out.—the emigration agents harass, accuse, flatter me; threaten the Indians; —to avoid the troops and armed forces at the seizure of the reserve, I reply that the Indians will not offer resistance. —On the 5th the government takes possession of my pre-empted church and house. —On the 4th I say Mass there again, the alter is dismantled, and the church's interior stripped amidst the Indians' sobs and my own tears. I bid farewell; we pray together once more for the success of missions, we sing: In thy protection do we trust . . . I depart.

The End of the Trail

Nearly two weeks after the journey began, Tipton and his men left the caravan at Danville, Illinois, and returned to Indiana. Judge William Polke, a prominent Indiana civil servant and politician who was federally appointed to conduct the removal, took charge of leading the Potawatomi the rest of the way to Kansas. Polke's enrolling agent, Jesse C. Douglas, who recorded the names of the Potawatomi on the journey, also provided a journal of the trip, commonly known as Polke's journal.

As they passed through central Illinois, the Indians received a lot of attention from the locals. One observer noted that the Indians wore their finest clothing and carried themselves with great dignity. The town of Jacksonville, Illinois, added to "the entertaining spectacle" by having a band play as the Indians passed through. Douglas wrote, "[T]he sight of an emigration or body of Indians is as great a rarity [for the citizens of Jacksonville] as a traveling Caravan of wild animals."

On October 10 the Potawatomi crossed the Mississippi on steam ferry boats and entered Missouri. It took the Potawatomi almost a month to traverse Missouri, which required crossing the Missouri River. The Indians touched Kansas soil on November 2 and reached their final destination of Osawatomie, Kansas, on November 4, 1838. They had traveled around 660 miles in two months.

The harsh journey took its toll. Of the more than 850 Potawatomi who set out from Indiana, around forty of them died—most of them children. Several days after arriving in Kansas, one of the chiefs insisted on making a statement to Polke. According to Polke, the chief said, "They had now arrived at their journey's end—that the government must now be satisfied. They had been taken from homes affording them plenty and brought to a desert—a wilderness—and were now to be scattered and left as the husbandsman scatters his seed."

Menominee died less than three years after arriving in Kansas and is buried there. Almost seventy years later, Indiana acknowledged that the Potawatomi chief had a legitimate claim to the land. In September 1909 the state erected a life-size statue of Menominee at Twin Lakes, southeast of Plymouth, Indiana, near the site of Menominee's vanished village.

Stricken with typhoid fever, Father Petit died while returning to Indiana from Kansas and was buried in Saint Louis, Missouri. He was just twenty-eight years old. In 1856 his body was moved to Indiana and his remains rest under the Log Chapel at the University of Notre Dame in South Bend.

Selected Bibliography

Cayton, Andrew R. L. *Frontier Indiana*. Bloomington: Indiana University Press, 1996.

Collins, Gail. *William Henry Harrison*. The American Presidents. New York: Times Books/Henry Holt and Co., 2012.

Cooke, Sarah E., and Rachel B. Ramadhyani. *Indians and a Changing Frontier: The Art of George Winter*. Indianapolis: Indiana Historical Society in cooperation with the Tippecanoe County Historical Association, 1993.

Edmunds, R. David. *The Potawatomis: Keepers of the Fire*. Norman, OK: University of Oklahoma Press, 1978.

———. *The Shawnee Prophet*. Lincoln, NE: University of Nebraska Press, 1983.

———. *Tecumseh and the Quest for Indian Leadership*, 2nd ed. New York: Pearson and Logman, 2007.

Glenn, Elizabeth, and Stewart Rafert. *The Native Americans*. Peopling Indiana 2. Indianapolis: Indiana Historical Society Press, 2009.

"History." Little River Wetlands Project. http://www.lrwp.org /page/history.

Jackson, Marion T., ed. *The Natural Heritage of Indiana*. Bloomington: Indiana University Press, 1997. "Journal of an Emigrating Party of Pottawatomie Indians, 1838." *Indiana Magazine of History* 21, no. 4 (December 1925): 315–36.

Madison, James H. *Hoosiers: A New History of Indiana*. Bloomington: Indiana University Press; Indianapolis: Indiana Historical Society Press, 2014.

McKee, Irving. "The Centennial of 'The Trail of Death.'" *Indiana Magazine of History* 35, no. 1 (March 1939): 27–41.

———. *The Trail of Death: Letters of Benjamin Marie Petit*. Indianapolis: Indiana Historical Society, 1941.

Nabokov, Peter. *Native American Testimony: A Chronicle of Indian–White Relations from Prophesy to the Present, 1492–1992*. New York: Viking, 1991.

O'Maley, Elizabeth. *Bones on the Ground*. Indianapolis: Indiana Historical Society Press, 2014.

Rafert, Stewart. *The Miami Indians of Indiana*. Indianapolis: Indiana Historical Society, 1996.

Simons, Richard S. *The Rivers of Indiana*. Bloomington: Indiana University Press, 1985.

Sugden, John. *Tecumseh: A Life*. New York: Henry Holt and Co., 1997.

Tanner, Helen Hornbeck, ed. *Atlas of Great Lakes Indian History*. The Civilization of the American Indian 174. Norman, OK: University of Oklahoma Press and Newberry Library, 1987.

"Trail of Death." Fulton County [Indiana] Historical Society. http:// www.fultoncountyhistory.org/TRAILOFDEATHHOMEPAGE .html.

Van Bolt, Roger H. "The Indiana Scene in the 1840s." *Indiana Magazine of History* 47, no. 4 (December 1951): 333–56.

Essential Questions

1 What groups, tribes, or native peoples lived on the land that would become Indiana during the 1700s to 1830s?

2 In general, what were some major differences between native cultures and European cultures?

3 What was the nature of French–Indian relations? What factors contributed to their relationship?

4 How and why did native interactions with the British and later the Americans differ significantly from native interactions with the French?

5 In what ways did the cultures of native groups in Indiana change as a result of contact with the Europeans and Americans?

6 How did different individuals and/or tribes respond to the increasing threats to their culture and lands posed by American settlers?*

7 What strategies did the Americans use to address what they viewed as the Indian menace and to secure land for settlement? What were the effects of these strategies on the native population?*

See student activities related to this question.

Activity 1: Little Turtle and Tecumseh

Introduction: In this chapter, you read about how contact with French, British, and Americans resulted in profound changes to native life. However, it is important to remember that Indiana's native people responded in multiple ways; different tribes and even different individuals within tribes responded to threats to their lands, lives, and cultures in different ways. Little Turtle and Tecumseh provide examples of the different courses of action native people followed in an attempt to protect and preserve the lives and customs of their people. Though having previously enjoyed some significant victories over the American forces, the Miami people, led by Little Turtle, suffered

a major defeat by American General Anthony Wayne in 1794 at the Battle of Fallen Timbers. Little Turtle urged other Indian chiefs to sign the resulting Treaty of Greenville; he was convinced that the Americans would leave the Indians alone after they signed over territory that included two-thirds of Ohio and a narrow strip of southeastern Indiana. According to an excerpted speech in an early biography of Little Turtle, he told his people:

> We have beaten the enemy twice under separate Commanders. We cannot expect the same good fortune always to attend us. The Americans are now led by a Chief who never sleeps; the night and the day are alike to him and during all the time that he has been marching upon our village notwithstanding the watchfulness of our young men we have never been able to surprise him. Think well of it. There is something whispers to me, it would be prudent to listen to his offers of peace. (Young, 84)

Many Indians disagreed with Little Turtle's words, but some followed his plea and signed the Treaty of Greenville.

Little Turtle urged his people to make peace with the Americans; however, the Shawnee warrior Tecumseh, and his brother Tenskwatawa, the Prophet, tried to convince Indians of various tribes to join a confederation that would take up arms against the Americans. They saw that the Treaty of Greenville had been disastrous for native peoples, causing them to become more and more dependent on Americans who sought to destroy native culture. They responded to the devastation they saw in native life and the American deception they perceived by joining with British forces and fighting against the Americans during the War of 1812. In a speech to British Major General Henry Proctor during that war, Tecumseh urged an attack on the Americans, noting:

> The Americans have not yet defeated us by land; neither are we sure that they have done so by water; we therefore wish to remain here and fight our enemy, should they make their appearance. If they defeat us, we will

then retreat with our father [Proctor]. . . . Father, you have got the arms and ammunition which our great father [the British king, George III] sent for his red children. If you have an idea of going away, give them to us, and you may go and welcome, for us. Our lives are in the hands of the Great Spirit. We are determined to defend our lands, and if it be his will, we wish to leave our bones upon them. (Drake, 189)

Tecumseh believed his people could only be saved by taking up arms.

▶ **Consider the excerpt of Little Turtle's speech:**

1 What reasons does Little Turtle give for thinking the Miami should sign the Treaty of Greenville?

2 Based upon what you have read about the situation in which the Miami found themselves in 1794 following the Battle of Fallen Timbers, do you agree with Little Turtle's conclusions or not? Would you advise signing the treaty?

3 Review the section of chapter text about Little Turtle, the Treaty of Greenville, and its effects. In retrospect do you think that Little Turtle and others should have signed the treaty or not?

▶ **Consider Tecumseh's remarks to Major General Proctor:**

1 How does Tecumseh justify his/the confederation's continued armed resistance against the Americans?

2 Based upon what you have read about the state of relations between Tecumseh and the Prophet's followers and the Americans in the early 1800s, do you agree with the choice to keep fighting? Why or why not?

3 Tecumseh died on October 5, 1813, at the Battle of the Thames near present-day Chatham, Ontario, in Canada. For all intents and purposes, Indian resistance east of the Mississippi River ended with Tecumseh's death. Would you say that native groups fared better under Little Turtle's approach or under Tecumseh's approach?

▶ **Imagine a conversation between Little Turtle and Tecumseh. How would each justify his response to the American threat? What would each hope to save or gain using his approach—land, the lives of his people, the peoples' culture or way of life? Record your imagined conversation in writing or work with a partner, each expressing one side of the debate. Be sure to base your conversation on what you have learned about Little Turtle, the Miami, and Tecumseh, the Prophet, and their coalition. Try to make an emotional plea about how you think you are helping your people by leading them in this direction.**

Activity 2: The Trail of Death

Introduction: As pointed out in the chapter introduction, an important consideration for historians studying this era is that the vast majority of written accounts are from the European or American perspective rather than from the native perspective. Documents relating to the removal of the Potawatomi from Indiana to Kansas reflect this absence of the native voice. We have to look to the writings of white observers for a firsthand account of the Trail of Death. Father Benjamin Marie Petit, a French Catholic missionary to the Potawatomi, accompanied the tribe on its journey to reservation lands in Kansas. In letters he wrote to Bishop Simon Bruté we get a sense of the hardships endured by the Potawatomi. In one letter, addressed to Bruté and marked "Osage River, Indian Country, November 13, 1838," Petit writes:

The United States flag, carried by a dragoon; then one of the principal officers, next the staff baggage carts, then the carriage, which during the whole trip was kept for the use of the Indian chiefs; then one or two chiefs on horseback led a line of 250 or 300 horses ridden by men, women, children in single file, after the manner of savages. On the flanks of the line at equal distance from each other were the dragoons and volunteers [soldiers], hastening the stragglers, often with severe gestures and bitter words. After this cavalry came a file of forty baggage wagons filled with luggage and Indians. The sick were lying in them, rudely jolted, under a canvas which, far from protecting them from the dust and heat, only deprived them of air, for they were as if buried under this burning canopy—several died thus. (McKee, 99)

Although clearly still biased (note the use of the word "savages"), Petit provides a sympathetic account of the Potawatomi's ordeal.

▶ Re-read this excerpt from Petit's letter and pay special attention to his description of the plight of the stragglers and the sick. Compose a Haiku poem (see instructions below) written from the perspective of a Potawatomi being marched to Kansas.

> **Haiku Instructions:** Haiku is a traditional Japanese form of poetry that distills a subject down to its essence. Haiku poems are three lines long and adhere to the following syllable count: The first line contains five syllables; the second contains seven syllables; and the third contains five syllables.

▶ Compile a class anthology of your poems or hold a poetry reading session in which you can share your poems if you wish.

Activity References

Drake, Benjamin. *Life of Tecumseh and of His Brother, the Prophet, with a Historical Sketch of the Shawanoe Indians.* Cincinnati: Anderson, Gates, and Wright, 1858.

McKee, Irving. *The Trail of Death: Letters of Benjamin Marie Petit.* Indianapolis: Indiana Historical Society, 1941.

Young, Calvin M. *Little Turtle, the Great Chief of the Miami Indian Nation: Being a Sketch of His Life Together with that of Wm. Wells and Some Noted Descendents.* Indianapolis: Sentinel Printing, 1917.

Indiana Pathways

The first American settlers in Indiana traveled through forests such as this and followed trails made by Indians. The Buffalo Trace, a trail stamped out by generations of buffalo migrating from the area that became Jeffersonville to the one that became Vincennes, might have looked similar to this wide trail in the fall.

2

American Expansion across the Appalachian Mountains

"Old America seems to be breaking up, and moving westward."

— *Morris Birkbeck, English immigrant, 1817*

During the late eighteenth century, the population on the East Coast was growing. People were having large families, and more immigrant groups from England, Scotland, Ireland, and Germany were steadily arriving. The people needed more land, and they knew where to find it—the western frontier.

Even before the Americans defeated the British, they had been eyeing with longing the land west of the Appalachian Mountains. Beyond the mountains was a frontier with vast acres of land seemingly ripe for clearing and planting. For many young families who wanted their own farms, the West held out the promise of a better future.

In its Proclamation of 1763, the British government had insisted that the colonists stay east of the Appalachians. This restriction was one of the many grievances that sparked the Americans' fight for independence. Motivated by victory over the British redcoats during the American Revolution and inspired by George Rogers Clark's dazzling victory on the Wabash in 1779, the Americans were determined to cross the Appalachians and settle the land all the way to the Mississippi River.

After the Americans won the Revolutionary War the British could no longer hinder American expansion, but settling the West was still not going to be easy. Native Americans considered the land beyond the Appalachians theirs to hunt, fish, and farm. At first, some welcomed newcomers from the East, especially as traders. Enterprising men such as William Conner created homes and prospered among the Indian people. However, as more and more settlers arrived and began to build log cabins and clear woodland for farming, the Native Americans began to regard them as invaders.

Indian resentment toward American settlement led many tribes to turn to the British, who controlled Canada, for help in repelling the invaders. To the natives who joined the British, the ensuing War of 1812 offered the possibility that British and Indians fighting together could stop the Americans' westward expansion. Indian war parties took up weapons. Armed with British hatchets and rifles, they were a major obstacle to western settlement.

In September 1812 Indian warriors attacked the settlement of Pigeon Roost in present-day Scott

Violence on the Frontier

Peace was not easy for officials of the Indiana Territory to enforce. Violence often broke out between Native Americans and settlers. Each group was responsible for brutality during this period. In these two drawings artist William Vawter depicts atrocities committed by both sides. Although Native American leaders surrendered numerous perpetrators from their tribes to American authorities, American murderers often escaped punishment due to community support for their actions.

County, Indiana, killing twenty-four men, women, and children. Settlers fled to a nearby fort or crossed the Ohio River to escape the violence. Realizing the British were furnishing the Indians with arms and ammunition, many believed, as a woman in Vincennes wrote on October 10, 1811, that the Indians were "deceitful in the extreme." The Pigeon Roost massacre and the end of the War of 1812 marked the end of serious Indian violence in Indiana, but it did not end violence against Indians.

Nearly twelve years later in spring 1824, five white men attacked and brutally murdered nine Indian men, women, and children who had set up camp near Fall Creek in Madison County. Despite one of the English-speaking Indian woman's calls for mercy in the name of Jesus, the white men responded by shooting her in the back and clubbing her head.

At this time it seemed unlikely to many that white men would ever be arrested and convicted for killing Indians. Native Americans were largely considered savages, undeserving of American justice. Nevertheless, the accused were brought to trial in a log cabin in Pendleton. Four men were convicted of murder and sentenced to death. Three of these men were hanged

on the banks of Fall Creek in front of a large crowd that included some of the murdered Indians' relatives. Nearing the last minute, Indiana Governor James B. Ray rode in and pardoned eighteen-year-old John Bridge Jr. because of his youth, even though he had plunged a butcher knife into one of the Indians.

This trial in the fledgling state of Indiana marked the first legal execution of whites for murdering Indians in America. Three judges were involved. Two were locals, elected by their neighbors: attorney Samuel Holliday and a local blacksmith, Adam Winchell, who made the iron shackles for the prisoners. The presiding judge, William Wick, who had been elected by the Indiana state legislature, made a passionate statement as he passed sentence:

By what authority do we hauntingly boast of our being white? What principle of philosophy or of religion establishes the doctrine that a white skin is preferable in nature or in the sight of God to a red or black one? Who has ordained that men of the white skin shall be at liberty to shoot and hunt down men of the red, or exercise rule and dominion over those of the black?

During much of this period, a government policy of acculturation was in place, which sought to "civilize" the Indians by teaching them to live and farm like white families. Little Turtle and other chiefs asked President Thomas Jefferson for plows, hoes, and livestock to be sent to the Miami and Potawatomi. Jefferson did so in order to encourage American farming methods and to encourage the Indians to abandon their hunter–warrior way of life. This was not only a strategy used by the federal and territorial governments. Some religious missionaries also promoted American-style agriculture, the removal of liquor, and Christianity. For example, Quaker missionary Philip Dennis set up a model farm on the Wabash River where he showed Indian men how to use a plow

and horse. At the same time he urged women to work inside the home. However, Indian men refused to farm because they considered it women's work; and Indian women refused to give up farming. Few accepted a Christian God. Thus, attempts at assimilation mostly failed.

Because many Indians refused to adapt to the American way of life, many government officials and Americans concluded that they needed to be removed west of the Mississippi River. By the late 1820s removal became the favored Indian policy, even before President Andrew Jackson officially proclaimed it in 1830. Prior to 1816 Indiana's Territorial governor, William Henry Harrison was following this policy as he negotiated treaty after treaty with Native American tribes in order to purchase their lands for the United States.

Indian land cession treaties and removal gradually opened Indiana for white settlement. Americans flooded across the Appalachians, down the Ohio River, and across the trails. But even as they wanted more land, settlers also wanted the protections of the new American democracy.

Moving West

As Native American treaties and removal opened large tracts of land in Indiana, white settlers eagerly traveled to claim it. These early immigrants often traveled with their belongings and their livestock by flatboat along the Ohio River, as shown in this lithograph from the 1830s.

Early Americans Move West

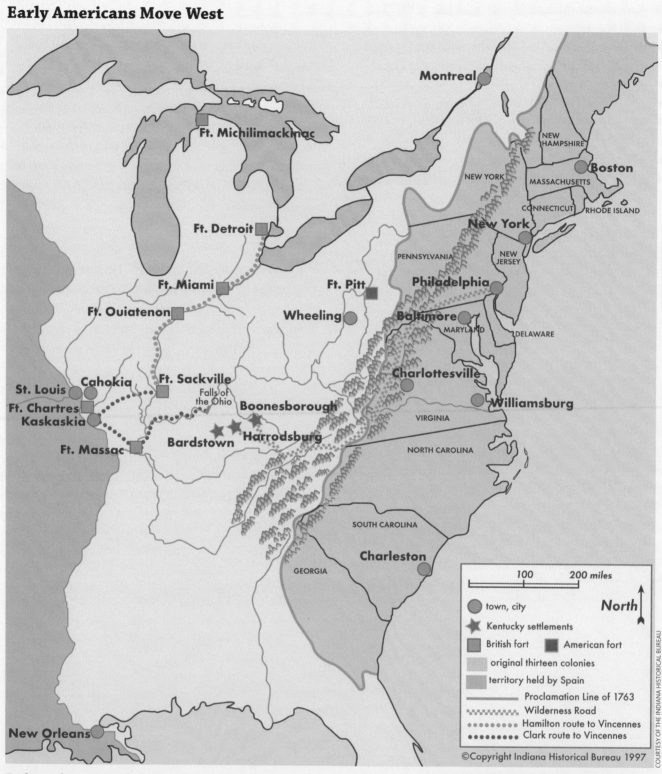

Early settlers to North America's western lands were forced to overcome many natural obstructions, including the Appalachian Mountains, marked in blue on this map. Many traveled west along the Wilderness Road that went through the Cumberland Gap in the mountains. By the 1770s much of North America was claimed by Britain, Spain, and the newly created United States. Yearning for more land, Americans encroached upon the British-claimed territory, both with military skirmishes and with settlers who claimed land by squatting on it. George Rogers Clark was instrumental in attaining American territory north of the Ohio River, due to his taking of Fort Sackville (present-day Vincennes, Indiana) in February 1779. This map appeared in *The Indiana Historian* in December 1997.

The American Constitution and Bill of Rights contained the promise of good government for the states. The Northwest Ordinance of 1787 and the creation of the Indiana Territorial government in 1800 expanded that promise to the western frontier. Indiana's Constitution of 1816 declared that "all power is inherent in the people." These gradual steps toward stable government, democracy, and rights were essential for settlers in the West to create America's nineteenth state—Indiana.

The democracy was far from perfect. Women and African Americans were denied full rights of citizenship, including the right to vote. Some settlers in the Indiana Territory even wanted to bring their slaves with them—a controversial subject long before the Civil War (1861–65). It would be a long time before there was a semblance of justice and equality for all.

The men featured in this chapter are celebrated as heroes. George Rogers Clark, Anthony Wayne, William Henry Harrison, and William Conner achieved greatness militarily, politically, and financially. However, remember that it took many ordinary men and women to shape Indiana's history; it could not have been done by a handful of heroes. Some people fought the British during the Revolution or in the War of 1812, while others fought the Indians at the Battle of Fallen Timbers and at Tippecanoe. Most were farmers who purchased land the federal government sold them cheaply. On sections of 80 or 160 acres they farmed to provide for their large families. Hopeful for a better future, Hoosier pioneers created Indiana together, alongside the heroes of their days.

2.1

George Rogers Clark and the Fall of Vincennes

[I] Whispered to those near me to [do] as I did—ameediately took some water in my hand [,] poured on Powder [,] Blacked my face [,] gave the war hoop [,] and marched into the water without saying a word.

— *George Rogers Clark, from his memoir*

Making of a Hero

George Rogers Clark was only twenty-seven years old at the time of his victory at Fort Sackville in present-day Vincennes, Indiana, but he was well on his way to becoming an American hero. The tall, rugged Virginian had already proven himself to be an aggressive warrior. In the year leading up to his triumph at Vincennes, he had captured the British posts of Cahokia and Kaskaskia in the Illinois country along the Mississippi and the Vincennes post near the Ohio on the Wabash. He also had ambitions to take Fort Detroit, Britain's main fort in the West.

The British had essentially ignored Fort Sackville at Vincennes, which they had won from the French in 1763, because they were preoccupied with the rebelling colonies on the East Coast during the American Revolution. Clark's men claimed the fort in August 1778 after a Catholic priest from Kaskaskia persuaded Vincennes' residents, many of whom were French or French-Indian, to sign an oath of allegiance to the Americans. Rumors that France was planning to aid the fledgling American government in its war against Great Britain helped to convince residents in the British-held posts that it was wise to side with the Americans; and the many French and French-Indian residents of the back country were also keen to defeat the British. When news of Fort Sackville reached Lieutenant Governor Henry Hamilton, the top British officer at Fort Detroit, he resolved to take back Vincennes for the British Crown.

Hamilton and the Indians

Hamilton forged powerful alliances with the Indians in the region. In return for supplies and arms, Indians raided white settlements to discourage American expansion—a goal the Indians and the British shared. An Irishman by birth, Hamilton had become skilled at negotiating with the Indians by operating on terms familiar to them. Americans called him the "hair-buyer general," accusing him of accepting white scalps in trade with the Indians. In his defense, Hamilton claimed that he told the Indians not to harm women and children. But warfare in the western wilderness lacked enforceable rules—the concept "crimes against humanity" had not yet been invented.

Battle of Fort Sackville

Hamilton set off for the Maumee–Wabash route from Detroit with approximately 30 British soldiers,

Crossing the Wabash

The march from Kaskaskia to Fort Sackville in February 1779 was miserable for George Rogers Clark and his men, complete with freezing rain and mud. This portion of Ezra Winter's mural immortalizing the trek idealizes Clark as a hero. The mural hangs in the rotunda of the George Rogers Clark Memorial in Vincennes, Indiana.

Hamilton Surrenders

Frederick C. Yohn's *The Fall of Fort Sackville* depicts the surrender of British-held Fort Sackville by Henry Hamilton to George Rogers Clark just outside the fort's walls. Indiana's schools celebrate George Rogers Clark Day on February 25 to commemorate his victory in 1779.

60 Indian warriors, and 145 mostly French-Canadian militia. The crossing at the portage was difficult, but as the force's forty boats sped down the Wabash River they attracted additional support from Indian tribes in the area. By mid-December, Hamilton's troops had reached Fort Sackville and retaken Vincennes.

When Clark discovered that Hamilton was at Vincennes, he was seriously concerned. His force numbered only 170 men, and he knew that if he waited until spring to attack Fort Sackville, Hamilton's forces would greatly outnumber his own. He decided that his only hope of victory was a midwinter surprise attack.

As Clark's men drew close to Vincennes in February 1779, they were running out of steam. They had traveled 180 miles, mostly on foot, and their supplies were almost gone. Clark's strategy was to lead by example, and it worked. When his tired and frozen militia balked at plunging into the freezing water of a flooded plain to reach Fort Sackville, Clark was the first man in. To fire up his troops even more, Clark blackened his face with gun powder and let out an ear-splitting war cry.

Hamilton was indeed surprised. Not expecting to fight until spring, he had allowed a large number of his troops to go home for the winter, as was convention in eighteenth-century warfare. When the Americans began to fire on Fort Sackville, Hamilton discovered that the bulk of his Canadian troops as well as the townspeople had deserted him. He was surrounded, outnumbered, and had no choice but to surrender.

Clark showed Hamilton and his followers a gruesome example of what happened to those who crossed him. His men dragged four pro-British Indians to the fort gate where they tomahawked and scalped them and threw their bloody corpses into the Wabash. The

Americans hoisted their flag over the fort and renamed it Fort Patrick Henry after the governor of Virginia who had approved Clark's western expedition against the British and their Indian allies. Clark took Hamilton prisoner and sent him under armed guard to Virginia where he remained in prison for a number of years enduring harsh conditions. Although Clark's plans to capture Fort Detroit failed, his stunning victory at Vincennes, on February 24, 1779, helped secure the Northwest Territory for the United States. It also sent a clear message: The Americans intended to step up their game until all of the land was theirs.

The "Hair-Buyer General"

Henry Hamilton was often called the "Hair-Buyer General" due to rumors that he paid for white scalps from Indians. This 1812 cartoon, created by William Charles, lambasts the practice of British officers paying bounties for American scalps during the War of 1812. On the left an Indian gives a British officer a bloody scalp while holding a rifle with a sign reading "Reward for Sixteen Scalps." On the right, another Indian is in the process of scalping an American soldier. In the background two Native Americans and two British soldiers dance gleefully around a campfire. In reality, scalping was practiced by both sides, but rarely. Americans often used the topic as a form of propaganda to exaggerate the atrocities of their enemies.

Clark's Legacy

Clark looms large in Indiana history. In the early twentieth century, Hoosiers spared no expense honoring his achievements. On Monument Circle in Indianapolis, Clark's statue stands heroically as the "Conqueror of the Country Northwest of the Ohio River from the British." In 1936 President Franklin Delano Roosevelt dedicated the grandest Clark monument of all, a massive Roman-style temple in Vincennes that cost $2,500,000. There, a twelve-ton, seven-and-a-half-foot bronze statue of the young Clark towers over visitors, a representation of his larger-than-life presence. On the monument's walls there are seven oil murals that depict the story of Clark's expedition. Artist Ezra Winter and six assistants labored on the murals for two and a half years. In 1966 the George Rogers Clark Memorial became part of the National Park Service. Clark's heroic status continued into the late twentieth century. In 1975 the Indiana General Assembly proclaimed February 25 as George Rogers Clark Day to be celebrated each year in schools across the state. In 1979 millions of Hoosiers displayed state license plates on their cars commemorating Clark.

The George Rogers Clark Memorial website includes the statement, "The truly great heroes of history age well and provide guidance for the future." For today's historians, this means considering Clark's achievement in a broader context than people did in the past. It is undeniable that Clark was brave, and to those whose cause he served, heroic. However, he also believed that the only way to fight Indians was "to excel them in barbarity." In today's more balanced consideration of Clark, he becomes more human and less a bronze statue of an eighteenth-century super hero.

2.2

Indiana from the Northwest Ordinance through Statehood

"There shall be neither Slavery nor involuntary Servitude in the said territory."

— *Northwest Ordinance of 1787, Article VI*

After the Americans freed themselves from British rule with the Treaty of Paris in 1783, they were eager to expand their new nation. However, they confronted a huge obstacle: the Indians stood firm on the land the Americans wanted. The new federal government was confident that it could solve the Indian problem, so it began to create policies that would make the western land, once settled, part of the new nation. Conquering and opening the West meant access to boundless new resources the young nation needed. Americans felt that the sooner this could happen, the better.

The Battle of Fallen Timbers

By the mid-1780s settlers were slowly but steadily moving north of the Ohio River. The Indians reacted by conducting raids against white settlements in

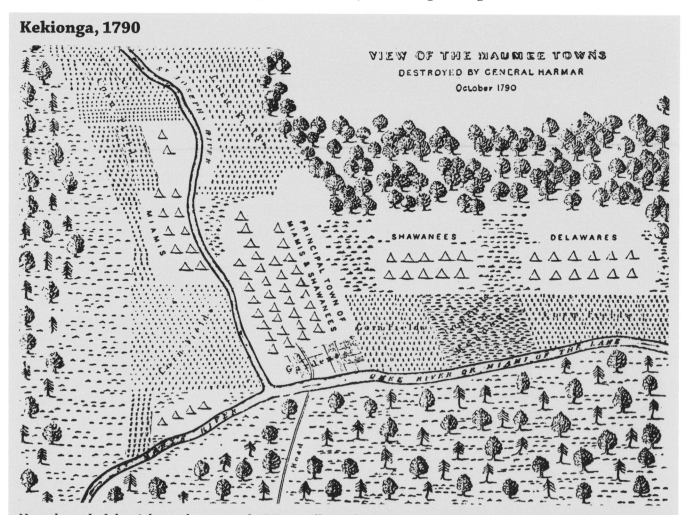

Kekionga, 1790

VIEW OF THE MAUMEE TOWNS
DESTROYED BY GENERAL HARMAR
October 1790

Near the end of the eighteenth century the Miami village of Kekionga, near the Maumee–Wabash Portage, was a center of trade and the home for many tribes, including Shawnee and Delaware. This map, drawn by American officer Lieutenant Ebenezer Denny in 1790 after General Josiah Harmar's forces failed to capture Kekionga, shows how the tribes lived alongside each other and where their corn was planted. After his victory against Kekionga's warriors at the Battle of Fallen Timbers, General Anthony Wayne established a fort at Kekionga and the area was known thereafter as Fort Wayne. (Bert Joseph Griswold and Mrs. Samuel R. Taylor, *Pictorial History of Fort Wayne* [Chicago: Robert O. Law, 1917])

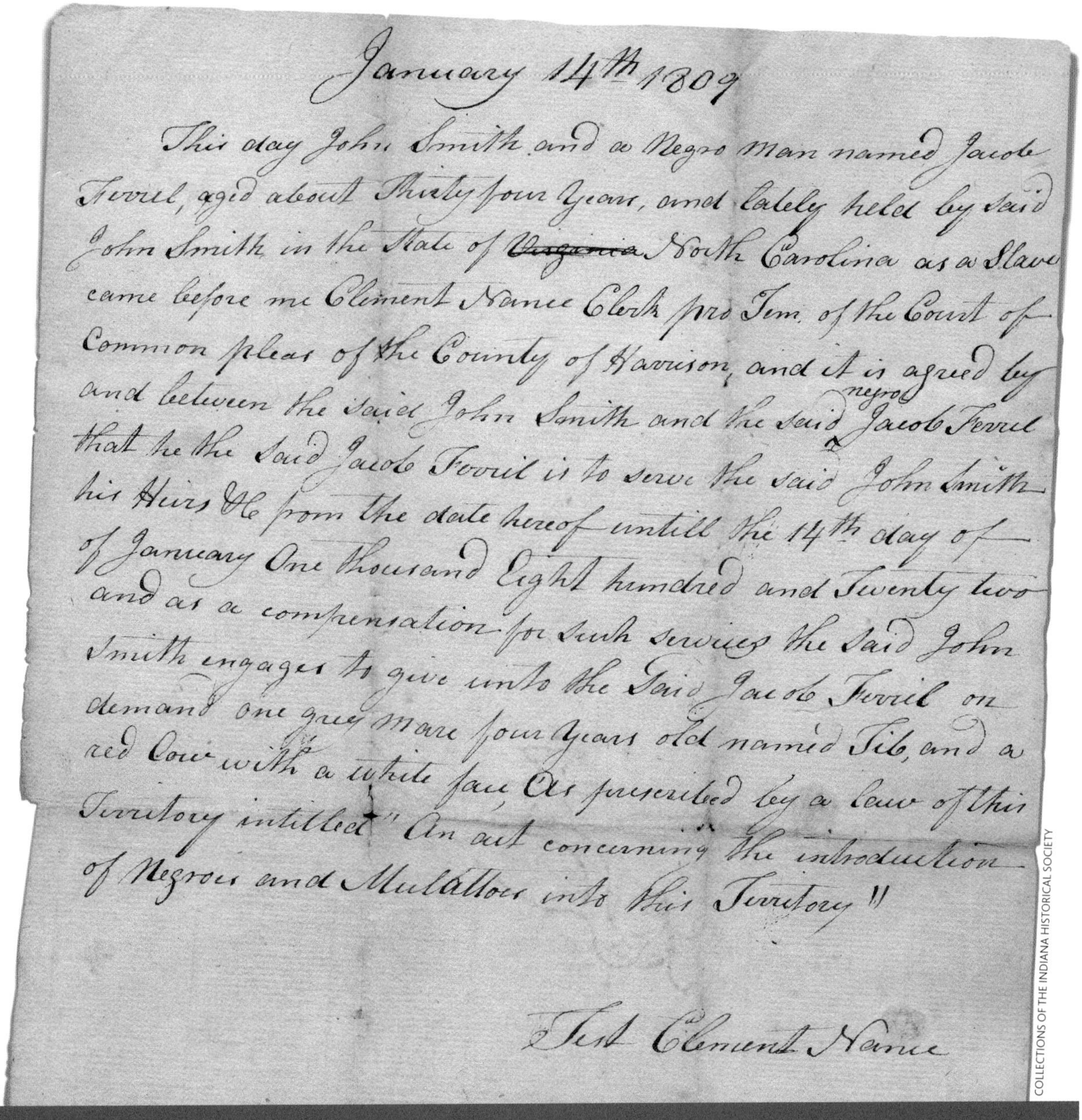

January 14th 1809

This day John Smith and a Negro man named Jacob Ferrel, aged about Thirty four Years, and lately held by said John Smith in the State of ~~Virginia~~ North Carolina as a Slave came before me Clement Nanee Clerk pro Tem. of the Court of Common pleas of the County of Harrison, and it is agreed by and between the said John Smith and the said negro *Jacob Ferrel that he the said Jacob Ferril is to serve the said John Smith his Heirs &c from the date hereof untill the 14th day of January One thousand Eight hundred and Twenty two and as a compensation for such services the said John Smith engages to give unto the said Jacob Ferril on demand one grey mare four Years old named Tib, and a red Cow with a white face, As prescribed by a law of this Territory intitled "An act concerning the introduction of Negroes and Mulattoes into this Territory"*

Test Clement Nanee

Indentured Servitude

Although slavery was outlawed in the Northwest Ordinance of 1787, Indiana passed an indentured servitude law in 1805, which circumvented rules against slavery by allowing slaves to be brought into Indiana for long periods of time as "indentured servants." Transcribed here is an 1809 document that traded thirteen years of Jacob Ferrel's working life for a horse and a cow. According to the indenture, Ferrel was to gain his freedom in 1822.

January 14th 1809

This day John Smith and a Negro man named Jacob Ferrel, aged about Thirty four years, and lately held by said John Smith in the state of ~~Virginia~~ North Carolina as a Slave came before me Clement [Nanee/Nance], Clerk pro Tem. of the Court of Common pleas of the County of Harrison, and it is agreed by and between the said John Smith and the said negro Jacob Ferrel that he the said Jacob Ferrel is to serve the said John Smith his Heirs &c from the date hereof until the 14th day of January 1822 and as a compensation for such serving the said John Smith engages to give unto the said Jacob Ferrel on demand one grey mare four years old named [Tib], and a red cow with a white face, as prescribed by a law of this territory entitled "An act concerning the introduction of Negroes and Mulattoes into this Territory."

Clement [Nanee/Nance]

present-day Kentucky and on the north side of the Ohio River. Settlers protected themselves the best they could, but they also begged the American government for help.

To solve the Indian problem in Indiana Territory and open it to American settlement, the government realized that it was essential to gain control of the portage between the Wabash and Maumee Rivers. This land break between the two rivers was the location of Kekionga, a meeting ground of the Miami, known to the Americans as Miamitown. Kekionga served as the base of an Indian confederation, consisting of the Miami and other tribes. The Americans had conducted two major military expeditions against Kekionga, but both had failed. A confederacy of tribes, led by Miami Chief Little Turtle, defeated the Americans in bloody battles near that site in 1790 and 1791.

The tide turned in favor of the Americans in 1794 at the Battle of Fallen Timbers. In a grove of trees felled by a storm near the Maumee River, U.S. General Anthony Wayne led the third and largest expedition against Kekionga's forces and won a decisive victory. Wayne, whom Little Turtle referred to as "the chief who never sleeps," won the battle in about an hour with fewer than one hundred total fatalities — twenty-six Americans, and about twice that many Indians.

After The Battle of Fallen Timbers, Wayne built a fort on the site of Kekionga and named it after himself. Fort Wayne was evidence of Americans gaining control over the critical Maumee–Wabash Portage. Little Turtle and many other chiefs saw the handwriting on the wall and decided it was in their best interests to accommodate the Americans and maintain peace. Many of them donned white man's clothing, acquired land, and practiced white

Development of the Indiana Territory

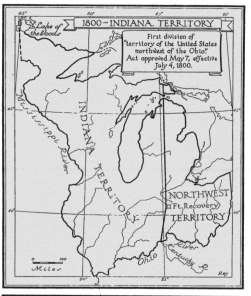

This map shows the evolution of the Indiana Territory from 1800 to 1809. (R. Carlyle Buley, *The Old Northwest Pioneer Period, 1815–1840* [Indianapolis: Indiana Historical Society, 1950], 62–64)

man's customs; some accepted annuities, or payments, from the U.S. government. Little Turtle even accepted an African American slave as payment for helping negotiate a treaty with Native Americans. Stalwart resistors, such as Tecumseh, however, remained steadfast and fought the American invaders.

The Northwest Ordinance of 1787— a Roadmap to Statehood

In order for the American federal government to guarantee that the western lands were settled in an orderly fashion, it needed to devise a workable plan. There were many options, and there was plenty of debate over what that plan would be. In 1787 the American government came up with a policy that would be a win-win for the westerners and the country as a whole.

The Northwest Ordinance, which laid the foundation for government in the West, is considered by today's historians an example of federalism at its most pragmatic and intelligent. The ordinance allowed for the gradual transfer of power from the federal government to a group of western territories until a democratic balance was struck.

At first the ordinance established a single government for the Northwest Territory, which included all land northwest of the Ohio River and east of the Mississippi River, but it also provided for eventual division of the territory into three to five smaller territories. There were three stages of government for each territory. In the first the federal government appointed a governor, a secretary, and three judges for the territory. Residents of the territory enjoyed the same rights and privileges as the thirteen original states, including freedom of religion, trial by jury, and other rights of free Americans. In the second stage, the territory was allowed to elect the lower house of the territorial legislature. This stage was reached when five thousand free adult males in the territory owned at least fifty acres of land each. Though the territorial legislature could choose a delegate to Congress to speak on the territory's behalf, the delegate was not allowed to vote. When a territory had sixty thousand inhabitants, it had reached the third stage and could petition for

statehood. In a controversial provision, the ordinance prohibited slavery in the emerging territories.

The Indiana Territory

The Indiana Territory was created in 1800 and lasted sixteen years. Originally, it extended from the Ohio River to the southern border of Canada, west to the Mississippi River and east to the boundary with what would become Ohio. When it was founded, the territory had a total white population of 5,641 which was concentrated around Clark's Grant (eventually Clarksville) on the Ohio River and in Vincennes, the territorial capital. During the thirteen years between legislating for the Northwest Territory and the creation of the Indiana Territory, settlers had often voiced their disgruntlement at being governed by a leader who had been given near total control; they demanded more democratic government at the territorial stage. Thus, when the Indiana Territory was partitioned off the Northwest Territory, the law was changed to allow the second stage of government to occur when the majority of freeholders wanted it—not when five thousand free adult males in the territory owned at least fifty acres of land each.

By 1810 the population of the Indiana Territory had grown to 24,520 residents. However, the territory was smaller in geographical size, due to the splitting off and creation of the Michigan Territory in 1805 and the Illinois Territory in 1809. Because newcomers settled in southeastern Indiana as well as along the Wabash River in southwestern Indiana, Hoosiers moved their capital from Vincennes to the more central location of Corydon in 1813.

The Move to Statehood

From the beginning there was disagreement in the Indiana Territory about the mode of government and it only got worse. Residents were unhappy with the concentration of power that rested with the territorial governor, William Henry Harrison. After some pressure, Harrison agreed to allow a vote for moving to the second, or representative, stage of territorial government in 1804.

In addition to the desire to be more self-governing, many people in the Indiana territory did not want slavery. However, the French settlers at Vincennes had owned slaves as early as the mid-eighteenth century, and despite the prohibition of slavery in the Northwest Ordinance, the institution continued.

Harrison and some wealthy landowners who were pro-slavery passed an indentured servant law in 1805. This law enabled those with slaves to bring them into the Indiana Territory and hold them as "indentured servants" for long periods of time. John Badollet, one of the territory's most fervent antislavery spokesmen, angered Harrison when he drafted and circulated a petition to the U.S. Congress in 1809 describing slavery as: "A system outraging at once the laws of natural justice, the principles of our institutions, the maxims of sound policy, and the holy religion we profess."

In 1810 the antislavery forces repealed the 1805 indenture law in the territorial general assembly. At this time, people in the Indiana Territory felt it was time to move toward statehood. The Indiana House first petitioned Congress for statehood in 1811, but the War of 1812 stalled the movement. The push for statehood was revived in 1815, when the Indiana Territory had a population of 63,897, more than the Northwest Ordinance required for statehood.

Statehood!

Jonathan Jennings led the pro-statehood group. He was a critic of Harrison and had been outspoken against slavery. Congress responded positively to the statehood cause. On April 19, 1816, it passed an Enabling Act that provided for an election of delegates to a convention that could form a state constitution.

The Indiana Constitutional Convention was held in Corydon in June 1816. In summer heat and humidity, the forty-three delegates sometimes met in the shade of a large elm tree. They studied the state constitutions of neighboring Ohio and Kentucky, and they also grappled with issues unique to Indiana. The convention had a share of delegates that were pro-slavery, but a majority of the delegates were anti-slavery and their ideas prevailed.

The Constitution of 1816 represents the clearest statement of values and beliefs of early pioneer Indiana. It opened with a bill of rights guaranteeing Hoosiers freedom of worship, press, and speech, and the right to bear arms and to assemble peaceably. Voting was restricted to white male citizens over the age of twenty-one who had lived in the state for at least one year; women and African Americans were not allowed to vote. The constitution also contained the promise of a free education for all citizens—a very progressive inclusion for the era. Mindful of the conflict over slavery, the delegates at Corydon made it a point to declare in the constitution, "There shall be neither slavery nor involuntary servitude in this state."

The new constitution was signed on June 29, 1816, and took effect immediately. In November 1816 Jennings was elected the first governor of the state of Indiana. On December 11, 1816, President James Madison signed the congressional resolution admitting Indiana to the Union as its nineteenth state. It was now up to Hoosiers to define their place in the American nation.

The Constitution Elm

Delegates met in the summer of 1816 in Corydon to write Indiana's first constitution. Occasionally they moved outside to the shade of this tree, known as the "Constitution Elm." The tree's branches were trimmed in 1925 due to disease. The wood and shavings were preserved and made into souvenirs; in 2000, remnants were used in a display case for both of Indiana's constitutions at the Indiana Statehouse in Indianapolis. The remaining portion of the trunk is on display in a sandstone monument in Corydon.

Tecumseh and Harrison at Grouseland

In August 1810 Tecumseh and William Henry Harrison met on the grounds of Harrison's home, in Vincennes. At one point, tensions boiled over when both parties drew their weapons, as this lithograph illustrates. The hostility was resolved without violence, and talks resumed. However, neither man gained ground in the talks and the Battle of Tippecanoe and the War of 1812 soon followed.

2.3

William Henry Harrison (1773–1841)

"The introduction of Slavery into this territory continues to be the Hobby horse of the influential men here."

— *John Badollet, Register of the Land Office of Vincennes, to Albert Gallatin, Secretary of the U.S. Treasury, August 31, 1805*

Few men had as large an impact on Indiana during the pioneer era as William Henry Harrison. He was a complex individual who possessed many admirable qualities and accomplished a great deal in his adopted state, but he also had a knack for irritating modest, practical Hoosiers. One thing is certain—Harrison's actions in Indiana distinguished him on the national stage when he was a young man. He subsequently built on the accomplishments of his Indiana years to attain the highest office in the land, President of the United States.

Early Life

Harrison was born to a prominent Virginia family on February 9, 1773. One of his paternal ancestors was elected to the governing council in Jamestown in the 1630s. His father Benjamin, who owned a vast plantation, signed the Declaration of Independence. Harrison attended Hampden–Sydney College for three years where he received a classical education, focusing on Greek, Latin, logic, and debate. His parents then sent him to study medicine in Richmond and later in Philadelphia. In spring 1791 Harrison's father died and he discovered that his family was having financial difficulty and could not continue to pay for his education.

Harrison joined the army at the age of eighteen and became knowledgeable about Indians and the state of affairs on the western frontier. In 1794 he served bravely at the Battle of Fallen Timbers as General Anthony Wayne's aide-de-camp. From that point forth, Harrison was on the fast track to success.

In 1795 Harrison met Anna Symmes, the beautiful, twenty-year-old daughter of Colonel John Symmes, a distinguished Revolutionary War colonel. It was love at first sight. Anna and Harrison married soon after, despite Colonel Symmes's disapproval; he did not want his favorite daughter to marry a soldier. Nevertheless, it was a happy marriage and the couple had ten children.

Governor of the Indiana Territory

In 1800 President John Adams appointed twenty-seven-year-old Harrison to be the first governor of the new Indiana Territory. Harrison and his family, which by that point included three young children, moved to Vincennes, a settlement with around one thousand residents, many of whom were of French and/or Indian descent. By 1805 they had built an opulent thirteen-room brick mansion, with hand-carved woodwork and a grand staircase. Harrison named his home Grouseland and staffed it with former slaves with whom he had signed indentured servitude contracts. This conspicuous show of wealth would come to haunt Harrison. To the local population it marked him as an elitist and an outsider.

Harrison's pro-slavery stance also made him unpopular with the majority of the population in the Indiana Territory. In 1802 he used his clout to call a territorial convention to consider repealing Article VI of the Northwest Ordinance, which prohibited slavery. Although this attempt failed, in 1805 Harrison and the territorial judges passed a law that allowed slaves to be brought into the Indiana Territory as indentured servants. In time, however, the anti-slavery movement in Indiana proved to be stronger than Harrison and the pro-slavery forces. In 1810 the general assembly repealed the indentured servitude law; and when the territory gained statehood five years later, slavery and involuntary servitude were banned.

Harrison and the Indians

Even though his East Coast ways and pro-slavery stance alienated many people in the Indiana Territory, Harrison continued to please his superiors in Washington, DC, especially in the area of Indian relations. Between 1803 and 1809 Harrison served President Thomas Jefferson by shrewdly negotiating

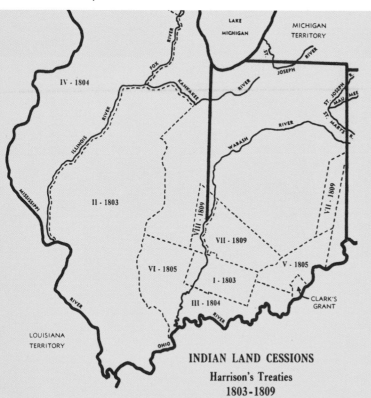

INDIAN LAND CESSIONS

Harrison's Treaties
1803-1809

  I. June 7, 1803, at Fort Wayne, with the Delawares, Shawnee, Potawatomi, Miami, Eel Rivers, Wea, Kickapoo, Piankashaw, and Kaskaskia.
 II. August 13, 1803, at Vincennes, with the Kaskaskia.
III. August 18 and 27, 1804, at Vincennes, with the Delawares and Piankashaw.
 IV. November 3, 1804, at St. Louis, with the Sauk and Foxes.
  V. August 21, 1805, at Grouseland, with the Delawares, Potawatomi, Miami, Eel Rivers, and Wea.
 VI. December 30, 1805, at Vincennes, with the Piankashaw.
VII. September 30, 1809, at Fort Wayne, with the Delawares, Potawatomi, Miami, Eel Rivers, and Wea.
VIII. December 9, 1809, at Vincennes, with the Kickapoo.

In 1803 U.S. President Thomas Jefferson tasked William Henry Harrison with quickly obtaining land east of the Mississippi River. Harrison proved capable; within six years he had secured most of modern-day Illinois and southern Indiana through treaties with the Native Americans. This map shows the areas obtained through the treaties, the locations where the treaties were negotiated, the dates they were signed, and the tribes who signed them. (John D. Barnhart and Dorothy L. Riker, *Indiana to 1816: The Colonial Period*, The History of Indiana 1 [Indianapolis: Indiana Historical Society and Indiana Historical Bureau, 1971], 377) many treaties with Miami, Potawatomi, Delaware, Shawnee, and other tribes, opening millions of acres of land to white settlement in Indiana and Illinois. Harrison was skillful at identifying the most persuadable chiefs and using them to divide and conquer more resistant ones. When necessary, he rewarded chiefs who agreed to cede land on his terms with gifts and bribes. He also reminded them of the invincibility of the Americans.

Harrison's negotiating tactics worked with many Indian chiefs, but not Tecumseh, the powerful Shawnee chief, who defiantly refused any terms Harrison offered. These two men—arguably the most powerful in the West—met several times, including at Harrison's home Grouseland in August 1810. Tensions always ran high at their meetings; at one Tecumseh called Harrison a liar, and Harrison responded by drawing his sword. No blood was shed during that incident, but it soon would be.

In fall 1811 Harrison felt it was urgent to squelch the Indian rebellion fueled by Tecumseh and his brother Tenskwatawa, known as the Prophet. When he knew that Tecumseh was away from Prophetstown recruiting Indians to join his growing anti-American confederation, Harrison decided to make his move. On November 6 Harrison's militia of about a thousand men camped along the Wabash River, planning to strike Prophetstown at daybreak. Instead, the Indians attacked before dawn, ineptly led by the Prophet. Two hours of fierce fighting concluded with an Indian retreat. Although Harrison proclaimed the Battle of Tippecanoe a total victory, it was far from it. Almost one-fifth of his men were dead or wounded. Harrison was unscathed in the battle, except for a bullet hole in his hat.

War of 1812

When the War of 1812 broke out, Harrison resigned his post as Governor of the Indiana Territory and rejoined the army. After a series of swift promotions, he attained the position of brigadier general. In fall 1813 Harrison successfully retook the fort at Detroit, which had been surrendered to the British the previous year. Then he and his army pursued British troops working in collaboration with Tecumseh in Ontario, Canada. There, at the Battle of the Thames, Tecumseh died, and Harrison emerged a hero. In May 1814 Harrison resigned from the army and left for Ohio, where his family had been living in his absence, but returned to the army to negotiate post-war treaties with the Indians at the request of President James Madison.

Political Career Continues

From his farm and large home on the Ohio River, named North Bend, Harrison earned a reputation as an advocate for veterans, a generous host, and a civic leader. In 1816 he filled the seat of an Indiana congressman who had resigned, marking the launch of a new political career. During his time in Congress, he continued to champion the cause of wounded veterans and widows of men who died in combat. He did not seek reelection in 1819, but that same year he agreed to run for the Ohio State Senate and won. After his stint in the state legislature, he returned to Washington in 1825 as one of Ohio's two U.S. senators.

In 1829 Harrison returned to Ohio after serving as an ambassador to Colombia for a brief time. He threw himself into various business ventures, many of which failed. He constantly felt the financial strain of trying to support a large family and applied for positions that would bring in extra income. In 1831 he ran for the United States Senate and lost, and for a time it looked as if his political career was over. Five years later, though, Harrison was in the thick of national politics.

Presidential Campaign

Harrison's presidential campaign of 1840 was a brilliant public relations model that is still emulated by politicians today. His famous slogan, "Tippecanoe and Tyler, too," was a catchy phrase with very little substance, yet it is still remembered today. Tippecanoe, of course, referred to Harrison's victory in battle against the Indians. The Whig Party, on which ticket Harrison was running, chose John Tyler of Virginia to be Harrison's vice presidential running mate.

The Whigs promoted Harrison's "pioneer virtues" in lavish parades with symbols such as log cabins and hard cider, knowing that they would appeal to the American populace, which was primarily rural and hard-working. In contrast, his opponent Martin Van Buren was portrayed as a wine-drinking rich man and a Washington insider. A quick glance at today's presidential campaigns shows how enduring this marketing ploy turned out to be. A contemporary biographer of Harrison wrote, "The log cabin image grew to be so popular that it became almost imperative for every Whig politician to find a log cabin in his history."

A Short-Lived Presidency

Finding out who won the 1840 presidential election took several weeks in the era before electronic voting machines. Voting began on October 30 and continued until November 18. When all of the votes were counted, the result was an Electoral College landslide for Harrison, who won 234 votes to Van Buren's 60. The Whigs also gained control of Congress.

Harrison rode his favorite horse Whitey to his inauguration in Washington, DC, on March 4, 1841. Although it was a cold, wet day in the capital, Harrison wore no overcoat and waved his hat at the crowds. At the age of sixty-eight, he would be the oldest president sworn into office until Ronald Reagan in 1980. Another record that Harrison set was the length of his inaugura-tion speech. It lasted almost two hours—the longest of any President of the United States through at least 2013.

The many hours Harrison spent in the cold and slush on inauguration day took its toll. He soon contracted pneumonia. None of the favored medical methods of the day—bleeding, cupping, opium, castor oil, camphor, wine or brandy—improved his condition. Harrison died on April 4, 1841, exactly one month after he took office. Anna (Symmes) Harrison, who never wanted her husband to run for president, never entered the White House.

Harrison had a grand and dignified funeral, a credit to the American people who had not mourned a sitting president before. His body lay in state in the White House in a glass-topped coffin where thousands of citizens filed past to pay their respects. In the funeral procession, Harrison's horse trotted without a rider to symbolize the fallen leader. At Anna's request, Harrison's final resting place was near her father's grave in North Bend, Ohio.

Harrison's grandson, Benjamin, was elected president in 1888. Benjamin's presidential campaign, organized from his home in Indianapolis, adopted many of the features of his grandfather's 1840 log cabin campaign. As of 2013 Benjamin Harrison was the only grandson of a former president to hold the office.

"Tippecanoe and Tyler, too!"

During the 1840 political campaign for the presidency, Harrison and his political party, the Whigs, branded him as a common "man of the people." This campaign advertisement shows just that: Harrison is standing outside a log cabin, sharing hard cider with soldiers, reminding voters of Harrison's participation in the War of 1812. Supporters flooded voters with similar posters and badges. In reality, the Whigs were misrepresenting Harrison. He was well-educated, from an established Virginia family, and lived in a luxurious house in North Bend, Ohio. The tactic worked, and Harrison won the election.

2.4

William Conner (1777–1855)

"Profit was the one continuity in William Conner's otherwise eclectic life."

— John Lauritz Larson and David G. Vanderstel, Indiana Magazine of History, *1984*

Early life

Born in present-day Ohio, William Conner was the third son of Richard Conner and his wife Margaret. Margaret had been a captive of the Shawnee from childhood, and when Richard ransomed her in order to marry her, he promised the Shawnee their firstborn son. In 1771 James, their firstborn, arrived. The Conners gave him to the Shawnee and ransomed him back a short time later.

The Conner family lived for the most part in Ohio, but they also moved around the Northwest frontier, living among Moravian missionaries and Christian Shawnee and Delaware. Richard supported his family by trading with the Indians and working as an interpreter between the Indians and settlers in the area. During the Revolutionary War, the Conners followed the Moravians to what is now Michigan, where Richard founded Macomb County and the city of Mount Clemens, the county seat.

Richard lived to the advanced age of eighty-nine and was quite successful; he acquired thousands of acres of land and established an important trading post in southeastern Michigan. He left his family very well-off when he died. All of his sons inherited land, but William and his brother John, who was two years older than William, were restless to leave Michigan and seek their own fortunes. In 1800 they traveled south to the Indiana Territory.

In the Indiana wilderness the Conner brothers became licensed traders who dealt with the Delaware Indians near the west fork of the White River, a convenient location for fur trade and commerce. In 1802 William married Mekinges, the daughter of Delaware chief William Anderson, whose name gives evidence to the prevalence of intermarriage between whites and Indians. The Conners moved about twenty-five miles from Anderson's village and had six children.

Having an Indian wife earned Conner special status and trust among the Indians, which proved useful in his business ventures. He emulated his father's lifestyle and became a successful trader and interpreter. For about a decade William and John built a robust business trading with the Indians, taking advantage of the long relationship the Conners had established with them over two generations.

Agent of Removal

By 1811 William Conner was using his connections with the Indians to help the United States government acquire Indian land. Conner aided William Henry Harrison in his mission to get the Indians to cede their land by using his interpretive skills to assist in treaty negotiations that worked to the Americans' advantage.

People today sometimes wonder what was going through Conner's mind during this time, because his personal life was full of contradictions and conflict. He was married to an Indian woman and his children were half Indian, yet he enlisted with General Harrison's troops to fight against the Indians and the British in the War of 1812. He was present at the crucial Battle of the Thames and helped identify the mutilated body of the great Shawnee warrior Tecumseh. After the war was over, Conner resumed his role as an agent of the federal government, serving as interpreter when Americans negotiated treaties with the Indians. In this way, he played an essential role in the process of Indians

William Conner

This portrait of William Conner was painted by Jacob Cox, ca. 1850.

Conner House

Located on two hundred acres in Hamilton County, Indiana, Conner Prairie is a living history museum, occupying the land of William Conner's original home (pictured here). In Conner's time the acreage was surrounded on three sides by the White River, which flooded the grounds early each spring. The floods left a layer of rich soil and kept trees from growing evenly, making the land ideal for planting. Whereas most settlers in Hamilton County had to spend a great deal of time and energy clearing land of forest before they could plant crops, Conner's prairie was ready for agriculture.

In 1934 Eli Lilly, an Indianapolis businessman who was president of the pharmaceutical manufacturer Eli Lilly and Company, discovered that William Conner's home had fallen into disrepair. He bought the Conner homestead and began to finance its restoration. Lilly began producing historic pageants at the site and invited the

public, believing this was an engaging way for Hoosiers to learn about their pioneer heritage.

Lilly lived to see the creation of 1836 Prairietown, a fictitious pioneer community with a blacksmith shop, a pottery shop, a schoolhouse, and more. Prairietown is "populated" by staff in historic costume demonstrating the ways early Hoosier pioneers lived. Visitors to Prairietown are invited to join them in tasks such as chopping wood, throwing pots, and caring for farm animals. When Prairietown was first created in the 1970s, it was a unique approach to learning about history. Since then, many sites around the world have created "living history" experiences modeled on Prairietown.

Conner Prairie Interactive History Park continues to change with the times in order to bring historical experience to life in the twenty-first century. The Smithsonian Institution's only Indiana affiliate, it has received many awards for its innovation in teaching history, including the National Medal for Museum and Library Service in 2010. In recent years, new hands-on exhibits, such as the 1859 Balloon Voyage and "Civil War Journey: Raid on Indiana," have been added and are enjoyed by thousands of visitors of all ages each year.

COLLECTIONS OF THE INDIANA HISTORICAL SOCIETY

ceding, or signing over, their land to the government.

In 1818, two years after Indiana became a state, Conner was present at the signing of the Treaty of Saint Mary's. This document set the terms for the removal of the White River Delaware, which included his wife Mekinges and their children. Rather than leave for Missouri with his family and start his trading business anew, he gave them supplies for their long journey and stayed in Indiana. He left no personal record to explain his decision, so we can only speculate about it. It is possible that Conner chose to stay behind because he

could see the boundless opportunities to make a fortune in Indiana, now that the land was fully available to white enterprise. By contrast, in Missouri he might have to start over as a trader and might never enjoy opportunities such as those available in Indiana. On one 1829 public record—a petition seeking clarification of a title to some of his land—Conner portrayed himself as a neutral or even benevolent bystander to the Indian removal process in Indiana, stating that "he had lived among the Indians, and fed them when they had not the means to do it; and at all times was engaged in preparing their minds for the sale of their land to the United States."

A Frontier Capitalist

Three months after Mekinges and their children headed west, Conner married Elizabeth Chapman, a seventeen-year-old white woman who was the step-daughter of a recent settler. At forty-four, William was considerably older than his bride, but he was intent on starting a new life in the growing white community. The couple had ten children.

In 1823 Conner replaced his log cabin on the White River with a large brick house. Conner's home was the grandest and most important building in the region. In 1823, when Hamilton County was founded, the house served as the seat of its government, a courthouse, and a post office. Conner was the county's first treasurer.

Because he was one of the first white men in the area and played a key role in treaty negotiations with the Indians, Conner was able to acquire a great deal of land. He was fortunate in his business dealings; nearly all his ventures were successful, and eventually he became a very wealthy man. Over the course of his long life Conner continued to expand his empire in many ways. He remained active in Indian affairs; even

License to Trade with Miami Indians

BY WILLIAM HENRY HARRISON,

GOVERNOR OF THE INDIANA TERRITORY, AND SUPERINTENDANT OF INDIAN AFFAIRS.

WHEREAS *Bennoist Bizayou* of the county of *Knox* hath made application for permiſſion to trade with the *Miamis* nation of Indians, and hath given bond according to law, for the due obſervance of all the laws and regulations for the government of the trade with Indians that now are, or hereafter may be enacted and eſtabliſhed, licenſe is hereby granted to the ſaid *Bennoist Bizayou* to trade with the ſaid *Miamis* nation, at their town *on the Wabash* and there to ſell, barter and exchange with the individuals of the ſaid nation, all manner of goods, wares and merchandizes, conformably to the laws and regulations aforeſaid; but under this expreſs condition and reſtriction, that the ſaid *Bennoist Bizayou* ſhall not, by *his* ſervants, agents or factors, carry or cauſe to be carried to the hunting camps of the Indians of ſaid nation, any ſpecies of goods or merchandize whatſoever, and more eſpecially ſpirituous liquors of any kind; nor ſhall barter or exchange the ſame, or any of them, in any quantity whatever, on pain of forfeiture of this licenſe, and of the goods, wares and merchandize, and of the ſpirituous liquors which may have been carried to the ſaid camps, contrary to the true intent and meaning hereof, and of having *his* bond put in ſuit: and the Indians of the ſaid nation are at full liberty to ſeize and confiſcate the ſaid liquors ſo carried, and the owner or owners ſhall have no claim for the ſame, either upon the ſaid nation, or any individual thereof, nor upon the United States.

This licenſe to continue in force for one year, unleſs ſooner revoked.

GIVEN under my hand and ſeal, the *Thirtieth* day of *December*, in the year of our Lord one thouſand eight hundred and *Seven*.

Willm Henry Harrison

Trade with Native Americans was a lucrative business. William Conner and other traders needed to procure a license such as this one from Indiana Territorial Governor William Henry Harrison before undertaking business.

though most of the Indians had been removed west, there were still land disputes with those who remained behind. For decades, Conner continued to prove useful in negotiations and acquired more and more land. At the time of his death in 1855, he owned more than four thousand acres in Hamilton County. He also engaged in retail trade, manufacturing, town building (he founded Noblesville), and politics. One historian points out that although William served three terms in the state legislature from 1829 to 1837, he was not by nature a political animal. He saw politics as a means to an end—building a road, developing land, and, above all, creating personal profit.

Legacy

William Conner died at the age of seventy-eight and is buried in Crownland Cemetery in Noblesville, near many of his descendants. Toward the end of his life, in addition to being recognized as one of the wealthiest and most prominent citizens in Indiana, Conner was considered a living historical figure. People often asked him to tell stories about his experiences on the frontier and about his life with the Indians. In old age, Conner was one of the few people alive who had experienced the territory's transition from wilderness to a rapidly developing state—and he was not just a witness to this transformation, he was an agent of it. On the other hand, Conner and other Americans who were among the first to live alongside the Indians, brought American civilization with them, which eventually resulted in the destruction of the Indians' way of life.

In light of William Conner's profound impact on Indiana and Hamilton County in particular, it is appropriate that Conner Prairie, his former home, has become a living history center where Hoosiers can learn more about the man and his times.

Selected Bibliography

Barnhart, John D., and Dorothy L. Riker. *Indiana to 1816: The Colonial Period*. The History of Indiana 1. Indianapolis: Indiana Historical Bureau and Indiana Historical Society, 1971.

Birkbeck, Morris. *Notes on a Journey in America from the Coast of Virginia to the Territory of Illinois*. 4th ed. London: Severn and Co., 1818. Internet Archive.

Cayton, Andrew R. L. *Frontier Indiana*. Bloomington: Indiana University Press, 1996.

Cleaves, Freeman. *Old Tippecanoe*. New York: Charles Scribner's Sons, 1939.

Collins, Gail. *William Henry Harrison*. The American Presidents. New York: Times Books/Henry Holt and Co., 2012.

Crawford, Mary M., ed. "Mrs. Lydia B. Bacon's Journal, 1811–1812." *Indiana Magazine of History* 40, no. 4 (December 1944): 367–86.

Dora, Bob. "Along the Wabash: Dora Family History Leads Back to Indiana's Earliest Recorded European Settlers." *The Hoosier Genealogist: Connections* 50, no. 2 (Fall/Winter 2010): 68–79.

Gaff, Alan D. *Bayonets in the Wilderness: Anthony Wayne's Legion in the Old Northwest*. Norman, OK: University of Oklahoma Press, 2004.

Indiana Historical Bureau. "George Rogers Clark: Winning the Old Northwest." *The Indiana Historian* (December 1997).

Horsman, Reginald. "William Henry Harrison: Virginia Gentleman in the Old Northwest." *Indiana Magazine of History* 96, no. 2 (June 2000): 125–49.

Larson, John Lauritz, and David G. Vanderstel. "Agent of Empire: William Conner on the Indiana Frontier, 1800–1855." *Indiana Magazine of History* 80, no. 4 (December 1984): 301–28.

Madison, James H. *Hoosiers: A New History of Indiana*. Bloomington: Indiana University Press; Indianapolis: Indiana Historical Society Press, 2014.

Merriam, John M. *The Legislative History of the Ordinance of 1787*. Worcester, MA: American Antiquarian Society, 1888.

Mills, Randy K. *Jonathan Jennings: Indiana's First Governor*. Indiana Biography Series. Indianapolis: Indiana Historical Society Press, 2005.

Murphy, David Thomas. *Murder in Their Hearts: The Fall Creek Massacre*. Indianapolis: Indiana Historical Society Press, 2010.

Sheehan, Bernard W. "The Characters of Henry Hamilton and George Rogers Clark Compared." In *Indiana History: A Book of Readings*, compiled and edited by Ralph D. Gray, 38–44. Bloomington: Indiana University Press, 1994.

———. "'The Famous Hair Buyer General': Henry Hamilton, George Rogers Clark, and the American Indian." *Indiana Magazine of History* 79, no. 1 (December 1984): 1–28.

Taylor, Robert M., Jr., ed. *The Northwest Ordinance, 1787: A Bicentennial Handbook*. Indianapolis: Indiana Historical Society, 1987.

Thornbrough, Gayle, ed. *The Correspondence of John Badollet and Albert Gallatin, 1804–1836*. Indiana Historical Society Publications 22. Indianapolis: Indiana Historical Society, 1963.

Waller, George M. *The American Revolution in the West*. Chicago: Nelson–Hall, 1976.

Essential Questions

1 How did the British and native groups work together in an attempt to halt the westward movement of Americans?

2 How did the Battle of Fallen Timbers mark a turning point in the Americans' pursuit for Indian lands?

3 What was the result of the American attempt to Americanize native peoples?

4 How did the policy of Indian removal affect the Indiana frontier?

5 What roles did the following individuals play in securing Indian lands for settlement:

  A George Rogers Clark

  B William Henry Harrison

  C William Conner

6 How did the Northwest Ordinance of 1787 provide a path to statehood for the territories it established?

7 Why was slavery a divisive issue during Indiana's territorial period and how was the issue resolved in the 1816 constitution?*

See student activities related to this question.

Activity 1: The Issue of Slavery in Indiana Territory

Introduction: As Indiana progressed along the path toward statehood mapped out in the Northwest Ordinance of 1787, the issue of whether or not to allow slavery became a divisive one. Slaves were brought to Indiana by French settlers before the Northwest Territory was established. However, in Article VI, the Northwest Ordinance forbade slavery in the territories it established.

Article VI was circumvented by many settlers who owned slaves, including the territorial governor, William Henry Harrison. The pro-slavers urged that this article be removed.

As you have read, Harrison and other pro-slavery advocates were opposed by an anti-slavery contingent including John Badollet. Badollet's reasons for opposing slavery were based on morality. He stated:

> [Slavery is] *"a system outraging at once the laws of natural justice, the principles of our institutions, the maxims of sound policy, and the holy religion we profess."* (Thornbrough, 334)

On the other hand, Harrison and many others in the territory felt that slavery was practical and economically advantageous. Harrison and a delegation of pro-slavers sent a petition (referred to as a "memorial") to a committee of the fourteenth United States Congress led by John Randolph of Virginia. In this memorial, they asked that Congress repeal Article VI of the Northwest Ordinance, thus allowing slavery to exist in the Indiana Territory. Randolph responded to Harrison and the other petitioners with the following statement:

> *The Committee to whom the memorial of the Indiana Convention, Gov Harrisons Letter, &c* ~~are referred~~ *were referred, reported,*

> *That the rapid population of the State of Ohio sufficiently* evinces *in the opinion of your Committee that the labour of slaves is not necessary to promote the growth and settlement of Colonies in that region. That this labour,* demonstrably *the dearest of any, can only be employed to advantage in the cultivation of products more valuable than any known in that quarter of the U. States: That the Committee deem it highly dangerous and* inexpedient *to impair a provision wisely calculated to promote the happiness and prosperity of the N. Western Country and to give strength and security to that extensive frontier. In the salutary operations of this sagacious and benevolent restraint, it is believed*

that the inhabitants of Indiana, will at no very distant ~~period~~ day, find ample remuneration for a temporary privation of labour and of immigration.
(William Henry Harrison Papers)

Glossary

Evinces: Clearly shows; makes evident

Demonstrably: Obviously

Dearest: Most expensive or highest-priced

Inexpedient: Inadvisable; not recommended

Provision: A clause in a legal document

Calculated: Carefully thought out or planned

Salutary: Promoting a beneficial purpose; wholesome or healthful

Sagacious: Wise or intelligent

Benevolent: Intended to benefit or help others

Restraint: The act of controlling; In this case, restraint refers to the prohibition on slavery

Remuneration: Reward as in money

Privation: The act of being deprived of something, hardship

▶ **After you have had a chance to read both the quotation by John Badollet and the U.S. Congressional Committee's response to the memorial by Harrison and the pro-slavery advocates, take a few moments to put both statements into your own words.**

1 Rewrite Badollet's description of slavery (below) in the form of a tweet. Remember that you may only use 140 characters in your tweet! Be persuasive and focus on encouraging your followers to oppose slavery for the same reasons you do.

[Slavery is] a system outraging at once the laws of natural justice, the principles of our institutions, the maxims of sound policy, and the holy religion we profess.

2 Consider the following: What answer does the committee give to the request that slavery be allowed in the Indiana territory? What reasons does the committee give for its decision? Using your own words, rewrite as a tweet each of the sentences below from the committee's response to the pro-slavery memorial.

A That the rapid population of the State of Ohio sufficiently *evinces* in the opinion of your Committee that the labour of slaves is not necessary to promote the growth and settlement of Colonies in that region.

B That this labour, *demonstrably* the *dearest* of any, can only be employed to advantage in the cultivation of products more valuable than any known in that quarter of the U. States.

C That the Committee deem it highly dangerous and *inexpedient* to impair a *provision* wisely *calculated* to promote the happiness and prosperity of the N. Western Country and to give strength and security to that extensive frontier.

D In the *salutary* operations of this *sagacious* and *benevolent restraint*, it is believed that the inhabitants of Indiana, will at no very distant ~~period~~ day, find ample *remuneration* for a temporary *privation* of labour and of immigration.

3 Compare Badollet's statement about why slavery should not be allowed to the committee's justification for the prohibition of slavery. Which argument do you believe is more powerful, Badollet's emotional one or the committee's rational one? Which do you think might have been more powerful at the time (1803)?

4 What do you predict William Henry Harrison's reaction to these statements was? Imagine that Harrison follows both Badollet's and the committee's Twitter handles. What would he tweet in response to each?

▶ Alternately, choose to write a journal entry from the perspective of either John Badollet or William Henry Harrison in response to news of the committee's decision to continue the ban on slavery in the Indiana territory.

Activity 2: Indentured Servitude

Introduction: Although the U.S. Congressional Committee chose to uphold Article VI and continue the ban on slavery in the Indiana Territory, Governor Harrison and the pro-slavers achieved a victory a few months later. In 1803 Harrison and the three judges who comprised Indiana Territory's legislative body passed a bill allowing indentured servitude in the territory.

▶ On page 41 of chapter two, you may view a scan of an indenture dated 1809 that bound Jacob Ferrel, "a negro man," to serve John Smith for a period of thirteen years. Read the document and answer the following questions:

1 Does indentured servitude differ from slavery in practice or just in name?

2 Was this act just a maneuver for Governor Harrison to get around the 1803 ruling of the Congressional Committee?

▶ Next, read the Seventh Provision of Article XI of the 1816 Constitution for the State of Indiana, which states:

There shall be neither slavery nor involuntary servitude in this state, otherwise than for the punishment of crimes, whereof the party shall have been duly convicted. Nor shall any indenture of any negro or mulatto hereafter made, and executed out of the bounds of this state be of any validity within the state.

▶ Take a few minutes to write a journal response to this provision, considering the following questions:

1 How does it make you feel that the 1816 constitution expressly prohibits slavery?

2 Do you think this provision settled the debate once and for all?

3 Where could you look to determine if slavery and indentured servitude ended in Indiana with the 1816 constitution?

Activity References

Thornbrough, Gayle, ed. *The Correspondence of John Badollet and Albert Gallatin, 1804–1836*. Indiana Historical Society Publications 22. Indianapolis: Indiana Historical Society, 1963.

John Randolph to William Henry Harrison, March 2, 1803. William Henry Harrison Papers and Documents, 1773–1841, M 0364, box 1, folder 9, Indiana Historical Society.

3

Pioneers and Politics

"At this time was the expression first used 'Root pig, or die.' We rooted and lived and father said if we could only make a little and lay it out in land while land was only $1.25 an acre we would be making money fast."

— Andrew TenBrook, 1889

The pioneers who settled in Indiana had to work hard to feed, house, and clothe their families. Everything had to be built and made from scratch. They had to do as the pioneer Andrew TenBrook describes above, "Root pig, or die." This phrase, a common one during the pioneer period, means one must work hard or suffer the consequences, and in the Indiana wilderness those consequences could be hunger. Luckily, the frontier was a place of abundance, the land was rich, the forests and rivers bountiful, and the pioneers knew how to gather nuts, plants, and fruits from the forest; sow and reap crops; and profit when there was a surplus.

The Westward Movement

Thousands of people crossed the Appalachian Mountains and traveled the rivers and trails to the new state of Indiana in the first decades of the nineteenth century. This westward movement featured three general streams of migration. The largest stream was from the South. Next in size were pioneers from the Mid-Atlantic states, mostly Pennsylvania and New York. Smallest was the movement from the New England states. Southerners tended to settle mostly in southern Indiana; the Mid-Atlantic people in central Indiana; the New Englanders in the northern regions. There were exceptions. Some New Englanders did settle in southern Indiana, for example.

Pioneers filled up Indiana from south to north like a glass of water fills from bottom to top. The southerners came first, making homes along the Ohio, Whitewater, and Wabash Rivers. By the 1820s people were moving to central Indiana, by the 1830s to northern regions. The presence of Indians in the north and more difficult access delayed settlement there.

Because they came earliest and in the largest numbers southerners from Virginia, North Carolina, and Kentucky were especially important in early Indiana, many of them Scots-Irish from the Appalachian Mountains. Their way of speaking, preparing food, and building barns made these Hoosiers different from those who would come later to the north. Although they were from the South, most were not plantation aristocrats. They knew nothing of breezy verandas or fancy balls. Most, like young Abe Lincoln's family, were too poor to own slaves.

Settling Indiana

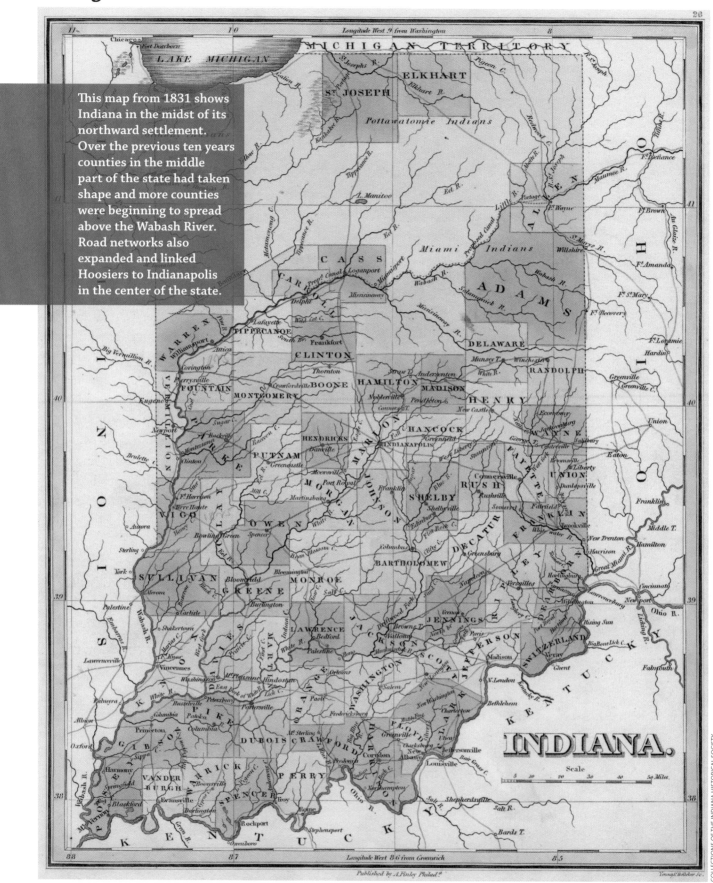

This map from 1831 shows Indiana in the midst of its northward settlement. Over the previous ten years counties in the middle part of the state had taken shape and more counties were beginning to spread above the Wabash River. Road networks also expanded and linked Hoosiers to Indianapolis in the center of the state.

Nearly all came because they had heard that Indiana had abundant, cheap, and fertile land. Most settlers agreed with the fictional pioneer woman who told her husband as he went off to buy land, "'Git a plenty while you're a gittin'," figuring that land would probably never be cheaper than it was at that place and time.

Many pioneers believed that land would not only provide their living but also lay the foundation for freedom, equality, and democracy. Those American ideals were important to pioneers. After crossing through southern Indiana in 1818 Englishman Morris Birkbeck concluded, "The simple maxim, that a man has a right to do any thing but injure his neighbour, is very broadly adopted into the practical as well as political code of this country."

Among those seeking a better life in Indiana were African American pioneers. Free blacks and escaped slaves sought the same opportunities as white pioneers. Many black families moved to Indiana from the same neighborhoods in Kentucky or North Carolina. The process of moving from one place and settling together in another place is called chain migration. White pioneers also moved as links in a chain.

African Americans knew that many Quakers were against slavery and that some had a dedication to their freedom and well-being. Thus, black pioneers sought out Quakers and created all-black communities near them. The Beech Settlement in Rush County had a population of nearly four hundred African American settlers by the 1830s. In 1831 one black farmer wrote back to relatives in North Carolina that his hogs had increased in number from four to fifty in a year, boasting, "If you could be here I could go with you in some fields that would make you open your eyes."

Other black communities included Roberts Settlement in Hamilton County, Lyles Station in Gibson County, and the Huggart Settlement in Saint Joseph County. In addition to creating lives of their own, some of these settlers helped slaves escape on the Underground Railroad.

Making Homes in the Wilderness

The movement west was family centered. Brothers, sisters, and cousins often settled in the same county. Most new settlers were young men and women. Childbearing began as early as age seventeen. A new baby every other year meant a high birth rate and large families. Couples had no reliable birth control. As important, children were needed as workers on the family farm.

Shelter was one of the pioneer family's first concerns. Log cabins became homes and the symbol of pioneer life. Men cut logs, often of

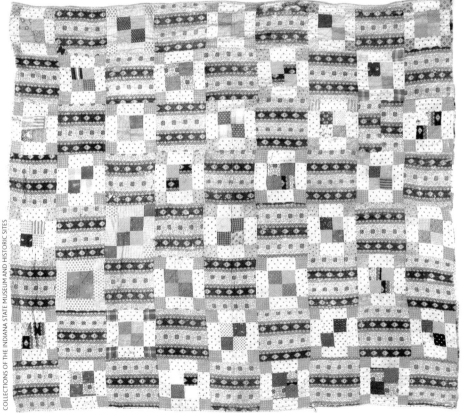

Pioneer Quilt

During Indiana's pioneer period women sewed quilts from whatever fabric was at hand. This double-nine patch-pieced quilt was sewn by a woman in the Crawfordsville area between the 1820s and 1850s.

tulip poplar—later named the state tree—and notched them at the ends so that corners were secure. In the spaces between the logs a mixture of clay, mud, and smaller pieces of wood filled the gaps. Along one wall they cut a door and sometimes a window, and along another wall they built a fireplace and chimney. The floor was dirt. Pioneers built log cabins with few tools and no nails, yet they offered good shelter. Within the log walls could be heard the everyday sounds of life—laughter and anger, work and storytelling, dying and giving birth.

Food was also a primary concern. Without any store-bought food, men hunted deer, wild turkeys, and small game such as squirrels. The wild game that women prepared for most meals was supplemented by nuts, berries, honey, and other food from the forests.

Clearing the land of massive trees to plant crops was the pioneer's hardest work. The ax was an essential tool. Families planted vegetables as well as flowers near their cabins. Corn, which grew well in Indiana, was the most important crop. Women turned corn into all kinds of dishes such as corn pone, a flat bread made from corn meal and water, cooked in a skillet over a fire; mush made from corn meal and water or milk to a consistency much like grits or porridge; and Johnny cakes, which were like corn pancakes. Many pioneers grew weary of eating these corn dishes. More appealing to some was whiskey, which also was made from corn, although one traveler complained that it "smells somewhat like bedbugs."

Hogs were everywhere on the frontier—wild and domestic—and deserve a place alongside the log cabin as central to pioneer life. The pigs that pioneers kept as livestock also ate corn and grew fat. Early winter butchering was a time for celebration because families knew they would have fresh meat for weeks. They salted or smoked most of the pork so it lasted for months.

Pioneers made their own clothing. Early settlers wore deerskins, much like Native Americans. One later wrote: "I recollect of wearing one pair of buckskins winter and summer Sundays and

all times for two years." Later, women made clothing from flax and wool. The sounds inside cabins often included the hum of a spinning wheel. Women also made quilts for warmth in the winter. These quilts are now some of the most cherished of pioneer handicrafts. Men made shoes for their families, too, with no difference between left and right, one reason pioneers often went barefoot. Few early pioneers wore underwear.

The Pioneer Legacy

Pioneers wanted a better life than they had back in Pennsylvania, Massachusetts, or Virginia. By and large, the Indiana frontier was a place of success for most. The woods, streams, and fertile land provided food, clothing, and shelter for those willing and able to work. Pioneers believed progress was achieved through hard work. Few starved. Most wanted to move as soon as possible from crude log cabins and corn mush to better lives.

By the middle of the nineteenth century the pioneer era was nearly over. Hoosiers had cleared and planted most of Indiana's land. Those who could afford it had built and moved into brick homes. Stores were built, and the new Hoosiers bought shoes, underwear, and many other items. Immigrants had built canals and railroads, connecting Hoosiers to people far away and increasing commerce. A cookbook published in New Albany in 1851 is suggestive of this emerging way of life in Indiana. It contains recipes for oysters and lemon punch.

Moldboard Plow

Like the quilt, the plow was an essential item for a pioneer family. Moldboard plows, such as the one shown here that was used to farm near Frankfort in Clinton County, helped pioneers plant crops such as corn that fed not only the family but also the livestock on their farm.

COLLECTIONS OF THE INDIANA STATE MUSEUM AND HISTORIC SITES

PAINTING IN THE COLLECTIONS OF THE INDIANA STATE MUSEUM AND HISTORIC SITES

The Hoosier's Nest

Marcus Mote (1817–1898) painted *The Hoosier's Nest*, based on an idyllic pioneer scene depicted in a poem of the same title by John Finley, published widely in 1833. When Finley wrote his poem, people were already beginning to feel nostalgic about the passing of pioneer days. Celebrating the promise the pioneers felt coming to the Indiana frontier, Finley wrote:

Blest Indiana! In thy soil
Are found the sure rewards of toil,
Where honest poverty and worth
May make a Paradise on earth

Finley went on to describe how a pioneer:

Erects a cabin in the woods,
Wherein he stows his household goods.
At first, round logs and clapboard roof,
With puncheon floor, quite carpet proof,
And paper windows, oiled and neat,
His edifice then complete.
When four clay balls, in form of plummet,
Adorn his wooden chimney's summit.

Settlers from the three migration streams: from the South, the Mid-Atlantic in the East, and New England in the Northeast mixed with immigrants from Germany and Ireland to create a distinctive culture for the nineteenth state. Together, they became Hoosiers, with nuances that made them different than people from other states. Later generations would celebrate Indiana's pioneers as heroic people. However, most were not so different from people of our own time. Some were lazy or selfish; some had bad luck; but most lived good lives.

Pioneer Hoosiers set down the patterns and beliefs that persist to our day. They believed in freedom. They wanted the democracy and good government that had been promised in Indiana's 1816 Constitution and later in the Constitution of 1851. Pioneers wanted progress, which sometimes required government help, as in the Internal Improvements Act of 1836 that initiated the building of canals and roads. Hoosiers also wanted opportunities for their children. Some Hoosiers, such as Caleb Mills, thought a public school system would provide opportunities for generations to come.

3.1

Abraham Lincoln, Hoosier

We reached our new home about the time the State came into the Union. It was a wild region, with many bears and other wild animals still in the woods. There I grew up.

— *Abraham Lincoln autobiography, 1859*

The Lincolns Move to Indiana

Among the early pioneer families to move to the new state of Indiana in 1816 was the Thomas Lincoln family. Thomas, his wife Nancy, daughter Sarah, and son Abraham "Abe" had been living in Kentucky. They came to Indiana because it was easy to claim its abundant, rich farmland and because the state prohibited slavery. Thomas disdained the institution of slavery as would Abe when he matured.

The Lincolns crossed the Ohio River with their meager belongings in November or December when their son was seven years old. After crossing the river, they traveled about twenty miles by horse-drawn wagon through the wilderness. There were no roads to Spencer County, Indiana, where Thomas had secured 160 acres near Little Pigeon Creek. The trip took two weeks. When the Lincolns reached their destination, their first priority was to build a log cabin, which they did with the help of their pioneer neighbors.

The area around Little Pigeon Creek was teeming with wildlife. Passenger pigeons, now extinct, were then so plentiful the area was named after them. There were also wild turkeys, raccoons, deer, and many other animals that ended up on the Lincolns' table at mealtime. Thomas taught Abe, who was tall and strong for his age, how to wield an ax, as every set of capable hands was essential to prospering in the Indiana wilderness. Abe also knew how to use a rifle, but he soon discovered that he disliked killing. When he was around eight years old, he shot at some wild turkeys through a crack in the wall of the family's log cabin. He killed one of them and never after "pulled a trigger on any larger game."

Early Life and Loss

Abraham Lincoln's experiences growing up may sound strange and exotic today, but his boyhood was typical for his place and time. Like all boys on the Indiana frontier, Lincoln did his share of grueling manual labor, and he was familiar with the perils of living in the wilderness. In the early 1800s, Hoosiers had fresh memories of the bloody altercation with the Indians at the Battle of Tippecanoe. Wild animals were also a clear and present danger. In an 1846 poem, the future president wrote about his Indiana experience, depicting a frightful place:

When first my father settled here,
'Twas then the frontier line:
The panther's scream, filled night with fear
And bears preyed on the swine.

Life expectancy in Lincoln's Indiana was much shorter than it is today, due to disease and poor medical care. One of the greatest tragedies in Lincoln's tragedy-filled life occurred in October 1818, almost two years after his family moved to Indiana. At the age of thirty-four his mother, Nancy Hanks Lincoln, contracted milk sickness and died. We now know the disease is caused by drinking contaminated milk from a cow that has eaten white snakeroot plant, which produces a fatal toxin. The week before, Nancy's aunt and uncle, Thomas and Elizabeth Sparrow, who had migrated to Indiana and lived near the Lincolns, also died of the disease. Milk sickness claimed the lives of thousands of people in the Ohio River Valley in the early nineteenth century. When Lincoln helped his father build his mother's coffin, he was just nine years old. Today, thousands of people each year visit Nancy's grave at the Lincoln Boyhood National Memorial in Spencer County.

A year after his mother's death, Lincoln had a near-death experience of his own when a stubborn horse kicked him in the forehead at a nearby mill. So severe was the blow, the miller thought the boy was dead and summoned Thomas Lincoln, who took his seemingly lifeless son home. After lying unconsciousness for a day, Abe regained full command of his faculties. The accident had a profound impact on him, and he referred to it often in his adult life.

An Education "by littles"

Nancy Lincoln had kindled a love of learning in her son that was nurtured by his stepmother Sarah "Sally" Bush Johnston, who married Thomas Lincoln the year after Nancy's death. Sally quickly recognized Abe's exceptional intelligence and encouraged him to read and feed his insatiable curiosity. Sally brought a few books of her own to the Lincoln home, which her stepson devoured, often reading late into the night. She saw to it that he took advantage of every opportunity to attend school, although the chances to do so were few and far between. In frontier Indiana, children were most likely to attend school only a few weeks in the winter, when farm chores were not pressing. In an 1859 autobiographical sketch, referring to himself as "he," Lincoln wrote of his education, "The aggregate [combined total] of all his schooling did not amount to one year. He was never in a college or Academy as a student; . . . What he has in the way of education, he has picked up."

In Indiana, Lincoln attended school "by littles," meaning he only went to school intermittently between the ages of eleven and seventeen. He was fortunate to have a few teachers who recognized his intellectual abilities and took special interest in him. It was probably a teacher who loaned him *The Life of Washington* by Mason Locke Weems, a book that greatly influenced the future president. Teacher Azel Dorsey, who was a resident of Spencer County, helped Lincoln master mathematics. One of the most important artifacts we have today from Lincoln's early life is the 1824–26 sum book in which he wrote his multiplication tables. A leaf from Lincoln's sum book is in the collections of the Indiana Historical Society and another is at Lilly Library at Indiana University.

Later in his life, Lincoln regretted what he referred to as his "defective" education while growing up in Indiana. He compensated for the lack of educational opportunities by reading everything he could. He once told his friend Joshua Speed, "I am slow to learn and slow to forget what I have learned—My mind is like a piece of steel, very hard to scratch any thing on it and almost impossible after you get it there to rub it out." During Lincoln's lifetime, Indiana would make considerable strides toward creating a free public education system available to all Hoosier children.

Westward Moving Settlers

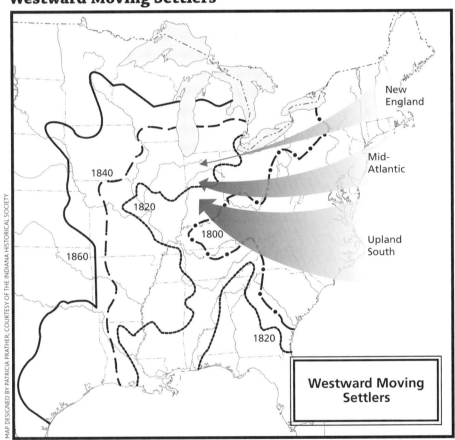

MAP DESIGNED BY PATRICIA PRATHER, COURTESY OF THE INDIANA HISTORICAL SOCIETY

This map illustrates how settlers from different portions of the country moved into Indiana. Where they settled in their new state often reflected where they had come from. New Englanders tended to settle in the north while settlers from the Mid-Atlantic states settled in the central part of Indiana. Pioneers such as the Lincoln family from the Upland South—Kentucky, Tennessee, Virginia, and the Carolinas—tended to settle in the southern part of Indiana. The arrows indicate that the larger migration stream was from the South followed by settlers from the Mid-Atlantic states. The fewest pioneers to Indiana during this period were from New England.

A Life-Changing Adventure

In January 1828, a few weeks before Lincoln's nineteenth birthday, his almost twenty-one-year-old sister Sarah, who had married Aaron Grigsby in August 1826, died in childbirth. She and her stillborn child were buried near Little Pigeon Primitive Baptist Church in what is now Lincoln State Park. Lincoln and Sarah were always extremely close, and her death was another devastating blow.

Several months after Sarah's death, a local storekeeper hired Lincoln to travel with his son by flatboat to New Orleans to sell grain and cured pork. Lincoln jumped at the chance. The two young men began their trip on the Ohio River near Rockport. It was Lincoln's first venture away from the lands of his childhood, Kentucky and Indiana, and it exposed him to parts of the country that he only knew about through his voracious reading.

Lincoln found the two-month-long flatboat journey exciting, eye-opening, and at one point, dangerous. Along the coast of Louisiana, thieves attacked the flatboat, but Lincoln and his companion scared their assailants away by pretending to have guns.

New Orleans was a bustling, multi-cultural city, unlike anything the two Hoosier lads had ever experienced. Before they went home, they explored the city. Lincoln did not leave a written account of what he saw there, but most of his biographers believe that he must have seen slave markets as they were a common scene in this major southern port. The young men returned to Indiana by steamboat, which added another dimension of excitement to their adventure.

In March 1830 Thomas Lincoln sold his land in Spencer County and moved his family to Illinois. Abe, now an adult of twenty-one, decided to accompany them. The Lincolns crossed the Wabash River, swollen by spring rains, at Vincennes and settled on the Sangamon River near

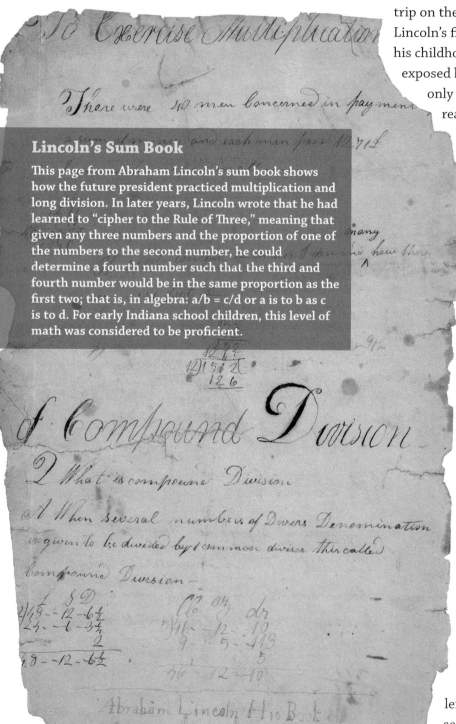

Lincoln's Sum Book

This page from Abraham Lincoln's sum book shows how the future president practiced multiplication and long division. In later years, Lincoln wrote that he had learned to "cipher to the Rule of Three," meaning that given any three numbers and the proportion of one of the numbers to the second number, he could determine a fourth number such that the third and fourth number would be in the same proportion as the first two; that is, in algebra: $a/b = c/d$ or a is to b as c is to d. For early Indiana school children, this level of math was considered to be proficient.

Decatur, Illinois. Lincoln would live in Illinois for three decades, until he left in 1861 for his inauguration as the nation's sixteenth president. He visited Indiana only once before that time, to campaign for Henry Clay, the Whig presidential candidate in 1844. The visit made a powerful impression on Lincoln, inspiring him to write a ninety-six-line poem that begins:

> *My childhood home I see again,*
> *And gladden with the view;*
> *And still as mem'ries crowd my brain,*
> *There's sadness in it too.*

As Lincoln's poem attests, Indiana had a profound impact on him. He moved here when he was seven and lived here until he was twenty-one, the ages when his intellectual, moral, and psychological foundations were formed. Although he was six feet four inches tall, Lincoln looked like a stereotypical Hoosier with his long muscular arms. Walt Whitman, the American poet who wrote "O Captain! My Captain!" about Lincoln, also said of the president's appearance, "He has a face like a Hoosier Michel Angelo, so awful ugly it becomes beautiful." Many people wonder how Lincoln the young pioneer from Indiana became Lincoln the great leader in the darkest episode in our nation's history. There is no simple answer, but as one historian has remarked, "Although Lincoln left Indiana behind, his life as a Hoosier pioneer never went away."

Lincoln Boyhood National Memorial

The Lincoln Boyhood National Memorial in Spencer County, about forty-five miles east of Evansville, is the site of the farm where Abraham Lincoln lived with his family from 1816 to 1830. In Indiana, Lincoln grew from boy to man, acquiring the convictions and strength of character that equipped him to lead the United States through the Civil War and distinguish him as one of the nation's greatest presidents.

The State of Indiana preserved and administered Lincoln's boyhood home for decades. In 1962, one year before his assassination, President John F. Kennedy signed a bill authorizing that Lincoln's boyhood home be designated a national memorial.

The visitor center in Lincoln Boyhood National Memorial features five sculptured limestone panels depicting scenes from Lincoln's life. Artifacts pertaining to frontier life are also on exhibit. Visitors can walk trails leading to a working pioneer homestead called the Lincoln Living Historical Farm, the burial site of Lincoln's mother, Nancy Hanks Lincoln, and the Lincoln cabin site.

3.2

Connecting Indiana: Building Early Roads and Canals

The road traveled over today was execrable. At all the creeks there are steep precipitous banks of hard clay, which are really dangerous. I was twice thrown out of my wagon at these pitches, and many places were so bad that I dared not ride at all.

— *J. Gould, twenty miles from Indianapolis, journal entry, 1839*

There was nothing romantic about being a pioneer. The first settlers in Indiana were generally subsistence farmers, meaning they used much if not all of the crops and livestock they produced for food, clothing, and other items for the family. This could mean that their needs were only minimally met. However, pioneers did not want to just scratch out a living. After they were settled, Hoosiers began producing a surplus of corn and hogs. These commodities were in demand outside of Indiana, but first the pioneers had to find a way to reach those markets. Hoosiers also wanted the same conveniences and comforts that people in the East enjoyed. Isolation of its citizens from the rest of the country was one of the biggest obstacles the young state of Indiana had to overcome. Consequently, connecting Hoosiers with each other and with the rest of the United States became a critical public goal between statehood in 1816 and the Civil War in the 1860s.

The Crossroads of America . . . Not!

In the early 1800s, Indiana transportation routes were extremely crude and slow. Many roads were nothing more than dirt trails that followed animal paths, such as the Buffalo Trace from New Albany to Vincennes or the Old Sauk Indian Trail across the Calumet Region. Some routes had been hacked out of the wilderness by soldiers during expeditions against Indians.

After statehood, citizens expected government to take action to improve roads. The federal Enabling Act of 1816 promised Indiana three percent of the proceeds from the sale of public land within its borders to be used for transportation infrastructure. In 1821 the state general assembly allocated the money to build two dozen state roads, many reaching to Indianapolis, the new state capital. This plan spread the limited resources too thin. It might have been better if the state had planned a few main roads than a lot of inferior ones.

Michigan Road was a main highway that brought better north-south transportation to Indiana. The Potawatomi Indians gave up a strip of land north of the Wabash and additional parcels of land to construct the road in 1826. Ironically, this made it easier to remove the Potawatomi in 1838. It also stimulated white settlement in Northern Indiana. Fully opened in 1836, the road connected the northern harbor of Michigan City to centrally-located Indianapolis and to the booming town of Madison on the Ohio River.

The National Road was the other major road that served Indiana. Started in 1811 by the federal government, it stretched from Cumberland, Maryland, to the West. It reached Wheeling, Virginia (now West Virginia), in 1818, moved through Ohio, then crossed into Indiana in the 1830s, connecting Richmond, Indianapolis, Terre Haute, and many smaller towns. Much of it today is U.S. 40.

Even major roads such as Michigan Road and the National Road were often in bad shape, with tree stumps protruding. In spring and fall rainy seasons, mud made the roads impassable. One traveler on horseback from the Ohio River to Bloomington wrote that his journey took him through "the most ill-looking, dark-coloured morasses, enlivened by streams of purer mud crossing at right angles" and that his goal was to find mud that had "at least some bottom."

The extreme Indiana seasons helped or hindered transportation depending on the mode. Hot dry weather favored road travel but hindered travel by river or other streams; whereas wet seasons were good for water travel, but made roads largely unusable.

River Travel

Like the Indians before them, Hoosier pioneers were river-centric. They built their first farms and towns near the Ohio, Whitewater, Wabash, and White Rivers, and along the streams that flowed into these major rivers. Rivers were the best way for farmers to get their goods to market, but Indiana's rivers were little help in getting goods to the largest markets on the East Coast. The Appalachian Mountains blocked the way east, and many of the rivers flowed in the wrong direction—south-westward. As a result, few Indiana goods reached markets in New York and Philadelphia.

Early trade from Indiana mainly moved south to New Orleans via flatboats (wide, rectangular boats with flat bottoms) on the Ohio and Mississippi Rivers.

A trip from Indiana to Louisiana by flatboat could take two or three months, depending on the weather and depth of the rivers. From New Orleans, sailing vessels took goods up the coast to Atlantic seaports. Flatboats provided Indiana's main tie to the national market until the mid-nineteenth century. Flatboats were temporary, one-way craft. Once a flatboat reached its destination and the crew sold the goods, they dismantled the boat and sold the lumber. The flatboat crew, usually Hoosier farm boys, such as young Abe Lincoln, then took the opportunity to see the sights in New Orleans before they set off for home. Keelboats provided some upriver navigation. Strong crewmen with poles painstakingly navigated these sturdy, flat-bottomed vessels with pointed prows (front of boat). Transport by keelboat was limited to lightweight or valuable goods, such as coffee, sugar, salt, and molasses. No other cargo was worth the hassle.

After the War of 1812, the revolutionary technology of steamboats provided transportation. Steamboats could travel upriver and navigate shallow waters. They were also much faster than flatboats or keelboats, making the trip from New Orleans to Indiana in eight days. Steamboats on the Great Lakes contributed to the growth

EARLY ROUTES OF TRANSPORTATION

South Bend
Valparaiso
Ft. Wayne
Logansport
WABASH AND ERIE CANAL
MICHIGAN ROAD
Wabash River
Lafayette
Richmond
Indianapolis   NATIONAL ROAD
NATIONAL ROAD 1829
First Rail Road 1834
Connersville
Terre Haute
Shelbyville
WHITEWATER CANAL
WABASH AND ERIE CANAL
White River
Madison and
Indianapolis R.R. 1847
MICHIGAN ROAD
Madison
Vincennes
Washington
First Stage Line Route
White River
Ohio River
PRESENT DAY COUNTY BOUNDARIES ARE SHOWN
Wabash River
1820
New Albany
Evansville

ROADS & TRAILS:
━━ Major
── Other

0   20   40 miles

ROBERT C. KINGSBURY, AN ATLAS OF INDIANA (1970)

This map illustrates road, railway, and canal networks across Indiana as well as the major rivers. Rivers provided one way to transport goods and people. In the 1820s and 1830s many main roads were laid followed by canals in the 1830s through 1853. However, the ambition of connecting Indiana by water was never fully realized due to the state's economic difficulties. By the 1840s railroads were adding to Indiana's transportation network.

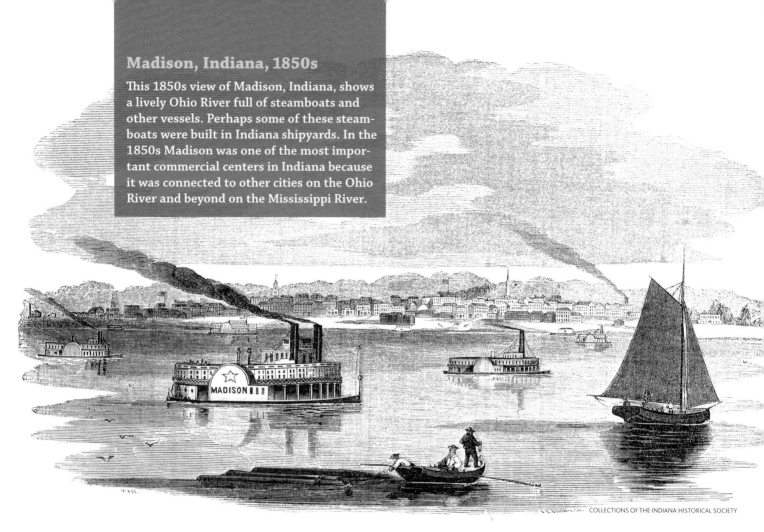

of cities in northern Indiana including Michigan City and South Bend, the latter connected to Lake Michigan by steamboats on the Saint Joseph River. Ohio River towns such as Madison and Evansville also grew because of steamboat traffic.

However, steamboats did not solve all of Indiana's water transportation problems. It was still almost impossible to reach Indianapolis by water. In 1831 one steamboat was left high and dry when it got stuck on a sandbar in the shallow White River trying to reach the state capital.

Canal Mania

Indiana's growing population demanded that the government do something about improving transportation in the state and increasing access to the outside world. In New York the Erie Canal had been completed in 1825. This event started a canal boom in the Old Northwest. Indiana dreamed of connecting Lake Erie with the Ohio River via the Wabash and Maumee Rivers.

In 1827 the federal government financed Indiana's first major canal project, the Wabash and Erie Canal. Work began on the project in the Fort Wayne area in 1832 and moved downstream along the Wabash River. Jesse L. Williams, the chief engineer, supervised skilled artisans who built locks, culverts, and aqueducts. More than a thousand laborers, many of them Irish immigrants, performed the backbreaking work of digging and moving dirt with pickaxes and shovels. Fighting frequently erupted between the Catholic and Protestant Irish workers, reenacting Old World feuds between the two groups. The several jiggers of whiskey they received each day in pay, along with their monetary wages, may have helped fuel the hostilities.

The opening of the Wabash and Erie Canal as far south as Huntington was marked on July 4, 1835, with a grand celebration of speeches and toasts. Canal mania spread throughout the state. Every region wanted its own canal.

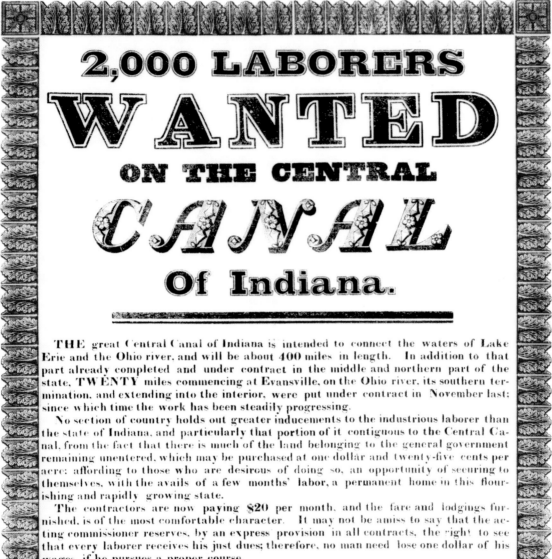

Recruitment Poster

This 1837 advertisement calls for laborers to build the Central Canal, which was part of the Internal Improvements Act of 1836. The plan was for this canal to go from Peru in the northern part of the state, through Indianapolis, to Evansville on the Ohio River in the south. Canal construction required massive amounts of work: from the first surveys of the land, to engineers designing bridges, to laborers removing trees and digging out the canal. Canal laborers worked long hours and were exposed to the natural elements and disease. Yet for the many workers who were new immigrants in Indiana, the ad also held out the possibility of a permanent home in the "flourishing and rapidly growing state."

The Internal Improvements Act of 1836

In 1836 the state legislature passed the Internal Improvements Act, to-date the most daring piece of legislation passed in Indiana's history. The goals outlined in the act were ambitious, optimistic, and, in retrospect, unrealistic. But had the act achieved everything it set out to do, it would have catapulted Indiana out of its pioneer condition of isolation. The act laid the plans for three major canal projects:

1 Extending the Wabash and Erie Canal from Lafayette to Terre Haute

2 Building the Whitewater Canal in the southeastern part of the state, to link the National Road and the Ohio River

3 Constructing the Central Canal, which would run from the Wabash and Erie Canal near Peru southward to Indianapolis and down to Evansville

The Act also promised a paved road from New Albany to Vincennes and the construction of a railroad from Madison to Lafayette via Indianapolis.

To pay for all these projects, the legislature authorized ten million dollars to be borrowed at five percent interest. With East Coast and British investors on board, the prospects for revolutionary transformation looked promising.

All of the projects initiated by the act came to a screeching halt in 1839 when the nation experienced a financial panic and severe depression. Consequently, the projects that the Internal Improvements Act of 1836 had promised were left incomplete. Even worse, by 1841 Indiana was bankrupt and could not even pay the interest on its internal improvements debt. Unhappy creditors hired lawyer Charles Butler to negotiate repayment. In 1847 the state legislature and Butler reached an agreement, stipulating that Indiana would pay half of its debt and the creditors would take stock in the canal projects.

The episode heaped embarrassment and international scorn on Indiana. A London newspaper denounced the state as "the land of promise for all the knavery and thievery in the known world." Hoosiers were so horrified by the outcome of the Act of 1836 that they inserted a clause in the Constitution of 1851 that restricts the state from going into debt.

Even though the 1836 projects were not completed and caused the state's financial ruin, they did have some positive consequences. It turned out that even unfinished canals were better than none. During the 1840s and 1850s large quantities of goods and passengers were transported on the Wabash and Erie Canal, and it provided a means for northern Indiana to ship goods to northeastern markets. When it was finally completed in 1853, the Wabash and Erie Canal was 468 miles long, which made it the longest canal in the country. It stimulated the growth of many Indiana cities, including Fort Wayne, Peru, Logansport, Delphi, and Lafayette. The Whitewater Canal, completed in 1846, was less advantageous to the state, but it did increase farmers' profits and helped develop towns such as Connersville, Brookville, and Lawrenceburg.

The "can do" spirit behind the Internal Improvements Act of 1836 was part of the pioneer optimism that had stimulated Indiana's development in the first half of the nineteenth century. The unfortunate timing of the country's economic crash and other factors derailed an over-ambitious plan that had envisioned sweeping improvements across the state. It was perhaps the last time that Hoosiers would place such immense faith in the hands of government. After the 1836 debacle, Indiana preferred to limit government and allow private enterprise a wide berth—an attitude that persists today.

3.3

Development of Indiana's Educational System

It shall be the duty of the General assembly, as soon as circumstances will permit, to provide, by law, for a general system of education, ascending in a regular gradation, from township schools to a state university, wherein tuition shall be gratis, and equally open to all.

— *1816 Indiana State Constitution, Article IX, Section 2*

Early Pioneer Education

In the first half of the nineteenth century, Hoosier pioneers had limited access to schooling. Most of them were lucky if they learned the "3 Rs"—reading, 'riting, and 'rithmetic. As in so many other aspects of pioneer life, the family's economic progress was the central focus. Children learned the basics of farm life such as hunting, building shelter, planting and harvesting, spinning and sewing, and cooking from their parents. Parents might also have taught their children how to read, write a few words including their names, and do simple arithmetic.

Church and Sunday school were places where children were able to learn and practice reading and writing. Sermons, hymns, and scripture introduced young people to words and concepts that became, as in Abraham Lincoln's case, permanent parts of their vocabulary and thought. The first Sunday schools appeared in Indiana in the 1810s, and by 1829, the state had more than one hundred of them. Religiously motivated individuals and groups got them up and running, believing that the frontier sorely needed both Christianity and education. Protestant denominations—Methodists, Baptists, and Presbyterians—led the way with Sunday school education. Methodists were the greatest in number, but Presbyterians, often educated in the East, made a big impact on not only religious education but education in general. In Indiana education reformer Caleb Mills was the most influential Presbyterian in this regard.

III. LESSON THIRD.

Same subject continued.

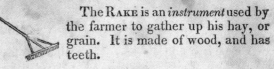

The RAKE is an *instrument* used by the farmer to gather up his hay, or grain. It is made of wood, and has teeth.

KEYS are made of iron, or copper. They are used to *lock* or unlock doors, trunks, &c.

This is a LEAF of the oak, which is one of the largest trees that grow. Men *build* ships of the oak.

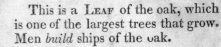

HIVES are houses made for *bees*, in which they make their honey. They are made of wood or straw. People sometimes make hives with glass windows, so that they can look in and see the bees making honey.

Where is the boy who does not love to fly the KITE? It should be made very light. You must not le it get *tangled* in the limbs of trees.

DEFINITIONS.

Instrument—a tool.
Lock—to make fast.
Build—to make, to construct.
Honey-bee—the bee that makes honey.
Tangled—caught.

B

Elementary Reader

This page from *The Elementary Reader to Accompany Webster's Spelling Book* (1835) shows the kind of textbook young Hoosier children studied if they were able to go to school. This book taught spelling and reading using illustrations for words and definitions. As students progressed, they moved on to readers with moral stories and poems to read aloud with emphasis on proper pronunciation, enunciation, and pauses.

Books were scarce on the frontier, so the Bible may have been one of the only books that a Hoosier pioneer child ever read. There was a void in secular, or non-religious, Indiana educational opportunities. Even though the 1816 state constitution had promised that the state would create a general education system that would be open to all citizens, progress was slow to non-existent at first. Common schools, similar to today's public schools, were locally created and funded, meaning they were funded by the town or township, not the state. Nowhere were they free and open to all. There were no state standards, nor were there schools to train teachers. Therefore, the ability of teachers varied greatly, and they received very low pay. Schooling was catch-as-catch-can for Hoosier children. In 1840 the state discovered how serious an educational problem it had.

The 1840 Census

"The name Hoosier [remained] the synonym for ignorance."

— *Author Charles W. Moores, 1905*

The federal census of 1840 revealed that less than one-quarter of Indiana children between five and fifteen attended school. Additionally, about one in seven adult Hoosiers could not read or write. Indiana's literacy ranked eighteenth among the twenty-eight states in the Union—lower than all northern states and four southern states. In part, Indiana's high illiteracy rate was due to the scant education in the Upland South—Kentucky, Tennessee, and the Carolinas—which had been home to many Hoosier pioneers. Not surprisingly then, southern Indiana counties had the highest illiteracy rates since many of the settlers in the area had come from the Upland South. But in the broader sense, the state's illiteracy was the result of its failure to deliver on the promise of free education for all in its 1816 constitution. The 1840 census was a call to action for education reformers, who began an energetic campaign to create a true system of public education.

Caleb Mills (1806–1879)

Caleb Mills, one of Indiana's greatest education reformers, served as Indiana's superintendent of public instruction from 1854–55. Mills also helped establish Wabash College, where he taught Greek for forty-four years.

Caleb Mills, "One of the People"

"Let us shut our eyes no longer to the teachings of experience. Let us have a system based on the broad and republican principle, that it is the duty of the State to furnish the means of primary education to the entire youth within her bounds."

— *Caleb Mills, to the Indiana General Assembly, December 6, 1847*

Caleb Mills, a New England Presbyterian missionary, was determined to bring both religion and education to the frontier. A graduate of Dartmouth College and Andover Theological Seminary, he arrived in Crawfordsville in 1833 to head a Presbyterian school that became Wabash College. Although Mills had been an advocate for public education before the 1840 census revealed the embarrassing statistics about Hoosier education, he emerged as the leading advocate of a state system of public education after the census report was published.

Between 1846 and 1852 Mills wrote and distributed six eloquent and elaborately argued messages to the state legislature and signed them simply as "One of the People." They are arguably the most important documents ever written on the subject of education in Indiana. He listed the causes of Indiana's backwardness as "want of competent teachers, suitable school books, a proper degree of interest in the community on the subject, adequate funds, and the method of procuring such funds." He argued for the necessity of state and township school taxes, stating, "There is but one way to secure good schools, and that is to pay for them."

Pressured by Mills and other reformers, Indiana's General Assembly submitted a statewide referendum, calling for eligible citizens to vote on the question of whether to enact taxes sufficient

New Harmony

New Harmony on the Wabash River in what is now Posey County presented an intriguing alternative to the values and lifestyle of frontier Indiana. From 1814 to 1827 two utopian groups that believed in the perfectibility of society settled in New Harmony, one after the other. The first group, the Harmonists, were Christians who believed that the second coming of Christ was near. They also believed in and practiced free education, but it is the second utopian group that has had a lasting influence on Indiana's education.

In 1824 industrialist Robert Owen bought New Harmony and traveled from England to the fledgling state of Indiana, intending to create a new way to educate and better society. The Owenites, as his followers were called, believed in abolishing private property and in equality between white men and women. Their plan required that all members work and contribute as they were able and equitably divide the material and cultural rewards. Though the community quickly failed economically, some of its ideas were implemented in Indiana by a couple of the community's members. Owen's son, Robert Dale Owen, advocated strongly for publicly funded schools, served three terms in the Indiana state legislature (1836–38), and was a delegate at the constitutional convention of 1850–51.

William Maclure, often referred to as the father of geology, came to Indiana as a business partner with Robert Owen and stayed when Owen left.

Maclure supported education that was free and open to all, and he led the New Harmony schools. In 1838 Maclure founded the Working Men's Institute, seeking to provide a place where laborers and their families could further their knowledge. He went on to establish Working Men Institutes across Indiana. Although none but the original remains, the others were often the first free public libraries in their communities and provided the base for many of the public libraries in Indiana today.

The Working Men's Institute in New Harmony, Indiana, is now the oldest operational library in Indiana and is also a museum. Though the library was originally housed in a church, it was moved to this building in 1894.

to provide at least three months of free, common-school education for all children. The 1849 referendum did not pass by a landslide, but it did pass. The referendum had a loophole that required a majority vote in each county to approve it in order for it to take effect in that county. Sixty-one counties approved it, and twenty-nine rejected it. This mixed response hindered the efforts to create a statewide common school system.

Mills's efforts impacted Indiana's 1851 constitution, which established a system of common schools and resulted in the passage of the 1852 Free School Law. The 1852 law mandated that counties statewide provide at least three months of free common-school education and set up a system to administer it. The law also levied a state tax to help fund public education equally throughout the state. Unlike the 1849 act, this law had no loophole or escape clause to let individual counties opt out. Scholars and educators alike consider the Free School Law of 1852 the most significant accomplishment of Indiana's common-school movement. Mills became the second superintendent of Indiana public schools in 1854.

The Persistence of Pioneer Thinking

While many school supporters regarded education as the means to provide equal opportunity for all Hoosiers, many of Indiana's pioneers viewed state-supported education as a step that would lead to a more centralized government. They reasoned that this would result in less local control over communities and eventually to a loss of individual freedom. Some pioneers even argued that taxes were the greatest obstacle to what they considered was their God-given right to pursue prosperity freely.

Formal education was also not necessarily met with a welcoming attitude regardless of who paid for the schools or how; some pioneers felt that it was not practical for life on the frontier. But Mills and other reformers knew that in order for Indiana to move beyond the pioneer era and toward a more sophisticated society and economy, skills other than rudimentary farming skills were needed.

In twenty-first century Indiana, there is a sense of déjà vu about the arguments for and against school funding and public schools. Many aspects of public education that vexed pioneer Indiana resonate every time today's Hoosiers face a new school referendum. As citizens weigh the pros and cons of raising taxes to support public schools, they question whether taxes are the best way to balance the school budget. Some voters ask if cutting subjects that they consider less essential, such as art and foreign languages, would accomplish the same thing.

Some parents resent being told what subjects their children must study or which schools their children must attend. Many of these parents educate their children at home. Other voters support school vouchers that allow parents to choose their children's schools, while pulling money away from less desirable schools. Thus, even with a statewide school system, the questions of how young Hoosiers should be taught and who should do so remain open for debate.

3.4

1851 Constitution

TO THE END, that justice be established, public order maintained, and liberty perpetuated; WE, the People of the State of Indiana, grateful to ALMIGHTY GOD for the free exercise of the right to choose our own form of government, do ordain this Constitution.

— *Preamble, Indiana State Constitution of 1851*

Indiana's Constitution of 1816 served the pioneer generation well, but by the 1840s, Hoosiers felt that it needed revising. All other states carved from the Old

Northwest were rewriting their constitutions, beginning in the 1840s, and Indiana had specific concerns it wanted to address. Hoosiers thought the general assembly could function more efficiently. They were also still reeling from the internal improvements investment of 1836 that had bankrupted the state. In the 1849 election a clear majority of voters favored a new constitution, with a vote of 81,500 for and 57,418 against.

The Constitutional Convention of 1850–51

On October 7, 1850, 150 elected delegates met in the Hall of the House of Representatives in the state capitol in Indianapolis for the constitutional convention of 1850–51. The composition of the convention largely mirrored the state's population at the time, except that the delegates were all white men. Since Indiana was an agrarian, or farming, state, 42 percent of the delegates were farmers. One-fourth

Indiana's 1851 Constitution

Much like the Constitution of the United States, Indiana's 1851 constitution contains a Bill of Rights that follows the preamble quoted at the beginning of this section. Indiana's Bill of Rights begins:

WE DECLARE, That all men are created equal; that they are endowed by their CREATOR with certain unalienable rights; that among these are life, liberty and the pursuit of happiness; that all power is inherent in the People; and that all free governments are, and of right ought to be, founded on their authority, and instituted for their peace, safety, and well being. For the advancement of these ends, the People have, at all times, an indefensible right to alter and reform their government.

Does the first line of Indiana's Bill of Rights sound familiar? It should; it directly quotes the Declaration of Independence. The constitution of 1851 reflects how men and women were seen differently at that time. In 1984 the phrase "all men are created equal" in Indiana's Bill of Rights was changed to "all people are created equal."

were lawyers, and there were a few doctors and people from other walks of life. Of the 150 delegates only 13 were native Hoosiers; 74 were born in the South, 57 in other northern states, and 6 in foreign countries. Because the Democratic Party was strong in Indiana, two-thirds of the delegates were Democrats and one-third were Whigs.

The four-month convention was a lively affair. The delegates worked hard, but they also had fun. Many told jokes and stories, a favorite Hoosier pastime. One newspaper reported that the delegates spent "hour after hour . . . in fun, revelry, vulgar anecdotes, stamping, hallooing, &c."

When the convention ended on February 10, 1851, after 127 days, the resulting document did not significantly alter state government, but its revisions had lasting impact. The voting public approved the new constitution in the election of 1851, and it immediately went into effect. The 1851 Indiana State Constitution has been the basic operating manual for state and local government for more than a century and a half. For a few months of every year, when the state legislature is in session, the original copy is on display at the statehouse in Indianapolis.

1851 Constitution and Public Will

The new constitution addressed a variety of issues. Confirming the basic Hoosier distrust of government power and enthusiasm for local control, it provided for popular election of state judges rather than political appointments. It granted the vote to immigrants who expressed intent to become citizens and who had resided in the United States for one year and in Indiana for six months. The constitution also reinforced the desire for popular, common sense democracy by proposing that all bills and resolutions "be plainly worded, avoiding as far as may be practicable the use of technical terms in Latin or any other than the English language."

Most important, the 1851 constitution addressed two issues on the public radar in the 1840s—the state's massive debt caused by the Internal Improvements Act of 1836, and the need for better public education as indicated in the 1840 census data that revealed Indiana's high illiteracy rates. Because the state was still in austerity mode, delegates established biennial (every other year) legislative sessions of sixty-one days to save money. The delegates also wrote a provision in the new constitution prohibiting the state from incurring debt, a provision that would limit options in changing times in the future. The delegates' sentiment was so strong on this point that there was little room for compromise. Democrat delegate Daniel Read, an Indiana University professor, argued that the state's credit should never be risked on another massive project. He stated that business should be put in the hands of private companies, and not in what he perceived to be the incapable hands of the government. Read said, "Public debt is a hydra [multi]-headed monster, which is always springing forth in some new form, and under some new pretext. Cut it off in the

nation,—straitway, it shoots forth in the States—cut it off in the States—it comes forth in the counties— cut it off in the counties—and it steals forth in the form of town or city bonds."

Another delegate, Schuyler Colfax, a Whig journalist from South Bend, who later served as Ulysses S. Grant's vice-president, stated that the only way Indiana should go into debt again was by a vote of the citizens in the state. Colfax explained, "The past history of our State is the best argument in favor of this amendment . . . as we have suffered more than other States from the results of imprudent debt, which still hangs over us, impairing our prosperity, and impeding our progress and advancement as a State."

Thanks to the efforts of Caleb Mills and other education reformers such as convention delegate Robert Dale Owen from New Harmony, public endorsement of state-wide common schools was finally strong enough that the new constitution established a permanent fund to support schools and provided for a state superintendent to head the school system. The 1851 constitution paved the way for the 1852 Free School Law, and a new day dawned for Indiana public schools.

Woman's Rights Association of Indiana

In 1851 the Woman's Rights Association of Indiana was founded on the principle of women's suffrage, the right to vote. In 1852 the association passed resolutions that affirmed women should have the same opportunities as men including education, equal pay for employment, and basic citizenship rights. In 1859 Dr. Mary F. Thomas and Mary Birdsall addressed the Indiana General Assembly to petition for these rights. Thomas stated that women should "assert their right to the elective franchise, and the privileges growing out of it, as the basis of all other rights." However, the General Assembly did not seriously debate the possibility of suffrage until the 1880s.

Women's Rights or Lack Thereof

The new constitution left large parts of the state's population out of the equation. Only white men could vote, and married women were barred from owning property. At the convention, Robert Dale Owen proposed an amendment to grant married women the right to own property. Opponents warned that social chaos would result if women had equal property rights; they argued that women should remain in the home and raise children. Delegates cited biblical scripture to

Preamble and Constitution OF THE *Suffrage* WOMAN'S RIGHTS ASSOCIATION OF INDIANA.

WHEREAS: The subject of Woman's Rights is founded upon the eternal rock of Truth, and as unceasing and untiring activity is absolutely necessary for the promulgation of information regarding woman's condition, needs and claims; and as united action and permanent organization further the cause most efficiently, we, whose names are hereunto subscribed, unite together under the following constitution:

Art. I. This society shall be known by the name of the Indiana Woman's Rights Association.

Art. II. The officers of this society shall consist of a President, Vice Presidents, Corresponding and Recording Secretaries and Treasurer, whose duties shall be such as devolve upon such stations, and they shall be elected annually.

Art. III. The Secretary, further, shall be requested to report annually upon the general condition of woman and the efforts made for her elevation.

Art. IV. Persons shall be appointed at each annual meeting to report upon each of the following subjects: Woman's Labor and Remuneration, Woman's Legal Condition, Woman's Social Position, and Woman's Education.

Art. V. This society shall meet annually at such time and place as shall hereafter be determined upon.

Art. VI. This society does advise the organization of District societies throughout the State.

Art. VII. This constitution may be altered or amended at any regular meeting of the society.

refuse women equal rights, "Paul says that the husband is the head of the wife even as Christ is the head of the Church, and that wives are to subject themselves unto their husbands."

Women in the visitors' galleries witnessed Owen's proposal go down in flames, but they were grateful for his efforts. Fifteen women led by Sarah T. Bolton, a noted poet, honored Owen with a testimonial. They presented the New Harmony reformer with an engraved silver pitcher on the floor of the House, the first time women were allowed in the space.

Although newspapers mocked the gesture of the women who honored Owen, more women began to be involved in the fight for equal rights. At an anti-slavery meeting in Henry County, Amanda Way, a young Quaker woman, changed the subject from slavery to women and called for a meeting to discuss women's rights. In October 1851 Hoosier women gathered in Dublin, Wayne County, for the state's first women's rights convention. Way told the convention: "Unless women demand their rights politically, socially, and financially, they will continue in the future, as in the past, to be classed with negroes, criminals, insane persons, idiots, and infants." The convention resulted in the formation of the Woman's Rights Association of Indiana, which, over many years, took the first steps toward winning equality for women in Indiana. Almost seventy years would pass before American women gained the right to vote.

Zerelda G. Wallace (1817–1901)

In 1881 the Indiana General Assembly voted to approve a constitutional amendment granting voting rights, suffrage, to women. Although the resolution ultimately failed to become law after a second round of voting, it was thanks to suffragists such as Zerelda Wallace and May Wright Sewall that the resolution got so far in the assembly. Born in Kentucky, Wallace came to Indianapolis when she was a young woman. She married and raised a family, including her well-known stepson Lew Wallace (see Chapter 4). After her children were grown, Wallace became active in the Suffrage and Temperance, anti-alcohol, Movements. The sexism, or prejudice, she faced publicly as president of the Woman's Christian Temperance Union led her to become an ardent suffragist. In 1878 Wallace and other prominent Indianapolis men and women formed the Indianapolis Equal Suffrage Society. Wallace also served as president of this organization, which lobbied Indiana legislators to support suffrage before the 1881 vote. Wallace remained active on a national scale following this defeat; but unfortunately, she did not live to see women gain the right to vote in 1920.

Selected Bibliography

Abraham Lincoln: A Living Legacy—A Guide to Three Abraham Lincoln National Park Sites. Virginia Beach, VA: Donning, 2007.

Arndt, Karl J. R. *George Rapp's Harmony Society, 1785–1847.* Philadelphia: University of Pennsylvania Press, 1965.

Baer, M. Teresa. "Loyalty, Morality, and Uniformity: Indiana's Search for a Cohesive Society through Public Schooling. *Journal for the Liberal Arts and Sciences* 17, no. 1 (Fall 2012): 11–33.

Bartelt, William E. *There I Grew Up: Remembering Abraham Lincoln's Indiana Youth.* Indianapolis: Indiana Historical Society Press, 2008.

Berthoff, Rowland. "'A Little Nonsense Now and Then': Conventional Humor in Indiana, 1850." *Indiana Magazine of History* 90, no. 2 (June 1994): 109–26.

Boone, Richard G. *History of Education in Indiana.* 1892. Reprint, Indianapolis: Indiana Historical Bureau, 1941.

Carmony, Donald F., ed. "From Lycoming County, Pennsylvania, to Parke County, Indiana: Recollections of Andrew TenBrook, 1786–1823." *Indiana Magazine of History* 61, no. 1 (March 1965): 1–30.

———. "Historical Background of the Restrictions against State Debt in the Indiana Constitution of 1851." *Indiana Magazine of History* 47, no. 2 (June 1951): 129–42.

———. *Indiana, 1816–1850: The Pioneer Era.* The History of Indiana, vol. 2. Indianapolis: Indiana Historical Bureau and Indiana Historical Society, 1998.

Crumrin, Timothy. "Women and the Law in Early 19th-Century Indiana." Conner Prairie Interactive History Park, https:// www.connerprairie.org/Learn-And-Do/Indiana-History /America-1800-1860/Women-And-The-Law-In-Early-19th -Century.aspx.

Eggleston, Edward. *The Hoosier School-Master: A Novel.* 1871. Reprint, Bloomington: Indiana University Press, 1984.

Fatout, Paul. *Indiana Canals.* West Lafayette: Purdue University Studies, 1972.

Fowler, H., convention reporter. *Report of the Debates and Proceedings of the Convention for the Revision of the Constitution of the State of Indiana.* Indianapolis: A. H. Brown, 1850. Internet Archive, https://archive.org/details /reportdebatesan00indigoog.

Full Text of the 1816 Constitution. Indiana Commission on Public Records. IN.gov, http://www.in.gov/icpr/2778.htm.

Gould, J. "Wanderings in the West in 1839." *Indiana Magazine of History* 30, no. 1 (March 1934): 71–103.

Hall, Baynard Rush. *The New Purchase or Seven and a Half Years in the Far West.* Princeton, NJ: Princeton University Press, 1916.

Haller, Steve. "The Meanings of Hoosier: 175 Years and Counting." *Traces of Indiana and Midwestern History* 20, no. 4 (Fall 2008): 4–13.

Kettleborough, Charles. *Constitution Making in Indiana: A Source Book of Constitutional Documents with Historical Introduction and Critical Notes.* Vol. 1. 1916. Reprint, Indianapolis: Indiana Historical Bureau, 1971. Indiana Historical Bureau and Indiana Supreme Court, 1816 constitution, http://www .in.gov/history/2460.htm; 1851 constitution, http://www .in.gov/history/2473.htm.

Kingsbury, Robert C., and John M. Hollingsworth. *An Atlas of Indiana.* Bloomington: Geography Department, Indiana University, 1970.

Lincoln, Abraham. *The Collected Works of Abraham Lincoln.* Edited by Roy P. Basler, et al. 9 vols. New Brunswick, NJ: Rutgers University Press, 1953–55.

Lindley, Harlow, ed. *Indiana as Seen by Early Travelers.* Indianapolis: Indiana Historical Bureau, 1916.

Madison, James H. *Hoosiers: A New History of Indiana.* Bloomington: Indiana University Press; Indianapolis: Indiana Historical Society Press, 2014.

McCord, Shirley S., comp. *Travel Accounts of Indiana, 1679–1961.* Indianapolis: Indiana Historical Bureau, 1970.

Mills, Caleb. *An Address to the Legislature of Indiana at the Commencement of Its Session, December 6, 1847, upon Popular Education.* Indianapolis: John D. Defrees, 1848. Internet Archive, http://www.archive.org/stream /anaddresstolegi00milgoog#page/n4/mode/2up.

Moores, Charles W. *Caleb Mills and the Indiana School System.* Indianapolis: Wood–Weaver Printing, 1905.

Newman, Otho Lionel. "Development of the Common Schools of Indiana to 1851." *Indiana Magazine of History* 22, no. 3 (September 1926): 229–76.

Osborn, Elizabeth R. "The Influence of Culture and Gender on the Creation of Law in Antebellum Indiana, Ohio, and Kentucky." PhD diss., Indiana University, 2004.

Peterson, Dr. "Rule of Three." The Math Forum at Drexel. Drexel University, http://mathforum.org/library/drmath /view/60822.html.

Pitzer, Donald E., ed. *Robert Owen's American Legacy: Proceedings of the Robert Owen Bicentennial Conference.* Indianapolis: Indiana Historical Society, 1972.

Reese, William J., ed. *Hoosier Schools, Past and Present.* Bloomington: Indiana University Press, 1998.

Reynolds, David S. "Lincoln and Whitman." History Now: American History Online. The Gilder Lehrman Institute of American History, https://www.gilderlehrman.org/history-by-era /american-civil-war/essays/lincoln-and-whitman.

Sandweiss, Lee Ann. "Was Lincoln a Hoosier?" *Indiana University Alumni Magazine* 70, no. 4 (January/February 2008): 46–51.

Vincent, Stephen A. *Southern Seed, Northern Soil: African–American Farm Communities in the Midwest, 1765–1900.* Bloomington: Indiana University Press, 1999.

Warren, Louis A. *Lincoln's Youth: Indiana Years, 1816–1830.* Indianapolis: Indiana Historical Society, 1991.

Essential Questions

1 What was the pattern of pioneer migration into Indiana? Where did settlers to Indiana come from, and what attracted them to the state?

2 Describe the conditions on the Indiana frontier.

3 Why was the development of transportation routes such a critical need in pioneer Indiana? Name at least two important land and/or water route improvement projects.

4 How did the Internal Improvements Act of 1836 get the state of Indiana into trouble? What is a lasting consequence of this situation?*

5 How did education reformer Caleb Mills attempt to strengthen Indiana's education system and realize, or achieve, the ideal of free public education set forth in the 1816 constitution?*

6 What lasting impacts did the Owenites, a utopian community in New Harmony, have on Indiana?

7 How did the 1851 constitution address the issues of public debt and free public education?

8 How did the 1851 constitution fail Hoosier women?*

See student activities related to this question.

Three Key Issues in the 1851 Constitution

Chapter three relates the trials, triumphs, and tribulations that Hoosiers experienced during the pioneer era. As more people flooded into Indiana, the state needed to develop a stronger infrastructure, such as roads and canals. Indiana also needed institutions, such as public schools, to serve the people of the state. As Hoosiers attempted to build transportation and educational systems capable of serving the growing population, it became clear that the 1816 constitution needed to be updated.

The revised 1851 constitution addressed important issues, such as public debt and free public education, but it also brought into question the state of civil rights for female Hoosiers. Through the activities below, which can be completed individually as self-contained mini-lessons or together as a group project, you will take a look at what Indiana's 1851 State Constitution has to say about the issues, and you will take a stand on the issues yourselves.

Activity 1: Public Debt

▶ Reread section 3.2 of chapter three, which addresses the Internal Improvements Act of 1836. With a partner, discuss how this piece of legislation impacted Indiana.

▶ Now, read Article X, Section 5 of the 1851 constitution, which states:

No law shall authorize any debt to be contracted, on behalf of the State, except in the following cases: to meet casual deficits in the revenue; to pay the interest on the State debt; to repel invasion, suppress insurrection, or, if hostilities be threatened, provide for the public defense.

▶ Talk with your partner about how this provision was designed to prevent a situation similar to the canal debacle.

Much has been made recently of the size of the national debt. Some people argue that government spending is out of control and programs such as Medicare (the federal health insurance program for people age sixty-five and older) must be slashed to rein in the national debt. Others argue that while spending should be scrutinized, increasing revenues—for example, through higher rates on the highest tax brackets—is a solution that helps address the problem without harming society's disadvantaged.

▶ What do you think? Should the federal government follow Indiana's lead (more than 160 years later) and amend the U.S. Constitution to stipulate that the federal government cannot incur any new public debt? Why or why not? Discuss this with your partner or write an individual journal entry in which you answer these questions and reflect on how Article X, Section 5 of Indiana's 1851 constitution helps to shape Indiana's budget today.

Activity 2: Free Public Education

▶ Reread section 3.3 of chapter three, which addresses the development of Indiana's educational system. With your partner, reflect on the state of the educational system in Indiana in 1840 as reported in the census of that year. How does the reality of 1840 compare with the ideal set forth in the 1816 constitution:

It shall be the duty of the General assembly, as soon as circumstances will permit, to provide, by law, for a general system of education, ascending in a regular gradation, from township schools to a state university, wherein tuition shall be gratis, and equally open to all.

▶ Consider the implications of the lack of a public education system.

1 Who receives an education when free schooling is not available?

2 How would the lack of an educational system affect the development of the state at large?

▶ Article VIII, Section 1 of the 1851 constitution states:

Knowledge and learning, generally diffused throughout a community, being essential to the preservation of a free government; it shall be the duty of the General Assembly to encourage, by all suitable means, moral, intellectual, scientific, and agricultural improvement; and to provide, by law, for a general and uniform system of Common Schools, wherein tuition shall be without charge, and equally open to all.

In Article VIII, Section 2, the constitution also sets aside money from various state and township funds and authorizes the levying of "Taxes on the property of corporations, that may be assessed by the General Assembly for common school purposes."

1 What provisions did the 1851 constitution make for schools?

2 Do you think that making further provisions for free public schooling should have been a priority for the drafters of the 1851 constitution? Why or why not?

▶ The wording of the educational sections of the 1851 constitution reflected the success of reformer Caleb Mills's campaign to strengthen the commitment to free public education. It also set the stage for the passage of the 1852 Free School Law, which made it mandatory for the state to provide at least three months of free, compulsory common-school education. In addition, the 1852 law levied a state tax to help fund public schools.

1 What arguments were offered against a government-controlled educational system?

2 Do you agree with these arguments? Why or why not?

▶ Today, education reformers are looking for ways to improve the public school system. The use of school vouchers to allow students to attend private schools using public tax money has become a hot-button issue. Some support this move, saying Hoosiers should have the right to decide what schools their children attend and that the tax money set aside to educate a student should follow him or her to the parents' school of choice. Others say these provisions weaken public schools by diverting funds away from them.

1 What do you think Caleb Mills would think about school vouchers?

2 What would those Hoosiers think who were opposed to the education provisions of the 1851 constitution and the 1852 Free School Law?

3 Choose a side of this issue to argue in a debate and work with a partner who will argue the other side of the debate. Acting as someone from 1851— either a supporter of common schools such as Caleb Mills—or a person who opposes a statewide system of public schools—prepare your pro or con arguments. Share these with your partner so that he or she can provide feedback that may help you strengthen your statements. Then, come back together for a class debate with one-half of the class representing the pro position and the other half representing the con position. Let your teacher determine which side presents a more convincing argument.

Activity 3: Women's Civil Rights

Introduction: The convention that gathered to draft Indiana's 1851 constitution was composed exclusively of white men. Not only were there no female delegates to the convention, Hoosier women at the time lacked suffrage, meaning that they, like the state's African Americans, did not enjoy the right to vote. Furthermore, married women could not own property. Upon marriage, a woman's personal property legally passed to her husband.

Hoosier women found an ally in Robert Dale Owen from New Harmony, who introduced a section to the 1851 constitution that would have allowed married women to own property. Owen's proposal was adopted three times, but each time was recalled and eliminated. Although married women finally achieved the right to own property in 1853, the 1851 convention did not take this step. The 1851 constitution extended suffrage to white male immigrants who had been in the United States for at least a year and living in Indiana for at least six months and were professing an intention to become a U.S. citizen. However, Hoosier women did not achieve the right to vote until 1920.

▶ With a partner, discuss how the 1851 constitution failed to afford Hoosier women equal opportunities.

1   Do you think that the 1853 law that awarded married women property rights could have been achieved without the groundwork laid by Robert Dale Owen's proposed section of the 1851 constitution? Why or why not?

2   Why do you think some Hoosiers opposed allowing married women to own property?

The published report of the debates of the constitutional convention includes remarks made by both Robert Dale Owen in support of married women's property rights as well as remarks by William R. Haddon against such rights. Owen indicated that the right to acquire, possess, and protect property was specifically mentioned in the U.S. constitution and applied to American women as well as men. Haddon said that bestowing this right created a slippery slope to the rights of representation and suffrage for women. He argued that women did not possess "the necessary degree of political knowledge" because their domestic duties directed their attention elsewhere, limiting "their knowledge in matters of civil government." (*Report of the Debates and Proceedings*, 462–70)

▶ Create a poster urging Convention delegates to vote for or against property rights for married women. Make sure that your poster uses images that express visually the arguments of the side you are representing.

▶ Imagine a conversation between Owen or a Hoosier woman and Haddon about this issue. With your partner, create a short skit representing this conversation. Perform your skit for the class.

Activity References

Fowler, H., convention reporter. *Report of the Debates and Proceedings of the Convention for the Revision of the Constitution of the State of Indiana*. Indianapolis: A. H. Brown, 1850. Internet Archive, https://archive.org/details/report debatesan00indigoog.

Kettleborough, Charles. *Constitution Making in Indiana: A Source Book of Constitutional Documents with Historical Introduction and Critical Notes*. Vol. 1. 1916. Reprint, Indianapolis: Indiana Historical Bureau, 1971. Indiana Historical Bureau and Indiana Supreme Court, 1816 constitution, http://www .in.gov/history/2460.htm; 1851 constitution, http://www .in.gov/history/2473.htm.

Recruitment Poster for Black Soldiers

This recruitment poster for African American soldiers illustrates that the question of slavery was at the forefront of the Civil War. At the end of 1863 African American soldiers in Indiana formed the Twenty-eighth Regiment of United States Colored Troops. Many USCT soldiers were former slaves who were fighting for the freedom of those still enslaved.

FREEDOM TO THE SLAVE

PUBLIC SCHOOL

Enlistment of Colored Soldiers 1864

4

Abolition and Civil War

Slavery, the Nation's greatest curse, was wiped from existence after four years of hard service.

— *A Hoosier veteran of the Civil War*

Slavery was indeed America's greatest curse, and the Civil War its greatest crisis. Before the war, Hoosiers argued long and hard about slavery and race. Could their nation endure half slave and half free? Were blacks worthy of justice and equality? These questions rocked Indiana as they did all states. Eventually war came, a war of great heroism and of great tragedy.

Less Equal Hoosiers

For the most part, Hoosiers were grateful that their Constitution of 1816 prohibited slavery. Most felt slavery was the South's problem, not Indiana's. Many believed, too, that blacks, slave or free, were inferior to whites. Indiana laws denied free black men and women the right to vote, to give testimony in a trial with whites, or to marry a white partner. Whites often permitted blacks to take only the least desirable jobs.

One racial problem in Indiana as in other states was deciding who was black. In 1840 the Indiana legislature officially defined an African American by the one-eighth rule—if a person had one black great-

grandparent and seven white great-grandparents, then that person was officially considered to be black. It was a strange genealogy.

Some white Americans even wanted blacks to move to Africa. In 1829 some Hoosiers who believed in this movement, formed the Indiana Colonization Society, which provided aid for emigration. Colonization was a bit like Indian removal—both were designed to get rid of a people whites did not want. Some who supported colonization felt that it would be helpful to ex-slaves. Colonization was voluntary, however. Fewer than a hundred black Hoosiers chose an unknown Africa over Indiana.

The most extreme statement about race came in Indiana's Constitution of 1851. Article XIII stated that "No negro or mulatto shall come into or settle in the State." Voters overwhelmingly approved closing the state's borders to all but white newcomers. Still, a few spoke against Article XIII. South Bend newspaper editor Schuyler Colfax was one of these people. He predicted that future generations would "burn with shame" at the exclusion provision and argued for "equal and exact justice, regardless of creed, race, or color."

Sometimes there was white violence against African Americans. Most notable was the mob that severely beat black abolitionist Frederick Douglass when he spoke in Pendleton in 1843. African American Hoosiers responded to white prejudice by creating communities of their own. Black settlements in rural Indiana and black neighborhoods in towns offered friendly faces and mutual support. So did churches, particularly the African Methodist Episcopal Church.

Hoosiers Debate Slavery

Most white Hoosiers preferred to ignore slavery. Some abhorred slavery but saw no way to end it. A small minority was more radical. They insisted on abolishing the evil institution by whatever means necessary. A Fourth of July orator in Fort Wayne in 1835 pointed to "the gross inconsistency of styling ourselves the friends of the rights of man while we hold within our own borders millions of human beings in absolute and degrading servitude." Events in the 1850s caused many Hoosiers to move toward antislavery positions.

Sparks began to fly with the federal Fugitive Slave Act that was part of the Compromise of 1850, a series of bills dealing with the question of slavery. The compromise defined which new western states could decide to be slave states and which states would be free of slavery, in an attempt to balance the growing country with half slave states and half free states. The Fugitive Slave Act backed slave catchers who tried to capture runaway slaves in both slave and free states. Along with other abolitionists, Hoosiers who assisted escaping slaves were liable to harsh penalties. A writer in a Madison newspaper claimed the new law was "the most tyrannical and unjust enactment that ever disgraced the annals of any country, pagan or Christian."

As Hoosiers learned of the plight of fugitive slaves from

COLLECTIONS OF THE INDIANA STATE ARCHIVES

Indiana's Negro Register

After Hoosiers endorsed Article XIII of the 1851 Constitution that barred African Americans from coming into or settling in Indiana, African Americans who already lived in Indiana had to register in their county of residence. This page from a "Register of Negroes and Mulattoes" from Franklin County in southeastern Indiana shows that county clerks recorded places of birth and residence; they also recorded names, ages, and physical descriptions for each individual.

PAINTING BY ADOLPH METZNER, COURTESY E. BURNS APFELD

Return from Picket Duty, Green River, Kentucky, February 1862

Captain Adolph Metzner, a German immigrant and member of Indiana's Thirty-second Volunteer Infantry, an all-German American regiment, recorded many of his and his regiment's experiences in sketches and paintings. In this painting Metzner illustrates the conditions the soldiers endured, such as the heavy snow shown here. The soldiers of the Thirty-second also endured brutal combat in battles at Shiloh and Missionary Ridge in Tennessee, among others.

newspaper reports and Harriet Beecher Stowe's novel, *Uncle Tom's Cabin*, they became more agitated. Many had been content with the Democratic Party's position to let slavery alone. Now, growing numbers wanted to stand against the Fugitive Slave Law and the evils of slavery. These antislavery Hoosiers joined other Americans to form the new Republican Party.

In the late 1850s Republican strength increased in Indiana. However, few antislavery Republicans were radical abolitionists. Abolitionists believed not only in abolishing slavery but also in ending racial discrimination and segregation. Most Republicans were mainly concerned with ending slavery. They disapproved of violence such as abolitionist John Brown's 1859 raid on the federal arsenal at Harpers Ferry, Virginia.

Morgan's Raid

In this illustration General John Hunt Morgan and his raiders are pillaging the town of Salem, Indiana, on July 10, 1863. The raiders burned down the town's depot, cut off their communications, and demanded ransom from merchants. Morgan's Raid was the only significant Confederate attack in Indiana during the Civil War.

Brown and others aimed to steal guns and ammunition from the arsenal and give them to slaves. Few Hoosiers supported abolitionists such as John Brown. Still, one Hendricks County Republican wrote that Brown "is looked upon as a martyr in a cause not legal but just."

Nevertheless, Democrats attacked Republicans as radical abolitionists and champions of racial equality. There was much talk of states' rights (the right for people in a state to choose whether the state legalized slavery or outlawed it) and of economic differences between North and South due to business based on slave labor versus business based on paid labor. At the center of the controversy was slavery. When Republicans carried Indiana and the nation in the 1860 elections—the year Abraham Lincoln was elected president—tensions boiled over and led to war.

War Comes

Soldiers of the southern confederacy fired on American forces at Fort Sumter in South Carolina in 1861, forcing a war few Hoosiers wanted. Once the war began, Indiana joined the Union and fought, sending off a higher percentage of soldiers from the state's population than nearly any other Union state. Hoosiers fought in all major battles, from Antietam (Maryland) and Gettysburg (Pennsylvania) to Vicksburg (Mississippi) and Shiloh (Tennessee).

Among the most honored units was the Nineteenth Indiana Volunteer Infantry Regiment, part of the famed Iron Brigade. On the first day of battle at Gettysburg, the Nineteenth Indiana, wearing the distinctive tall black hats of the brigade, stood their ground against charging Confederates. The brigade's heroism that day allowed the Union time to seize the high ground and win victory in the Battle of Gettysburg two days later.

Most had expected a short and easy war; it turned out to be long and bloody. More than 25,000 Hoosiers died from disease and/or wounds. One Owen County family had six men in uniform. Four did not come home.

Most of the men who joined were young and single. Many served alongside friends and neighbors, some in ethnic units such as the Thirty-second Indiana formed of German Americans. Some men deserted; some got into trouble. Nearly all soldiers were home-sick and nearly all grumbled about the hardship of war, including "crackers with maggots in them, maybe half a finger long." Despite many hardships, most soldiers continued to fight for their homes and for the Union. Back home in Indiana women took on farm chores and jobs that men had done. Many helped the war effort by establishing aid societies or serving as nurses.

Copperheads Threaten the Union

The Civil War produced the most bitter politics in Indiana's history. On the hot seat was Oliver P. Morton, Indiana's Republican governor. He was among those Union governors most supportive of President Lincoln's strong stand against the Confederacy, viewing it as southern treason. However, a growing number of Hoosiers opposed Morton. Some had ties to the South, the origin of many of Indiana's pioneers (brothers really did fight against brothers in some cases). Some questioned the high cost of war as bodies returned home. Some Democrats charged that Morton and Lincoln were power-hungry dictators. Congressman Daniel Voorhees from Terre Haute compared Lincoln to England's King George III.

Two issues gave Democrats their ammunition. One was the draft. As fewer men volunteered to serve, Indiana began to draft men into the army. Forcing men to fight was not the democratic way, many argued. In several towns anti-draft protesters committed violence, even murder. The second issue was Lincoln's Emancipation Proclamation, which freed slaves in Confederate states. Morton argued that freeing slaves owned by Confederates was a strategy aimed at crippling the Confederacy—just as blockading southern ports and destroying southern crops and railroads was aimed to cripple the Confederacy. Democrats attacked emancipation as unconstitutional and as a threat to white supremacy. Adding insult to the Democrats' perceived injury, Lincoln and Morton began to put black men in Union blue.

Deep divisions erupted. Some communities celebrated the Fourth of July in separate groups, one for pro-war Republicans, the other for anti-war Democrats. The harshest opposition came from Copperheads, the Republican nickname for an outspoken group of anti-war Democrats. Republicans likened them to snakes in the grass, who, in opposing the war effort, would aid the Confederacy.

When a Confederate cavalry unit under John Hunt Morgan invaded southern Indiana in July 1863, some assumed that Copperheads there would join him. But, as the rebels swept north to Corydon and on to Versailles, they drew scorn and resistance, not sympathy. There were indeed some Copperheads in Indiana but fewer than Morton or the Republicans had feared.

Despite Democratic opposition, Hoosiers cast majority votes for Morton and Lincoln in 1864. The state continued its contribution to the war and to the 1865 victory at Appomattox Courthouse in Virginia.

Indiana's role in the Civil War was complex and even contradictory. Sometimes labeled the most southern of northern states, Indiana offered strong military support to the Union in the war. While devoted to the nation, Hoosiers divided bitterly over the policies of Morton and Lincoln. Convinced of the racial inferiority of blacks, many still concluded that slavery had to end.

4.1

Antislavery Agents and the Underground Railroad

Our house was always a welcome stopping place for Antislavery speakers as well as for fugitive slaves.

— *An Indiana Quaker abolitionist*

Many early Hoosiers regarded slavery as a violation of the laws of God and man. At the same time, few whites in pioneer Indiana proposed to interfere in the South's "peculiar institution," as it was called, and fewer still proposed to correct racial inequalities within Indiana.

The Underground Railroad in Indiana

Some Hoosiers did assist slaves fleeing the South on what came to be called the Underground Railroad. The Underground Railroad was neither underground nor a physical railroad, but even today there are people who believe those were its characteristics. Although a few well-known white abolitionists received credit for helping fugitive slaves escape on this "railroad," there are many anonymous unsung heroes—mostly African Americans and Quakers—who did most of the work and took many of the risks. The Underground Railroad did not have maps or signs to follow; it only worked because it was a secret and ever-changing network.

Escaping slaves crossed the Ohio River and passed through Indiana river towns; Madison was the most important. One historian wrote, "Nowhere on the Ohio River was the contest between the forces of freedom and those of slavery more heated—or more violent—than in Madison, Indiana." Fleeing slaves may have met any of a number of free blacks in Madison's Georgetown neighborhood. Elijah Anderson, John Tibbets, George DeBaptiste, and Wilbur H. Siebert are some of the blacks from Georgetown who are known to have helped runaway slaves. As escaped slaves moved north from the river, they headed toward African American and Quaker communities. On the Underground Railroad, risk and courage fueled runaway slaves and those helping them. Armed slave hunters were more than willing to use violence to return slaves—who were considered to be stolen property—back to their southern owners.

Today, guides at historic Indiana sites proudly point out rooms and cellars that once possibly sheltered fugitive slaves. This public recognition of the clandestine enterprise makes it easy to forget how subversive the Underground Railroad actually was. Harboring and helping escaped slaves was an illegal response to slavery, a form of civil disobedience against the prevailing white attitudes of the time. Most whites

Historic Georgetown District in Madison, Indiana

COURTESY OF THE INDIANA DEPARTMENT OF NATURAL RESOURCES, DIVISION OF HISTORIC PRESERVATION AND ARCHAEOLOGY

Georgetown was an African American neighborhood in Madison, Indiana, established by free blacks in the 1820s. The brick house on the right was home to William Anderson, one of several known black conductors for the Underground Railroad. Anderson wrote, "My two wagons, and carriage, and five horses were always at the command of the liberty-seeking fugitive." At one point Anderson was arrested for helping runaways, and although the court released him, he had to sell this house to pay for the trial's costs. The building on the left is the African Methodist Episcopal Church that Anderson helped to found. Today, a majority of the buildings dating from 1830–65 still remain as part of the Georgetown Historic District.

HANNAH TOLIVER

Emancipation Proclamation (1863) did not free slaves in Kentucky. In April 1864, Hannah Toliver, a free black woman living in Jeffersonville, was arrested for aiding a fugitive slave from Kentucky. In May, she was convicted and sentenced to seven years in the Kentucky Penitentiary. She was pardoned January 5, 1865 and returned to Jeffersonville.

(Continued on other side)

Hannah Toliver Marker

This historical marker commemorates Hannah Toliver, who risked her freedom to help fugitive slaves, despite the dangers it presented. Toliver was one of a group of forty-four individuals sentenced to the Kentucky Penitentiary for aiding slaves. The Indiana Historical Bureau placed this marker in Jeffersonville, Indiana, in 2008. It is one of several such markers across the state commemorating the Underground Railroad.

disapproved of the Underground Railroad and the extreme approach to abolishing slavery it embodied. One activist regretted that "'nine out of every ten men I would meete would condem me for such conduct.'"[10]

Levi and Catharine Coffin

Among white Hoosiers, Quakers took the leading role in aiding slaves fleeing north on the Underground Railroad, often stepping in after African Americans provided assistance. The Quaker humanitarian Levi Coffin was among the most well-known "conductors" on the line. From Coffin's home at Newport (today Fountain City) in Wayne County, he and his wife Catharine (White) Coffin assisted nearly two thousand fugitives traveling through the Midwest to freedom in Canada. Legend has it that a frustrated slave catcher once called Coffin the "president of the Underground Railroad" because of his success helping runaway slaves, and the nickname stuck.

One of seven children and the only son, Coffin was born into an abolitionist Quaker family in North Carolina on October 28, 1798. According to his published memoir *Reminiscences*, Coffin became aware of slavery around age seven, when he saw a gang of black men chained together and learned that they had been taken away from their wives and children. Seventy years after that incident, he wrote, "As I listened, the thought arose in my mind 'How terribly we should feel if father were taken from us.'" He became an abolitionist on the spot. At age 15, he assisted a free African American who had been kidnapped and sold into slavery to

regain his freedom by encouraging other abolitionists, including his parents, to take up the case in court.

By the 1820s the North Carolina legislature had blocked nearly every avenue Quaker antislavery activists used to help slaves to freedom. Like many others in the Friends neighborhood where he lived, Coffin decided to leave the state and head to the Ohio Valley region. In 1826 he settled with Catharine, his wife of two years, and their infant son in Newport, a Quaker community in Indiana.

Coffin established a successful dry goods store in Newport. His business also branched off into hog butchering and linseed oil production. He was soon one of the town's most respected citizens, and his home was one of the busiest stops on the Underground Railroad. Most of the Coffins' neighbors were unwilling to get involved with the risky business, but some eventually pitched in to help. In his *Reminiscences,* Coffin explained, "Friends in the neighborhood, who had formerly stood aloof from the work, fearful of the penalty of the law, were encouraged to engage in it when they saw the fearless manner in which I acted, and the success that attended my efforts. . . . Some seemed really glad to see the work go on, if somebody else would do it."

Coffin's position as a Newport civic leader and prominent businessman helped deflect attention from his subversive activity. He was thankful that his businesses were profitable enough to cover the considerable expenses incurred by his Underground Railroad work.

Levi and Catharine were always ready to spring into action when fugitive slaves came to them for help. Catharine was just as committed as her husband. She worked tirelessly mending clothes for the many runaway slaves that came to their home with nothing but rags on their backs. Seldom would a week pass without a knock on their door in the middle of the night. "Outside in the cold or rain there would be a two-horse wagon loaded with fugitives, perhaps the greater part of them women and children."

In addition to helping many escaped slaves, the Coffins also helped start schools for children of African American families that settled in the area. Prominent abolitionists passing through Indiana sought the Coffins out, including Frederick Douglass, who stayed with them several days. The Coffins' reputation was so extensive that some scholars believe the couple was the inspiration for the courageous abolitionist couple the Hallidays in Harriet Beecher Stowe's classic novel *Uncle Tom's Cabin*.

In 1847, at the urging of other antislavery activists, Coffin moved to Cincinnati where he opened a warehouse that handled cotton goods, sugar, and other products produced by free labor. He had leased his Newport house and planned to return to Indiana once he got the new business established. The Coffins' large Cincinnati home became a major center for the Underground Railroad in that city. Fugitive slaves sometimes hid there in plain sight. Catharine cleverly created costumes disguising many of them as servants or even as Quaker women.

During the Civil War, although the Coffins were Quakers, a Christian sect that believed in pacifism and non-violence, they supported the Union cause. They volunteered at Cincinnati's war hospital, helping to care for wounded soldiers; and they moved many of the soldiers into their home to recuperate. Coffin

Levi and Catharine Coffin

Levi and Catharine Coffin helped hundreds of slaves to freedom from their homes in Newport (Fountain City), Indiana, and Cincinnati, Ohio.

was also a leader of the Western Freedmen's Aid Commission, which raised money to provide food, clothing, money, and other assistance to newly freed slaves. In one year, having traveled to England and other European countries to speak with antislavery sympathizers, Coffin raised more than $100,000 for this cause.

With the passage of the Fifteenth Amendment in 1870, granting African American men the right to vote, Coffin wrote, "I resigned my office and declared the operations of the Underground Railroad at an end." In September 1877, one year after the publication of *Reminiscences*, Coffin died at his Ohio home. At the time of his death, Coffin was not a wealthy man, but he was always willing to give his last dime to the abolitionist cause. The crowd at his funeral at the Cincinnati Friends Meeting House was so huge that many had to wait outside. Four of Coffin's eight pallbearers were African Americans. In 1902 the African American community of Cincinnati erected a six-foot-tall monument at Coffin's grave in the city's Spring Grove Cemetery.

In 1967 the State of Indiana purchased and restored the Coffin house, an eight-room Federal-style brick home in Newport (Fountain City), Indiana. The house's second floor bedroom has a small hidden door leading to a crawlspace where as many as fourteen fugitive slaves once hid. The house is a National Historic Landmark and is open to the public.

PHOTO BY EARL CONN

Wagon at the Levi Coffin House

At the Levi Coffin House Museum visitors can see this false-bottomed wagon. Wagons such as these carried many fugitive slaves northward. This photo illustrates how slaves were hidden in a concealed compartment by piling cargo around them. Approximately seven slaves could fit into this cramped space at one time. Today visitors can tour the Levi Coffin House, a National Historic Landmark, in Fountain City, Indiana.

4.2

Hoosier Attitudes toward Slavery

No negro or mulatto shall come into or settle in the State.

— 1851 Indiana State Constitution

At the beginning of the 1850s, people in Indiana held less militant antislavery views than people in most northern states, reflecting the state's large southern-born population. Few Americans in the mid-nineteenth century, including abolitionists, believed in racial equality; and many Hoosiers had little sympathy for African Americans in general. In 1851 a great majority of white males in Indiana voted according to their prejudices.

Article XIII of the Indiana State Constitution of 1851 prohibited African Americans from moving to and settling in the state. Although a handful of delegates at the 1851 constitutional convention spoke against Article XIII, it passed by a 93 to 40 vote. Then the Indiana electorate voted on Article XIII; 113,828 voted in favor of exclusion and 21,873 voted against it. The exclusion act was linked to the colonization act, which sought to send blacks already living in Indiana to Africa. So enthusiastic was the Indiana General Assembly that it appropriated funds to encourage African American colonization. Few black Hoosiers showed interest in the scheme as they had been born in the United States, some in Indiana, and had lived here their entire lives.

The Divided Democrats

In the early 1850s the Democratic Party dominated Indiana politics. The party strongly believed in states' rights, the right for people in a state to choose whether the state legalized slavery or outlawed it. Democrats supported the Compromise of 1850, which defined which new western states could decide to be slave states and which states would be free of slavery, in an attempt to balance the growing country with half slave and half free states. They also supported the Fugitive Slave Act that made assisting an escaping slave a crime and gave power to the slave catchers in the North.

As the decade progressed, Indiana's Democrats split into two factions, weakening the party and allowing for the rise of the Republican Party in the state. The smaller faction of the Democrats organized around Joseph A. Wright, Indiana's governor from 1849 to 1857. Jesse D. Bright, U.S. Senator from Indiana from 1845 to 1862, led the other, larger faction. Wright was a moderate who claimed that Indiana "knew no North, no South." Bright, on the other hand, was a vigorous defender of slavery.

Jesse D. Bright, States' Rights Democrat

Born in 1812 in New York, Jesse David Bright moved with his family to Madison, Indiana, at age eight. He married Mary Turpin of Kentucky and became a lawyer and politician. Propelled by the sheer force of his personality and large physical stature, Bright's career was on the fast track by the time he was in his twenties.

Adamantly proslavery and a believer in states' rights, Bright represented the majority of Indiana's Democrats in 1850. The passage of the Fugitive Slave Act that year catalyzed, or sped up, a split in the party with Bright and his proslavery colleagues on one side and more moderate Democrats on the other. In the U.S. Senate, Bright supported the Compromise of 1850. Hoosier sentiment was mostly behind the compromise; however, an increasing number of people

LIBRARY OF CONGRESS PRINTS AND PHOTOGRAPHS DIVISION, LC-DIG-PPMSCA-26777B

in Indiana disagreed with the Fugitive Slave Act. By the late 1850s Bright's political luster had dimmed for several

Jesse D. Bright

Jesse D. Bright, a Democrat from Indiana, served as a United States Senator from 1845 to 1862.

Oliver P. Morton

Oliver P. Morton was Indiana's governor from January 1861 to January 1867. He was the first Indiana-born man to hold the governorship. This full-length portrait of him was painted by Marion N. Blair in 1865.

He wrote a letter to Confederate president Jefferson Davis on behalf of a friend who was an arms dealer. The letter reads as follows:

Washington, March 1, 1861

MY DEAR SIR: Allow me to introduce to your acquaintance my friend Thomas B. Lincoln, of Texas. He visits your capital mainly to dispose of what he regards a great improvement in fire-arms. I recommend him to your favorable consideration as a gentleman of the first respectability, and reliable in every respect.

Very truly, yours,

JESSE D. BRIGHT

To His Excellency JEFFERSON DAVIS, President of the Confederation of States.

When this letter surfaced, the U.S. Senate accused Bright of disloyalty. During the hearing, Bright spoke in his own defense and explained that he did not realize that war was imminent at the time he wrote the letter, nor did he recognize Davis's presidency, in spite of how the letter addressed Davis. On February 5, 1862, the U.S. Senate expelled Bright by a vote of thirty-two to fourteen.

After his expulsion, Bright realized that he had no hope of being re-elected in Republican-dominated Indiana. He settled back on his farm in Kentucky, and his land near Jefferson, Indiana, became the home for Jefferson General Hospital, one of the largest Civil War hospitals in the Union. Bright was elected to the Kentucky state legislature. He died in Baltimore in 1875.

Oliver P. Morton and the Rise of Republicans

Slavery rose to the top of several issues that attracted Hoosiers to the Republican Party. Those who joined the new party were increasingly certain that the expansion of slavery was wrong and that Congress had the obligation to bar it from America's western territories. Those who would become Republicans emerged in

reasons, including the fact that more Hoosiers were gravitating toward an antislavery stance.

In 1860 Bright owned twenty-one slaves on his farm in Gallatin County, Kentucky. He opposed the Civil War on the grounds that it was a form of coercion and should not be used to keep the states unified. As if that position was not unpopular enough with a pro-Union Congress, Bright committed a blunder in 1861 that ultimately ruined his political career in Indiana.

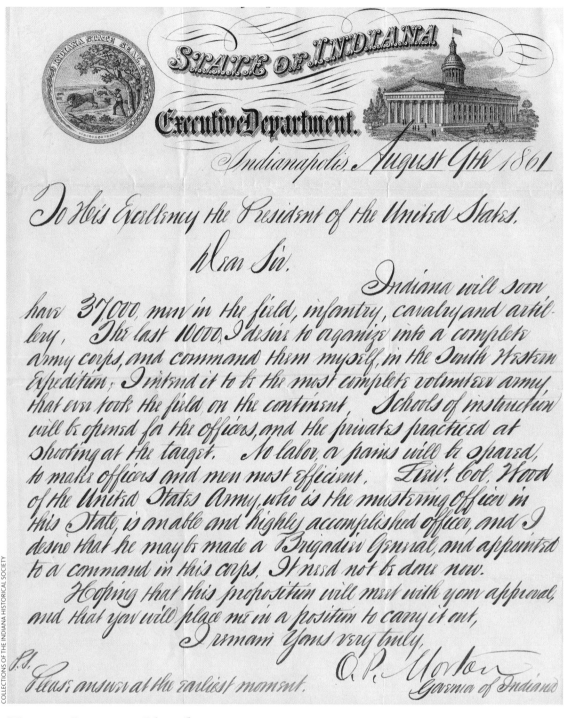

Morton Letter to Lincoln

On August 8, 1861, Governor Oliver P. Morton sent a letter to President Abraham Lincoln concerning Indiana's manpower contribution to the Union war effort. In the letter Morton wrote, *"Indiana will soon have 37000 men in the field, infantry, cavalry and artillery. The last 10000 I desire to organize into a complete army corps, and command them myself, in the South Western Expedition. I intend it to be the most complete volunteer army that ever took the field on the continent."*

fiery opposition to the Kansas–Nebraska Act of 1854, and formed the People's Party. The Kansas–Nebraska Act gave the power to decide whether or not slavery would be permitted in new territories to the citizens of the territories, rather than dictating a balance of slave to free states. That year, the new party won nine of Indiana's eleven U.S. congressional seats. Democratic congressmen from the state's southernmost districts won the other two seats. By 1856 the People's Party had transformed into the Republican Party.

Among the new Republicans was Oliver P. Morton, who would rise to become one of the most important governors in Indiana history. Once a Democrat, Morton switched to the Republican side because of his growing antislavery beliefs. This lawyer from Centerville had superb political and leadership skills that helped him become governor in 1861.

Governor Morton became one of President Lincoln's strongest war supporters. His energy and intelligence made him very successful at raising troops and supporting soldiers in the field. His political intensity caused him to stand firm against the Democratic opposition. Even when Democrats had a majority in the state legislature, Morton was able to outmaneuver them and enact the policies he wanted.

With the outbreak of the Civil War, Indiana made an enormous contribution to the Union side. This might not have been the case if a Democrat such as Bright had been controlling the state in 1861. Governor Morton answered Lincoln's call for troops by immediately sending ten thousand Hoosier men, and he responded to all other calls by filling or exceeding the quota. Indiana ranked second among the northern states in relative size of manpower contribution. Nearly two-thirds of the state's slightly more than 300,000 men of military age served. Indiana regiments mainly fought in the eastern and western campaigns and served with distinction in many of the War's major battles, including Bull Run (Virginia), Antietam (Maryland), Vicksburg (Mississippi), Gettysburg (Pennsylvania), and the Confederate surrender at Appomattox Courthouse (Virginia).

After the war Morton served in the U.S. Senate and became a strong supporter of constitutional rights for African Americans embodied in the national Reconstruction laws and constitutional amendments. His intense dislike of the Democratic Party by this time led him to characterize it as treasonous.

Indiana, a Microcosm of America on Slavery Issue

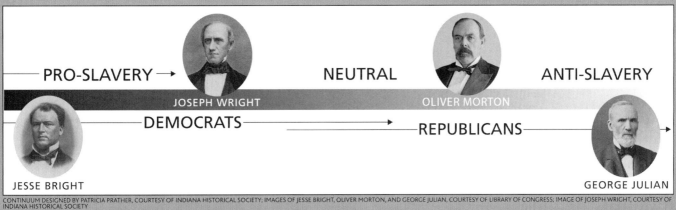

PRO-SLAVERY →   NEUTRAL   ANTI-SLAVERY

JOSEPH WRIGHT   OLIVER MORTON

DEMOCRATS → REPUBLICANS

JESSE BRIGHT   GEORGE JULIAN

Hoosiers argued passionately about slavery. Some continued to remain neutral even after the Civil War began. Even Republicans disagreed. Some were reluctant to go as far as Morton, but he was a moderate compared to Congressman George Julian, a fervent abolitionist. Although Julian was not a Quaker, he represented the heavily Quaker-populated area of the Whitewater Valley in eastern Indiana and always wanted to move faster toward emancipation than most of his fellow Hoosiers.

Before the outbreak of the Civil War, Indiana's population reflected the wide range of opinions on slavery that existed in the thirty-four United States, from proslavery represented by Jesse Bright, to Julian's radical abolitionism. Most Hoosiers were somewhere in the middle of the spectrum, agreeing with moderate Democrat Joseph Wright. Over time, many, like Morton, shifted their position to move toward an antislavery stance, although few became as militantly abolitionist as Julian.

4.3

Indiana's Black Civil War Regiment

We left our wives and little ones to follow the stars and stripes from the Lakes to the Gulf, with a determination never to turn back until it should be proclaimed from Washington that the flag of the Union waved over a nation of freemen.

— *Chaplain Garland H. White, Twenty-eighth USCT*

President Abraham Lincoln's Emancipation Proclamation on January 1, 1863, which freed slaves in the Confederate states, unleashed heated outrage among many Hoosiers. Here was the most extreme threat to white supremacy the state and nation had ever faced. By contrast, Hoosier soldiers were increasingly inclined to accept emancipation. Marching through the South, they saw firsthand the reality of slavery and the arrogance of slaveholders. Hoosier troops also witnessed the eagerness of freed slaves to help the Union cause and even, on occasion, their humanity. One Indiana soldier wrote this single-sentence entry in his diary in 1862: "The negro question is <u>the</u> question."

Creation of the Twenty-eighth Regiment USCT

Black men were not allowed to enlist in the United States Army until May 1863 when the War Department issued General Order 143, creating the United States Colored Troops. African American Hoosiers began helping the Union by enlisting for military service in other states because Indiana had no black regiment. In a letter dated November 30, 1863, the War Department authorized Governor Oliver P. Morton to organize a black regiment. The Twenty-eighth Regiment United States Colored Troops was officially formed in Indiana on December 24, 1863.

At first Congress set the pay of black soldiers at "ten dollars per month and one ration, three dollars of which monthly pay may be in clothing." White soldiers were paid "$13 per month, and an allowance of clothing of $3.50 per month, and one ration each."

In June 1864 Congress equalized the pay for blacks and whites.

In Indianapolis, several men took the lead in recruiting Indiana's only black regiment: Calvin Fletcher, an antislavery city leader and friend of Governor Morton, Reverend Willis R. Revels, pastor of the Bethel African Methodist Church, and Garland White, an African Methodist Episcopal (AME) pastor who became the Twenty-eighth regiment's chaplain. Together they recruited more than five hundred men, forming six companies. Most officers of these regiments were white; Garland White, with the rank of captain, was a rare exception.

The Twenty-eighth regiment trained at Camp Fremont in Indianapolis. Captain Charles S. Russell, who had fought valiantly at Antietam (Maryland, September 1862), Chancellorsville (Virginia, April–May 1863), and Gettysburg (Pennsylvania, July 1863), was in charge of drilling the troops. In April 1864 Russell received orders to take the regiment to the East Coast where it was to serve with other black troops under Major General Ambrose E. Burnside. Four days before they departed, the troops paraded through the streets of Indianapolis, creating an impressive spectacle. The *Indianapolis Daily Journal* reported:

> *Their marching, carriage of arms, &c., were features very creditable to their officers and instructors, and were, indeed, as good as is generally seen in old troops. They walk erect, and bear themselves as men who have rights and dare to maintain them. Captain Russell is quite popular with the battalion, and will soon lead them to the field.*

Chaplain Garland H. White

Born into slavery around 1829 in Virginia, Garland H. White became the property of Robert Toombs, a lawyer from Georgia, when he was a young man. Toombs, a proslavery Democrat, took White to Washington, DC, as his personal valet. While in the nation's capital, White acquired some rudimentary reading and writing skills. He also made the acquaintance of other politicians, some of them abolitionists. White escaped from bondage and made his way to Canada where he lived in a black community of former slaves. While living there he furthered his education and became a minister of the AME Church.

White had been a pastor in Toledo, Ohio, and an army recruiter before he traveled to Indianapolis to enlist in the Twenty-eighth UCST in 1863. He also worked to recruit other African Americans to the unit and became the regiment's chaplain in September 1864. As chaplain, he was an officer with the rank of captain and one of only fourteen black chaplains in the Union's 149 black regiments.

While serving with the Twenty-eighth, White wrote a series of letters to the *Christian Recorder*, an AME newspaper. The letters contain a wealth of information that details the regiment's wartime experiences, both in everyday life and on the battlefield. They are among the few eyewitness accounts by black soldiers in existence. White was an excellent writer. His letters include clear, emotionally-wrenching descriptions of the Battle of the Crater (Petersburg, Virginia, July 1864), the fall of Richmond (Virginia, April 1865), and the Twenty-eighth Regiment's ordeal in southern Texas. In one especially moving letter, White describes the events in Richmond shortly after it fell in defeat. The Twenty-eighth was among the first Union troops to enter Richmond. The officers and men of the Twenty-eighth asked White to give a speech there in the street, and he "proclaimed for the first time in that city freedom to all mankind." Immediately afterward, White states, "The doors of all the slave pens were thrown open, and thousands came out shouting and praising God and father or master Abe, as they termed him."

In the newspaper article, White speaks of yet another miracle that awaited him that day:

Among the many broken-hearted mothers looking for their children who had been sold into Georgia and else-where, was an aged woman, passing through the vast crowd of colored people, inquiring for a man by the name of Garland White, who had been sold from her

Isom Ampey

Isom Ampey was born in Wayne County, Indiana, and served in the Fifty-fourth Massachusetts Volunteer Infantry Regiment USCT with his brother Thomas Ampey. The two brothers mustered into the unit in May 1863—seven months before Indiana formed the Twenty-eighth Regiment USCT. Their younger brother George enlisted in the Twenty-eighth Regiment in December 1863. Of the three brothers, Isom and George survived the war. Thomas was killed at a battle at Fort Wagner, South Carolina, in July 1863.

when a small boy. . . . Some of the boys . . . soon found me, and said: "Chaplain, here is a lady that wishes to see you.". . . "This is your mother, Garland, whom you are talking to, who has spent twenty years of grief about her son." I cannot express the joy I felt at this happy meeting of my mother and other friends. . . . I have witnessed several such scenes among the other colored regiments.

On January 8, 1866, White spoke proudly at the public ceremony in Indianapolis honoring the Twenty-eighth USCT. He returned to his family in Ohio after the war.

DESCRIPTIVE LIST OF DESERTERS from the 28th Regiment of Colored Troops

Men of Co K.

to serve for the term of 3 years from the

No	NAME	RANK	CO	DESCRIPTION					WHERE BORN		RESIDENCE WHEN ENLISTED	OCCUPATION	ENLISTED OR ENROLLED		
				AGE	HEIGHT (Feet / Inches)	COMPLEXION	EYES	HAIR	STATE OR KINGDOM	TOWN OR COUNTY			WHEN	WHERE (Town and State)	BY WH—
1	Elias H Bliss	Capt	K	22	5 7	Light	Grey	Brown	Vermont	Johnson	Calais Vt	Farmer	Sept 13/64	near Petersburg Va / Washington	Press
	Thomas Latchford	1 Lieut	K										Aug 28/64	near Petersburg Va	Press
2	Henry Oviatt	2 Lieut	K	24	5 8½	Light	Gray	Brown	New York	Hornellsville	Grant Co. Mo	Farmer	Sept 23d	near Petersburg Va	Press
1	Watley William	Serg		25	5 8½	Blk	Blk	Blk	Maryland			Laborer	July 29/64	Baltimore Md	Draf
2	Davis Andrew	Serg		24	6 1	Bro.	Blk	Blk	"	Rockville		Laborer	July 30	E Mills Md	"
3	Rogers Chas	3		25	5 10	Blk	Blk	Blk	Virginia			"	July 28	Baltimore Md	Subs
4	Monroe James	4		21	5 3	Blk	Blk	Blk	"			"	July 31	"	"
5	Snavely Chas W			24	5 8	Blk	B.	"	"			Butcher	June 24/64	Frederick Md	"
1	Maulsby John B	Corp		17	5 5	"		"	Delaware			Laborer	July 24/64	Missouri	"
2	North Thomas			30	5 7	Dark	Hazel	Brown	Maryland	Centreville		" "	" 30	E Mills Md	Draf
3	Johnson Thomas			26	5 11	Blk	Blk	Blk	Virginia	Alexandria		Teamster	" 30	" "	Subs
4	Enloes William			28	5 8	Bro	"	"	"			Laborer	" 28	Baltimore Md	"
5	Pea Robert			19	5 6½	Blk			"			"	" 29	"	"
1	America Henry	Musc		27	5 8	Bro	"	"	Maryland	Anna Arndl		Woodcutter	July 30	E Mills Md	Dra
2	Archer Richard			23	5 7	Blk	"	"	Virginia	Loudon		Waiter	" 30	Baltimore	Sub
3	Brooks John			28	5 5	"	"	"	C			Laborer	" 28		"
4	Boston Daniel			21	5 8¼	"	"	"	S Carolina Raleigh			Teamster	" 29	E Mills Md	"
5	Berry John								No Carolina	Raleigh		Teamster	" 29	E Mills Md	"
6	Branch John			20	5 8½	Bro.	"	"	No Carolina	Raleigh		Teamster	" 29	E Mills Md	Subs
7	Berry John			22	5 7	Blk	"	"	Maryland			Farmer	" 28	Centreville	Subs
8	Brown Matthew			18	5 1½	"	"	"	Mississippi			Laborer	" 28	Jeffersonville	"
9	Brown William			23	5 7	"	"	"	Va			"	" 23	Baltimore	"

Twenty-eighth USCT Muster List

This is part of one of several muster lists for Indiana's Twenty-eighth Regiment. This and other muster lists provide a record of each soldier enlisted in a regiment and include categories for name, place of birth, occupation, enlistment location, and other descriptive information.

The Siege of Petersburg and the Battle of the Crater

[The] earth began to shake, as though the hand of God intended a reversal in the laws of nature. This grand convulsion sent both soil and souls to inhabit the air for awhile, and then return to be commingled forever with each other.

> — *Chaplain Garland H. White, August 8, 1864, describing the Battle of the Crater*

After leaving Indianapolis, the Twenty-eighth USCT went to Washington, DC, and then on to Alexandria, Virginia, for further training. They headed southeast from Alexandria and began engaging in fierce combat, suffering many losses. From July 1864 to April 1865, they participated in the Siege of Petersburg, as part of General Burnside's Ninth Army Corps.

teers, (Colonel *Chas L Russell* ,) called into the service of the U. S. by _____
_____ , 186 , (date of muster into service.)

MUSTERED IN.			LAST PAID.		BOUNTY.		CLOTHING ACCOUNT.		DESERTED.		WHERE PROBABLY TO BE FOUND.	REMARKS.
WHERE. (Town and State.)	BY WHOM.	PERIOD.	BY PAYMASTER.	TO WHAT TIME.	PAID $.	DUE $.	DATE OF LAST SETTLEMENT.	TOTAL MONEY VALUE OF CLOTHING DRAWN SINCE LAST SETTLEMENT.	WHEN.	WHERE.		
near Petersburg Va	Capt Dimmock	3 yrs	pay due from	Muster								Appointed Aug 20/64 assigned Sept 18th/64 to Co K to fill original vacancy
near Petersburg Va	Capt Dimmock	3 years	pay due from	Muster								Transferred to Adjutant Sept 22/64 Appointed Aug 20/64 assigned Aug 28th/64 to Co K to fill original vacancy
			pay due from	Muster								Appointed Sept 16/64 assigned Sept 23/64 to Co K to fill vacancy occasioned by
Baltimore	Capt Blumenberg	3 yrs	pay due from	Draft				24.79				
"	" Burnside	"	" "	"				13.13				
"	" Blumenberg	"	" "	"				24.79				
"	"	"	" "	"				24.79				
Frederick Md	" Smith	"	" "	"				13.89				
Wilmington Del	" Wilmer	"	" "	"				18.36				
Rockville Md 3 Dis Md	"	"						13.13				
E Mills Md	Capt Burnside	"	" "	"				13.18				
Baltimore	" Blumenberg	"	" "	"				24.79				
		"	" "	"				24.79				
Prince Geo Co Md 5 Dist Md		"	" "	"				13.13				
E Mills Md	Capt Burnside	"	" "	"				13.18				
Baltimore	Lt Cathcart	"	" "	"				21.65				
	Capt Blumenberg	"	" "	"				24.79				
E Mills Md	" Burnside							13.13				
Indianapolis Ind	Lt Cleto							25.36				
Indianapolis	Capt Cathcart							25.36				
Baltimore	Capt Cathcart							21.65				

Men of the Twenty-eighth participated in a daring plot that had tragic consequences. Directed by Lieutenant Colonel Henry Pleasants, Union officer and engineer, they tunneled 585.8 feet to place dynamite under a Confederate fortification near Petersburg. The theory was that a controlled explosion would destroy the fort and give the Union troops a clear path to Richmond, the Confederate capital.

The explosion took place, but not as planned. A faulty fuse delayed the explosion for an hour. When the blast finally occurred, it killed 278 Confederates and created confusion among the Union troops. Attempting to take the fort, Union leaders ordered their men to charge forward, causing the soldiers to rush forward into the crater. Confederate troops rallied and began to shoot into the pit, slaughtering the men of the Ninth Corps. Captain Russell's black troops suffered terrible losses in what came to be known as the Battle of the Crater. Total casualties (killed, wounded, captured, or missing) numbered 3,798 for the Union and 1,491 for the Confederates.

President Lincoln ordered an investigation to determine the cause of the tragedy. Seventeen days of testimony concluded that it was the result of defective leadership and planning. Captain Russell told the court that the botched plan cost him almost half of his men and seven out of eleven officers. General Burnside took the brunt of the blame, even though he was acting on orders from his superior, Major General George G. Meade. Burnside was relieved of his command and was not called to duty for the rest of the war. Congress eventually exonerated Burnside and blamed Meade for the debacle.

The failed plan at the Battle of the Crater delayed the capture of Richmond, Virginia, by almost nine months. Finally, on April 3, 1865, the Union army, which included troops from the Twenty-eighth Regiment, took the city. After Confederate General Robert E. Lee surrendered to Union General Ulysses S. Grant, the Twenty-eighth Regiment was assigned to guard Confederate prisoners at two large facilities, one in Virginia the other in Maryland. One Confederate prisoner wrote that being guarded by black troops made the prisoners' "Southern blood boil."

The Twenty-eighth USCT in Texas

Although April 9, 1865, marked the official end of the war, there were many "hot spots" in the country, especially in Texas, where there were still Confederate strongholds. The Twenty-eighth USCT and more than twenty-five other African American regiments received orders to help restore peace in Texas.

The troops were psychologically and physically unprepared for what awaited them along the Rio Grande–Mexico border. After fighting so long and bravely to unite the nation, they expected to return to their families. Instead they found themselves in deadly summer heat with inadequate provisions. Some men of the USCT died of disease. Fifteen soldiers who survived the Battle of the Crater died in Texas before the end of 1865. The *Christian Recorder* printed a letter from Chaplain White on October 21, 1865, describing the harsh conditions the troops endured:

> *No set of men in any country ever suffered more severely than we in Texas. Death has made fearful gaps in every regiment. Going to the grave with the dead is as common to me as going to bed. . . . I have spent a great portion of my time at the hospitals, and I never witnessed such fearful mortality in all my life. I have not seen a lemon, peach, apple or pear, nor corn enough over all that part of the country through which we have passed, to fatten a six months' pig.*

The Twenty-eighth Regiment left Texas in November 1865 and headed home by river boats on the Mississippi and Ohio Rivers. On January 6, 1866, the regiment of 950 men and 33 officers arrived in Indianapolis. Two days later they were honored at a public ceremony acknowledging their heroism and contribution to the war effort. The *Indianapolis Daily Journal* summarized the event as a pleasant occasion and "a large nail in the great platform of equal justice." The men of the Twenty-eighth Regiment then returned to their civilian lives, perhaps glimpsing that collectively and individually they were standard bearers for a long march toward civil rights.

COLLECTIONS OF THE INDIANA WAR MEMORIAL COMMISSION

Flag of the Twenty-eighth Regiment USCT

On the battlefield it was the job of a few soldiers to carry the regiment's flag into battle. Battle flags were used to keep regiments together, and regiments took pride in their flag and rallied around it. Many of Indiana's Civil War battle flags are preserved today at the Indiana War Memorial Museum in Indianapolis.

No.

Corpus Christy Texas; Sept. 4th 65

My Dear Brother

I now take hold of my pen to tell you that am well and that I receivd your welcom letter last night after dark I was glad to here from you again and that you was well, I hope your health remains good, But I am sorry that I have to inform you that James is sick and at hospital he has had a very severe attack of the scurvy which complaint is pervailing with us to an alarming extent he has been at the hospital about 3 weeks and is now very low even past walking about I went to see him this morning and it was thought he was mending but slowly, I also got a letter from home at the same time I got yours it was the first I have heard from home for 2 months all wer in common health and you may that I feel better then common to day on account of the letters

Trail Brothers Correspondence

Many families with able-bodied sons and husbands contributed more than one soldier to the war effort. In this letter William Trail Jr. writes to his brother David. William was a soldier in Indiana's Twenty-eighth Regiment USCT while David served in Tennessee's Fourteenth Regiment USCT. When William wrote this letter in September 1865, the Twenty-eighth was stationed in Texas, and the Fourteenth in Tennessee. In the letter William talks about his family, reports on news and conditions in Texas, and sends greetings. At one point he writes, "*It has been the camp talk all along that we wer[e] going to be mustered out of service in a little while but such talk dont take any effect on me anymore[.] I only hope to get home when my time is out.*" William did return home to Henry County in a few months and later owned a farm in Greensboro, Indiana. Although William and David both survived the war, two other Trail brothers who had fought in the Twenty-eighth Regiment did not. Benjamin F. Trail was killed at Petersburg, Virginia, on July 30, 1864; and James Trail died at Corpus Christi, Texas, September 24, 1865—twenty days after William's letter, which states that James was suffering from scurvy and could no longer walk.

4.4

Hoosier Officers and Ordinary Soldiers

The dead & wounded lay So thick that we could not help Steping on them.

— Hoosier soldier Joshua Jones in a letter to his wife, 1862

Hoosier soldiers of all stripes and stars experienced the Civil War in searing, visceral ways. Officer and infantryman alike saw men bayonetted or blown to bits. A general sitting in his polished saddle knew he was ordering his troops into enemy fire, which meant certain death for many. The average Hoosier farm boy who enlisted suffered the hardships of war every minute he managed to survive—from maggot-riddled food, to wet blankets, to long marches. Indiana sacrificed 25,028 men during the Civil War. Deaths from battle numbered 7,243, while 17,785 Hoosier soldiers died of disease, a bleak commentary on sanitary and medical conditions in military camps and on battlefields.

Stories of three Hoosier Civil War heroes—one officer and two common soldiers—illustrate the war they endured.

Lew Wallace (1827–1905)— Officer, Politician, Author

In the nature of things Freedom and Slavery cannot be coexistent. . . . I could not bring myself to defend the institution of slavery . . . my sympathies would side with the fugitive against his master. In all nature there was nothing more natural than the yearning for freedom.

— Lew Wallace, from his autobiography

Lewis "Lew" Wallace was born into a prominent, upper-middle class family on April 10, 1827, in Brookville, Indiana. When Lew was ten, his father David Wallace was elected the sixth governor of Indiana, and the family moved to Indianapolis. Like other boys of his social class, Wallace received a good education, although he did not show much interest in school. He

General Lew Wallace

Colonel Lew Wallace commanded the Eleventh Indiana Infantry Regiment, known as the Zouaves, from the beginning of the Civil War until he was promoted to brigadier general in September 1861. After the war he had a long political and diplomatic career. Today he is best-known as the author of *Ben-Hur*, his second of three novels. After a stint as ambassador to Turkey (1881–85), Wallace returned to Crawfordsville, Indiana, and built a study on his property that was completed in 1898. There he read and wrote until he died on February 15, 1905, at the age of seventy-seven. He is buried in Crawfordsville Oak Hill Cemetery. The study still stands and is home to the General Lew Wallace Study and Museum, which is open to the public.

was interested in the military, however. In 1846, at age nineteen, Wallace raised a volunteer regiment to serve under Zachary Taylor in the Mexican–American War. After the war, he earned a law degree, met Abraham Lincoln, and met and married Susan Elston in Crawfordsville in 1852. Wallace's first foray into politics was in 1856, when he was elected to the state senate on the Democratic Party ticket. Later, like many others in a split Democratic Party, he moved to the Republican Party.

When the Civil War erupted in 1861, Governor Oliver P. Morton appointed Wallace to organize the first six Indiana regiments. A smart, cool-headed commander on the battlefield, he rose quickly through the ranks to the position of major general. On April 6 and 7, 1862, Wallace led the Third Division, Army of the Tennessee, in the Battle of Shiloh in Tennessee, under the command of General Ulysses S. Grant. A mishap occurred at that battle that haunted Wallace the rest of his life. On the first day of fighting, Grant sent an aide to Wallace with written orders, instructing him to move his troops to support General William Tecumseh Sherman's division. However, due to miscommunication in the orders, Wallace's division arrived at its position after the fighting was nearly over. The Union suffered terrible casualties that day, but ultimately won the battle with ample support from Wallace's division on the second day. The Shiloh fiasco humiliated Wallace and besmirched his otherwise impeccable service record. Today Civil War buffs and historians still debate what happened at Shiloh on April 6, 1862.

Wallace continued to serve after Shiloh, most significantly at the Battle of Monocacy in Maryland, when his troops saved Washington, DC, from being invaded by Confederate troops. He was also appointed by President Andrew Johnson as a member of the commission that tried the conspirators who assassinated Abraham Lincoln.

After the Civil War, Wallace returned to Indiana and built a large house in Crawfordsville. He began to devote more time to writing fiction and continued to serve his country in politics and as a diplomat. He completed his most famous novel *Ben-Hur* while serving as Governor of the New Mexico Territory (1878–81). Published in 1880, *Ben-Hur* was the best-selling novel of the nineteenth century, selling more copies than Harriet Beecher Stowe's *Uncle Tom's Cabin*. Wallace garnered as much, if not more, fame for his novel than for his Civil War record.

Ambrose Bierce (1842–1913?)— Soldier, Author

According to degree of exposure, their faces were bloated and black or yellow and shrunken. The contraction of muscles which had given them claws for hands had cursed each countenance with a hideous grin. Faugh! I cannot catalogue the charms of these gallant gentlemen who had got what they enlisted for.

— *from "What I Saw of Shiloh" by Ambrose Bierce*

Like Lew Wallace, Ambrose Bierce became a famous author after the Civil War, but that is about all the two men have in common. Born on June 24, 1842, in the Western Reserve of Ohio, Bierce was the youngest of ten children in an impoverished family. When Bierce was around six years old his family moved to Warsaw, Indiana, where they had a hardscrabble farm—with little money and poor soil. Although Bierce's parents were poor, they valued education and

had books at home. Intelligent and headstrong, Bierce became the apprentice of an abolitionist newspaper editor when he was fifteen.

Bierce was living in Elkhart when the Civil War broke out. He enlisted with Elkhart's Company C, Ninth Indiana Volunteers. By the end

Ambrose Bierce

Ambrose Bierce was a Civil War soldier, journalist, and short-story writer who disappeared in 1913 while on his way to report on the Mexican Civil War.

of the war, Bierce, who had reenlisted several times, attained the rank of major. He fought in a half dozen key battles, including Shiloh and Missionary Ridge in Tennessee, and Pickett's Mill in Georgia. In 1864 he was shot in the head at the battle of Kennesaw Mountain, Georgia. The wound plagued him for the rest of his life.

The massive carnage Bierce experienced at Shiloh as part of the Ninth Indiana deeply traumatized him. Today, he might be diagnosed with Post-Traumatic Stress Disorder (PTSD). The stories based on his Civil War experiences (and nightmares) are considered among the finest of their type in American literature. Hoosier author Kurt Vonnegut, a World War II veteran and author of *Slaughterhouse Five*, wrote, "I consider anybody a twerp who hasn't read the greatest American short story which is '[An] Occurrence at Owl Creek Bridge,' by Ambrose Bierce. . . . It is a flawless example of American genius."

After the Civil War, Bierce was a journalist, newspaper columnist, and wrote in many literary genres, but he could not manage to live a stable life. As one historian wrote, "Bierce never seemed able to locate a place for himself in the world outside of war." His marriage ended and two of his three children died before him. In 1913, after the publication of his *Collected Works*, Bierce packed his bags and toured the Civil War battlefields he had fought on fifty years earlier. In the fall of that year he headed to Mexico, intending to imbed himself in Pancho Villa's army as an observer/reporter of the Mexican Civil War. After posting a letter on December 26, 1913, Ambrose Bierce vanished without a trace. A century later his disappearance remains an unsolved mystery.

Hardee Hat

Members of Indiana's Nineteenth Regiment Volunteer Infantry—part of the famed Iron Brigade—wore these tall, dark hats called Hardee Hats instead of the more common blue or grey kepis, caps with flat tops and horizontal brims.

Joshua Jones (1838–1862)—Farmer, soldier

Though details about Joshua Jones's life before his service in the Civil War are not clear, he may have grown up on a farm near Muncie, Indiana. In March 1859, when he was twenty-one, Jones married Celia Gibson. Their only child, George, was born a year later.

When the Civil War began, Jones, like thousands of other Hoosier men and boys, enlisted to fight for the Union. Jones joined the Nineteenth Indiana Volunteer Infantry on July 29, 1861, and served with the regiment until his death on September 30, 1862. The Nineteenth Indiana was part of the Iron Brigade, one of the most celebrated units of the Civil War. What little historians know about the lives of enlisted men in the Iron Brigade they owe to the letters and diaries written by Jones and a handful of other ordinary soldiers.

Jones wrote most of his letters to Celia. In intimate detail, with shaky spelling and grammar, Jones writes about his wartime experiences and feelings—homesickness, boredom, discomfort, fear, and

GAR Reunion

These veterans of the Civil War gathered in Auburn, Indiana, in 1913 to commemorate the Battle of Stones River, Murfreesboro, Tennessee, that took place from December 31, 1862, to January 2, 1863. After the Civil War, organizations such as the Grand Army of the Republic (GAR), to which these men belonged, provided a support network for veterans and enjoyed political influence that helped veterans and their families. The GAR also held encampments that included camping out, formal dinners, and memorial events. GAR events were held all across the northern states every year between 1866 and 1949.

patriotism. He also tries to lift Celia's spirits and advise her as she struggles to run their farm and take care of their baby son. Along with photographs and locks of his hair, he sends Celia the promise of "a Sweet time when I get home."

By 1862 Jones's letters take on a more pessimistic tone. He frequently mentions the possibility of dying. In a letter to Celia on September 6, 1862, Jones expresses frustration about not receiving a letter from other friends and relatives for a long time. "Can it be possible that they have all forgotten me," he asks his wife. Continuing, Jones tells Celia, "While you was going about the house or in your bed aSleep I was Either laying on the Battle field in the Raine or Seting up anodding[.] it Rained three days[.] you have no Idea what we have to go through."

Two weeks later, at Antietam in Maryland, a Confederate musket ball shattered Jones's ankle. He lay behind enemy lines without medical attention for two days. A few days later he died. Celia, now a young widow, subsequently received a letter from a surgeon in the Nineteenth Indiana offering her this meager comfort, "His remains were decently buried in a cemetry near by & a board placue at his head with his name & regt engraved upon it."

Celia remained in the Muncie area for the rest of her life and remarried when she was sixty-five years old. After she was widowed for the second time, she lived with her son and daughter-in-law. Celia had kept all of Jones's Civil War letters and left them to her son and grandchildren when she died.

A Nation Reunited but Forever Changed

Memories of the nation's most tragic war would endure. On Monument Circle in Indianapolis stands the majestic Soldiers and Sailors Monument. In towns and cemeteries across the state, other memorials and statues mark the tragedy. As times changed, many Hoosiers began to honor the war's great achievement of ending the nation's greatest curse—slavery. Many began to see the necessity of justice and equality for all.

At Gettysburg, a little town in Pennsylvania where Hoosiers in tall dark hats had fought and fallen alongside their Iron Brigade compatriots during early July 1863, the president who grew up in southern Indiana gave a speech to dedicate the cemetery built for all the Union soldiers who had died during the battle. In all, some 51,000 Union and Confederate soldiers were wounded, missing, or dead after that battle. In his southern Indiana accent, President Lincoln gave a short but memorable speech about the war, which would rage on for another year and a half. His speech gave meaning to the many lives that had been sacrificed and powerful meaning to the war—resolving that "these dead shall not have died in vain; that the nation, shall have a new birth of freedom, and that government of the people by the people for the people, shall not perish from the earth."

Selected Bibliography

Berwanger, Eugene H. "'Absent So Long from those I Love': The Civil War Letters of Joshua Jones." *Indiana Magazine of History* 88, no. 2 (September 1992): 205–39.

Bierce, Ambrose. *Shadows of Blue and Gray: The Civil War Writings of Ambrose Bierce*. Edited by Brian M. Thomson. New York: Tom Doherty Associates, 2002.

Boomhower, Ray E. *The Sword and the Pen: A Life of Lew Wallace*. Indianapolis: Indiana Historical Society Press, 2005.

Bowen, Ken, comp. and ed. "Roster of the 54th," in *Written in Glory: Letters from the Soldiers and Officers of the 54th Massachusetts*, http://54th-mass.org/about/roster/.

Clark, George P., and Shirley E. Clark. "Heroes Carved in Ebony: Indiana's Black Civil War Regiment, the 28th USCT." *Traces of Indiana and Midwestern History* 7, no. 3 (Summer 1995): 4–17.

Coffin, Levi. *Reminiscences of Levi Coffin*. Cincinnati: Western Tract Society, 1876. Making of America, http://quod.lib.umich .edu/m/moa/abt8668.0001.001?view=toc;q1=indiana.

Compiled Military Service Records of Volunteer Union Soldiers Who Served with the United States Colored Troops Infantry Organization, 14th through 19th. Washington, DC: National Archives and Records Administration, 2003. Internet Archive, https://archive.org/stream/compiledmilitary0011unit#page /n0/mode/2up.

Etcheson, Nicole. *The Emerging Midwest: Upland Southerners and the Political Culture of the Old Northwest, 1787–1861*. Bloomington: Indiana University Press, 1996.

———. *A Generation at War: The Civil War Era in a Northern Community*. Lawrence: University of Kansas Press, 2011.

Griffler, Keith P. *Front Line of Freedom: African Americans and the Forging of the Underground Railroad in the Ohio Valley*. Lexington: University Press of Kentucky, 2004.

Guelzo, Allen. "Ambrose Bierce's Civil War: One Man's Morbid Vision." *Civil War Times* 44, no. 4 (October 2005): 22–29. Historynet.com, http://www.historynet.com/ambrose -bierces-civil-war-one-mans-morbid-vision.htm.

Gugin, Linda C., and James E. St. Clair, eds. *The Governors of Indiana*. Indianapolis: Indiana Historical Society Press in cooperation with the Indiana Historical Bureau, 2001.

Hunter, Lloyd A., ed. *For Duty and Destiny: The Life and Civil War Diary of William Taylor Stott, Hoosier Soldier and Educator*. Indianapolis: Indiana Historical Society Press, 2010.

"The Indiana Constitution." *Indiana Historian* (June 2002). Indiana Historical Bureau, http://www.in.gov/history/2409 .htm#government.

"Indiana's 28th Regiment: Black Soldiers for the Union." *Indiana Historian* (February 1994). Indiana Historical Bureau, http:// www.in.gov/history/files/7023.pdf.

Kettleborough, Charles. *Constitution Making in Indiana: A Source Book of Constitutional Documents with Historical Introduction and Critical Notes*. Vol. 1. 1916. Reprint, Indianapolis: Indiana Historical Bureau, 1971. Indiana Historical Bureau and Indiana Supreme Court, 1816 constitution, http://www .in.gov/history/2460.htm; 1851 constitution, http://www .in.gov/history/2473.htm.

Madison, James H. "Civil War Memories," *Indiana Magazine of History* 99, no. 3 (September 2003): 198–230.

———. *Hoosiers: A New History of Indiana*. Bloomington: Indiana University Press; Indianapolis: Indiana Historical Society Press, 2014.

Miller, Edward A., Jr. "Garland H. White, Black Army Chaplain." *Civil War History* 43, no. 3 (September 1997): 201–19.

Moore, Wilma L. "The Trail Brothers and their Civil War Service in the 28th USCT." Indiana Historical Bureau, http://www .in.gov/history/4063.htm.

Nation, Richard F., and Stephen E. Towne, eds. *Indiana's War: The Civil War in Documents*. Athens: Ohio University Press, 2009.

Poinsatte, Charles R. *Fort Wayne during the Canal Era, 1828–55: A Study of a Western Community in the Middle Period of American History*. Indianapolis: Indiana Historical Bureau, 1969.

Price, Nelson. *Indiana Legends: Famous Hoosiers from Johnny Appleseed to David Letterman*. Cincinnati: Emmis Books, 2005.

Regan–Dinius, Jeanne. "Escaping Slavery: Discovering Indiana's Underground Railroad Connections," *The Hoosier Genealogist: Connections* 52, no. 1 (Spring/Summer 2012): 15–25.

Richter, William L. "'It Is Best to Go in Strong-Handed': Army Occupation of Texas, 1865–1866." *Arizona and the West* 27, no. 2 (Summer 1985): 113–42. Journal of the Southwest Article Stable, JStor, http://www.jstor.org/stable/40169408.

Smith, Timothy B. "Why Lew Was Late." *Civil War Times* 46, no. 10 (January 2008): 30–37.

Stephens, Gail. *Shadow of Shiloh: Major General Lew Wallace in the Civil War*. Indianapolis: Indiana Historical Society Press, 2010.

Terrell, William H. H. *Report of the Adjutant General of the State of Indiana*. 8 vols. Indianapolis: A. H. Connor, 1865–69.

Thornbrough, Emma Lou. *Indiana in the Civil War Era, 1850–1880*. The History of Indiana 3. Indianapolis: Indiana Historical Society, 1989.

———. *The Negro in Indiana: A Study of a Minority*. Indianapolis: Indiana Historical Bureau, 1957.

Vanderstel, David G. "The 1851 Indiana Constitution." Indiana Historical Bureau, http://www.in.gov/history/2689.htm.

Vonnegut, Kurt. *Man Without a Country*. New York: Random House, 2007.

Vosmeier, Matthew N. "Jesse D. Bright." Indiana Historical Bureau, http://www.in.gov/history/3998.htm.

Wallace, Lew. *Lew Wallace: An Autobiography*, 2 vols. New York: Harper and Brothers, 1906.

White, Garland H., Letters published in *Christian Recorder*. Philadelphia, PA: African Methodist Episcopal Church, 1864–65.

Yannessa, Mary Ann. *Levi Coffin, Quaker: Breaking the Bonds of Slavery in Ohio and Indiana*. Richmond, IN: Friends United Press, 2001.

Essential Questions

1 In what ways did Hoosiers try to keep African Americans out of Indiana in the few decades prior to the Civil War?*

2 How did African American Hoosiers respond to this systematic racism?

3 What factors contributed to the rise of the antislavery Republican Party and the decline of the Democrats in Indiana in the 1850s?

4 What actions did some Hoosiers take to show their opposition to slavery? Name some prominent Hoosier abolitionists.

5 Other than slavery and states' rights, what issues caused political division between Indiana Republicans and Democrats during the Civil War?

6 What contributions did the Twenty-eighth United States Colored Troops (USCT) make to the Union cause?*

7 Describe the experience of war like for Indiana Civil War soldiers?

See student activities related to this question.

Indiana Before and During the Civil War

In this chapter, you read about the many complexities and contradictions apparent in Civil War Indiana. Chief among the contradictions is the fact that a state that had actually tried to bar African Americans from settling within its borders in its 1851 Constitution contributed so many soldiers and resources to the fight to abolish slavery and defend the Union. While most Hoosiers remained deeply convinced of the inferiority of African Americans, they also came to see slavery as an evil that had to be stopped. Many Hoosiers did not agree with President Abraham Lincoln's decision to allow African Americans to

fight as Union soldiers; nonetheless, the state sent more than five hundred free black men to battle as part of the Twenty-eighth Regiment USCT. Despite the treatment they received from many white Hoosiers, black soldiers fought valiantly to defend the Union and abolish the institution of slavery.

In the following two activities, you will consider the complexities of Civil War-era race relations in Indiana in greater detail. As you do so, think about how Indiana evolved from a state banning African Americans in 1851 to one that, albeit reluctantly, commissioned and armed black Hoosiers to defend Indiana and the nation.

Activity 1: Article XIII of the 1851 Indiana State Constitution

Introduction: Article XIII of the 1851 Indiana State Constitution stated, "No negro or mulatto shall come into or settle in the State, after the adoption of this Constitution." To our modern sensibilities, this article seems preposterous. However, many Hoosiers in 1851 had a fear of the two races mixing, and tension over the issue of slavery ran high. This article enjoyed wide public support and passed by a vote of 113,828 to 21,873 when the changes to the constitution were put to a vote. (Vanderstel)

▶ Consider the following arguments favoring the ban on black immigration into Indiana that prefaced Article XIII when it was presented to Indiana's voting public:

A majority of the convention were of opinion, that the true interests alike of the white citizens of this State and of its colored inhabitants, demanded the ultimate separation of the races; and that, as the Negro cannot obtain, among us, equal social and political rights, it is greatly to be desired that he should find a free home in other lands, where public opinion imposes upon color neither social disabilities nor political disfranchisement. (Indiana Constitutional Convention, 971)

▶ Next, consider an opposing viewpoint from Schuyler
Colfax, a Whig newspaperman from South Bend and
delegate to the state's constitutional convention:

*The slave States drive the free negroes from their
borders, and the free States declare they shall not come
within their limits. Where shall the negro go? He has
not the means to transport himself to his native land,
or rather the land of his ancestors, whence . . . let us remember—we must remember—he came not of his own
will. The lust and avarice of the white man stole them
from their homes, herded them in the slave factories,
doomed them to the horrors of the "middle passage,"
and landed them on our shores to live the bondman's
life of unrequited toil. He was dragged from his home,
and now by the accidents of life a portion of the race
find themselves free but ordered off the earth by constitutional provisions, like the one now before this Convention. Where shall the negro go? Into the Ohio River!
. . . Let us not adopt such measures as we shall hate to
look back upon, from the future; such provisions as we
shall burn with shame to see inscribed on the first page
of our organic law. Let us do equal and exact justice,
regardless of creed, race, or color. If we value liberty let
us not step beyond the Declaration of Independence and
declare its sublime truths a living lie.* (Fowler, 458)

▶ With a partner, discuss the following questions:

1 How did the supporters of Article XIII claim that
barring the settlement of African Americans in
Indiana was a benevolent (good-hearted) move?

2 Why do you think they gave that reasoning for the
inclusion of Article XIII?

3 Do you think that Colfax's appeal is emotional,
logical, or both?

4 Colfax's statement, "Let us not adopt such measures as we will hate to look back upon, from the
future; such provisions as we will burn with shame
to see inscribed on the first page of our organic
law," provides food for thought. Does Article XIII
cause you to "burn with shame" that Hoosiers in
1851 thought it necessary and good to bar African
Americans from the state?

5 On your own, imagine and write a Facebook post
reporting the passage of Article XIII of the 1851
Constitution. Write responses to this post that
might come from Colfax, African American Hoosiers, white pioneers, or delegates supporting the
article. In doing so, accurately express the arguments given above, and perhaps offer others, in
simple, everyday language.

Activity 2: The Twenty-eighth USCT

Introduction: The Trail family sent four brothers to fight in the USCT. William Trail Jr., Benjamin, and James served in Indiana's Twenty-eighth Regiment USCT, while David served in Tennessee's Fourteenth Regiment USCT. All four brothers fought valiantly for the Union cause, but only William and David returned from the war. A letter dated September 4, 1865, from William, who was then stationed in Texas, to his brother David, stationed in Tennessee, offers a glimpse into the life of an African American Civil War soldier. It is among the few documents in existence today that was written from the perspective of an enlisted black soldier. Read the following excerpt of the letter, the first page of which appears on page 103 (spelling and grammar are from original; punctuation added for clarity):

> I was glad to here from you again and that you was well, I hope your health remains good, But I am sorry that I have to inform you that James is sick and at hospital[.] he has had a very severe attack of the scurvy which complaint is pervailing with us to an alarming extent[.] he has been at the hospital about 3 weeks and is now very low even past walking about[.] I went to see him this morning and it was thought he was mending but slowly. . . .
>
> We left Indianola on the 10th of Aug" and got here on the 12th[.] we are some better situated here[.] we can [get] plenty of water to drink and of a better quality[.] My company has left the camp of the regiment and mooved close up to town to do provost duty[.] we have been at this since the middle of last week but we have not had to kill any rebel yet[.] what few remain about here are perfectly sivell[.] There are plenty of rumers that the pay master will be along this week but we always have plenty of good newse but little of it comes to pass[.] I am not caring very much whither I get

payed until my time is out[.] I am getting used to doing without money and it don't go so hard as it used to. It has been the camp talk all along that we wer going to be mustered out of the service in a little while but such talk don't take any effect on me any more[.] I only hope to get home when my time is out, it is now over half out. (Trail)

▶ As a class, discuss the conditions under which William is serving in Texas (consider availability of food and drink, medical care, payment, and so forth). Keep in mind that the letter is written more than four months after the Civil War has officially ended.

Later on in his letter, William writes, *"I tell you this is an out of the way place[.] I havent seen a news paper since I"ve been in Texas and except just what I see I know as little about what is going on in the US as I do about what is going on in the moon."*

▶ Imagine that David has mustered out, or finished his military service, and has returned home to Henry County, Indiana, to farm. Using library books, journal articles, and reliable Internet sources, such as the Center for History and New Media at George Mason University website (http://chnm.gmu.edu/), the Civil War@Smithsonian website (http://www.civilwar.si.edu/), and the PBS website (http://www.pbs.org/), gather information about the events of late 1865:

1 President Andrew Johnson's presentation of his plans for "Reconstruction"

2 The passage of the Mississippi "Black Code"

3 The election of Benjamin Butler, radical Republican, to Congress

4 The establishment of the Ku Klux Klan in Tennessee

5 The establishment of the Joint Committee of Fifteen on Reconstruction

▶ Write a return letter from David to his brother William describing the current events in the United States in the fall of 1865. With the Civil War officially at an end, what do you think David found or experienced upon his return to Indiana? Do you think he felt gratitude from white Hoosiers for his service? Might he have experienced racism and discrimination upon his return? How would he have described this to William? How would you go about determining if your hypotheses are correct concerning post-Civil War race relations in Indiana?

Activity References

Fowler, H., convention reporter. *Report of the Debates and Proceedings of the Convention for the Revision of the Constitution of the State of Indiana*. Indianapolis: A. H. Brown, 1850. Internet Archive, https://archive.org/details/reportdebatesan00indigoog.

Indiana Constitutional Convention, *Journal of the Convention of the People of the State of Indiana, to Amend the Constitution*. Indianapolis: A. H. Brown, 1851. Available at Google Play.

Kettleborough, Charles. *Constitution Making in Indiana: A Source Book of Constitutional Documents with Historical Introduction and Critical Notes*. Vol. 1. 1916. Reprint, Indianapolis: Indiana Historical Bureau, 1971. Indiana Historical Bureau and Indiana Supreme Court, 1816 constitution, http://www.in.gov/history/2460.htm; 1851 constitution, http://www.in.gov/history/2473.htm.

Trail, William. William Trail Jr. Letter, 1865, SC 2883. Indiana Historical Society.

Vanderstel, David G. "The 1851 Indiana Constitution." Indiana Historical Bureau, http://www.in.gov/history/2689.htm.

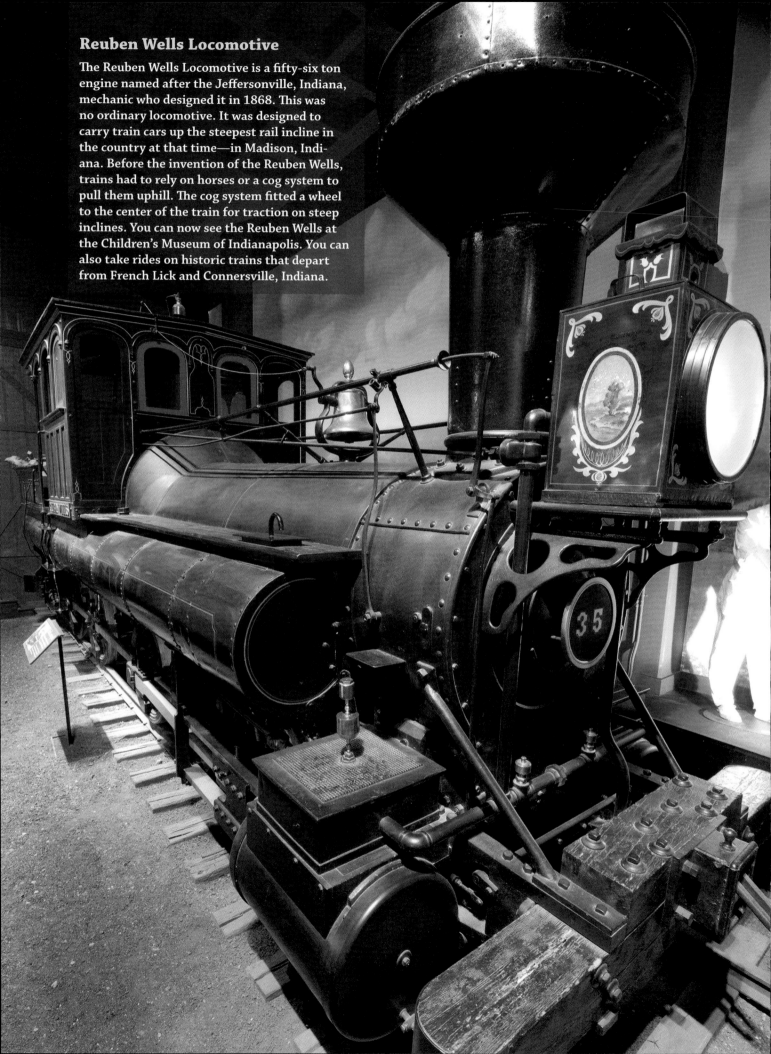

Reuben Wells Locomotive

The Reuben Wells Locomotive is a fifty-six ton engine named after the Jeffersonville, Indiana, mechanic who designed it in 1868. This was no ordinary locomotive. It was designed to carry train cars up the steepest rail incline in the country at that time—in Madison, Indiana. Before the invention of the Reuben Wells, trains had to rely on horses or a cog system to pull them uphill. The cog system fitted a wheel to the center of the train for traction on steep inclines. You can now see the Reuben Wells at the Children's Museum of Indianapolis. You can also take rides on historic trains that depart from French Lick and Connersville, Indiana.

5

The Age of Industry Comes to Indiana

[The] new kind of young men in business downtown . . . had one supreme theory: that the perfect beauty and happiness of cities and of human life was to be brought about by more factories.

— Booth Tarkington, The Magnificent Ambersons *(1918)*

Life changed rapidly for Hoosiers in the decades after the Civil War. Old ways withered in the new age of industry. As factories sprang up, hopes rose that economic growth would make a better life than that known by the pioneer generations. Economic growth there was. United States census workers counted more and more miles of railroad track, tons of steel, and crates of shoes and canned tomatoes.

Hoosiers were at the center of this unprecedented growth. By the end of the nineteenth century Indiana was among the top ten manufacturing states in the nation. It was, along with other midwestern states, America's industrial heartland—the envy of the world.

Origins of Growth

At the center of economic growth and change was the railroad. Bands of iron and steel crossed the state to link farms and factories to markets. Massive steam locomotives pulled long lines of freight cars loaded with commercial goods and passenger cars to towns such as Terre Haute, Indianapolis, and South Bend, transforming them with more people, more business, and more available goods to purchase.

New kinds of manufacturing also powered growth. Before the Civil War most families made their own food, clothing, soap, and shoes. Blacksmith shops and small factories produced a few special items, such as wagons and plows. Small flour and grist mills were the embodiment of pioneer manufacturing. In the late nineteenth century businessmen built large and complex factories that were at the cutting edge of innovation and productivity. The number of workers under one roof grew from a handful to hundreds and thousands, producing an immense output of items for sale. At the Pennsylvania Railroad shops in Fort Wayne, employees manufactured more than twelve thousand freight cars between 1867 and 1917.

Size mattered. A small number of big businesses began to dominate the Hoosier economy. By 1919 Indiana's 302 largest manufacturing companies— which together represented only 4 percent of the total number of manufacturing establishments in the state—employed 58 percent of the state's workers and produced 72 percent of its total value of manufactured goods. Locally owned small businesses continued but played diminished roles in economic growth. The future belonged to big business.

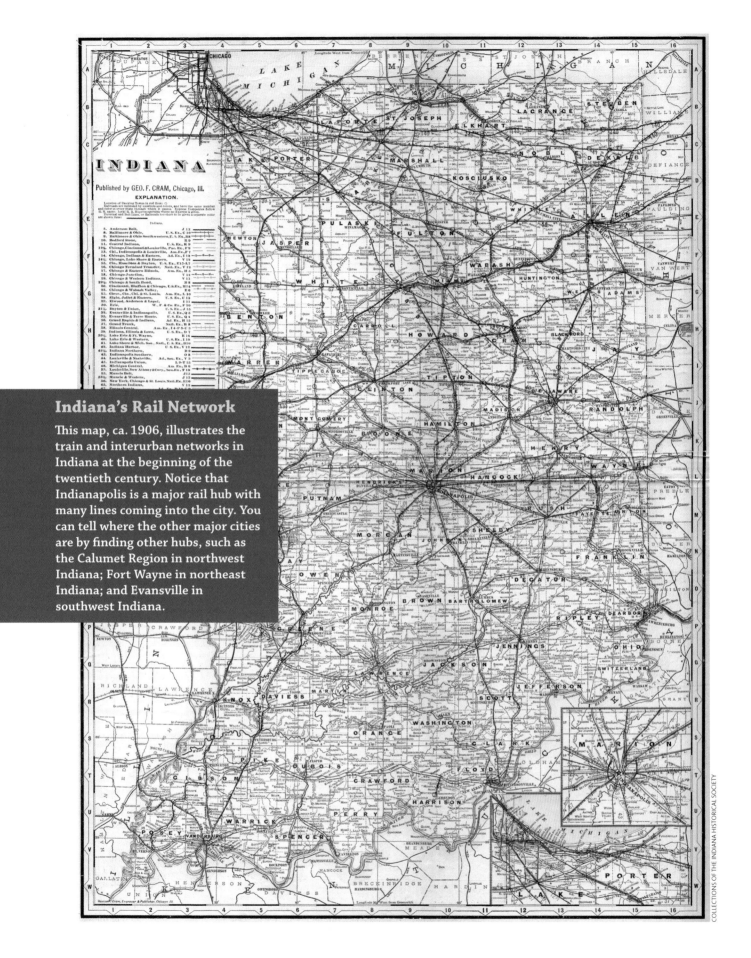

Indiana's Rail Network

This map, ca. 1906, illustrates the train and interurban networks in Indiana at the beginning of the twentieth century. Notice that Indianapolis is a major rail hub with many lines coming into the city. You can tell where the other major cities are by finding other hubs, such as the Calumet Region in northwest Indiana; Fort Wayne in northeast Indiana; and Evansville in southwest Indiana.

Even as Indiana became a major manufacturing state, it continued as one of the nation's top agricultural producers. New technologies changed agriculture, too. Farmers adopted new methods and more machinery to grow more crops with less labor. Farm and factory became linked, as factories began to manufacture farming equipment and process crops into canned goods.

Everyday Consequences

Economic growth often meant a better life. Log cabins gave way to wooden frame and brick houses. Cast iron stoves replaced the open fireplace to cook food. Spinning wheels went to the attic as women and their families wore store-bought clothing. Villages grew into towns and even cities. In the new restaurants in Indianapolis, Fort Wayne, and Evansville it was possible to eat fresh oysters, oranges, and lettuce in winter.

Life changed for many Hoosiers. More children went to school. Congregations built larger churches, often around bustling courthouse squares. Amusement parks opened. Baseball teams formed. Main street stores offered all sorts of gaudy merchandise.

There was more time for cultural activities. Indeed, some labeled the decades around 1900 as a Golden Age because of the outpouring of literature and art. The poetry of James Whitcomb Riley, the Pulitzer Prize-winning novels of Booth Tarkington, and the paintings of T. C. Steele attracted state and national admiration.

Public libraries sprang up across the state, many funded by local citizens and also by Andrew Carnegie, the steel magnate. By the early twentieth century Indiana had more Carnegie-funded libraries than any other state.

Just as some Hoosiers reaped more benefits from these changes than others, some parts of the state thrived more than others. Central and northern Indiana prospered more than hilly, southern Indiana, where there were fewer railroads and factories. Indianapolis and the Calumet Region, the northwestern section of Indiana, became the centers of industrialization, with growth also in South Bend, Fort Wayne, and Muncie.

Industrial growth also brought harm to the environment. Factories dumped their waste directly into rivers, as did most town sewers. The Wabash, White, Ohio, and other rivers became grossly polluted. Smoke

Montani Grocery Store

This 1905 photograph of the Montani Grocery Store in Indianapolis's City Market shows how industrialization affected every aspect of the Hoosier way of life. In this image you can see advertisements for coffee, tea, pickles, olive oil, spices, baked beans, and chocolate. All of these items would have been shipped from different places all over the country. These items provided dietary variety for Hoosiers as well as providing easily accessible convenience items.

poured from factories—a sign of progress, many believed—but it was also a threat to cleanliness and health. As Booth Tarkington's hometown of Indianapolis embraced manufacturing and grew into a city, the novelist lamented it, stating that as Indianapolis "heaved and spread, it befouled itself and darkened its sky."

Finally, the age of industry brought troubling questions about the role of government. Should government interfere with the marketplace? Should government regulate railroads, prevent young children from working in factories, or limit pollution of water and air? Initially, Hoosiers tended to answer no to these questions. Most preferred a government that was small and weak. Most put protecting individual freedom at the top of government responsibilities rather than forcing people to do this or that. Yet, massive industrialization with its unprecedented changes pushed more Hoosiers to call for regulation.

For some traditional Hoosiers there remained doubts about the new age of noisy railroads, smoky factories, and congested cities. Hoosier poet James Whitcomb Riley captured this sentiment in 1895:

You kin boast about yer cities, and their stiddy growth and size, / And brag about yer County-seats, and business enterprise, / And railroads, and factories, and all sich foolery— / But the little Town o' Tailholt is big enough for me!

Fast forward ninety years. At the end of the twentieth century (and even today), some Hoosiers still agree with Riley. Singer-songwriter John Mellencamp echoed the poet's feelings in the lyrics to his 1985 hit song, "Small Town":

Got nothing against a big town
Still hayseed enough to say
Look who's in the big town
But my bed is in a small town
Oh, and that's good enough for me

Inland Steel Workers

In this 1942 image steel workers stand in front of the Inland Steel Harbor Works in East Chicago, Indiana. Factories such as this often employed immigrants who moved into surrounding neighborhoods. The haziness in this photograph makes it easy to realize the negative effects of industry—dangerous working conditions, smoky skies, and polluted waterways.

COLLECTIONS OF THE CALUMET REGIONAL ARCHIVES, INDIANA UNIVERSITY NORTHWEST

5.1

Indiana in the Railroad Age

The transportation of our people is at the mercy of men who never see us, who know nothing of us, and care nothing for us.

— Indianapolis Daily Journal, *February 27, 1873*

Railroad construction in Indiana began booming in the late 1840s to early 1850s, as it did in the rest of the nation. In just one generation, pioneer modes of transportation were partially replaced with this dependable, rapid phenomenon.

Completed in 1847, the Madison and Indianapolis (M&I) was the state's first major railroad, stretching from the Ohio River to the capital city. The M&I's north-south route was distinctive from later railroads, which ran east-west. Its route illustrates two characteristics of early Indiana railroads: (1) they were feeder lines intended to help—not replace—river transportation, and (2) Indianapolis, a major destination for many, was a magnet, drawing the metal rails to it, and eventually becoming a hub with many spokes. [See Indiana's Rail Network map on page 116.]

The New Albany and Salem Railroad (later known as the Monon) was the longest of the early Indiana railroads. It ran for 288 miles and connected the Ohio River with Lake Michigan. When the line was completed in 1854, Indiana had eighteen railroad companies that had laid more than 1,400 miles of track. Most were short-line railroads of fewer than 100 miles. Small-town politicians, businessmen, and farmers could see the economic advantages for their town being on a railroad line. An unconnected town could not prosper, and would eventually fall behind and die.

Madison and Indianapolis Railroad

The president of the Madison and Indianapolis Railroad released this document about railroad operations when his company took over building the Madison–Indianapolis line in 1843. The entire line was opened in 1847. Along the top of this document is a picture of an early steam locomotive, likely from around the 1830s, pulling railroad cars that look similar to stagecoaches.

Railroads became the nation's first big businesses. Early Indiana railroads eventually hooked up with the vast national networks when the great east-west trunk lines moved from New York, Philadelphia, and Baltimore to connect with Chicago and Saint Louis. The Pennsylvania and the New York Central were the two largest systems. By 1920 these two companies operated almost half of Indiana's 7,812 miles of track.

In spite of the convenience and economic benefits the railroads provided, they also had many critics. Hoosier farmers with only one line serving their area complained bitterly of the resulting unfair monopoly rates they were charged to ship their produce and goods. Other people resented the Eastern control, or, as one critic expressed it, control by "combinations foreign to our State, whose local interests and business sympathies are elsewhere than in Indiana." The choices made by the Pennsylvania Railroad in its headquarters in Philadelphia, Pennsylvania, had lasting effects on Hoosier towns and on much of the state.

In general, northern and central Indiana benefitted more from the expanding railroad networks than did the southern part of the state, where the hilly terrain made it more difficult and expensive to lay track. Tunnels and bridges cost big bucks. In Greene County, in the southwest part of the state, the Tulip Trestle (also known as the Greene County Viaduct) was the state's longest and most spectacular railroad bridge and cost much more than track laid on flat lands to the north.

Tulip Trestle

The Tulip Trestle, also known as the Greene County Viaduct, was built in 1906—a year before this photograph was taken—near Bloomfield, Indiana. The bridge, one of the longest of this type in the world, stretches nearly half a mile over the fields below and is still in use today.

Indianapolis, the Railroad Hub

Indianapolis bids fair to become the largest inland capital in the Union.

> — *Lafayette and Indianapolis Railroad Company Annual Report, 1851*

Before the 1850s, Indianapolis was the state's political center, but it was significantly behind cities such as Madison and New Albany in industry. However, the town's central location was ideal for the new mode of transportation—the railroad. In 1847, when the M&I Railroad connected Indianapolis with the Ohio River, Indianapolis quickly evolved from an ordinary country town to a city with an expanding population and economic activities. This sudden growth was no flash in the pan. By 1860 Indianapolis was the focal point of the state, tying together all corners of the state because it was the center of Indiana's railroad system. According to historian Carl Abbott, Indianapolis "was the nerve-center where churchmen argued dogma, reformers planned crusades, and politicians scratched each others' backs."

Everyone knows that when it comes to real estate, it's all about "location, location, location." The railroads turned Indianapolis's central location from an arguable disadvantage in terms of its accessibility to a strategic advantage. Not only did the railroads connect the city to all parts of the state, they made it accessible to neighboring states. This resulted in economic as well as cultural growth.

The completion of the M&I spurred a manufacturing boom in Indianapolis by reducing the cost of coal transport from the Ohio River. Factories sprang up to process everything from pork to lumber and to produce machinery, furniture, carriages, and other goods.

City promoters argued that because it was within a half-day journey of eighty of the state's ninety-two counties, Indianapolis was an ideal site for "any Institution or business that looks to the patronage of the people of the State." Newspapers supported the city's bid to host the 1860 Republican Convention and argued for moving Indiana University to Indianapolis. However, as successful as the city was in many areas, Abraham Lincoln received his party's 1860 nomination at the Republican National Convention in Chicago and Indiana University remained in Bloomington.

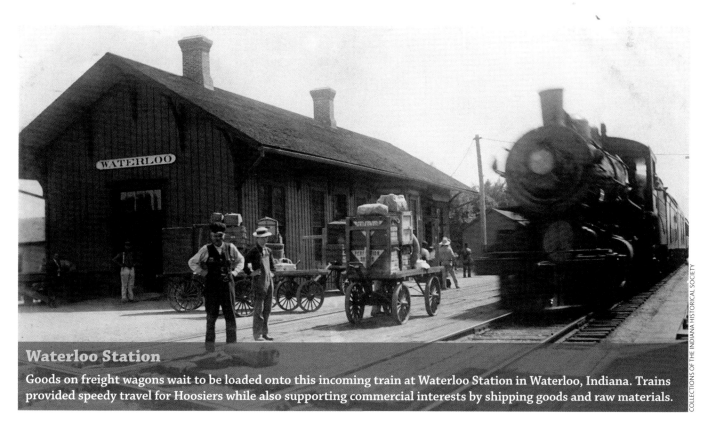

Waterloo Station

Goods on freight wagons wait to be loaded onto this incoming train at Waterloo Station in Waterloo, Indiana. Trains provided speedy travel for Hoosiers while also supporting commercial interests by shipping goods and raw materials.

Interurban Traction Terminal

Passengers gather at the Traction Terminal, the interurban hub in Indianapolis. Before automobiles were readily available, interurbans were a way for people to commute from their homes in smaller towns to Indianapolis. These people may have been commuting to work, shopping, or conducting other business in the capital city.

The Rise of Interurbans

The interurban business has developed into a great industry in Indiana, furnishing employment for a great army of men at very good wages. It is also very advantageous to travelers. They can come or go at any hour of the day, where previously they had to spend half their time waiting for trains.

> — *Fred B. Hiatt,* Indiana Magazine of History, *September 1909*

After the innovation of steam-powered locomotives and railroads, the next development in transportation was the quieter electric-powered cars of the interurban. The first interurban lines opened in the 1890s and were specifically designed for the short distances between towns and cities. In 1914 there were 1,825 miles of interurban rails in Indiana—second only to Ohio.

The first interurban entered Indianapolis on January 1, 1900, and the city soon emerged as the center of the state's extensive interurban system. By 1910 thirteen lines and nearly 400 trains daily served the city. The Terre Haute, Indianapolis and Eastern Traction Company alone stretched 402 miles from the eastern to the western border of the state and linked Indianapolis with cities such as Crawfordsville, Danville, Frankfort, Lafayette, Lebanon, and Martinsville, as well as extending from Terre Haute in three directions, to Clinton and Sullivan, Indiana, and to Paris, Illinois. Most of the lines stopped at the Indianapolis

Traction Terminal, on the corner of Illinois and Market streets. Designed by the famous architecture firm of D. H. Burnham and Company, the Traction Terminal comprised two massive buildings. One was a shed for interurban cars. The other was a modern nine-story office building that provided many conveniences for travelers, including a restaurant, stores, barbershop, and a ticket office and waiting room.

Interurbans Phased Out

The use of interurbans declined after World War I. There were many accidents on the lines. The worst occurred in Wells County in 1910 when a head-on collision killed forty-two people. Few new lines were built after 1911 because there was little potential for profit. The growing popularity of the automobile and motor buses also presented a major threat to interurbans. The electric railways limped through the 1920s until the Great Depression hit in 1929 and dealt the final blow.

In 1941 the last interurban train departed the Traction Terminal, and the majestic building became the main bus station. By the late 1960s, its train shed was destined for the wrecking ball, and in 1972, the Traction Terminal Building was also demolished. All that remains of the razed landmark are two stone eagles that once stood at the entrance to the train shed. Today, they guard the steps of the former Indianapolis City Hall, built in 1910 on Alabama Street.

5.2

Changes in Agriculture

Oh, the moonlight's fair tonight along the Wabash,
From the fields there comes the breath of newmown hay

— *Paul Dresser, "On the Banks of the Wabash,*
Far Away" (1897)

In 1913 Hoosiers designated "On the Banks of the Wabash" by Paul Dresser their state song. It was a nostalgic choice. Freshly mown hay and hog pens remained, but farming and rural life had been changing for decades.

Though Indiana remained a farm state, fewer men were working on farms—from 66 percent of Hoosier men working on farms in 1850 to only 31 percent in 1920. Manufacturing, transportation, trade, and urban service jobs gradually replaced farming as the main ways Hoosiers made a living.

Mechanized Farming

Down on the farm, pioneer methods were giving way to modern methods as farmers acquired new, labor-efficient machinery. By the 1880s farmers began replacing wooden plows with iron and steel plows, specifically James Oliver's chilled-iron plow, produced in the world's largest plow factory in South Bend. They also began using seed drills to sow seeds, mechanical mowers to cut hay, and reapers to harvest. With the new machinery, came more horses. Replacing human power with horse power meant that a single man could farm more acres. Steam power also increased productivity, especially with the massive threshing machines that separated grain from chaff.

Such changes were happening throughout Indiana, but they were concentrated in the northern and central parts of the state, where the land was flat and fertile. Farming in southern Indiana lagged behind. Due to the hilly terrain and poor soil quality, southern Indiana farmers had less money to invest in new technology

The Oliver Chilled Plow

Early pioneer plows were made of wood and later ones from cast iron. They were heavy, often difficult to use, and the metal was subject to breakage in hard soil full of rocks, stumps, and roots. In 1857 James Oliver, a Scottish immigrant in South Bend, Indiana, patented a new kind of plow using steel and iron and a new cooling process that created a durable blade that would stay sharp over many uses. His factory in South Bend produced thousands of plows per year and sold them to farmers across the country during the late-nineteenth and early-twentieth centuries. In these images, ca. 1885, you can see the Oliver Chilled Plow at work.

and so used traditional methods far longer than their northern counterparts. With fewer railroads and less industry, southern Indiana grew even more distinctive.

Farming as Big Business

At county fairs and agricultural societies, farmers learned about new farm technology and techniques. In 1852 the first state fair presented exhibits and awards for examples of new agriculture. The farming network expanded with help from media, too. Farm magazines such as the *Indiana Farmer*, established in 1866, informed farmers of new developments, as did organizations such as the Indiana Corn Growers Association and the Patrons of Husbandry, generally known as the Grange.

Founded in 1869, Purdue University was the epicenter of formal agricultural knowledge. Researchers there experimented with new farming methods, published bulletins, and worked with the federal government and farm organizations. In 1913 the Indiana General Assembly began to fund a statewide network of county agents—full-time resident advisers to local farmers—to spread Purdue's innovative knowledge and methods about agriculture that enabled more food to be grown on less ground.

By World War I, the typical Hoosier farmer was part of a complex national, even international, economic system, dependent on railroad agents, elevator operators, bankers, agricultural implement manufacturers, and market conditions. In 1919 the Indiana Farm Bureau formed to lobby state government for farm interests. Since weather and market economies made farming risky, farmers pleaded for government safety nets, such as those that would eventually be provided by the New Deal agricultural programs in the 1930s. In subsequent decades, federal farm subsidies included loans, disaster relief, price supports, and insurance. Critics argued that government subsidies helped the biggest farms and wealthiest farmers and neglected those who needed help most.

By the end of World War II, Indiana farms were increasing in size while declining in number. The traditional 160-acre farm had not been profitable for some time. As smaller farms failed, their land was absorbed by larger farms. In 1950 the U.S. census counted only two hundred Hoosier farms of more than a thousand acres. By 2007 there were almost four thousand farms in Indiana with more than a thousand acres. The number of small farms continued to decline. The federal

Threshing, 1910

After harvesting wheat or other cereals, farmers had to thresh the plants—meaning that they had to separate the edible grains (seeds) from the inedible stalks. Steam machines like those shown here sped up and simplified the process that previously had been done by hand. The machines blew the leftover stalks into large piles for future use and collected the grain in wagons or bags to be sold at market.

agricultural census of 2012 showed that Indiana lost 2,200 farms between 2007 and 2012.

In 1985 Hoosier rock-and-roll legend John Mellencamp and fellow musicians Willie Nelson and Neil Young organized the first Farm Aid concert to raise awareness that the traditional family farm was endangered, not only in Indiana but throughout the Midwest. By 2013 the organization had raised more than 43 million dollars to help small farms in crisis. At that time, Mellencamp said, "We're still doing Farm Aid because it is contributing. It's doing a job."

Changes in Rural Life

As farming changed, so did life on the farm. Railroads, interurbans, and automobiles, along with telephone lines, lessened the isolation of rural living. Farm families were now able to enjoy the best aspects of urban society. By 1920 almost half of Indiana's farm families had a car and two-thirds of them had a telephone.

Farm women especially welcomed the changes brought by modern transportation and communication. Their lives had been more isolated and lonely than those of their husbands because they had been spending long hours cleaning, cooking, and sewing without the aid of technology such as washing machines, dryers, electric stoves, and ready-made clothing. Mail order companies such as Sears, Roebuck, and Company and mass-produced consumer goods alleviated some of the drudgery of rural living for many farm women and lessened their workload. With free time that their mothers and grandmothers could only have dreamed of and the ability to visit by phone or

car, farm women were able to have a social life off the farm, joining women's clubs, volunteering at churches and libraries, and enjoying other activities.

Like their mothers, farm children and teenagers enjoyed the expanded social and cultural opportunities. Many young men and women left family farms for towns and cities and never looked back—either because they preferred city life or because there was not enough work available in rural areas as the number of farms declined and mechanization took the place of many farm workers. This rural to urban migration was so large that it became a subject of discussion for farm groups. The 1910 census underscored this concern when it showed that the number of rural Hoosiers declined for the first time. By 1920 Indiana's urban population surpassed that of its rural population.

EXTENSION BULLETIN No. 76
(Reprint Third Revised Edition)

January, 1929

PRACTICAL HOG HOUSES FOR INDIANA

The modified gable individual hog house.

Essentials of a Good Hog House

Warmth.—A reasonably warm hog house saves feed. The sow and the pigs should not be required to apply any more of their feed to warming the body than necessary.

Dryness.—A well drained floor, a tight roof and proper ventilation are essential to dryness. A damp house is usually cold, and it provides excellent conditions for harboring disease germs.

Purdue University Department of Agricultural Extension
J. H. Skinner, Director, Lafayette, Indiana
Co-operative Agricultural Extension Work. Acts of May 8 and June 30, 1914

The *Purdue Extension Bulletin*

The *Purdue Extension Bulletin* was issued by the Purdue University Department of Agricultural Extension. In this 1929 issue the focus was on building practical hog houses. Farmers could read this for tips, measurements, and sketches that would help them build a better hog house. This and other issues of the bulletin informed farmers about topics ranging from soybeans to insects to keeping their cows healthy.

In the late nineteenth century, some people in Indiana worried that modern advances were tilling under Hoosier pioneer traditions and modest values, along with rural life. But the majority saw a better future coming through steady but gradual progress and adaptation. One historian called this a "bifocal vision of progress" wherein "Those who criticized Indiana's slowness to change blamed farmers," and "those who boast[ed] of the state's stability praised them."

Canning

With the widespread availability of canned food, beginning in the 1880s, the eating habits of Americans changed. By 1900 home canning was also becoming commonplace. Farmers and home gardeners could now grow more crops and not worry about waste, and they could eat vegetables and meat all year long.

Farm Hicks No More— The Era of Modern Farming

Brainpower has replaced horsepower as the central ingredient of success on our farms.

— *Earl L. Butz, "Agriculture— An Industry in Evolution" (1966)*

By the end of World War II, most Hoosier farmers had moved toward sophisticated agricultural practices. They could no longer be stigmatized as farm hicks. New farm equipment, seeds, fertilizers, and methods would prevail on Indiana farms into the last decades of the twentieth century.

Agricultural change improved the state's and the nation's general welfare—for the most part. There was more food, cheaper food, and a greater variety of food. But by the late twentieth century there was also a growing concern about food production methods. As studies showed that chemical fertilizers and pesticides were harmful to the environment, there was a backlash against them and against biotechnology, due to fears that it would prove harmful as well. Some favored organic foods and locally grown foods cultivated by traditional methods of crop rotation and use of manure.

Rachel Peden, a Hoosier farm wife and author whose work appeared in the *Indianapolis Star* and *Muncie Evening News* from the 1940s to the 1970s, once described a pitch-in dinner at her beloved Maple Grove Church in Monroe County that would make any reader hungry. Peden wrote that the church ladies brought "fried chicken, baked ham, chicken and dumplings, beef and new potatoes, new peas, tomatoes, tossed salad, coleslaw, green beans, baked beans, butter beans," and "at least ten kinds of pies and cakes." All the food was home-grown and homemade. Many twenty-first century Hoosiers, whose diets mainly consist of factory-processed food and fast food, can only imagine the tantalizing smells and tastes at that pitch-in dinner at Maple Grove Church.

5.3

Industrialization

They had a mania for factories; there was nothing they would not do to cajole a factory away from another city; and they were never more piteously embittered than when another city cajoled one away from them.

— *Booth Tarkington,* The Magnificent Ambersons *(1918)*

The water-powered flour and grist mills that processed corn and wheat from nearby fields in the mid-nineteenth century faded into history when the railroads came. Railroads brought new kinds of businessmen who built factories that used steam power, then electricity, and finally the internal combustion engine to mass-produce iron and steel, glass, electrical machinery, railroad cars, and automobiles. The new products did not replace meat and grain processing, but they soon dominated Indiana's economy.

The Indiana Gas Boom

"I was ten years old when they discovered it. Overnight, towns with five hundred people shot up to five thousand. They thought the gas would last forever, that the millennium had come."

— *Jared Carter, "Natural Gas Boom, Tipton County"*

The discovery of natural gas in east-central Indiana in 1886 jump-started the region's industrialization. Within a few years, an eleven-county area became one of the main centers of heavy industrial production in the United States. Towns in the gas belt, including Anderson, Kokomo, and Marion, successfully enticed eastern companies to relocate with promises of free land and free access to the gas, which could be transformed into electricity. Muncie lured the Ball Brothers Company, a fruit jar factory, from Buffalo, New York, and it soon became the largest glass canning-jar factory in the world. These previously modest towns became bustling cities with established business districts and expanded residential neighborhoods.

In 1900 Indiana was the nation's leading producer of natural gas. Other manufacturing also thrived. The United States census for that year ranked Indiana second among all the states in glass production, third in wagons and carriages, fourth in iron and steel products, fifth in agricultural implements, ninth in paper and wood pulp, and tenth in foundry and machine shop products.

COLLECTIONS OF THE INDIANA HISTORICAL SOCIETY

Gas Well Flambeaux, ca. 1900

This gas well in Blackford County is flaring, a process by which a gas well is set on fire, perhaps to prepare the well for a new pipeline or even as a marketing promotion. Today allowing gas wells to flare is strictly regulated all over the world because of pollution and waste.

The Boom Goes Bust

They walked with a swagger—proud of the way they wasted it. They let the streetlamps burn night and day. Too much trouble to hire a man to go around and put them out each morning.

— *Jared Carter, "Natural Gas Boom, Tipton County"*

Despite Indiana's status as the nation's top natural gas producer in 1900, by 1890 state geologists were reporting a decline in supply. For more than a decade wells and flambeaux, the flames that were lit by the gas to show that it was flowing from the wells, had burned twenty-four hours a day, seven days a week—wasting approximately one hundred million cubic feet of gas each day. The conservation wake-up call came too late and was largely ignored through the 1890s.

The Indiana General Assembly passed legislation penalizing wasteful practices, and some companies complied. However, most consumers were too used to the inexpensive luxury to regulate their use. The horse was out of the barn, so locking the door did little good. The gas boom was over by around 1901.

Most of the gas works had closed by 1920. Some factories switched to using coal to fuel production. Although east-central Indiana never again achieved the same level of industrial supremacy it had experienced during the gas boom, it still remained a manufacturing center for most of the twentieth century. Today, the boom towns and cities of the old gas belt have a worn patina of the prosperity they enjoyed during their heyday.

Corporate America Comes to Indiana

With changes in technology came big business. Fewer companies produced more of Indiana's total manufactured products and employed the majority of its workers. These were companies with plants scattered in several cities, states, and even countries. Their names indicate their size and scope: United States Steel, American Can Company, International Harvester, and American Car and Foundry.

Big businesses utilized mass production methods, new technologies, large workforces, and a new managerial structure. Machines often replaced hand labor.

By 1917 machines at Eli Lilly and Company could turn out two and a half million capsules a day in the largest capsule factory in the world. Efficiency was the name of the game—on the factory floor and in the office. The Wooton Patent desk was a symbol of this new age of big business; it was manufactured in Indianapolis and sold as far away as England. The company promised its revolutionary desk would bring order to paperwork and management with "one hundred and ten compartments, all under one lock and key. A place for everything and everything in its place."

In the Home

A kitchen without a cabinet is like a farm without a plow.

— *The Hoosier Manufacturing Company, advertisement, ca. 1910*

Factories and other big businesses were not the only ones to benefit from new technology and innovation. Women went about their business in new ways, too. Time-saving devices and methods enabled them to do chores more efficiently.

COURTESY OF THE MINNETRISTA HERITAGE COLLECTION, MUNCIE, INDIANA

Ball Jar

Jellies and jams would fill this wide mouth half-pint Ball Special Jar that was produced between 1912 and 1923.

In the kitchen, the Hoosier Cabinet was the counterpart of the Wooton Patent desk. The first Hoosier cabinets appeared around 1900. A prototype of the cabinet was manufactured by a refurbished furniture factory in Albany, Indiana, near Muncie. Production of the Hoosier Cabinet moved to New Castle after a fire at the Albany factory. The Hoosier Cabinet had a lot of "bells and whistles" in the form of racks for storing dishes and spice jars, pullout shelves for storing pots and pans, utensil drawers, bins for storing flour, a built-in flour sifter, and an easily cleaned top of zinc or enamel. Its functional design saved the busy homemaker time and steps as she could do most of her food preparation standing at the cabinet. Later models were even more sophisticated and included meal-planning devices, daily reminders for grocery shopping, and helpful household hints.

Although the Hoosier Manufacturing Company was the first and best known producer of the Hoosier Cabinet, competing companies soon emerged and manufactured knock-offs. Nevertheless, the Hoosier Manufacturing Company effectively used twentieth-century mass marketing methods to sell the *original* cabinet. Eye-catching advertisements with clever slogans appeared regularly in publications with a female readership, such as *Ladies Home Journal*, *Good Housekeeping*, and *Better Homes and Gardens*.

Other manufacturers also marketed their products to women. In 1909 Muncie-based Ball Glass Works printed what would become the first *Ball Blue Book*, a guide to home-canning techniques. Unlike the pioneer woman, the twentieth-century homemaker could put up tomatoes from her garden in August and serve them to her family in February. What vegetables and fruits she didn't preserve herself, she could buy processed in cans from her local grocery store.

No Turning Back

The triumph of big business and industrialization changed the map. Industry tended to move north from the Ohio River and concentrate in a few urban areas. With the exception of Evansville, river towns in southern Indiana declined in manufacturing importance. Meanwhile, Indianapolis emerged as the state's center of manufacturing, a process that began with the railroads in the 1850s.

Indianapolis's industrial growth was relatively steady. However, industrial growth in Indiana's other major manufacturing area—the Calumet Region in northwestern Indiana—was more rapid and disrup-

"Saves Miles of Steps for Tired Feet"

The Hoosier Cabinet

The Hoosier Manufacturing Company promotes its Hoosier Cabinet in this ad from 1911. In this image you can see the built-in features of the cabinet, including the flour bin, flour sifter, spice racks, and other compartments. The company emphasized that the cabinet was an all-in-one package, so housewives could save "miles of steps" by not having to run around the kitchen. With the Hoosier Cabinet, kitchens, like factories, could be efficient workplaces.

Indiana Harbor Works Steel Mill

This steel mill in East Chicago, Indiana, ca. 1943, illustrates steel workers pouring molten steel into a mold. After the steel has cooled, it takes the form of a bar or block called an ingot. It is then cast into its final shape. This steel could have been used for military needs for World War II, or for building construction, railroad tracks, or some other purpose.

tive. The new industries of petroleum refining and steel production brought revolutionary changes to cities such as Gary. In 1906 the United States Steel Company founded Gary as the future home of its new factory and named it after the company's founding chairman, Elbert Henry Gary. Nearly three years later, United States Steel's Gary Works opened and was the largest and most efficient steel mill in the world. Freighters on the Great Lakes and a complex system of railroad lines transported iron ore and coal to the factory, and great quantities of finished steel moved out. By 1919 Lake County's industries generated more than one-fourth of the state's total value of manufactured product.

Manufacturing had replaced agriculture as Indiana's primary economic activity by 1920. Many of the people who worked in Indiana's factories alongside hundreds of other workers had pioneer parents and grandparents who had spent their days working alone in the fields or the house. Industrialization affected the lives of all Hoosiers. Growing numbers of people migrated from farms and villages to factories and cities. Abundant new jobs attracted African American workers from the rural south and new waves of immigrants from abroad, particularly from southern and eastern Europe and from Mexico. German, Polish, Czech, Russian, Spanish, and Yiddish accents mingled with those of the Deep South on factory floors.

Despite its progress, Indiana lagged behind its midwestern neighbors in most areas of manufacturing. Reasons for the lag are not clear. Hoosiers may have had a stronger attachment to farming and rural life, thus making the transition to manufacturing more gradual. Although Indiana lagged behind states such as Michigan, Ohio, and Illinois, manufacturing in Indiana grew more rapidly than in the nation as a whole, placing the state firmly among the leading manufacturing and agricultural states by the early twentieth century.

5.4

Labor

Those who produce should have, but we know that those who produce the most—that is, those who work hardest, and at the most difficult and most menial tasks, have the least.

— *Eugene V. Debs,* Walls and Bars *(1927)*

Not everyone shared equally in the growing economy. Many factory jobs brought low pay, long hours, unsafe working conditions, and frequent periods of unemployment. In 1881 the Indiana Department of Statistics published the first report on factory wages, which revealed that the average worker earned $1.00 to $1.50 for a ten- to twelve-hour workday. Skilled workers earned up to $4.50 a day. Ten-hour days and six-day work weeks were common. Industries with the longest working hours included manufacturing products such as gas, cement, paper and wood pulp, baked goods, and iron and steel. Steelworkers often worked seven days a week.

Some felt that state government should do more for workers, but political and industrial leaders of late-nineteenth-century Indiana were reluctant to interfere. Their stance was commitment to individual freedom and laissez-faire economics, a belief that the economy should be let alone without regulation. Only gradually did the state venture into the complex relationship between workers and employers.

Women in the Workforce

The sanitary condition of buildings in which girls were working are not generally at present what they should be to insure the best health and strength of employees.

— *Indiana, Department of Statistics, "Women Wage Earners of Indianapolis,"* Fifth Biennial Report, *1898–99*

Industrialization meant that more women worked in paying jobs outside the home. Although middle-class norms discouraged married women from working for pay, some single women with an education became store clerks or teachers. Women with less education worked in domestic service as maids or cooks; and many went to work in factories. In the factory, women worked in jobs specifically for women. Often the departments were even divided by gender. Industries that attracted the most women workers were garment factories, book binderies, paper-box plants, laundries, and pork-packing plants. In 1899 an Indiana state factory inspector's report revealed that female workers in the state's factories were paid about half what men earned for the same work. Working conditions were atrocious. The workers had to stand or sit for hours on end, often in environments with excessive noise, poor ventilation, unsanitary conditions, and lack of protective gear. Many factories qualified as firetraps—several stories high with overheated machinery and inadequate access to fire escapes.

Most industrial states responded to the needs of women workers before Indiana. It wasn't until 1913 that the Indiana General Assembly initiated a study of women's work. Conducted by the Department of Labor, the study focused on garment factories and retail stores, where nearly half of the women who worked outside the home were employed. Despite the study's documentation of long hours, low pay, and generally poor working conditions, the resulting legislation called for only modest reform.

Child Labor

Cheap labor means child labor; consequently there results a holocaust of the children—a condition which is intolerable.

— *Dr. Felix Adler, first meeting of the National Child Labor Committee, 1904*

Children were also a huge part of Indiana's industrial workforce, especially in the glass industry, coal mining, furniture making, and fruit and vegetable canning. As early as 1867 the state legislature passed laws prohibiting persons under age sixteen from working more than ten hours a day in cotton or woolen mills. For the next thirty years, additional attempts at child labor regulation were few and far between.

Kahn Tailoring Company

At this garment factory in Indianapolis in 1907 men and women are busy sewing, though they work at separate tables. Kahn Tailoring was founded in 1903 and produced men's suits as well as military uniforms. Owner Henry Kahn, a son of Jewish immigrants, hired hundreds of newly arrived Jewish immigrants in his factory and provided his employees with social services such as doctors and night school.

In 1897 the Indiana General Assembly passed two pieces of legislation that began to correct the situation. One law prohibited factory employment of children under the age of fourteen and stipulated that children under sixteen could work no more than ten hours a day. The legislature also passed the state's first compulsory school attendance law, requiring children between ages eight and fourteen to attend school for a minimum of twelve consecutive weeks each year.

However, the child labor laws were not well enforced. Some parents allowed their children to work at factories such as Muncie's Hemingray Glass Company, claiming that their families needed the children's wages. In 1904 Hemingray employed 150 workers under the age of sixteen. The owner vowed to fight "any attempt to pass a law prohibiting children under sixteen [from] working at night," since "it was better for them than running in the streets and did not hurt them anyway."

The most persuasive exposure of child labor conditions around the country came from the camera of Lewis Hine. In 1908 the National Child Labor Committee sent Hine to Indiana to photograph children working in factories. His powerful images of children working the night shift appeared in the *Indianapolis Star* and in reformers' reports. But, as Hine's colleague Edward Clopper pointed out, "The people of Indiana are slow to take hold of any movement."

A 1910 survey reported that Indiana ranked third highest for its proportion of child labor, below only Pennsylvania and Ohio. Only very gradually did state legislation address the worst abuses. In 1911 the general assembly passed a weak child labor bill. It extended the 1897 ban on employing children in factories under the age of fourteen to all other types of work except farming and domestic service. One exception to this ban was in the canning industry where children between twelve and fourteen were still allowed to work in the summer. It took another ten years (1921) for the general assembly to remove all industry exceptions, regulate which industries children could work in, and to set a rule that all workers between fourteen and sixteen had to have completed the eighth grade.

Lewis Hine Child Labor Photo

This Lewis Hine photograph from 1908 shows a boy taking boards away from a double cutoff machine, a type of saw in a woodwork factory in Peru, Indiana. As was typical of Hine's photographs, it shows a child involved in a dangerous task.

Eugene V. Debs and Workers Rights

And there's 'Gene Debs—a man 'at stands
And jes' holds out in his two hands
As warm a heart as ever beat
Betwixt here and the Jedgment Seat!

— *James Whitcomb Riley, "Regardin' Terry Hut" (1916)*

As the state government dragged its feet to improve working conditions, many workers decided to take matters into their own hands. During the 1850s and 1860s various trades attempted to form labor unions. After the Civil War several labor organizations joined forces to work for common goals, especially the eight-hour work day. Indiana's first widespread—and violent—labor action took place during the depression of the 1870s and involved striking coal miners, who shut down mining operations several times, particularly in Brazil in Clay County. The strikes were broken as management brought in black workers from the South, but armed clashes ensued and eventually, at least one black man was killed. The most important labor unrest involved the railroads, particularly in the great strike of 1877. As part of a national protest against reductions in pay, Indiana workers stopped trains in Evansville, Terre Haute, Indianapolis, and Fort Wayne.

Terre Haute's Eugene V. Debs (1855–1926) emerged as an iconic labor leader on the national stage in the early years of the twentieth century. Debs, who had worked on the railroad from the time he was fourteen, founded the American Railway Union in 1893. Within a year the organization had nearly 150,000 members. Debs gained national recognition and notoriety when he organized the Pullman Strike of 1894 in Chicago, which stopped all train movement west of Chicago as fifty thousand workers walked off the job because their pay had been cut by about 25 percent. His involvement in the strike earned him a six-month prison sentence on conspiracy charges. While in jail, Debs became a Socialist and his reputation as a working class hero grew. He ran for president five times as the Socialist Party's candidate. He even ran for president while serving his second prison term for an anti-war speech during WWI; he got more than 900,000 votes. Debs used his incarceration as an effective campaign strategy: his campaign buttons featured his convict number and his face behind bars.

Debs's ideas were radical for his day, but many entered the mainstream in the decades following the Pullman Strike. He advocated shorter workweeks, pension (retirement) plans, sick leave, medical benefits, and women's suffrage. Most Hoosiers respected Debs, and residents of his hometown Terre Haute generally treated him affectionately even if they didn't agree with his leftist politics. Debs and his friend, noted Hoosier poet James Whitcomb Riley, who tended to stay out of politics, frequently enjoyed a glass of good whiskey together. Riley visited Debs so often that the guest bedroom in the Debs house is still referred to as "the Riley room."

COURTESY OF THE EUGENE V. DEBS FOUNDATION

Eugene V. Debs for President!

Eugene V. Debs ran for President of the United States a total of five times. This campaign poster is from his second campaign when he received just under 3 percent of the total vote and lost to Theodore Roosevelt. His campaign platform was based on workers' rights and opposition to capitalism. Today the Debs house at 451 North Eighth Street in Terre Haute belongs to the non-profit Eugene V. Debs Foundation and is open to the public. Each year the foundation hosts a banquet to honor an individual whose work advanced causes to which Debs dedicated his life—workers' rights, social justice, and world peace.

COLLECTIONS OF THE INDIANA HISTORICAL SOCIETY

Diamond Chain Employees Unite!

In this 1913 flyer labor organizers call for employees of Indianapolis-based Diamond Chain Company, which manufactured bicycle chains, to organize into a union. Once in a union workers gained a voice at the negotiating table for safer working conditions, shorter work days and weeks, and better pay and benefits.

Selected Bibliography

Abbott, Carl. "Indianapolis in the 1850s: Popular Economic Thought and Urban Growth." *Indiana Magazine of History* 74, no. 4 (December 1978): 293–315.

Baer, M. Teresa. "From Tribal and Family Farmers to Part-Time and Corporate Farmers: Two Hundred Years of Indiana Agriculture." *Centennial Farms of Indiana.* Edited by M. Teresa Baer, Kathleen M. Breen, and Judith Q. McMullen. Indianapolis: Indiana Historical Society Press, 2003.

Bogle, Victor M. "Railroad Building in Indiana, 1850–1855." *Indiana Magazine of History* 58, no. 3 (September 1962): 211–32.

Butz, Earl L. "Agriculture—An Industry in Evolution." *Indiana: A Self-Appraisal,* edited by Donald F. Carmony. Bloomington: Indiana University Press, 1966.

Carter, Jared. "Natural Gas Boom: Tipton County." *Tipton Poetry Journal* 3 (Spring 2006): http://www.tiptonpoetryjournal .com//tpj_200605.html.

Debs, Eugene V. *Walls and Bars.* Chicago: Socialist Party, 1927.

Fletcher, Stephen J. "The Business of Exposure: Lewis Hine and Child Labor Reform." *Traces of Indiana and Midwestern History* 4, no. 2 (Spring 1992): 12–23.

Glass, James A. "The Gas Boom in East Central Indiana." *Indiana Magazine of History* 96, no. 4 (December 2000): 313–35.

Hiatt, Fred B. "Development of Interurbans in Indiana." *Indiana Magazine of History* 5, no. 3 (September 1909): 122–30.

Hiller, Nancy. *The Hoosier Cabinet in Kitchen History.* Bloomington: Indiana University Press, 2009.

Madison, James H. *Hoosiers: A New History of Indiana.* Bloomington: Indiana University Press; Indianapolis: Indiana Historical Society Press, 2014.

Peden, Rachel. *Rural Free: A Farmwife's Almanac of Country Living.* New York: Alfred A. Knopf, 1961. Reprint, Bloomington: Indiana University Press, 2009.

Phillips, Clifton J. *Indiana in Transition: The Emergence of an Industrial Commonwealth, 1880–1920.* The History of Indiana 4. Indianapolis: Indiana Historical Bureau and Indiana Historical Society, 1968.

Price, Nelson. *Indiana Legends: Famous Hoosiers from Johnny Appleseed to David Letterman.* Cincinnati: Emmis Books, 2005.

Riley, James Whitcomb. "The Little Town o' Tailholt." *Afterwhiles.* Indianapolis: Bowen–Merrill, 1895.

———. "Regardin' Terry Hut." *The Hoosier Book: Containing Poems in Dialect.* Indianapolis: Bobbs–Merrill, 1916.

Seigel, Peggy. "Industrial 'Girls' in an Early Twentieth-Century Boomtown: Traditions and Change in Fort Wayne, Indiana, 1900–1920." *Indiana Magazine of History* 99, no. 3 (September 2003): 231–53.

Simons, Richard S., and Francis H. Parker. *Railroads of Indiana.* Bloomington: Indiana University Press, 1997.

Tarkington, Booth. *The Magnificent Ambersons.* 1980. Reprint, Bloomington: Indiana University Press, 1989.

Thornbrough, Emma Lou. *Indiana in the Civil War Era, 1850–1880.* The History of Indiana 3. Indianapolis: Indiana Historical Bureau and Indiana Historical Society, 1965.

USDA. Census of Agriculture, 2012, http://www.agcensus.usda .gov/index.php.

Walters, Betty Lawson. "The King of Desks: Wooton's Patent Secretary." *Smithsonian Studies in History and Technology,* no. 3 (December 31, 1969): 1–32.

Essential Questions

1 How did railroads and the interurban system fuel economic growth in Indiana?

2 How did new technologies available in the late nineteenth and early twentieth centuries change agriculture and rural life?

3 In what ways did the economic growth of the Industrial Age improve the quality of life for Hoosiers? In what ways did industrialization negatively affect quality of life?

4 How did the economic growth of the Industrial Age bring into question the role of government in the lives of individual Hoosiers?

5 Where is Indiana's "gas belt"? How did the discovery of natural gas drive industrial growth in the state?

6 Why was the "gas boom" so short-lived?

7 How did the quest for efficiency change work and home life? Name at least one Indiana product that promised to increase efficiency at home, on the farm, or in the workplace.

8 What areas of Indiana experienced the most growth due to industrialization?

9 How did Hoosier workers experience industrialization? What particular challenges did women and children face in the workplace?

10 In what ways did Hoosier Eugene V. Debs try to improve the situation for laborers in Indiana and around the nation?*

See student activities related to this question.

Activity: Eugene V. Debs and Indiana's Labor Capital

Introduction: As noted in Chapter 5, the Industrial Age was an era of great promise and upheaval for Hoosiers. New products promised to improve quality of life; but life as people had known it changed drastically beginning in the 1870s. Natural resources and the hard labor of men, women, and children fueled economic growth. Many companies relocated to Indiana to take advantage of the state's natural resources, labor capital, and transportation networks. With rapid industrial growth came new concerns about the need for improved infrastructure (roads, bridges, and so forth), the rights of laborers (particularly of women and children), and the effects of large-scale manufacturing on the environment.

Though Hoosiers remained skeptical about government interference in private enterprise, some began to see a need for regulation. Terre Haute native Eugene V. Debs tried to counter the vulnerability of working people by organizing labor unions and advocating politically for laws protecting workers. His radical ideas landed him in jail but also brought him into the national political spotlight.

▶ Re-read the part of Section 5.4 devoted to Eugene V. Debs on pages 134–35.

▶ Next, read the poem below written by Mabel Ervin in 1894. Ervin's words were set to music by Mrs. Ione Hanna. The resulting song "This Grand Countrie" was dedicated to Eugene V. Debs. Read through the poem quickly and then carefully re-read it.

"This Grand Countrie"

What a grand and glorious country is this "free" America! / With its rich, expansive prairies, stately forests, flowery lea, / Largest lakes and longest rivers, tow'ring mountains, wildest sea— / With the mightiest of nations in this grand countrie! (1)

Fertile fields and fruitful gardens from a wilderness have sprung, / Mighty cities have arisen where before were vale and town / But what is all this grandeur, this magnificence to me / While a million men are starving in this grand countrie! (2)

Costly palaces and churches rear their lofty heads to heav'n; / Great achievements, vast adornments, show the wealth which God has giv'n; / Lakes and rivers deck'd with steamers, workshop, mine and all you see, / Yield a bounty to the wealthy in this grand countrie! (3)

The "iron horse" goes bounding from the mountains to the sea / And the telegraph sings merrily the news where'er you be / Yet upon the wings of "Progress" this sad story comes to me: / A million children hunger in this grand countrie! (4)

Here were gathered from all nations of the earth, both near and far, / The most bounteous gifts of nature, types of peace and spoils of war; / Cunning handiwork of ages brought from far across the sea / But far greater was the splendor of this grand countrie! (5)

Titled ladies deck'd with diamonds, courtly princes of the crown, / Came with men of fabled opulence and men of great renown / Where a million sad-eyed maidens toil in shop and factory / And can scarcely earn a pittance in this grand countrie! (6)

'Mid all this glare and glimmer, this magnificence, this wealth, / Where Want is slave to Plenty, where Fraud with step of stealth, / Holds back the arm of Justice—is there not some power to save / The poor and weak from famine, from tyrant, from knave? (7)

Are there not some men among us—men of years and men of youth, / Men who dare assail th'oppressor, men who dare uphold the truth, / Men who scorn a falt'ring coward, men to strike for Liberty, / Are there not some men of grandeur in this grand countrie? (8)

Lo! Behold a million working men, their banners lifted high! / You can see the fire of battle in each patriotic eye! / You shall hear their shout of vict'ry in the coming jubilee— / For those men shall be the rulers of this grand countrie! (9)

The general prosperity they quickly will promote; / To establish truth and equity their lives they will devote— / And the blessings of sweet Liberty the toilers all shall see / When this band of patriots triumph in this grand countrie! (10)

▶ With a partner, choose a stanza to illustrate through some kind of visual representation of the content. As a class, make sure each pair of students illustrates a different stanza so that all ten stanzas are depicted. As you and your partner work on your illustration, consider the following and answer these questions:

1 What or who is the subject or focus of your stanza (e.g., nature/the environment, industrialists, laborers, or others)?

2 Is the subject portrayed in a negative or positive light by the author? Cite specific evidence for your answer.

3 Are there any unfamiliar words in your stanza? Look them up and write down the definitions.

4 What is the message of your stanza and how can you show that visually? What symbols might you use?

▶ After you have completed your illustration, regroup with the other students in your class. In order from one to ten, each group should read their stanza and present their illustration to the class, explaining any symbols used.

▶ As a class, discuss the meaning that you have derived from Mabel Ervin's poem.

1 What specific examples of "progress" does the author give? Overall do you think she views this term positively or negatively? Why?

2 Do the song's words describe one America or two Americas? Cite evidence from the text to support your opinion.

▶ Remember that this poem is dedicated to Eugene V. Debs. Debs's name is not mentioned in the poem, but the last two stanzas speak of a group of men that will restore general prosperity and close the wealth gap in America.

1 Do you think the author, Mabel Ervin, sees Debs as one of these men? Why or why not?

2 The stanzas describe this group of men as a "band of patriots." How do you think the leaders of industry might respond to that characterization?

3 What reform policies did Debs include in his presidential campaign platforms that were intended to restore general prosperity and close the wealth gap in America?

4 What argument or reasoning did Debs's opponents offer against such reforms?

▶ Consider the 2014 debate over income disparity and increasing the minimum wage in the United States.

1 What do you think Debs would have to say about the wealth gap that exists in America today?

2 Would Debs support an increased minimum wage? Why or why not?

3 Who opposes/opposed a minimum wage? What are/were their arguments?

4 Do you support raising the minimum wage as a way to narrow the wealth gap? Offer your own arguments for or against this reform.

This 1912 song, with music written by Hoosier composer Albert von Tilzer, reflects how the automobile pervaded American culture during the early twentieth century. The sheet music cover gives a sense of the freedom and enjoyment cars offered Hoosiers and all Americans.

6

Immigrants, Cars, Cities, and a New Indiana

Indiana holds by the pioneering culture . . . old-fashioned
philosophies springing out of the soil and smelling of the pennyrile
and the sassafrack [mint and sassafrass].

— *Irvin S. Cobb, 1924*

In the late nineteenth century Indiana moved along with the nation, experiencing increasing immigration, rapid industrial change that came with a new invention—the automobile, and big city growth. Indiana developed a culture of its own. Hoosiers claimed to be the most American of Americans, but they also developed pride in being different from Texans or New Yorkers. They liked the Indiana way of doing things, including being fiercely independent and self-sufficient, intensely political and wary of the government, and community-focused. However, economic growth in the late nineteenth century changed the old ways. Change promised a better life, for some, but not all. Some Hoosiers welcomed the new era; some found the changes threatening.

The Indiana Way

At the time of the American Revolution, Indiana was settled by Indian groups and a few Catholic French fur traders and families of mixed French and Indian blood, mostly from tribes associated with the Miami. After winning their revolution with the British, Americans who had been born in the eastern United States began to move west. The ancestors of most of the Americans had come from England, Scotland, Wales, and the German principalities. Immigrants from Ireland and the German states started arriving in the early to mid part of the nineteenth century, and a few African Americans settled in the state, too, most near Quaker settlements.

By 1880 Indiana had become different than other states in an important way—Hoosiers were primarily American-born, white, and Protestant. Other states tended to have more immigrants, more ethnic groups, and more people of different religions. In 1880, 70 percent of Indiana's population had been born in the state. By 1920, 95 percent of Hoosiers had been born in the United States; 97 percent were white; and 75 percent of Indiana's church members were Protestants. There were also a few thousand Jews and a sizable number of Catholics. Regardless of nationality or religious affiliation, most Hoosiers lived in small towns or on farms.

Such homogeneity offered a foundation for building a Hoosier identity. Hoosiers could rightly think that they were all mostly alike and belonged together. Likely, too, this homogeneity contributed to a tendency to cling to old ways and question different and new ways. Hoosiers preferred slow and gradual change. They tended to reject revolutionary proposals and disruptive arrangements. Consequently, Hoosiers hesitated to embrace people and ideas different from the Hoosiers they knew and the Indiana way of doing things. Nevertheless, the late nineteenth and early twentieth centuries brought revolutionary changes. By the early twentieth century Hoosiers were grappling with "new" immigrants recruited by factories producing new types of products, such as the automobile.

New Hoosiers

One of the most obvious changes came as a new wave of immigration from southern and eastern Europe flooded into the United States at the end of the nineteenth century. Speaking Italian, Greek, Polish, and many other languages, newcomers generally made their way from ports in Boston, Massachusetts; New York City; Baltimore, Maryland; or New Orleans, Louisiana, to Indiana. Although the immigrant population in Indiana increased, immigrants accounted for no more than 10 percent of the state's total population—a smaller proportion than in other industrial states. Still, the immigrants had a large impact on native-born Hoosiers.

Hoosiers struggled to accept people unlike them from the start. Most of the state's Indians were sent away by the 1830s, and blacks were barred from entering the state in its 1851 constitution. The "old immigrants," the Irish and Germans, received cool or even hostile welcomes from native-born Hoosiers. They were different. Their language, their religion, their food, and their ways of doing things seemed strange. Would they and their children continue to be outsiders, or would they assimilate, that is, become like other Hoosiers? Long after they had assimilated, southern and eastern Europeans moved into the state, and Hoosiers asked these questions of the new groups. But even the least welcome of European immigrants had the chance eventually to become more like white, native-born Hoosiers.

African American Hoosiers

Unlike Irish Americans or Polish Americans, African Americans were not going to become "white." In 1850 about 1 percent of the people in Indiana were black. The small proportion of African Americans in Indiana was due in large part to generally held anti-black attitudes and discriminatory laws. Due to the ban on blacks in 1851, the proportion would change very little until after the Civil War. Blacks who did live in Indiana encountered challenges of race that persisted for generations.

During the 1870s many former slaves immigrated north to join relatives, find work, or just to get away from the South. Later in the century black people immigrated to Indiana for newly available factory jobs. By 1920 African Americans comprised nearly 3 percent of Indiana's population.

COLLECTIONS OF THE INDIANA HISTORICAL SOCIETY

Logansport Drugstore

Busjahn and Schneider's drugstore with a soda fountain in Logansport, Indiana, in the early twentieth century is an example of how the children of immigrants became part of their new communities. Part owner John Busjahn was the son of German immigrants and his partner, John Schneider, was the son of a German and a Canadian immigrant.

Evansville Barbershop

William H. Glover's Shaving Parlor in Evansville. Although job opportunities for African Americans in Indiana were often limited and most worked for low pay, some found higher paying work in factories or as small business owners.

In 1885 Indiana passed a civil rights act that promised all people could eat in any public restaurant, get a hotel room, or go to a theater. The problem was that the law was rarely enforced; discriminatory practices were still the norm. African Americans found ways to help each other, however. Despite an often hostile climate, they began to seek ways to enjoy the same rights as other Americans. By 1900 black Hoosiers had most of the same legal rights as whites. They still could not legally marry a white partner or serve in the state militia; but black men could and did vote.

Factory Jobs and City Lives

For most newcomers the pull to Indiana was the possibility of a job, a better job than back in Ireland or Italy or rural Mississippi. European immigrants and African Americans provided essential labor for Indiana's new factories and cities. Employers could often hire them at lower wages than white, native-born Americans.

Most of the new factories were in cities, so it was to the growing cities that the newcomers migrated. South Bend, Fort Wayne, Gary, Evansville, and Indianapolis pulled them in. Newcomers often lived with people of similar origin, clustered in separate neigh-

borhoods. Indiana cities became like patchwork quilts where Hoosiers sorted themselves by race, ethnicity, and class.

In his novel *The Magnificent Ambersons*, published in 1918, author Booth Tarkington wrote that in Indianapolis "all the women who wore silk or velvet knew all the other women who wore silk or velvet." Such wealthier, native-born Hoosiers knew each other, but usually not those people in their town who were poor, of foreign birth, or had dark skin. At the same time, a Polish American family in Indianapolis or South Bend knew mostly other Polish immigrants. They attended the same churches, shopped in the same stores, and joined the same organizations.

It would take time for Hoosiers of different backgrounds to learn to know each other—time to trust, respect, and even value differences. As much as traditional Hoosiers might have liked old ways, many gradually came to see benefits of new people and new technology. Newcomers brought their culture—food, music, and ideas—that added zest to Indiana's culture. New manufactured products brought jobs but also increasing prosperity to many, while new technology—especially the automobile—brought increasing freedom to most Hoosiers.

6.1

Immigrants Come to Indiana, 1850–1920

"Cooking, keeping house, and mending in the true German way are very much harder here. The good German wife also helps her husband in many tasks, which would never occur to a genuine Yankee woman."

— *German settler in Allen County, 1852*

Indiana seldom offered rags to riches for immigrants. Many groups came because conditions were very difficult in their native countries. Political upheavals in German lands, starting in 1848, forced many to leave. Widespread famine in Ireland drove thousands away from their homeland. Cheap and abundant land for farming and the enticement of jobs pulled the emigrants to America's shores. Even though cultural and economic circumstances in America limited upward mobility for many European immigrants, there was still enough work and freedom for many to hope that their future would be brighter if they crossed the Atlantic.

The Germans

German Americans settled in Indiana during the pioneer era and comprised more than half of the state's foreign-born population at the time of the Civil War. Governor Oliver P. Morton distributed a pamphlet in Germany detailing the advantages of settlement in Indiana in the 1860s. Some Indiana counties attracted large numbers of Germans, notably Dubois County in southern Indiana where a visitor would have heard the German language spoken on the streets, in churches, and in schools. Evansville, Indianapolis, and Fort Wayne were also magnets for large numbers of Germans.

There were so many German newcomers in the state by the 1850s that the legislature ordered the governor's message to be printed in German as well as English. In 1915 in Vanderburgh County, the grandchildren of immigrants who had come to Indiana before the Civil War were still confirmed in church services conducted in German. One woman recalled, "'If you weren't confirmed in German, you weren't confirmed. God didn't listen to you in the English language.'" German-language newspapers, schools, beer gardens, and social clubs helped preserve the homeland culture and make newly-arrived Germans feel at home.

Some German newcomers were Jewish. Although incidents of anti-Semitism occurred in Indianapolis, Wabash, and elsewhere, Jews and Christians interacted socially and in business but seldom intermarried. There were a few Jewish communities, including Ligonier in Noble County. By the end of the nineteenth century Ligonier came to be called "Little Jerusalem."

The Irish

In the mid-nineteenth century Irish immigrants were second in number to Germans in Indiana. By 1860 about 25,000 foreign-born Irish were living in Indiana. Many came during the canal craze of the 1830s and 1840s as workers to dig the canals. They also performed manual labor building railroads. The Irish in Indiana and other northern states formed regiments and fought in the Civil War—as did German Americans.

With the factory boom, many Irish moved to the larger cities in the northern and central part of the state. In Indianapolis, Fort Wayne, and South Bend blue collar, Irish factory workers were a common sight. Irish Catholics in these Indiana cities and elsewhere in the state formed their own parishes. They also formed ethnic associations, including units of the Ancient Order of Hibernians and Gaelic athletic clubs, which continued into the twenty-first century.

The New Immigrants

Other ethnic groups began to arrive en masse at the end of the nineteenth century. More came from southern and eastern Europe, from places that would

Turnvereine and the Athenaeum

Many of the Germans who immigrated to Indiana in the mid-nineteenth century sought freedom and relief from the failed democratic revolutions in their homeland. These immigrants were generally well educated, socially progressive, and believed that America was a place where they could freely pursue their ideals and retain their culture.

Many of the German immigrants who had fought for democracy to replace monarchy in German lands were dedicated to the teachings of Friedrich Ludwig Jahn, the founder of the Turner movement that promoted the idea that a healthy body and healthy mind were inextricably linked. Followers of the Turner movement founded *Turnvereine* in cities such as Fort Wayne and Indianapolis. *Turnvereine* were German gymnastics and cultural clubs, often in substantial custom-built brick buildings. Organized in 1865, the Fort Wayne Turners still thrive today and promote athletic and civic programs.

The building shown here, known today as the Athenaeum, was constructed between 1893 and 1898 in Indianapolis and is one of the finest examples of German Renaissance

Revival architecture in the Midwest. Designed by two American-born architects of German parentage, Bernard Vonnegut and Arthur Bohn, it served as home to the Indianapolis *Socialer Turnverein*, a "house of culture" for the mind and body. Known originally as *Das Deutsche Haus* (The German House), the building contained a gymnasium, locker rooms, meeting rooms, auditorium, bowling alleys, concert hall, beer garden, and classroom space. An ideal educational facility, in 1907 *Das Deutsche Haus* became home to the Normal College of the North American Gymnastic Union, America's oldest institution for training physical education teachers.

Anti-German sentiment during World War I prompted the *Socialer Turnverein* to change the building's name to the Athenaeum. In 1973 the National Register of Historic Places added the Athenaeum to its roster. In 1991 the building became the property of the nonprofit Athenaeum Foundation. Many consider the thoroughly renovated building one of Indianapolis's architectural jewels. Behind its beautiful façade, as of 2013, the Athenaeum was home to ten prominent cultural organizations.

become countries such as Italy, Hungary, Austria, Greece, and Poland, and fewer from northern and western Europe, from countries such as France, Spain, and England. This wave of new immigration reached a peak in the decade before World War I.

Hibernians in America

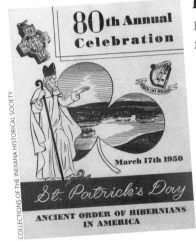

Irish Americans, as other immigrant groups, formed organizations to celebrate their heritage. The Ancient Order of Hibernians formed in Indiana in 1871 as a fraternal organization for Irish immigrants and their descendants. Members organized Saint Patrick's Day celebrations—even eighty years after the organization's beginnings, as evidenced by this souvenir booklet. In the nineteenth century, the Ancient Order of Hibernians also provided insurance support for its members and spoke up for Irish American interests.

Southern and eastern European languages, businesses, and customs were most visible in South Bend and the Calumet cities, such as Gary and East Chicago. South Bend's Studebaker Company and Oliver Chilled Plow Works recruited workers from Hungary. U. S. Steel attracted many Poles, Lithuanians, Croats, and Slovaks to Gary. Gas belt cities such as Muncie, Anderson, Kokomo, and Fort Wayne received fewer new immigrants than the northern most manufacturing cities, which was also true of Indianapolis and Evansville.

Just as the old immigrants, the Germans and Irish, had seemed different to earlier generations of Hoosiers, the new immigrants appeared strange to people born in Indiana. Many were poor, and because they could not speak English they appeared ignorant and backward. Many native-born could not imagine how these newcomers might one day become "real Hoosiers."

Casting Department Employees at Studebaker, ca. 1901

The Studebaker Manufacturing Company in South Bend, Indiana, employed immigrants from Hungary, Ireland, and other European countries.

Shapiro's Grocery and Deli, 1950

Max Shapiro serves Frania Kaplan, a German Jewish immigrant, in Shapiro's Deli in Indianapolis in 1950. Jewish and non-Jewish residents in Indianapolis stopped by Shapiro's for good corned beef and fresh rye bread, among other treats. Today, the more than one-hundred-year-old deli remains a draw for any food lover.

COLLECTIONS OF THE INDIANA HISTORICAL SOCIETY

Ethnic Hoosiers

In the end the ethnic history of Indiana and America proved immigrants and migrants could be embraced and accommodated despite their unique cultures.

— John Bodnar, Introduction, Peopling Indiana *(1996)*

Most immigrants lived in city neighborhoods among their own class and ethnic group. Eventually, some immigrant families improved their economic situation and moved out of the old neighborhood. German Jews in Indianapolis who had begun as peddlers and clerks on the south side moved to the north side. Eastern European and Russian Jews formed a vibrant community on the south side. There, in the first decade of the twentieth century, Louis and Rebecca Shapiro opened a grocery store of kosher foods. A century later, the fourth generation of their family owned iconic Shapiro's Delicatessen, serving more than one thousand hungry Hoosiers a day. In South Bend, Hungarian immigrants who worked in the Studebaker factory worshipped at Our Lady of Hungary Catholic Parish and School. Today, the parish's annual multicultural Harvest Fiestaval (fiesta and festival) raises funds to support the school and draws visitors from as far away as Detroit.

Descendants of immigrants who came to Indiana in the nineteenth and early twentieth centuries assimilated and today proudly consider themselves Hoosiers. In turn, Indiana recognized, adopted, and now fully celebrates the rich and diverse contributions of their cultures.

6.2

African American Hoosiers

*We feel that our real freedom dates only
from the day we entered Indiana.*

— *Meeting of North Carolina Exodusters (black emigrants),
Greencastle, Indiana, December 1880*

The ancestors of most African Americans, unlike those of European immigrants, did not come voluntarily to America's shores; they came as slaves. After the Civil War freed the slave population, conditions in the South worsened for thousands of black families, so they boarded trains and headed north. Many came to the growing industrial towns of Indiana. The state's African American population grew faster than its white population. By 1900 Indianapolis had the seventh largest black population among northern cities.

COLLECTIONS OF THE INDIANA HISTORICAL SOCIETY

Color Lines Limit Opportunity

"The Negro suffers every type and kind of discrimination in this state that he suffers anywhere, even jim-crow theaters and moving picture houses. In fact our pictures in the mile square—that is downtown—refuse absolutely to admit Negroes."

— *Freeman Ransom, Indianapolis attorney, 1933*

Even in the north, most African Americans found conditions of daily life difficult because of racial discrimination. Again and again they were turned away, excluded, and restricted from jobs and community life. Even Booker T. Washington, an educator and one of America's most respected black leaders, was turned away from a hotel when he came to Anderson, Indiana, in 1900.

Some Indiana towns became known as "sunset" towns, all-white places where it was understood that no black person would remain after the sun set. Worst of all, there were lynchings in Indiana. The most notorious occurred in Marion on August 7, 1930, when a mob of angry whites broke three black teenagers out of the Grant County jail and lynched (hung) two of them—Thomas Shipp and Abram Smith—on suspicion of murdering a white man and raping his girlfriend. It was the last lynching in Indiana. Sixteen–year-old James Cameron, who survived, later became a civil rights activist.

The major challenge facing black families was earning a living wage. The only jobs most men could find were for unskilled labor

African American Waiter

A black waiter serves white passengers in the dining car of an interurban in 1908. Due to discrimination, waiting tables was often one of the few jobs open to African American men.

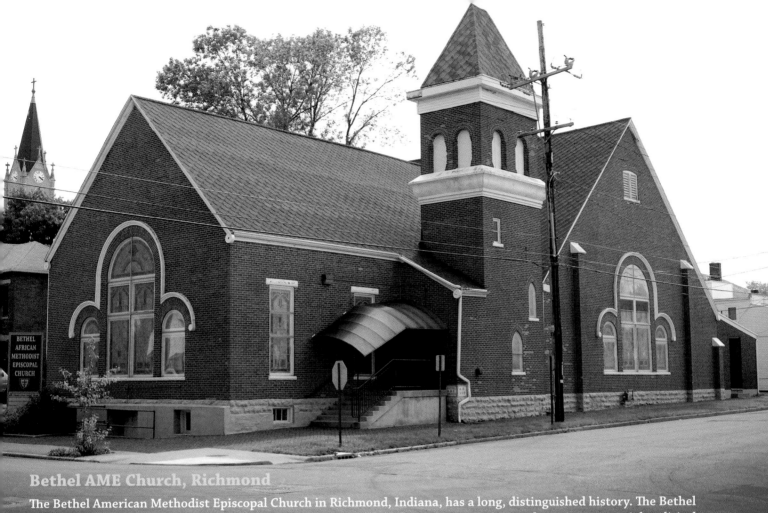

Bethel AME Church, Richmond

The Bethel American Methodist Episcopal Church in Richmond, Indiana, has a long, distinguished history. The Bethel congregation moved into this building in 1868. The church served many community needs, acting as a social, political, and cultural center for Richmond's African Americans. Ministers were also community leaders. For instance, James Townsend, who briefly served as Bethel's minister, went on to become one of Indiana's first black legislators in 1885.

as janitors, waiters, or hod carriers (laborers who carried supplies, such as bricks or plaster, to construction workers). Some black men found slightly better employment as barbers, blacksmiths, or railway workers. Very few labor unions welcomed black workers. While white women were finding low-paying jobs as sales clerks, telephone operators, and stenographers, black women often worked as cooks and maids. At L. S. Ayres, Indianapolis's largest department store, all elevator operators were black women; all porters were black men; all sales jobs were restricted to whites.

Color lines also ran through education. The common school movement in the mid-to late-nineteenth century excluded black children. Legislation from 1869 required school trustees to provide separate schools in areas with a sizeable black population—and integrated schools if not. Black elementary schools became commonplace in most Indiana communities with sizable

black populations. In addition, the southern Indiana towns of Madison, New Albany, and Evansville opened segregated high schools in the 1880s. During this period, educational opportunities for black children did expand and there was some racial integration. However, this was also the beginning of a separate and quite unequal system.

African American Response

"We need some action out here. I don't want riots or anything like that. But I do want justice for all, and I don't believe in any isms but Americanisms. I want my sixteen year old son to know the true meaning of Americanism by seeing it practiced toward men regardless of color."

— *Mayole Nelson, East Chicago, to secretary of NAACP, 1943*

Despite color lines and limited opportunities, a small middle class of African American Hoosiers

National Negro Business League

The Evansville branch of the National Negro Business League received third prize in the National Clean Up and Paint Up Campaign in 1923. The campaign encouraged citizens nationwide to clean up their communities. Evansville had several active African American leaders in the business community, including W. A. Goins, a funeral home owner and Dr. George Washington Buckner, a physician.

developed. In Indianapolis, Evansville, and elsewhere there were black businessmen and professionals—restaurant and barbershop owners, insurance agents, doctors, lawyers, teachers, ministers, and newspaper editors. The black middle class nurtured associations and institutions essential to African American communities. African American Hoosiers created their own groups because they were excluded from white organizations and because they valued the pride and well-being that came from racial solidarity. The African American churches stood at the center of black communities, not just as places of worship but also as places of social action. African American newspapers were also important. By 1900 Indianapolis had three—the *Indianapolis World*, the *Freeman*, and the *Recorder*. Black lodges, clubs, and fraternal orders also grew.

In 1909 the National Association for the Advancement of Colored People (NAACP) formed in New York City. Mary Ellen Cable, an educator, founded the first Indiana branch in Indianapolis in 1912 and served as its first president. NAACP branches subsequently organized in Gary, Evansville, Marion, Terre Haute, and Muncie.

Flossie Bailey, president of the Marion branch of the NAACP, is remembered for her courageous action before and after the 1930 lynching in her town. Bailey fearlessly tried to prevent the mob from murdering the young black men. After the horrendous deed occurred, she convinced local and state officials to bring the perpetrators of the crime to justice. Two of the accused lynchers were tried but acquitted by an all-white jury. Bailey's persistence resulted in the passage of a stricter anti-lynching law in 1931.

Madam C. J. Walker

"I got myself a start by giving myself a start."

— Madam C. J. Walker, 1917

Born to ex-slaves in Louisiana in 1867 and orphaned at age six, Sarah Breedlove knew loss, poverty, and back-breaking work. Before she was a teenager, Breedlove was a sharecropper and a laundress—two of the few jobs available to African American women.

Breedlove was a mother and widow by age twenty. When her husband died, she took her little girl, Lelia, to Saint Louis, Missouri, where she heard she could get work as a laundress. She lived and worked in that city for seventeen years, barely getting by. While in Saint Louis, Breedlove developed a formula to encourage hair growth and a way to straighten hair using a heated steel comb; both were designed specifically for black women. With these innovations Breedlove started her own business and sold her products door-to-door.

In 1905 Breedlove and Lelia moved to Denver, Colorado, where she worked as a cook for a pharmacist. While in Denver, Breedlove married a man named Charles Joseph Walker and applied his name to her products. She developed a successful mail-order business and soon saw the opportunity to expand.

In 1910 Sarah (Breedlove) Walker moved to Indianapolis to establish the headquarters of the Madam C. J. Walker Manufacturing Company of Indiana. She became the nation's first black woman millionaire. Walker became a powerful, influential, and generous social leader. She supported black schools and colleges, orphanages, the NAACP, and YMCAs, including the Indianapolis YMCA at Michigan and Senate in 1912. Educator, author, and presidential advisor Booker T. Washington dedicated this YMCA building in 1913.

After she became rich and famous, Walker frequently spoke to groups of African American women. On these occasions, she always emphasized that they needed to believe in themselves and be persistent. At one convention in 1913 she stated, "The girls and women of our race must not be afraid to take hold of business endeavor and . . . wring success out of a number of business opportunities. . . . I want to say to every Negro woman present: Don't sit down and wait for the opportunities to come. . . . Get up and make them!"

In 1916 Walker moved to New York City to have an East Coast base and expand her business internationally. She hired Vertner Tandy, New York City's first licensed black architect, to design a thirty-four-room mansion for her on the banks of the Hudson River. She named her home Villa Lewaro and furnished it with priceless art and antiques. Today it is a National Historic Landmark.

In 1919 Walker died at age fifty-one from complications of high blood pressure and kidney failure. Lelia (who had changed her name to A'Lelia) inherited Villa Lewaro and became president of her mother's business empire. The Walker Company is widely considered the most successful African American-owned business in the first half of the twentieth century.

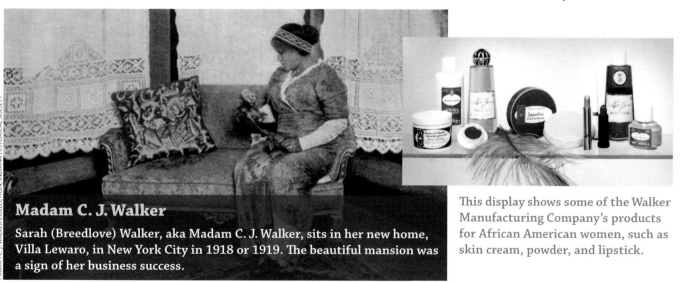

Madam C. J. Walker

Sarah (Breedlove) Walker, aka Madam C. J. Walker, sits in her new home, Villa Lewaro, in New York City in 1918 or 1919. The beautiful mansion was a sign of her business success.

This display shows some of the Walker Manufacturing Company's products for African American women, such as skin cream, powder, and lipstick.

6.3

Hoosiers Make Cars

"Highways and streets are not for the exclusive use of vehicles propelled by animal power."

— Indiana Supreme Court, 1901

Hoosiers have always loved cars. Early on, Indiana had more than its share of pioneering inventors and entrepreneurs who made horseless carriages. Later, the automobile changed many aspects of life in Indiana—where people lived and worked, what jobs they had, how they commuted to those jobs, and how they went about their daily lives. In essence, cars changed Indiana's economy and culture.

Elwood Haynes, Pioneer Automobile Maker

The discovery of natural gas in northern Indiana—back in the late [eighteen-] eighties—was responsible for the invention of the automobile.

— Robert Paterson, Gas Buggy (1933)

The inventive exploits of Elwood Haynes inspired the little-known 1933 novel *Gas Buggy* by Robert Paterson. Set in a fictional town modeled after Kokomo, Indiana, the novel is so obscure that a recent online search revealed that it was not in the Kokomo–Howard County Public Library. Today, Paterson is all but forgotten, but Haynes is still remembered as a significant American inventor whose gas-powered vehicle, appropriately named the Pioneer, put Kokomo at the forefront of early automobile production.

Haynes was born in Portland, Indiana, in 1857 and trained as an engineer in Massachusetts. He returned to Indiana and eventually moved to the natural gas fields of Jay and Howard Counties where he and other investors founded Portland Natural Gas and Oil Company in 1886. He superintended the laying of pipelines, drilling wells, and running the office's operations. Frustrated by the slowness of the horse and

buggy as he drove to survey the pipeline work, Haynes imagined a faster mode of transportation in the form of a mechanized vehicle. He settled in Kokomo and started building such a machine with the help of two mechanics, brothers Elmer and Edgar Apperson.

On July 4, 1894, Haynes test-drove his vehicle along the Pumpkinvine Pike near Kokomo. A year later he and the Appersons went into business together and started producing cars. Although Haynes–Apperson proudly used the slogan "America's First Car," others in America also made this claim. However, the Haynes–Apperson Company could certainly claim to be one of the first successful car manufacturers.

Haynes achieved other automotive "firsts." In 1899 he gained national attention for driving one of his cars from Kokomo to New York City, a distance of more than one thousand miles. In 1902 he entered a car in the first Long Island Non-Stop Contest and won a blue ribbon. After the Appersons left Haynes–Apperson to form a new company, Haynes renamed it the Haynes Automobile Company. Elwood Haynes died in 1925, not long after the last Haynes cars rolled off the assembly line.

Hoosiers Catch "Car Fever"

By 1910 the car was well on its way to becoming part of the Hoosier state's identity. One particular event sealed the deal—the Indianapolis 500. Two Indianapolis manufacturers, James Allison and Carl Fisher, led the effort to create the Indianapolis Motor Speedway as a way to test out new car models and celebrate them. The first Indianapolis 500 took place on May 30, 1911, and was wildly popular. Ray Harroun won the race in a locally-made Marmon Wasp that averaged 74.59 miles-per-hour.

As with many new inventions or forms of progress, there were naysayers who did not like cars or the noise and fumes they produced. The main character in Booth Tarkington's 1918 Pulitzer Prize-winning novel *The Magnificent Ambersons* spoke for these folks when he proclaimed that automobiles were "'a useless nuisance.'" "'They'll never amount

Elwood Haynes

In this 1894 photograph, Elwood Haynes sits in his first car, the Pioneer, one of the first cars to be powered by a small gasoline engine and one of the first to appear on American roads.

to anything,'" he stated. "'They had no business to be invented.'" The roar of many powerful car engines drowned out such opinions.

By 1919, 172 businesses in more than thirty Indiana towns were producing automobiles and auto parts, according to the U.S. census. Companies that once manufactured farm wagons, such as Studebaker in South Bend, transitioned to making cars. Other companies, such as the Auburn Automobile Company located in the northeastern Indiana town of Auburn, also emerged as successful car manufacturers. Businesses that supported the auto industry also developed in Muncie, Anderson, and Indianapolis, producing parts such as transmissions, generators, gears, and headlights.

A Major Automobile State

In the first decade of the twentieth century, Indiana, Ohio, and Michigan became the heart of the new American auto belt, with hundreds of manufacturers. Most of the small companies failed as the industry moved toward a big business model in the form of the "Big Three"—Ford, Chrysler, and General Motors—all based in Detroit. Some Indiana companies held on through the 1920s, but most went out of business. The Great Depression was the final blow for those that remained, including Marmon and Stutz. By 1930 fewer than 4 percent of Indiana-registered cars had been made in the state. Only South Bend's Studebaker hung on until 1963 when it, too, ceased production. Detroit, not Indianapolis, Kokomo, or South Bend, became the world's Motor City. The Big Three crushed all competition.

However, even with the rise of the Big Three, Indiana remained a major automobile state, behind only Michigan and, occasionally, Ohio in production. Dozens of auto parts factories dotted the Indiana landscape, mostly from Indianapolis to the north and east in Kokomo, South Bend, Marion, Fort Wayne, Muncie, and New Castle. Anderson was possibly the most auto-dependent town, where Delco-Remy and Guide Lamp, both suppliers for General Motors, employed thousands of workers by the late 1920s.

Changes Brought by the Automobile

An' ther hain't a day rolls by that somebuddy hain't sellin' ther sewin' machine, or ther home, or somthin' t' pay on an automobile.

— *Indiana humorist Kin Hubbard, 1923*

Although Bob Dylan did not release his song "The Times They Are a-Changin'" until 1963, the song might have been the anthem for the changes brought by the automobile. Cars altered America and Indiana in many significant ways. Most would agree that these changes had both positive and negative sides.

Even though some Hoosiers were perfectly happy with horses as a mode of transportation and were initially cautious about buying a car, automobile registrations doubled in the 1920s and horse-drawn traffic essentially disappeared from town squares. The car culture merged with the excitement of the roaring twenties. Young people were the first to embrace the new ways. Instead of waiting demurely in the front parlor for her boyfriend to call, a young woman heard the horn honk and ran out the front door to hop in the front seat. Off the couple sped to meet friends at a picnic or roadside restaurant. Country roads along rivers or between cornfields became lovers' lanes, causing handwringing and outcries from church and civic leaders, including one Muncie judge who called the automobile "'a house of prostitution on wheels.'"

Most Hoosiers embraced the new freedom that came with owning a car. They enjoyed driving to family dinners—or a diner—on Sunday after church, to the new state parks, or to visit friends in the next town. However, the freedom was not necessarily extended to Indiana's African American population. This is evidenced by *The Negro Motorist Green Book*, which was published in 1949 with the intent to give black travelers information that would keep them from running into difficulties. The guidebook listed the restaurants, gas stations, and lodging that welcomed African Americans in each state. Some hotels, restaurants, and other public places in Indiana turned away African Americans as late as the 1960s. In addition, during the early car era the Indianapolis 500 prohibited black drivers from competing. Despite this exclusion, African Americans still took part in Indiana's fascination with the automobile, organizing and racing in a separate "Gold and Glory Sweepstakes" at the state fairgrounds.

Lexington Motor Cars

One of many auto manufacturers that sprang up across Indiana was the Lexington Motor Company, which opened a plant in Connersville, Indiana, in 1910. The company developed the Lexington motor car, such as this model from 1923, and participated in auto races. Like many early motor companies, Lexington had financial troubles and went through multiple owners before Auburn Automobile Company, owned by Errett Lobban Cord, finally bought the company in 1927.

Marmon Wasp

In this Marmon Wasp, named for its bright yellow body and black trim, Ray Harroun won the first Indy 500 in 1911 with an average speed of 74.59 miles per hour. Since then, car technology continues to advance. Today's racing cars are not only safer, but would also leave the Marmon in the dust at speeds hovering around 220 miles per hour! You can see this car and others at the Indianapolis Motor Speedway Museum in Indianapolis.

IMS PHOTO

More cars meant the need for more roads and better roads, but many Hoosiers opposed the taxes required to pay for building them. At the end of World War I there were almost no paved roads in Indiana. In 1919 the Indiana General Assembly created the Indiana State Highway Commission, which made the state eligible for financing from the federal government to build new roads. By 1925 there were more than a thousand miles of paved roads in Indiana and by 1940 more than ten thousand miles. All of the roads were financed by federal aid and user taxes.

Cars and the roads they ran on put an end to interurbans. Like the horse and buggy, they soon became obsolete. By 1920, the light, electric-powered trains carried people and freight at low cost and good speed on some twenty-six hundred miles of rails in the state. But the scheduled stops of the interurban could not compete with the freedom cars offered to Hoosiers.

Although the Great Depression dealt a death blow to interurbans, automobiles survived and thrived. Even in the crippled economy, Indiana gasoline consumption in the 1930s remained above the 1929 level. Car registrations dipped slightly after the stock market crash in 1929 but began to rise by 1933.

Rise of Unions

Labor unions, which were organized to negotiate workers' pay, hours, and benefits, formed gradually in the auto industry. In the 1920s Indiana was generally hostile to unions. However, with the formation of the United Auto Workers (UAW) in 1935, union organizers energetically recruited skilled and unskilled workers in the auto industry. In South Bend employees at Studebaker and Bendix (a GM supplier) formed UAW locals and hosted the second national convention of the new auto union in 1936.

Union activity on behalf of workers stirred up a lot of unrest and sometimes violence as community and business leaders did their utmost to keep the unions out. The UAW generally targeted large, stable GM shops for protest activities such as strikes. In Anderson, where there were eleven thousand GM workers in a city of about forty thousand, a sit-down strike instigated by the national UAW at Guide Lamp in 1937 resulted in anti-union retaliation and violence. The strikers eventually won and forced GM to recognize the union. The UAW became a powerful national organization that soon brought benefits such as establishing an eight-hour work day, overtime pay, and paid vacations to its blue-collar workers.

Automobiles and the American Dream

The good pay and benefits that came along with union jobs made the American Dream seem possible. Americans strove to achieve the dream of gaining a comfortable life by working hard and playing by the rules. Like all Americans, Hoosiers wanted their piece of that dream. The American Dream made car ownership a necessity. Consequently, public transportation began to decline in major cities such as Indianapolis. New interstates crossed the state and ringed cities. Drive-in restaurants, banks, and movie theaters became common. Malls sprang up, taking away shoppers from the stores on Main Street. Suburbs of single-

Car Safety Ad

This safety poster reminded automobile drivers to take caution near interurban lines, such as the Dixie Flyer line between Jeffersonville and Indianapolis. Hoosiers, like all Americans, had to adjust to a world of cars. In the early twentieth century, driving was made more difficult by few paved roads and traffic lights. By the time this poster appeared around 1925, however, automobile infrastructure was improving.

family homes sprawled around large cities and then became cities themselves.

The American fascination with cars and the rapid consumption of oil and gasoline lasted well past the middle of the century. The future seemed bright for automobile manufacturing and consumption. But that imagined future relied on cheap gasoline. An oil embargo in 1973–74, in which Arab oil companies refused to export oil to the United States for political reasons, was a wakeup call—Americans needed to ponder a mode of transportation that consumed less than a gallon of gas every twelve miles. In the early twenty-first century, America is still fine-tuning its relationship to the automobile.

Bendix Strike

After the United Auto Workers union gained a foothold in Indiana in 1936 among workers in South Bend's Bendix Corporation, the local union went on strike in order for the UAW to gain recognition with Bendix. Men and women workers sat down in the factory and refused to work. On November 26, 1936, Bendix finally gave in and recognized the UAW as the workers' representatives in labor talks and disputes. This strike, the longest of its kind at the time, transpired without violence and influenced workers elsewhere to join unions.

6.4

Gary, A New City

And I saw workmen wearing leather shoes scruffed / with fire and cinders, and pitted with little holes / from running molten steel, / And some had bunches of specialized muscles around / their shoulder blades hard as pig iron, muscles / of their fore-arms were sheet steel and they looked / to me like men who had been somewhere.

— Carl Sandburg, "The Mayor of Gary," 1915

Steel on a Sand Dune

The peaceful dune lands in northwest Indiana known as the Calumet Region, once home to Indian tribes, French fur traders, and later pioneers, was the last part of the state to be developed industrially. Calumet is a French version of the Potawatomi name of the two main rivers in the area, the Grand Calumet River and Little Calumet River.

The Calumet Region's tranquility vanished when industrialists discovered the area in the late nineteenth century. Factories and oil refineries were built on swamplands and sand dunes along Lake Michigan. In 1889 Standard Oil built a refinery in Whiting, in the northern part of Lake County. Twelve years later Inland Steel built the gigantic Indiana Harbor Works in East Chicago. But these were just warm-up acts for the U. S. Steel Corporation's even more ambitious project. In 1906 the company broke ground on what became the world's largest state-of-the-art steel works and company town of its time. The town, named after U. S. Steel chairman, Elbert H. Gary, is Gary, Indiana.

In 1909 U. S. Steel's Gary Works opened. Great Lakes' freighters and a web of railroad lines brought coal and iron ore to the massive complex. Great quantities of finished steel moved out. Even though they were built on sand, one observer wrote in 1920 that Gary's mills were "'so solid, so permanent, so strong.'" With the output of other factories in nearby towns such as East Chicago, Whiting, and Hammond, Lake County produced more than one-fourth of the state's total value of manufactured product by 1919.

City of the Century

Gary is nothing more than the product of effort along practical lines to secure the right living conditions around a steel manufacturing plant.

— Eugene J. Buffington, Gary Land Company president, May 8, 1909

U. S. Steel hired designers and planners to make Gary an appealing model town for the company's skilled workers and supervisors. Gary had paved sidewalks, manicured lawns, churches, a library, a YMCA, and brick buildings in the business district. Workers were able to purchase their own homes on original lots. The town also had a thriving cultural life with an orchestra and theater groups. By 1908 U. S. Steel had

Freight trains connected industrial cities such as Gary to resource suppliers and steel customers. Early in the twentieth century commuter rails, such as the South Shore Line Interurban, connected the people of the Calumet Region to South Bend and larger cities such as Chicago.

Broadway, looking North from 7th Street, Gary, Ind.

Downtown Gary, 1920s

This 1920s scene of Broadway Street in Gary does not reveal that the business district was actually less than twenty-five years old at the time. The newly planned city boasted a host of stores and businesses rising above paved sidewalks.

spent more than $42 million on both the steel works and on town projects. Local boosters called Gary "'the Magic City'" and "'the City of the Century.'"

Gary city school superintendent William A. Wirt achieved national recognition by shaping the schools to the practical, everyday needs of society, particularly the industrial society of the Calumet Region. The "work-study-play" curricula included traditional academic subjects, vocational training, and physical education. The state legislature responded to the trend in 1913 by requiring schools in Indiana towns and rural areas to provide courses in vocational education, including agricultural education.

Like a giant magnet made of steel, Gary drew thousands of people who wanted a job in the massive steelworks. In the process, the city became a microcosm of America. African Americans came to Gary from the South; immigrants traveled to the city from eastern and southern Europe; and Mexicans crossed the nation's southern border and headed to Gary.

The Great Steel Strike of 1919

Although U. S. Steel put a lot of money and thought into creating a town for its workers, the company was less concerned about the harsh working conditions in the plants. Workers grew fed up working twelve-hour days, seven days a week. In September

1919 they protested by going on strike. The strike at Gary Works crippled the nation's steel industry. Fiercely anti-union, U. S. Steel refused to negotiate with workers and brought in strikebreakers—people who were willing to work where others were on strike—thus making the strike ineffectual. In this case the strikebreakers were mostly unskilled Mexican and African American workers.

Strikebreakers and police clashed with pro-union strikers, and the violence escalated. In October, fifteen hundred United States Army troops came to Gary to restore the peace. The strike ended in January 1920 with no concessions made by U. S. Steel. In 1923, under pressure from President Warren G. Harding, the company agreed to eight-hour work days. For the next two decades, there was little union activity in the steel industry.

The New Hoosiers of Gary

Fifty-two nationalities made their home in Gary by 1920. Specialty shops sprang up in ethnic neighborhoods. Polish meat markets displayed kielbasa and cured ham; Greek bakeries sold bread and cookies. The Europeans assimilated. Some of them moved out of Gary's factory jobs and into professional jobs. Doctors, lawyers, dentists, and architects had last names that ended with -vitz, -iski, -off, and -vich. Children

Emerson School, Gary, Indiana

At its inception, the Emerson School's Manual Training Department was one of the few in the state. Vocational training was part of the unique curriculum envisioned by Gary Schools superintendent William A. Wirt.

of foreign-born workers quickly learned English and spoke it without accents and acquired American slang and mannerisms; by the time they were in high school they were thoroughly Americanized.

On the south side of the original planned city of Gary, another Gary grew. Known as the "Patch," it was home to many African American and Mexican American unskilled laborers. The Patch did not have manicured lawns and stately buildings. Instead it had dilapidated boarding houses and saloons. African Americans and Mexicans experienced extreme discrimination. One Catholic priest told the Gary Rotary Club (a service organization comprised of professional people) in 1928, "'You can Americanize the man from southeastern and southern Europe,'" but you "'can't Americanize a Mexican.'"

Gradually, Mexicans settled in other towns in the Calumet Region and also in Saint Joseph, Allen, and Marion Counties and in scattered pockets across the state, even in small towns such as Ligonier, Huntington, and Clarksville. Hispanic grocery stores, small businesses, and Spanish-language churches appeared, and some second and third generation Mexican Americans moved into white collar and professional careers.

Changing with the Times

During its first fifty years Gary grew dramatically. The 1910 census reported a population of 16,802; by 1930 it had grown nearly six times larger with a population of 100,426. Founded as a steel town, Gary has always been a steel town. One historian noted "One of the results of this peculiar dependency upon one industry was that Gary, the 'instant city,' passed from birth to adolescence to middle age and into old age and decay in a mere seventy years."

Gary, more than many American cities, was hit hard in the 1970s by international competition in the steel industry, which forced it to update technology and lay off workers. Fluctuations in the national economy, including a troubled American auto industry and other variables, also played a part. With the need for fewer workers, Gary's population declined. Today it is around 80,000—less than half of what it was at the city's peak in 1960. Problems that hit many American "rust belt cities," areas distinguished by a decline in industry, aging factories, and a fall in population, hit Gary early and hard. These problems include white flight, the mass movement of white city-dwellers to the suburbs, crime, and decaying infrastructure, such as crumbling roads and sewers. In these ways, Gary is emblematic of how quickly the ups and downs of industry can change a city's economy and social dynamics.

Mexican American Family

A Mexican American family sits at the Gary Neighborhood House in 1939. The Neighborhood House helped immigrants settle into life in a new city by offering services such as sewing lessons, English classes, a nursery, and employment assistance. Mexican mutual aid societies also provided support with social opportunities and financial assistance.

Selected Bibliography

Bigham, Darrel E. *Reflections on a Heritage: The German Americans in Southwestern Indiana*. Evansville: Indiana State University, 1980.

Buffington, Eugene J. "Making Cities for Workmen." *Harper's Weekly* (May 8, 1909): 15–17.

Bundles, A'Lelia Perry. *On Her Own Ground: The Life and Times of Madam C. J. Walker*. New York: Scribner, 2001.

Dolan, Jay P. "Review of *The Irish: Peopling Indiana*, by William W. Giffin." *Indiana Magazine of History* 103, no. 3 (September 2007): 315–16.

Etcheson, Nicole. *A Generation at War: The Civil War Era in a Northern Community*. Lawrence: University of Kansas Press, 2011.

Fine, Sidney. *Sit-Down: The General Motors Strike of 1936–1937*. Ann Arbor, MI: University of Michigan Press, 1989. Reprint, 1991. Google Books, http://books.google.com.

Gray, Ralph D. *Alloys and Automobiles: The Life of Elwood Haynes*. Indianapolis: Indiana Historical Society, 1979.

———. "*Gas Buggy* Revisited: A 'Lost' Novel of Kokomo, Indiana." *Indiana Magazine of History* 70, no. 1 (March 1974): 24–43.

———. "The Man from Kokomo: Elwood Haynes and the Origins of the Automobile Industry in Indiana." *Traces of Indiana and Midwestern History* 6, no. 2 (Spring 1994): 12–17.

"History." The Athenaeum Foundation. http://www.athenaeum foundation.org/about-the-a/history/.

Holli, Melvin G. "Review of *City of the Century: A History of Gary, Indiana*, by James B. Lane." *Indiana Magazine of History* 75, no. 4 (December 1979): 358–59.

Keen, Judy. "Gary, Ind., Struggles with Population Loss." *USA Today* (May 18, 2011), http://usatoday30.usatoday.com/news /nation/2011-05-18-gary-indiana-revival_n.htm#.

Latham, Charles, Jr. "Madame C. J. Walker & Company." *Traces of Indiana and Midwestern History* 1, no. 3 (Summer 1989): 28–37.

Lynd, Robert S., and Helen Merrell Lynd. *Middletown: A Study in American Culture*. New York: Harcourt, Brace and World, 1929.

Madden, W. C. *Haynes–Apperson and America's First Practical Automobile: A History*. Jefferson, NC: McFarland and Company, 2003.

Madison, James H. "Flossie Bailey: 'What a Woman!'" *Traces of Indiana and Midwestern History* 12, no. 1 (Winter 2000): 23–28.

———. *Hoosiers: A New History of Indiana*. Bloomington: Indiana University Press; Indianapolis: Indiana Historical Society Press, 2014.

———. *Indiana through Tradition and Change: A History of the Hoosier State and Its People, 1920–1945*. The History of Indiana 5. Indianapolis: Indiana Historical Society, 1982.

———. *A Lynching in the Heartland: Race and Memory in America*. New York: St. Martin's–Palgrave, 2001.

McShane, Stephen G., and Gary S. Wilk. *Steel Giants: Historic Images from the Calumet Region*. Bloomington: Indiana University Press, 2009.

Mohl, Raymond A., and Neil Betten. *Steel City: Urban and Ethnic Patterns in Gary, Indiana: 1906–1950*. New York: Holmes and Meier, 1986.

The Negro Motorist Green Book. New York: Victor H. Green Publishers, 1949.

O'Hara, S. Paul. *Gary: the Most American of All American Cities*. Bloomington: Indiana University Press, 2011.

Phillips, Clifton J. *Indiana in Transition: The Emergence of an Industrial Commonwealth, 1880–1920*. The History of Indiana 4. Indianapolis: Indiana Historical Bureau and Indiana Historical Society, 1968.

Remy, Charles F., and John W. Donaker. *Reports of Cases Argued and Determined in the Supreme Court of Judicature of the State of Indiana*, vol. 156. Indianapolis: Levey Bros. and Company, 1901.

Rubenstein, James M. *Making and Selling Cars: Innovation and Change in the U.S. Automotive Industry*. Baltimore: Johns Hopkins University Press, 2001.

Sandberg, Carl. "The Mayor of Gary." In *Smoke and Steel*. New York: Harcourt, Brace and Howe, 1920.

"Strange Fruit: Anniversary of a Lynching." Radio Diaries: Extraordinary Stories of Ordinary Life. Special Series in *All Things Considered*, National Public Radio, http://www.npr.org /templates/story/story.php?storyId=129025516.

Taylor, Robert M., Jr., and Connie A. McBirney, eds. *Peopling Indiana: The Ethnic Experience*. Indianapolis: Indiana Historical Society, 1996.

Thornbrough, Emma Lou. "Breaking Racial Barriers to Public Accommodations in Indiana, 1935 to 1963." *Indiana Magazine of History* 83, no. 4 (December 1987): 301–43.

———. *Indiana Blacks in the Twentieth Century*. Bloomington: Indiana University Press, 2000.

Trautmann, Frederic. "'Life in the Wild': Three German Letters from Indiana, 1852–1853." *Indiana Magazine of History* 80, no. 2 (June 1984): 146–65.

Warne, C. E. *The Great Steel Strike of 1919*. Boston: Heath and Company, 1963.

Wissing, Douglas. "The Shapiro's Story." *Traces of Indiana and Midwestern History* 21, no. 4 (Fall 2009): 4–15.

Writers' Program. Indiana Federal Writers' Project. *The Calumet Region Historical Guide*. Gary, IN: Garman Printing, 1939. Internet Archive, https://archive.org/details /calumetregionhis00writrich.

Essential Questions

1 What is meant by the term "the Indiana way"?

2 What factors motivated immigrants to leave their home countries and settle in Indiana?

3 In the mid-nineteenth century, most of Indiana's immigrants came from what two countries? In what Indiana cities did these groups tend to settle?

4 Where did late-nineteenth-century immigrants to Indiana come from? In what Indiana cities did the "new" immigrants tend to settle?

5 What specific challenges did African American immigrants to Indiana face?

6 Who was Elwood Haynes?

7 Name at least three ways in which the automobile changed life for Hoosiers.

8 Why was Gary referred to as the "Magic City" or "City of the Century" in the early 1900s?*

9 Name two ways that life in Gary was less than ideal. What ultimately caused Gary's decline?*

See student activities related to this question.

Activity: Gary—City of Magic?

Introduction: Years of industrial growth and immigration brought significant changes to Indiana, a state in which agrarian traditions were strongly rooted. Conceived and built by the U. S. Steel Corporation as the world's largest steel works and company town, Gary embodied both the promise of economic growth and the accompanying social issues.

▶ Read the following description of the founding of Gary published in a souvenir pamphlet, *Gary 1917–1918:*

Such a location was found in the state of Indiana on the south shore of Lake Michigan, some 25 miles south of the city of Chicago. Here the company purchased a tract of over 9,000 acres with a frontage on Lake Michigan of seven miles. One thousand acres of this property, including a water front two miles in extent, was selected as the site of the new steel plant. The property was a dreary waste of drifted sand, entirely uninhabited and covered with a scanty growth of grass and scrub timber. It was an ideal location for the purpose, for on one side it was accessible to the ore carrying steamers of Duluth, [Minnesota] and on the other side it was served by several trunk railroads, over whose tracks the coke and limestone could be brought in and finished products hauled away, without any intermediate handling or trans-shipment. (Beaudette, 4–5)

▶ Consider the following questions and discuss your answers with a partner.

1 How does the author describe the natural state of the site on which Gary was to be built? Is the description of the undeveloped land positive or negative? How do you know? What words does the author use to show positive or negative points of view?

2 What factors made the site an ideal location for U. S. Steel to build its steel works?

▶ Now study the article below, which is included in *Gary 1917–1918*. After reading the article, complete the discussion questions that follow.

"Gary, the City of Magic, Steel and Energy"
by H. R. Snyder

Many pens have been employed during the past decade in attempting to write the story of Gary. One frequently finds reference made to this City in current literature as the Magic City, and it has attracted the notice of publicists, historians and philosophers, far and wide. Sometimes it is called "The Wonder City," for in eleven years, there has sprung up on the sand dunes on the shores of Lake Michigan, in Northern Indiana, a settlement which has grown so rapidly that it is now believed to number in round figures some 75,000 people. This cosmopolitan city is represented by the most diverse nationalities of any city of similar size in the world. Many well-educated men have been attracted to Gary and make up its official, secretarial, business and professional life. But the great bulk of our adult population is made up of the working classes, attracted here by the good wages and regular employment afforded them in the great steel mills that run day and night the year round. The tremendous demands for steel, iron, shells, shops, ships, bridge-stuffs, railway iron, cannon, guns, and all kind of construction materials have been especially heavy on the Gary mills during the past three years. Immigration from Southeastern Europe having been cut off by the great world war, now in progress, raging in that continent, mill labor has been attracted from other quarters, and thousands of colored men have come from the cotton States of the South.

This gives our City a remarkable diversity of population, as originally manual labor was performed largely by Slavs, Magyars [Hungarians], Poles, Lithuanians, Czechs, Greeks, Turks, Ingo Slavs, Roumanians and others of that great conglomerate peoples who inhabit the Balkans.

Gary is noted for its steel works, built by competent engineers, embracing the most modern, scientific and mechanical intelligence. It is claimed that the Gary plant, which had originally as its base, eight blast furnaces, but recently reinforced by four more, is the most efficient and productive iron and steel works now in existence. The open hearth is the heart of the immense, pulsating steel mills. . . .

The original plant, which covered one thousand acres, is constantly expanding, being supplemented by the Drawn Steel Works, the Tin Mills, a great new Tube plant, and additions to the original shops and furnaces.

▶ Discussion Questions: "Gary, the City of Magic, Steel and Energy"

1 According to the author of this article, what was the estimated population of Gary in 1917, eleven years after its founding?

2 What adjectives does the author use to describe Gary?

3 According to the author, immigrants from what nations made up the workforce in Gary's steel plants?

4 Based on your knowledge of immigration to Indiana and the United States at large, would these groups be part of the "old" wave of immigration or the "new" wave of immigration?

5 The author also mentions another group of people drawn to Gary by the promise of jobs. What group was that?

6 Make a prediction about how people from so many different backgrounds got along with each other. Years later, when some of the steel jobs left Gary, how do you suspect the competition for jobs affected relations between different ethnic groups?

7 Examine the photo on page 159 titled "Downtown Gary, 1920s." Do you think this is a photo of a prosperous city? What do you see that makes you say that?

8 Log on to Google Maps and look up Broadway between 6th and 7th Avenues in Gary, Indiana, today. How do these recent images compare to the 1920s image on page 159.

    A Do you think these are photos of a prosperous city? What do you see that makes you say that?

    B What do you suspect happened to cause the changes you see?

▶ Once you have completed the discussion questions, re-read the section of Chapter 6 about "The New Hoosiers of Gary" on pages 159–61. As noted there, many African Americans and Mexican Americans came to Gary in search of better-paying jobs and greater economic opportunity, but they encountered intense discrimination. Poet "Bob" Dyrenforth wrote of the promise of Gary in this verse that appears in the introduction to *Gary 1917–1918*:

> *City of the sands, most marv'lous,*
> *Built as mankind said could'st not be,*
> *Wonder of man's work, and progress,*
> *Gary—"Bee hive" of our country,*
> *Symbol of our land's achievement;*
> *City made and kept ideal,*
> *True American—thy progress,*
> *Gary—wonder of our nation!*

▶ How do you think an African American or Mexican American might have described Gary in a poem? Write a verse from the perspective of a member of a group that was not able to experience the promise of Gary in the same way as its white residents.

Activity Reference

Beaudette, E. Palma, *Gary, 1917–1918*. Gary, IN: E. Palma Beaudette, 1918.

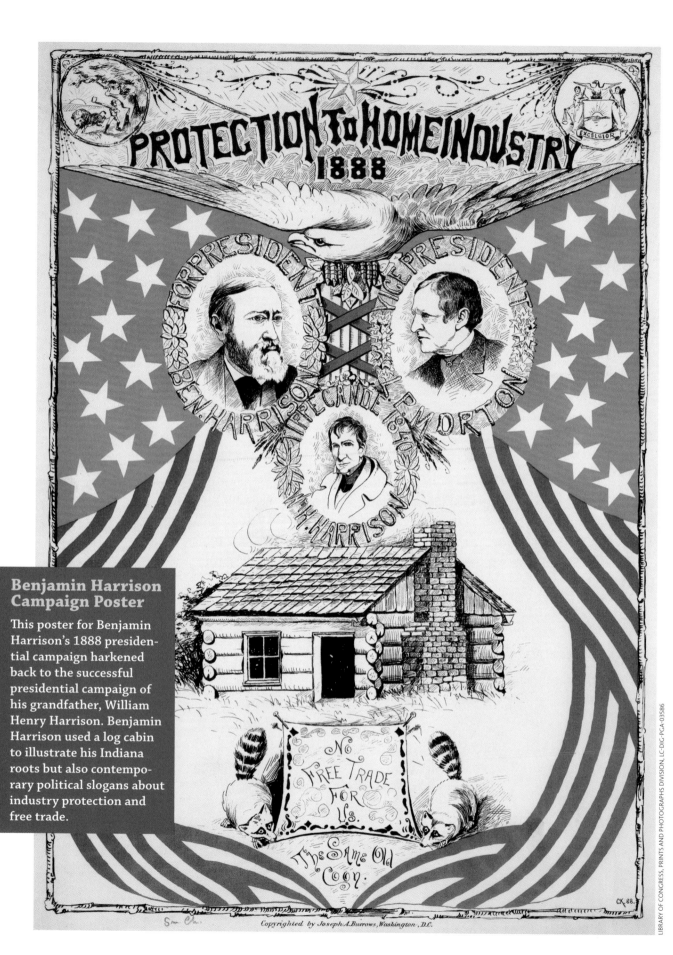

Benjamin Harrison Campaign Poster

This poster for Benjamin Harrison's 1888 presidential campaign harkened back to the successful presidential campaign of his grandfather, William Henry Harrison. Benjamin Harrison used a log cabin to illustrate his Indiana roots but also contemporary political slogans about industry protection and free trade.

7

Progressive Era Politics and Reform

We must turn to these new social and economic questions which have to do with the daily lives and happiness of human beings and which press for answer; questions that involve the righteousness of American business, a juster distribution of wealth by preventing dishonest accumulation of gain; questions that look to the physical, mental, moral upbuilding of all the workers in factory and on farm throughout the entire Republic.

— Indiana Senator Albert Beveridge to the Republican State Convention, 1906

Hoosiers loved politics. On the frontier they gathered eagerly for stump speakers and campaign hoopla. William Henry Harrison's log cabin campaign of 1840 was great fun, but politics could also be deadly serious, as in the Civil War era, when Indiana's political choices helped decide the future of the nation. In the late nineteenth century Hoosiers created their own style of politics to fit their beliefs. Politics became a means by which Hoosiers created an identity, a sense of belonging to the same state and caring about it.

Indiana's Intense Style of Politics

Hoosiers created a political culture that was among the strongest in the nation. They turned out in huge numbers to vote. From 1860 to 1900 an average of 91 percent of the state's eligible voters cast their ballot in presidential election years. This high turnout placed the state far ahead of its midwestern neighbors.

Hoosiers also showed unusually strong attachment to a political party. Nearly all Indiana voters were either Republicans or Democrats. They voted a straight ticket and rarely wavered—few Democrats ever voted for a Republican and vice versa. Intense partisan loyalty passed from father to son. Everyone knew there were Republican families and Democratic families. Politics was so intense, in part, because elections were always close. Often Hoosiers divided almost fifty-fifty in their choice of political party. Thus, a shift in a few votes could decide an election. Especially important for each party was to make sure all their loyal voters turned out on Election Day.

To encourage voter turnout, parties provided entertainment. Campaigns became raucous spectacles with parades, barbecues, songs, food, and often whiskey. Banners flew and campaign buttons appeared on coats. What fun it was as an election approached and each party sought to make sure its voters cast a ballot!

Indiana's close elections drew national attention to the state in presidential election years. Indiana was one of a handful of swing states that could tip the balance from one candidate to favor another on the basis of only a few thousand votes. Swing states were so very important because of the Electoral College. In order to win a majority of electoral votes, each party spent most of its time and money in Indiana and other swing states. There was no reason to campaign in the South, for example, since voters there always chose Democratic candidates. Likewise, there was no reason to campaign in New England, since New England states always voted Republican.

The national parties also sought the Indiana vote by putting a Hoosier on the national ballot, particularly as a vice-presidential candidate. These included Schuyler Colfax (1868), William H. English (1880), Thomas A. Hendricks (1876, 1884), Charles W. Fairbanks (1904, 1916), John W. Kern (1908), and Thomas R. Marshall (1912, 1916). Republican Benjamin Harrison was the only major-party Hoosier presidential nominee (1888, 1892). Harrison served as president from 1889 to 1893.

Political Issues and Progressive Reform

Beneath all the waving flags, buttons, and speeches were real political issues and real differences between the two parties. Indiana Democrats held to the Jefferson–Jackson tradition of individual freedom. They preferred small government and low taxes and claimed to represent the common man. They attracted particularly strong support among descendants of Upland southern pioneers in southern Indiana.

Republicans tended to expect more from government. They wanted local, state, and national governments to play a larger role in such areas as education, public health, women's rights, and prohibition of alcohol. Republicans believed government could make life better.

Political Event in New Albany

Political events could be grand affairs with waving flags and live music. State politician and attorney Evan Stotsenberg from New Albany spoke at this event, ca. 1895–1937.

Election Day with Suffragists

Suffragists and other citizens of Brookville, Indiana, gather on Election Day in this photo by Ben Winans, ca. 1900–1909. Although women would not have the right to vote until 1920, they could still be politically active. Here, women encouraged the male voters with signs that stated "Vote 'Yes' for Me" and "When you go in the booth think of us."

There were always new issues to influence parties and voters. An economic depression from 1873 to 1878 touched off a wave of reform across the country, involving farming, education, democratic methods, and the economy. Reformers came together to form the Populist Party in the 1890s. While the Populist Party attracted some notice in Indiana, most Hoosiers rejected this third party because its political and social ideas were radically different than the political beliefs they held traditionally. By 1896 the Populist Party joined the Democratic Party. Although the Populists were largely unsuccessful in Indiana, they laid the foundations for future Hoosier reformers.

New reform issues flooded the political arena in the first decade and a half of the twentieth century. Progressive reformers in both parties urged more government action to solve some of the negative consequences of urban and industrial growth. Progressives sought wide-ranging reform: stricter child labor laws, regulation of monopolies, a state income tax, public health measures, conservation of natural resources, prohibition of the sale of alcohol, and expanded democracy through direct primary elections, direct elections of United States senators, and women's suffrage. Progressives also sought the powers of initiative and referendum on the state level. Initiative gave citizens

FOR PRESIDENT,
WOODROW WILSON:
OF NEW JERSEY
FOR VICE-PRESIDENT
THOMAS R. MARSHALL:
OF INDIANA.

Woodrow Wilson and Thomas Marshall

This campaign illustration from 1912 features presidential candidate Woodrow Wilson on the left and vice presidential candidate Thomas Marshall on the right. Wilson and Marshall won and served from 1913 to 1921. Prior to serving at the federal level, Marshall had been governor of Indiana from 1909 to 1913.

ON TO WASHINGTON!

the power to propose laws and referendum allowed citizens to voice their opinions on proposed legislation.

Progressive reform issues bitterly divided Hoosiers. The Republican Party's progressive wing, led by Senator Albert Beveridge, eventually joined Theodore Roosevelt's new political organization, the "Bull Moose" Party. Standpat Republicans, who were staunchly conservative and resistant to change, saw little need for reform. This caused a split in the Republican Party that helped Democrats dominate Indiana's political stage between 1909 and 1916. It also ended Beveridge's political career since standpat Republicans turned their backs on the reformer.

The reform movement divided Democrats as well. However, Democrats found popular leaders such as Thomas Marshall who minimized conflict within the party by implementing programs of slow and cautious reform. As Indiana's governor (1909–1913), Marshall was described as a "'liberal with the brakes on.'" He sought modest progressive legislation that included some increased state regulation. Marshall also wanted the state to write a more modern constitution but this proposal failed. Marshall later served as Woodrow Wilson's vice president from 1913 to 1921.

Indiana's reformers brought many changes to the lives of Hoosiers. Progressives, many of whom were women, fought against alcohol as had Temperance crusaders for many decades. Progressives won a victory with new state and national prohibition laws. Progressives also took up the long-fought campaign for women's suffrage, which also ended victoriously in 1920 with the ratification of the Nineteenth Amendment to the U.S. Constitution.

Indiana at 100

Although there were certainly unsolved problems facing Hoosiers as they celebrated their centennial of statehood in 1916, there were also good reasons to be proud of Indiana. Economic growth had created a booming economy with factories pushing out goods and fields waving with corn. Cities bustled with new cultural and social opportunities. Indiana authors, such as Booth Tarkington and James Whitcomb Riley, and Indiana painters, such as T. C. Steele, were among the best in the nation. For many Hoosiers there was a singular contentment in their state during the new century. This feeling was captured in a poem published in an Indianapolis newspaper in 1919. The author, William Herschell, had been a young railroad worker and participated in the 1894 Pullman Strike before becoming a journalist. He titled his poem, reproduced below, "Ain't God Good to Indiana?"

> *Ain't God good to Indiana?*
> *Other spots may look as fair,*
> *But they lack th' soothin' somethin'*
> *In th' Hoosier sky and air.*
> *They don't have that snug-up feelin'*
> *Like a mother gives a child;*
> *They don't soothe you, soul an' body,*
> *With their breezes soft an' mild.*
> *They don't know th' joys of Heaven*
> *Have their birthplace here below;*
> *Ain't God good to Indiana?*
> *Ain't He, fellers? Ain't He though?*

7.1

Benjamin Harrison and Indiana-Style Politics

No other people have a government more worthy of their respect and love or a land so magnificent in extent, so pleasant to look upon, and so full of generous suggestion to enterprise and labor. God has placed upon our head a diadem and has laid at our feet power and wealth beyond definition or calculation.

— *Benjamin Harrison, 1889 Inaugural Address*

As of 2016, Benjamin Harrison (1833–1901) is the only U.S. president elected from Indiana and is the only grandson of a former president to be elected. He brought to the executive office legal expertise, military service, Christian principles, and a hefty measure of Hoosier pragmatism.

Ancestry and Early Life

Harrison descended from a prominent American family. His paternal great-grandfather, also named Benjamin Harrison, signed the Declaration of Independence and was the governor of Virginia. His grandfather William Henry Harrison, the hero of Tippecanoe and the nation's ninth president, died shortly after his inauguration when Benjamin was seven years old.

Harrison was born on his family's large farm in North Bend, Ohio, on August 20, 1833. He attended Farmer's College where he met his future wife, Caroline Scott, whose father taught at the school. After graduating in 1853 with a law degree from Miami University of Ohio, Harrison married Caroline. The young couple settled in Indianapolis the following year and subsequently had two children, Russell and Mary.

Before he was thirty, Harrison was on his way to becoming a pillar of the Indianapolis community. A devout Christian, he became an elder in the city's First Presbyterian Church at age twenty-eight. His law practice was also successful; he earned a reputation as a riveting courtroom speaker and served as the city's attorney. In 1860 Harrison ran as a Republican for his first political office, reporter of the state Supreme Court, and won. In this office he prepared summaries and accounts of the court's proceedings. He left the position when the Civil War erupted.

Civil War Hero

Harrison raised and trained the Seventieth Indiana Regiment at the request of Governor Oliver P. Morton. In 1862 he had the rank of colonel when the regiment deployed to join the U.S. Army in Louisville. For two years Indiana's Seventieth guarded railroads and did reconnaissance, exploring and reporting on enemy

Benjamin Harrison

Benjamin Harrison served as the President of the United States from 1889 to 1893.

President Benjamin Harrison Home

Benjamin Harrison's house in Indianapolis was not only where he lived with his family before and after his presidency but was also the scene of his "front porch" political campaign. Today the home is a National Historic Landmark and a popular house museum containing original Harrison furniture, which is open for tours and programs.

WELCOME

FRANK LESLIE'S
ILLUSTRATED
NEWSPAPER

Entered according to Act of Congress, in the year 1888, by Mrs. FRANK LESLIE, in the Office of the Librarian of Congress at Washington.— Entered at the Post Office, New York, N. Y., as Second-class Matter.

No. 1,731.—VOL. LXVII.]   NEW YORK—FOR THE WEEK ENDING NOVEMBER 17, 1888.   [PRICE, 10 CENTS. $4.00 YEARLY. 13 WEEKS, $1.06.

Harrison's Election Day

Frank Leslie's Illustrated Newspaper of November 17, 1888, depicts how Benjamin Harrison's supporters swarmed the yard of his Indianapolis home after he won the presidential election. His campaign was a "front porch" campaign in name only, as Harrison did not add a porch to the house until after he returned from the White House.

THE LATE ELECTION.—POPULAR DEMONSTRATION AT THE RESIDENCE OF GENERAL HARRISON, IN INDIANAPOLIS, IN HONOR OF HIS ELECTION TO THE PRESIDENCY.

FROM A SKETCH BY FRANK ADAMS — SEE PAGE 222.

territory for the army. In 1864 the regiment moved to the front lines of Major General William T. Sherman's Atlanta Campaign.

Harrison commanded troops and fought valiantly at numerous battles, including Resaca (Georgia, May 1864) and Peachtree Creek (Georgia, July 1864). While his regiment continued in General Sherman's campaign, Harrison was promoted to brigadier general and transferred to Tennessee to lead troops in the Battle of Nashville. After winning this battle, Harrison was sent to rejoin the Seventieth Indiana Regiment, but due to illness, he reached the regiment only after the war was over. In 1865 Harrison left the army and returned to civilian life a decorated war hero.

Legal Career

Benjamin Harrison was a typical citizen of the Hoosier capital and wished always to be known as such. It was his chosen home.

— Historian Ross Lockridge, 1938

Back in Indianapolis, Harrison picked up where he had left off before the Civil War. After serving out his term as State Supreme Court reporter, he resumed his law practice and was extremely successful. In 1881 alone Harrison tried six cases before the United States Supreme Court, which enhanced his national reputation.

By 1874 Harrison's income was large enough to build a sixteen-room brick home on a lot that he bought in 1868 at 1230 North Delaware Street. At the time the house was outside Indianapolis's city limits, but it is well within city limits today. In time, many prosperous Indianapolis citizens also made their home in the north part of the city. Today, the Benjamin Harrison Home is open to the public and hosts many exhibitions and events.

In 1876 Harrison ran for governor. Although he lost, he assumed the mantle of the state's leading Republican when Oliver P. Morton died the following year. Five years after running for governor Harrison was elected to the United States Senate. An outspoken advocate of legislation for veterans' benefits, such as pensions, he was referred to as the "soldier's friend."

The "Soldier-Citizen" and the 1888 Presidential Election

In 1888 the Republican Party chose "soldier-citizen" Benjamin Harrison as its presidential candidate. Harrison conducted his presidential campaign in a typical fashion for national politics of the time. Instead of roaming the nation giving speeches, he held a "front porch" campaign, delivering many of his most important speeches from his Indianapolis home. Harrison's adoring public grabbed many souvenirs from his family's home on Delaware Street, including sections of their white picket fence. His wife Caroline is said to have joked, "If we don't go to the White House we'll go to the poor house, with all of the repairs we'll have to make."

Go to the White House they did. Even though Harrison lost the popular vote by 90,000 votes, he defeated Democratic incumbent Grover Cleveland by carrying the Electoral College 233 to 168. Winning in New York and Indiana, both important swing states, sealed his victory. Harrison was called the "centennial president" because he was sworn in a century after George Washington's inauguration. His inauguration speech was brief compared to that of his grandfather, William Henry Harrison, who set the record for giving the longest inaugural speech in United States history.

President Benjamin Harrison, 1889–1893

Harrison's administration is considered among the most activist and reform-oriented in the nineteenth century. On his watch, some very important legislation passed, including the Dependent and Disability Pension Act (for veterans, 1890), the McKinley Tariff Act (1890), the Sherman Anti-Trust Act (1890), and a Meat Inspection Act (1891). Congress also expanded the size and scope of the United States Navy (1889–1901).

Harrison refused to travel to campaign for reelection in 1892 because Caroline was very ill. She lost a long battle with tuberculosis and passed away on October 25, 1892, two weeks before the general election. Harrison lost his bid for reelection to his former rival Grover Cleveland by a substantial margin.

Final Years

After leaving the White House, Harrison returned to private life in Indianapolis. Even though he traveled for speaking engagements and went to Europe on diplomatic missions, he always came back home to Indiana. In 1896 he married Mary (Lord) Dimmick, Caroline's niece, who was twenty-five years younger than him. Their daughter Elizabeth was born in 1897. In 1901 Harrison died from pneumonia at his home on Delaware Street. He is buried in Crown Hill Cemetery next to Caroline. When Mary died in 1948, she, too, was buried next to the late president.

Caroline Scott Harrison

Caroline Scott Harrison in an 1885 portrait likely painted by Lilly M. Spencer.

The Legacy of Caroline Scott Harrison

It has been said "that the men to make a country are made by self-denial;" and is it not true that this Society, to live and grow and become what we would desire it to be, must be composed of self-denying women? Our hope is in unity and self sacrifice.

— *Caroline Scott Harrison, Address to First Continental Congress, Daughters of the American Revolution, February 22, 1892, Washington, DC*

Long before her husband became president, Caroline Scott Harrison had a reputation as a genteel woman with artistic talents. In Indianapolis many admired her dedication to charitable causes, especially those associated with orphans and veterans.

As America's twenty-third First Lady, Harrison was a role model for subsequent First Ladies. She brought her appreciation of culture to the White House by introducing French language and art classes. Seventy years later First Lady Jacqueline Kennedy also filled the White House with art, from the visual to the performing arts. Harrison started the White House china collection, which Kennedy later took a special interest in. Harrison's "American made" inaugural gown was designed by Mary Williamson of Lafayette, Indiana. More than 120 years later, First Lady Michelle Obama made a commitment to wearing clothes created by American designers.

Harrison China

Caroline Scott Harrison
designed and painted the motif
of goldenrod and ears of corn on
this plate, which was part of her
White House china.

Harrison made America's first home a place that citizens could be proud of as well as a comfortable home for her family. Before the Harrisons moved in, the White House had fallen into neglect. Rats infested it, and it did not yet have electricity—situations that Harrison corrected. A gardener with a passion for orchids, Harrison used the White House's greenhouse and started the tradition of the first family having a decorated Christmas tree.

In 1890 Harrison became the President-General of the National Society, Daughters of the American Revolution (DAR), a genealogical organization for women who descend from patriots of the American Revolution. In February 1892 she invited the first

Continental Congress of the DAR to the White House for a reception and elegant dinner, which was served on the Harrison china that she had designed. Harrison gave a speech to her guests that evening—the first public address given by a sitting First Lady. A DAR historian and friend of Harrison's commented that it was a great self-sacrifice for Harrison to accept the honor of the office of President-General because even in 1890 the First Lady's health was in decline. In 1894 the Indianapolis DAR chapter was named after Harrison, who, shortly before her death in 1892 had urged a friend from Indianapolis to start a DAR chapter in her hometown. Today the Caroline Scott Harrison Chapter DAR has around 500 members.

7.2

Improving Hoosiers: Dr. John N. Hurty and Progressive Health Reform

"We must not cease our labors, as a body, until the citizens of this State have pure air to breathe, pure water to drink, unadulterated food and medicines, live in buildings that are not sources of infection to themselves or their neighbors, and have an intelligent body of agents to warn and protect them from preventable, indigenous, and importable causes of disease."

— Dr. Luther D. Waterman, MD, president of the Indiana State Medical Society, 1878

Hoosier moderation largely prevailed during Indiana's progressive era. Women's suffrage, prohibition, and public welfare challenged Indiana's preference for middle-of-the road policies. But in the area of public health, Indiana led the nation.

In 1881 the Indiana General Assembly created the Indiana State Board of Health to collect statistics and disseminate information about disease and sanitation in order to supervise the health of the state's citizens. In its first decade, the board's accomplishments were modest due to lack of funding and weak leadership. It primarily focused on establishing local health boards in counties and larger cities throughout the state.

Dr. John N. Hurty, Indiana's "Most Useful Citizen"

"Dr. Hurty has been called the most useful citizen of Indiana, and I am sure that no one that knows what he has accomplished will begrudge him this."

— Dr. W. E. Stone, President of Purdue University, 1915

In 1896 Dr. John N. Hurty became director of the Board of Health. He campaigned for improving sanitary conditions to prevent the spread of disease and made great advancements in public health reform. Three years later, the legislature passed Hurty's Pure Food and Drug Law, which prevented the sale of contaminated food and drugs. It was among the nation's first such state laws. Additional reforms by the legislature included state licensing and regulation of medical professionals and expansion of accredited medical education through creation of the Indiana University School of Medicine in 1908.

COLLECTIONS OF THE IUPUI UNIVERSITY LIBRARY SPECIAL COLLECTIONS AND ARCHIVES

John Hurty

John Hurty, head of the State Board of Health from 1896 to 1922, at work with his secretary Louise Lingenfelter in 1917. Posters concerning public health hang in the background. Hurty's views are expressed through one of the posters that states, "Hygiene can prevent more crime than any law."

```
```

Infant mortality plummeted thanks to Hurty's campaign that focused on the health and care of newborns. In 1914 the board printed thousands of copies of *The Indiana Mother's Baby Book* and distributed them to new moms around the state. The wildly popular "Better Babies Contest" held at the Indiana State Fair during the 1920s emerged from this outreach effort. In 1915 the American Medical Association ranked Indiana sixth nationally for the effectiveness of its public health programs largely because of Hurty's pioneering work.

Hurty's Youth

Born in Lebanon, Ohio, in 1852, John Newell Hurty was the son of Ann Irene and Josiah Hurty, a German-American schoolteacher who strongly believed in the benefits of cleanliness and fresh air. Hurty adopted his father's philosophy, which greatly influenced his career as a scientist and Indiana's first public health reformer.

In 1866 the Hurty family moved to Paris, Illinois, where John, age 14, met Colonel Eli Lilly, who was part owner of a local drugstore. Hurty became Lilly's apprentice three years later. Hurty took Lilly's advice and attended the Philadelphia College of Pharmacy. In 1873 Hurty joined Lilly in Indianapolis where he had opened a pharmaceutical laboratory with Dr. John Johnstone, a dentist.

In Indianapolis Hurty married Johnstone's daughter, Ethel, in 1877 and opened his own drugstore and laboratory at the corner of Ohio and Pennsylvania Streets two years later. Even in his early years in

INDIANA STATE BOARD *of* HEALTH

I AM DEATH

TO EARLY JOIN ME

BREATHE MUCH FOUL AIR.

DRINK ALCOHOLIC LIQUORS.

EAT MIDNIGHT SUPPERS.

EAT LOTS OF RICH FOOD.

BOLT YOUR FOOD OR WASH IT DOWN WITH LARGE AMOUNTS OF BLACK COFFEE.

NEGLECT YOUR BOWELS.

The State Board of Health released this grim poster in 1912 expressing its view of what constituted unhealthy behavior.

Indianapolis, Hurty was obviously concerned about public health. He performed a weekly analysis of the city's water supply and provided his findings to the Indianapolis Water Company. A proponent of education, Hurty was also a founding member of the state's first school of pharmacy at Purdue University where he occasionally taught. He remained friends with Lilly and was a pallbearer at the Colonel's funeral in 1898, when his own career was reaching its zenith.

"Dean of American Sanitarians"

During the twenty-six years Hurty directed the Indiana State Board of Health he zealously championed causes that made Indiana a national model for public health, thereby gaining a national reputation as a cutting-edge progressive reformer. Between 1899 and 1915 more than thirty-five laws were passed to improve the daily lives of Hoosiers. A few of these were the Drug Sample Law (1907)—which prevented drugs from being distributed freely; the Hydrophobia Law (1911)—that required that dogs receive the rabies vaccine; the Cold Storage Law (1911)—which regulated the temperature and time span food could be held in cold storage; and the Anti-Rat Law (1913)—that attempted to reduce the number of rats both for economic and public health reasons.

Sterilization Law and Eugenics

A person who is morally defective has no right to impose another defective on the human family. We take from them their lives when they are murderers—hang them, electrocute them—and it is not nearly so severe to take from them their right to procreate.

— *Dr. John N. Hurty, 1909*

Among the lengthy list of laws passed on Hurty's watch, one gave Indiana a dubious distinction—the 1907 Sterilization Law, which extended the state's quest for order and cleanliness to human behavior. The first of its kind in the nation, this *eugenics* law empowered penal and mental institutions to sterilize inmates deemed "criminals, idiots, imbeciles, and rapists." Supporters of the law hoped that sterilization would help improve the human race and decrease social problems.

The first year the law was in effect, doctors sterilized 119 men at the Indiana Reformatory in Jeffersonville and hundreds more later. Genetics was a new field of study and its research was widely accepted. Hurty relied on this new research; he was one of the first in the nation to give talks on "morons" and "making a better race." He claimed that "'all social problems, which we have assiduously tried to solve by education, care, cure and relief, are fast becoming recognized to be biological problems.'" Hurty was proud of Indiana's leadership in a movement that he considered a "higher hygiene, through which we can hope to better the race." Historian Alexandra Minna Stern notes, "Hurty praised his signature quarantine (1903), school sanitation (1911), and pure food and drug (1906) acts in the same breath as the . . . sterilization laws."

While eugenics crusaders in other states often targeted new immigrants from eastern Europe, Mexico, and China, Indiana more often deemed poor whites to be biologically unfit. The Committee on Mental Defectives researchers, comprised mostly of professional women, found many poor whites to research among the population of Southern Indiana. Families found in geographical edges of the hill country far from mainstream urban life struggled to cope with declining agricultural productivity and lived in extreme poverty.

In 1921 the Indiana Supreme Court overturned the 1907 eugenics law, but remnants of the crusade continued. The 1927 Holmes–Shake Bill legalized the "eugenical sterilization of mentally unfit confined to state institutions." The following year, sterilizations commenced at the Fort Wayne School for Feeble Minded Youth; more than 1,500 eugenics sterilizations were completed there through 1957. The law stood on the books until 1974 when Governor Otis Bowen finally repealed it.

In 2007, a century after the passage of Indiana's sterilization law, a group of scholars, community leaders, human rights activists, and artists convened at the Indiana State Library for a public symposium to examine the lasting impact of eugenics in the Hoosier state. The centennial included the exhibition *Fit to Breed? The History and Legacy of Indiana Eugenics, 1907–2007*, created by Indiana University and the Indiana State Archives, which was converted to a digital archive and published online the following year.

On April 12, 2007, the installation of a marker on the state library's east lawn recognized the 1907 eugenics sterilization law. The marker's intent was to raise public awareness of the practice of eugenics in Indiana history and to acknowledge some 2,500 Hoosiers who were sterilized against their will during the movement.

PETITION

To the Board of Trustees of the Muscatatuck State School:

The undersigned petitioner respectfully represents that he is the duly appointed and acting superintendent of the Muscatatuck State School.

That said institution has the care and custody of _____, a feeble-minded inmate thereof; that the said _____ was born _____ and was committed by or admission authorized through the proper authorities of ___Knox___ County, Indiana on the _____ day of _____, 19___, and has been an inmate of the Muscatatuck State School since the _____ day of _____.

That said _____ is definitely feeble-minded and incurable; and that it is the opinion of the petitioner that the welfare of the said _____ and society will be promoted by h_er_ sexual sterilization.

That your petitioner is informed and believes that _____ residing at ___Evansville, Indiana___ is related to said _____ as ___mother___ and is h_er_ nearest or next of kin.

Wherefore your petitioner prays that an order be made and entered by your Board authorizing and requiring Dr._____, a competent physician to sexually sterilize said _____ by performing on h_er_ the operation of salpingectony, ~~vasectomy~~.

Signed _____ Supt. Muscatatuck S. S.

State of Indiana)
Jennings County) SS

___Cliff Bemish___ being duly sworn upon oath says; that the matters and facts set forth in the foregoing petition are true as he verily believes.

Signed _____

Subscribed and sworn to before me this_____ day of _____

My Commission expires _____

_____ Notary Public

Muscatatuck Sterilization Petition

In 1940 the superintendent of the Muscatatuck State School petitioned to have a "feeble-minded" student of his school sterilized because, in his opinion, it would improve both the welfare of the student and society. This was not a lone case. Sterilizations of young people took place over several decades in the first half of the twentieth century until the sterilization law was repealed in the 1970s. [Names have been edited out of this petition.]

7.3

Albert J. Beveridge: Hoosier Reformer in the Nation's Spotlight

It is a noble land that God has given us; a land that can feed and clothe the world; a land whose coastlines would inclose half the countries of Europe; a land set like a sentinel between the two imperial oceans of the globe, a greater England with a nobler destiny.

— Albert J. Beveridge, "March of the Flag" campaign speech, Indianapolis, 1898

A Hard Worker from Humble Roots

Albert Jeremiah Beveridge was born on a farm in Highland County, Ohio, on October 6, 1862. After his father fought in the Civil War, he faced chronic financial difficulties. When he lost the farm, he moved his family to Illinois. There, Beveridge pieced together the equivalent of a high school education while doing hard labor as a farmer, railroad worker, and logger.

In 1881, with a few dollars in his pocket, Beveridge entered Indiana Asbury University (now DePauw University) at Greencastle, Indiana, where he distinguished himself as a superb, hard-working student. Industrious and organized, he accounted for every minute of his day, seldom spent time with his peers, and often slept only four hours a night in order to study. He was a talented speaker and debater, winning top prizes at school and in an interstate oratory contest.

In 1887 Beveridge married Katharine "Kate" Langsdale of Greencastle and embarked on a law career in Indianapolis. Beveridge seemed to prefer working on high-profile, public cases that dealt with issues of constitutionality, rather than those that required mostly behind-the-scenes research. His superiors in the Indianapolis legal world, including Governor Alvin P. Hovey and Indiana Supreme Court Judge Francis E. Baker, held the rising legal superstar in high esteem.

Albert Beveridge

This portrait of Albert Beveridge by Frances Johnston was taken in 1900, a year after Beveridge's election to the U.S. Senate. Beveridge grew more progressive during the ensuing decade.

From Indiana to Washington, DC

I shall fearlessly stand in the Senate of the United States for the business interests of this country, when that means the welfare of all the people; and I shall fearlessly stand for the labor interests of the land, when that means the prosperity of all the people; and I shall just as fearlessly stand against the demands of any class, when those demands do not involve the interests of the entire American people.

— *Albert J. Beveridge, speech upon inauguration to United States Senate, 1899*

Beveridge got his start in Indiana politics in 1884 when he began making stump speeches for Republican candidates around the state. He proved so sensational in this work that he frequently received speaking invitations from the party's candidates in neighboring states. Beveridge found himself part of a new genera-tion of Hoosier Republican leaders who appeared on the scene in the 1890s. His main rival for party promi-nence was Charles Warren Fairbanks, a man as cool and reserved as Beveridge was charming and gregari-ous. Known by his detractors as "the Indiana Icicle," Fairbanks was a wealthy lawyer and part owner of the *Indianapolis News*. He won a U.S. Senate seat in 1897, and in 1904 gained the vice-presidency as Theodore Roosevelt's running mate.

Despite their common party ties, Beveridge and Fairbanks differed on a number of political issues, among them the topic of American overseas expan-sion. Where Fairbanks was cautious about involve-ment in the affairs of other nations, Beveridge was an enthusiastic promoter of the new American empire. His famed "March of the Flag" speech of 1898, which

THE WALLS OF JERICHO.

Republican Cartoon by Udo Keppler, 1910

This political cartoon titled "The Walls of Jericho" illustrates Progressive members of the Senate, including Albert Beveridge, holding an ark with the words "Square Tariff Deal" printed on its side, protesting what they believed to be an unfair tariff bill supported by standpat Republicans. Tariffs were one of the many issues that caused a split in the Republican Party.

advocated expansion to Cuba, Puerto Rico, and the Philippines, helped propel him to the U.S. Senate the following year. At age thirty-six, he was one of the youngest senators in Congress.

Beveridge and Wiley: Among the Progressive Standard Bearers

In addition to American expansion overseas, Progressive-era reformers, such as Beveridge, called for widespread reform in domestic issues during the first fifteen years of the twentieth century. They argued for more vigorous government intervention to lessen the negative effects of industrial and urban expansion. Calls for reform touched on many aspects of daily life. For workers, Progressives demanded stronger child labor laws and workers' compensation laws. They demanded regulation of monopolistic business practices that hindered economic competition, especially with railroads. Reformers also sought conservation of natural resources through the formation of the national park system; expanded opportunities for democratic action through women's suffrage and primary elections, which would give voters a say in which candidates ran for office; and measures to protect public health.

Thanks to public health laws, an outbreak of salmonella or botulism from contaminated food is not an everyday occurrence and makes front-page news around the country today. In large part, we can thank two landmark bills that President Theodore Roosevelt signed into law in July 1906. Both laws gave the federal government the power to safeguard the American food and drug supply. Two progressive Hoosier reformers, Albert J. Beveridge and Harvey W. Wiley, were the driving forces behind those laws.

Beveridge sent Roosevelt a copy of Upton Sinclair's novel *The Jungle*, a graphic exposé of the revolting conditions in Chicago's meatpacking industry that created a national uproar upon its publication in 1906. With the president's support, he drafted the Federal Meat Inspection Act (FMIA) that mandated the inspection of all livestock, slaughterhouses, and meatpacking plants. At the time, the meat from the United States sold to other countries had to be inspected, but no

such safeguards existed for meat consumed by the American public. After an uphill battle in Congress, the FMIA passed. Exhausted, Beveridge wrote a friend, "I was about played out when Congress closed. I was not much more than a fish worm physically." Nevertheless elated and proud of his achievement, he concluded that the meat bill was "the most important exercise of federal power ever sanctioned by Congress."

Harvey J. Wiley, "father" of the Pure Food and Drug Act, was a highly respected chemistry professor and food analyst from Purdue University in Lafayette, Indiana, before accepting the post of chief chemist for the United States Department of Agriculture (USDA) in 1883. Wiley was unflagging in his long crusade for food and drug regulation. He released his research on food adulterants—food contaminants that are impure or injurious to the consumer—in USDA bulletins. His research on the impact of certain food preservatives on humans gained national attention. Wiley also worked with pure food activist Alice Lakey from New Jersey to prompt more than a million American women to write letters in support of the 1906 Food and Drug Act. The law is widely considered the hallmark piece of Progressive legislation and a victory for the American consumer. Also known as the Wiley Act, the law gave the Bureau of Chemistry—later reorganized as the Food and Drug Administration (FDA)—the power to regulate food production. Wiley was the FDA's first director.

As necessary as the reform laws seemed to progressive leaders such as Beveridge, these issues bitterly divided Hoosiers. Despite being too reformist for many Hoosier voters, Beveridge won his bid for reelection in 1905 as the Republican Party split in two. Indiana senators Beveridge and Fairbanks—one an outspoken reformer, the other a "standpat" conservative Republican—stood on opposite sides of the fence. Due to the split in the Republican Party, the Democratic Party dominated the national stage from 1909 to 1916. When Beveridge ran for a third term in the Senate in 1910, he lost. Historian Daniel Levine comments that Beveridge "was convinced that he had failed to be reelected in 1910 not because he had been too progressive but because the Republican party had not been progressive enough." A staunch supporter of President Theodore Roosevelt, Beveridge joined Roosevelt's new Progressive "Bull Moose" Party in 1912, hoping to resuscitate his political career. However, he lost a 1912 bid for Indiana governor and attempts to regain his senate seat in 1914 and 1922.

Beveridge in Later Years

After the failure of his 1912 gubernatorial bid, Beveridge turned to another of his interests, historical research and writing. He excelled at this as he had in all of his previous pursuits. Beveridge wrote a four-volume biography of U.S. Supreme Court Justice John Marshall, which won a Pulitzer Prize for biography in 1920. During the 1920s he was an active member of the American Historical Association (AHA). After completing two volumes of a planned four-volume study of Abraham Lincoln, Beveridge died in Indianapolis in 1927. His second wife Catherine (Eddy) Beveridge donated $50,000 to the AHA in Beveridge's memory in order to establish an award for the best book written in English on the history of the United States, Latin America, or Canada. The award is still given annually.

COURTESY OF THE FDA HISTORY OFFICE

Harvey Wiley

Harvey Wiley, a chemist at Purdue University who became chief chemist for the United States Department of Agriculture in 1883 is shown in a laboratory late in his career. Wiley was known as the "father" of the 1906 Pure Food and Drug Act.

FDA Cartoon

As this cartoon depicts, in the 1906 Pure Food and Drug Act, Harvey Wiley pushed for eliminating harmful additives in food and drugs, as well as "fake foods" and "quack remedies."

7.4

Albion Fellows Bacon: Indiana's Housing Reformer

I began to notice how the threads of the social problems, the civic problems and even the business problems of a city are all tangled up with the housing problems, and to realize that housing reform is fundamental.

— *Albion Fellows Bacon,* Beauty for Ashes *(1914)*

Women as well as men were activists for reform during the Progressive Era. Albion Fellows Bacon (1865–1933) was born and died in Evansville, Indiana, but her work in hometown housing reform had both state and national impact. With her upbringing and background, Bacon could have lived the sort of quiet, comfortable life enjoyed by many upper-middle class women of the late nineteenth and early twentieth cen-

turies. But one day in the late 1890s Bacon, a wife and mother in her thirties, visited a tenement in Evansville, and her life changed radically. Years later she said the experience removed the blinders she had been wearing. For the rest of her life, she dedicated herself to the job of improving housing for the poor—an arduous, uphill journey, especially for someone who did not even have the right to vote.

A Sheltered Early Life

Mary (Erskine) Fellows named her third daughter after her recently deceased husband, Reverend Albion Fellows, who is said to have died from pneumonia at age thirty-eight. The young widow soon moved with her daughters Lura, Annie, and newborn Albion, to rural McCutchanville near family. Bacon fondly remembered her idyllic childhood in southern Indiana, where her sheltered life revolved around school and church. She and her sister Annie were passionate about writing poetry and fiction and were thrilled when a couple of their early efforts were published.

In 1881 Mary and her girls moved back to Evansville. Bacon attended the city high school, where she excelled and graduated as class salutatorian. A talented artist, she was disappointed that her mother could not afford to send her to college as she had her older sisters. Instead, Bacon took a job as a secretary for her uncle, Judge Asa Iglehart, and eventually became a skilled court stenographer.

On October 11, 1888, Bacon, then twenty-three, married prosperous dry goods merchant Hilary Edwin Bacon at Trinity Methodist Church in a double ceremony with her sister, Annie, and Annie's groom William Johnston. Hilary and Albion soon settled in a pretty, spacious house on the edge of Evansville where, Bacon later recalled, "'My husband, my housekeeping, flowers, music, reading, my friends, and a pleasant social round, filled up the hours.'"

The couple welcomed their daughter Margaret in 1889, Albion Mary in 1892, and twins Joy and Hilary Jr. in 1901. Bacon was active in her church but avoided getting involved with local social and political issues of the day, wishing to "'exclude every ugly or blighting thing'" from her life. It was

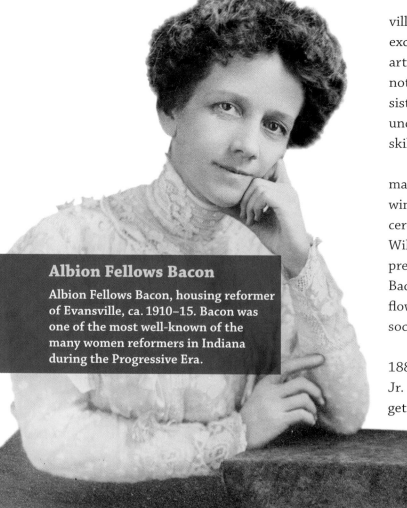

Albion Fellows Bacon

Albion Fellows Bacon, housing reformer of Evansville, ca. 1910–15. Bacon was one of the most well-known of the many women reformers in Indiana during the Progressive Era.

An Evansville Tenement, ca. 1914

This cramped tenement in Evansville illustrates just how terrible the conditions were in places where poor families lived. These were the conditions that Albion Fellows Bacon wanted to improve. This photo appears in the book Bacon wrote, *Beauty for Ashes* (1914), with the caption "Day shifts and night shifts used the same beds."

concern for conditions at her middle daughter's school that propelled her into civic activism—she led the fight to clean up a blighted lot to establish a safe playground on school grounds. Soon after, Margaret and Albion Mary contracted scarlet fever, a disease that in those days often proved fatal. Although Margaret and Albion Mary survived the fever, Bacon noticed that many of the poorer children in the school were sickly. For example, one child had a mother who had recently died from tuberculosis, a bacterial disease that is spread through the air. Bacon rolled up her sleeves and agreed to serve on the sanitation committee of the city's Civic Improvement Association.

A Force to Be Reckoned With

Sights and smells rose and assaulted me, choked and gashed me, and the scars remain yet. They will until my dying day. I had never dreamed that people lived like that in our city.

— *Albion Fellows Bacon, 1914*

Bacon was horrified by what she saw when she went to visit Evansville's tenements, where the city's poorest families lived. Women and children "boiled over every window and door" in dilapidated, garbage-ridden buildings, often with little running water. She had read about such tenement conditions in places such as New York City and Chicago, but she could not believe they existed in her city. She joined the city's Visiting Nurse Circle, the Evansville Flower Mission, the Working Girls' Association, and a local chapter of the Young Women's Christian Association (YWCA). Within a few years, state legislators would know her name.

In 1907 Bacon drafted a tenement regulation bill for Evansville that was eventually passed by the city council. The following year, she addressed the Indiana Conference of Charities and Correction in South Bend on the topic "The Housing Problem of Indiana." Using her Evansville bill as a model, Bacon gradually gained statewide support for a similar housing bill that would apply to the entire state. In January 1909 the homemaker and mother of four spoke before a joint session of the all-male State General Assembly, delivering an impressive, well-reasoned appeal. On March 3, 1909, Bacon's bill had garnered enough support to become a law, and Governor Thomas Riley Marshall signed the bill. The next day the *Evansville Press* headline declared, "Law Framed by Mrs. Bacon Now on Books."

AS A WAR MEASURE

The Country is Asking of Women Service	Women Are Asking of The Country
AS	
FARMERS	
MECHANICS	
NURSES and DOCTORS	
MUNITION WORKERS	
MINE WORKERS	
YEOMEN	
GAS MAKERS	
BELL BOYS	
MESSENGERS	ENFRANCHISEMENT
CONDUCTORS	
MOTORMEN	
ARMY COOKS	
TELEGRAPHERS	
AMBULANCE DRIVERS	
ADVISORS TO THE COUNCIL OF NATIONAL DEFENSE	
AND	
The Country is Getting It !	Are the Women Going to Get It ?

National Woman Suffrage Publishing Company, Inc. 154   171 Madison Ave., New York City

Women's Rights Poster

In the early twentieth century, women actively participated in community organizations and addressed political issues. Their move into the public sphere continued during the United States' involvement in the First World War in 1917 and 1918. Yet as this poster points out, for all that they contributed to the country, women still did not have the right to vote.

COLLECTIONS OF THE INDIANA HISTORICAL SOCIETY

Bacon considered her achievement merely a beginning. The 1909 bill had been watered down. For several years Bacon worked to build a stronger coalition to refuel Indiana's housing reform movement. In 1913, with a Progressive climate in state politics, she lobbied for nothing that "decency does not demand . . . simply light and air, water, drainage, provision for waste and a degree of privacy, without which decency is difficult and home life is impossible." On February 26, 1913, the General Assembly passed Senate Bill 118, making Indiana a leader in housing reform legislation.

Women's Suffrage

It was a point of pride with me to avoid all the little things that cause the reproachful remark "That's just like a woman," and to take all the fates of war, at least outwardly, in the calm impersonal way men do.

— *Albion Fellows Bacon,* Beauty for Ashes *(1914)*

Bacon was aware of other women reformers championing women's right to vote, but housing reform was always her top priority. She did not publicly hop on the women's suffrage bandwagon. One historian calls Bacon an "inadvertent" feminist. While she eventually endorsed women's suffrage, it was from a standpoint of practicality rather than from the basic sentiment of equality. Rather, for Bacon, women's votes were a means to an end—advancing many of the reforms she worked for.

Bacon remained a social activist, though she slowed down when her health began to decline. She passed away at home at age sixty-eight. Her daughter Joy put it simply, "Mother just burned herself out." She is buried in Evansville's Oak Hill Cemetery. Today, part of Bacon's legacy lives on in Evansville through Albion Flats, a historic housing unit downtown, and the Albion Fellows Bacon Center, a non-profit organization that works to eliminate domestic abuse.

Winning the Right to Vote

Industrialization affected women just as it did men. Time-saving devices aided women in doing household tasks that decreased the amount of time it took them to finish their work, making it possible for middle-class women to venture from their homes. Some women joined garden clubs and literary societies, while others were eager to improve their communities through charitable work and other forms of community housekeeping. The middle class women who participated in these efforts gained new skill sets in organization and publicity as well as in public speaking. Women civic reformers of Bacon's day applied these skills in a man's world to succeed in reaching their objectives in ways they felt would improve their cities—through housing reform, child labor regulations, prohibition, and women's rights.

Reform was gradual in the Progressive Era, but especially so in cautious Indiana. One by one, new laws improved life for Americans and awarded equal rights to a growing number of people. Although women did much of the heavy lifting in social reform, they did so without the right to vote. Finally, in 1920, thanks to the work of thousands of woman suffragists and social crusaders such as Albion Fellows Bacon, they gained that right with the Nineteenth Amendment to the U.S. Constitution.

Votes for Women Button, ca. 1900

Similar to politicians, suffragists used buttons and banners to spread their message.

Selected Bibliography

Bacon, Albion Fellows. *Beauty for Ashes.* New York: Dodd, Mead, and Company, 1914. Internet Archive, https://archive.org/details/beautyforashes01baco.

Barrows, Robert G. *Albion Fellows Bacon: Indiana's Municipal Housekeeper.* Bloomington: Indiana University Press, 2000.

Benjamin Harrison Presidential Site: Championing the Values and Legacy of the 23rd President, http://www.presidentbenjaminharrison.org/.

Bennett, Jeff, and Richard D. Feldman. "The Most Useful Citizen in Indiana: John N. Hurty and the Public Health Movement." *Traces of Indiana and Midwestern History* 12 (Summer 2000): 34–43.

Bennett, Lee F., ed. *Proceedings of the Indiana Academy of Science, 1916.* Fort Wayne: Fort Wayne Printing Company, 1917. Archive.org, https://archive.org/details/proceedingsofind1916indi.

Beveridge, Albert J. *The March of the Flag: Beginning of Greater America.* Indianapolis: N.p., 1898. Fordham University: The Jesuit University of New York, http://www.fordham.edu/halsall/mod/1898beveridge.asp.

Bodenhamer, David J., and Robert G. Barrows. *The Encyclopedia of Indianapolis.* Bloomington, IN: Indiana University Press, 1994.

Boomhower, Ray E. "William Miller Herschell." Indiana Journalism Hall of Fame, http://indianajournalismhof.org/2002/01/william-miller-herschell/.

Braeman, John. *Albert J. Beveridge: American Nationalist.* Chicago: University of Chicago Press, 1971.

Calhoun, Charles W. *Benjamin Harrison.* American Presidents Series. New York: Henry Holt and Company, 2005.

"Caroline Lavina Scott Harrison, 1832–1892: Mrs. Benjamin Harrison." Caroline Scott Harrison Chapter DAR, http://www.darindiana.org/csh/moment_in_history.html.

"FDA's Origin and Functions." Food and Drug Administration, http://www.fda.gov/AboutFDA/WhatWeDo/History/Origin/default.htm.

First Ladies Research. National First Ladies Library, http://www.firstladies.org/biographies/.

Foster, Harriet McIntire. *Mrs. Benjamin Harrison: The First President–General of the National Society of the Daughters of the American Revolution.* N.p., 1908.

Hahn, Patricia. "Orchids and Art." *Daughters of the American Revolution Magazine* (February 1993). Caroline Scott Harrison Chapter DAR, http://www.darindiana.org/csh/orchids.htm.

Harstad, Peter. "Thomas R. Marshall." In *The Governors of Indiana,* eds. Linda C. Gugin and James E. St. Clair. Indianapolis: Indiana Historical Society, 2006, 232–42.

Heritage. Lilly, http://www.lilly.com/about/heritage/Pages/heritage.aspx.

Hurty, John N. "Review of Public Health Work in Indiana." *Journal of the Indiana State Medical Association* 11, no. 5 (May 15, 1918): 1–7.

"Inaugural Address of Benjamin Harrison." The Avalon Project: Documents in Law, History and Diplomacy. Yale Law School, Lillian Goldman Law Library, in memory of Sol Goldman, http://avalon.law.yale.edu/19th_century/harris.asp.

Indiana Historical Bureau. "Public Health in Indiana." *The Indiana Historian* (March 1998). http://www.in.gov/history/files/publichealth.pdf.

Indiana State Board of Health Monthly Bulletin 14, no. 4 (April 1911). IUPUI Scholar Works, Indiana University–Purdue University, Indianapolis, https://scholarworks.iupui.edu/bitstream/handle/1805/2556/im-iumed-iph-1911-v14n4.pdf?sequence=1.

Indiana University and Indiana State Archives, 2008. *Fit to Breed? The History and Legacy of Indiana Eugenics, 1907–2007,* exhibition. Digital archive and timeline, http://www.iupui.edu/~fit2brd/.

Journal of the House of Representatives of the State of Indiana during the Sixty-First Session of the General Assembly. Indianapolis: William Burford, 1899.

Levine, Daniel. "The Social Philosophy of Albert J. Beveridge." *Indiana Magazine of History* 58, no. 2 (June 1962): 101–16.

Lockridge, Ross F. "Benjamin Harrison Memorial Home." *Indiana Magazine of History* 34, no. 3 (September 1938): 307–18.

Lockwood, Mary S., and Emily Lee Sherwood, *Story of the Records D.A.R.* Washington, DC: George E. Howard, 1906.

Lynch, William O. "Review of *Abraham Lincoln: 1809–1858*, by Albert J. Beveridge." *Indiana Magazine of History* 24, no. 3 (September 1928): 214–16.

Madison, James H. *Hoosiers: A New History of Indiana.* Bloomington: Indiana University Press; Indianapolis: Indiana Historical Society Press, 2014.

———. *Indiana through Tradition and Change: A History of the Hoosier State and Its People, 1920–1945.* The History of Indiana 5. Indianapolis: Indiana Historical Society, 1982.

McDonald, Michael. "Voter Turnout." United States Elections Project, George Mason University, Department of Public and International Affairs, http://elections.gmu.edu/voter_turnout.htm.

Parker, James R. "Beveridge and the Election of 1912: Progressive Idealist or Political Realist." *Indiana Magazine of History* 63, no. 2 (June 1967): 103–14.

"Pass Eugenics Bill: Measure to Permit Sterilization of Unfit Persons in State Institutions." *Kokomo Daily Tribune*, February 24, 1927.

Phillips, Clifton J. *Indiana in Transition: The Emergence of an Industrial Commonwealth, 1880–1920.* The History of Indiana 4. Indianapolis: Indiana Historical Bureau and Indiana Historical Society, 1968.

Pierce, Jennifer Burek. "Indiana's Public Health Pioneer and History's Iron Pen: Recollecting the Professional Idealism of John N. Hurty, 1896–1925." *Indiana Magazine of History* 106, no. 3 (September 2010): 224–45.

"Presidential Key Events: Benjamin Harrison." Miller Center, University of Virginia, http://millercenter.org/president/bharrison/key-events.

Price, Nelson. *Indiana Legends: Famous Hoosiers from Johnny Appleseed to David Letterman.* Cincinnati: Emmis Books, 1997.

The Revised Statutes of Indiana, vol. 3. Chicago: E. B. Myers and Company, 1892.

Sharp, Harry. "Vasectomy as a Means of Preventing Procreation in Defectives." *Journal of the American Medical Association* 53 (December 4, 1909): 1897–1902. ScholarWorks @ Georgia State University, http://scholarworks.gsu.edu/cgi/viewcontent.cgi?article=1003&context=col_facpub.

Stern, Alexandra Minna. "'We Cannot Make a Silk Purse Out of a Sow's Ear': Eugenics in the Hoosier Heartland." *Indiana Magazine of History* 103, no. 1 (March 2007): 3–38.

Stewart, Ernest D. "The Populist Party in Indiana." *Indiana Magazine of History* 14, no. 4 (December 1918): 332–67.

Taylor, Robert M., Jr., and Connie A. McBirney, eds. *Peopling Indiana: The Ethnic Experience.* Indianapolis: Indiana Historical Society Press, 1996.

Wedderburn, Alex. J. *A Popular Treatise on the Extent and Character of Food Adulterations.* Washington, DC: Government Printing Office, 1890. Internet Archive, https://archive.org/details/populartreatiseo00wedd.

Young, James Harvey. "Two Hoosiers and the Two Food Laws of 1906." *Indiana Magazine of History* 88, no. 4 (December 1992): 303–19.

Zavodnyik, Peter. *The Rise of the Federal Colossus: The Growth of Federal Power from Lincoln to F.D.R.* Praeger Series on American Political Culture. Santa Barbara, CA: ABC-CLIO, 2011.

Essential Questions

1 Why was the political culture in Indiana so intense in the late nineteenth and early twentieth centuries?

2 In general, what type of government did Republicans of this era favor? What about Democrats?

3 Why is President Benjamin Harrison's administration considered by historians to be "activist" or "reform-minded"?

4 How was the state of Indiana a national leader in public health laws and practices? What role did Dr. John N. Hurty play in making Indiana a leader in public health?

5 What does the term "eugenics" mean? How was this practice employed in Indiana?

6 What Progressive reforms did Indiana Senator Albert Beveridge advocate?*

7 Why did the Republican Party split in the early 1900s?

8 What type of Progressive reforms did Albion Fellows Bacon lobby for?*

See student activities related to this question.

Indiana's Progressive Leaders

Industrialization, urbanization, and immigration transformed the Indiana landscape in both positive and negative ways. In the early twentieth century, Progressive reformers of both the Republican and Democratic Parties tried to mobilize government to tackle some of the negative consequences of urban and industrial growth. Progressives looked for ways to balance democracy and capitalism and focused on making the world a better place through the democratic process. They attempted to tackle the problems of modern society such as living and working conditions for laborers, the power of corporations, and corruption in government. They also urged people to be active participants in the democratic process as well as in private clubs and organizations as they worked to achieve "the greater good."

Activity 1: Albert J. Beveridge and American Imperialism

Introduction: In 1898, as a result of the Spanish American War, the United States gained from Spain control of Guam and Puerto Rico. Also as a result of this war, Cuba gained its independence, and the United States won the ability to purchase the Philippine Islands for $20 million.

In the Indiana Republican Party, Progressive reformers were led by Senator Albert J. Beveridge. Beveridge is best known as a proponent of American imperialism—the extension of American territory and influence throughout the world. Beveridge urged Americans to expand by taking over the governments of other nations, by force if necessary. Read the following passage from Beveridge's famous 1898 campaign speech, a defense of imperialism, "The March of the Flag," and consider the questions below it.

The Opposition tells us that we ought not to govern a people without their consent. I answer, The rule of liberty that all just government derives its authority from consent of the governed, applies only to those who are capable of selfgovernment[.] We govern the Indians without their consent, we govern our territories without their consent, we govern our children without their consent. How do they know what our government would be without their consent? Would not the people of the Philippines prefer the just, humane, civilizing government of this Republic to the savage, bloody rule of pillage and extortion from which we have rescued them? And, regardless of this formula of words made only for enlightened selfgoverning people, do we owe no duty to the world? Shall we turn these peoples back to the reeking hands from which we have taken them? Shall we abandon them, with Germany, England, Japan hungering for them? Shall we save them from those nations, to give them a selfrule of tragedy?

▶ With a partner, note vocabulary that is unfamiliar to you. Use the context of the sentence and a dictionary or thesaurus to determine the meaning of new vocabulary. Then, answer the following questions on a separate piece of paper:

1 According to Beveridge, opponents of American imperialism argued that a governed people must provide what in order for their government to be just?

2 What examples does Beveridge supply to refute this argument?

3 Why does Beveridge describe American imperialism as "a duty to the world"?

4 How do you think the citizens of the Philippines and of Guam and Puerto Rico might have felt about Beveridge's comment that they needed to be rescued from "a selfrule of tragedy"?

5 How are the reasoning and attitudes displayed by Beveridge in this excerpt consistent with the Progressive *goal* to make the world a better place?

6 How are the reasoning and attitudes displayed by Beveridge in this excerpt inconsistent with the *means* used by Progressives to achieve this goal (for example, the democratic process; encouraging citizens to be active participants in their society).

Activity 2: Albion Fellows Bacon

▶ Examine the tenement photograph that appears on page 189. Albion Fellows Bacon originally published this picture in her autobiography *Beauty for Ashes*. Bacon, as you have read, also urged Progressive reforms. An Evansville resident, Bacon enjoyed a sheltered upper-middle class life until she visited an Evansville tenement house. There, she witnessed the deplorable conditions in which the poor lived. Although she did not have the right to vote, she began to push for reforms to housing laws that would control or outlaw unsafe and unhealthy living conditions. She played a pivotal role in getting Indiana housing laws passed in 1909, 1913, and 1917.

Mentally divide the photograph into four quadrants. For each section, take note of the objects you see. Then, answer the following questions on a separate piece of paper:

1 Based upon the objects you observed in the space, what room does this appear to be (for example, bathroom, kitchen, bedroom, etc.)? Or, does the space appear to have more than one main function? What do you see that makes you say that?

2 What adjectives would you use to describe the conditions in this tenement?

3 How many coats do you see hanging on the wall? How many chairs do you see? How many beds are there? Make a guess about how many people live here.

4 Does it appear that fresh air, light, and fresh water are available to the residents? Cite evidence for your answer.

5 What kinds of laws or housing codes might improve the living conditions in a tenement such as this?

▶ In 1914, following a visit to an Evansville tenement, Bacon wrote, "Sights and smells rose and assaulted me, choked and gashed me, and the scars remain yet. . . . I had never dreamed that people lived like that *in our city*." (Bacon, 88) After studying the image again, close your eyes and imagine how you might experience the space through your different senses. Write a journal entry describing the space using all five senses—sight, smell, sound, touch, and taste. Your description should be at least one page long.

Activity References

Bacon, Albion Fellows. *Beauty for Ashes*. New York: Dodd, Mead, and Company, 1914. Internet Archive, https://archive.org/details/beautyforashes01baco.

Beveridge, Albert J. *The March of the Flag: Beginning of Greater America*. Indianapolis: N.p., 1898. Fordham University: The Jesuit University of New York, http://www.fordham.edu/halsall/mod/1898beveridge.asp.

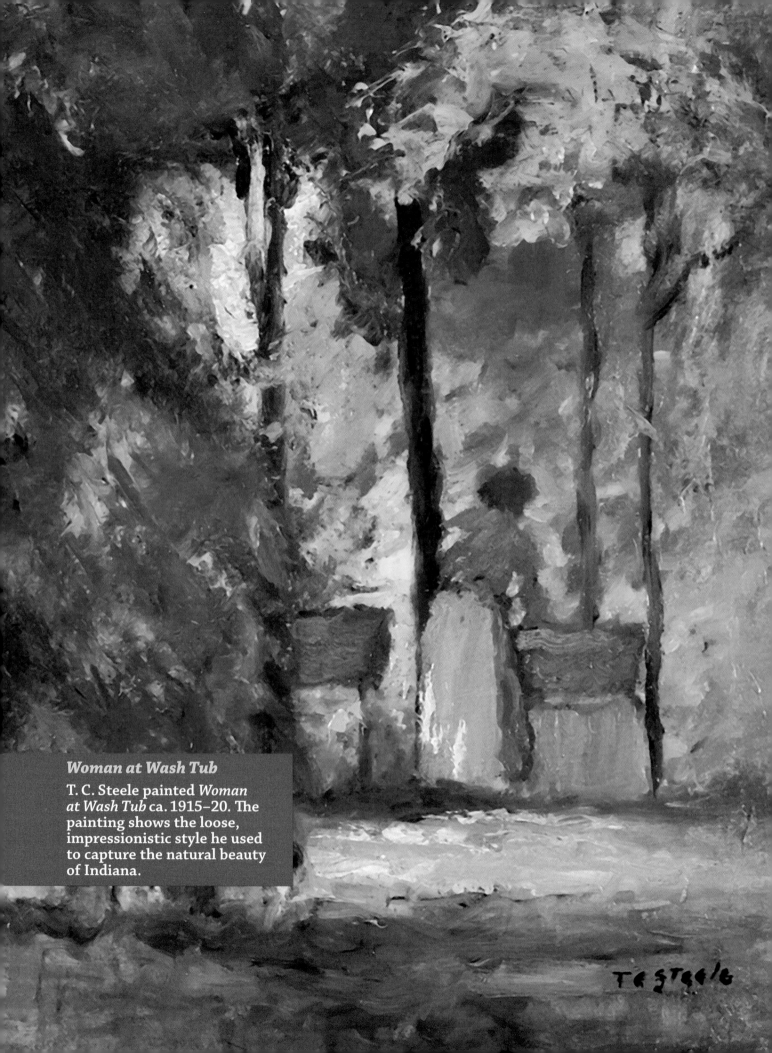

Woman at Wash Tub

T. C. Steele painted *Woman at Wash Tub* ca. 1915–20. The painting shows the loose, impressionistic style he used to capture the natural beauty of Indiana.

8

The Roaring Twenties

During no other period in the history of the world was there such a revolutionary change in the manners and customs of the American people, such a rising tide of prosperity, or such lawlessness. It was the decade of the gin-mill, the speakeasy, the flapper, flaming youth, bootleggers and gangsters.

— *"The Roaring Twenties" Saturday Spectator, Terre Haute, Indiana, November 11, 1939*

Everything seemed new and exciting in the 1920s. Change often meant progress, including improvements in daily life. Many Hoosiers now had radios, flush toilets, cars, telephones, sewing machines, and fancy stores jammed with enticing goods. But the changes also threatened traditional ways.

The "Roaring Twenties" followed a decade of contradictions, beginning with a golden age of the arts and closing with "a war to end all wars." The second decade of the twentieth century truly encompassed both the best of times and the worst of times.

A Golden Age?

Hoosiers had good reasons to be proud when they celebrated the state's one-hundredth birthday in 1916. Then and later they would look back on the last couple of decades of the nineteenth century and the first years of the twentieth as a Golden Age.

The turn of the twentieth century ushered in a Golden Age in art and literature in Indiana. Painters and writers seemed to spring from the Indiana soil. The number of best-selling books by Indiana authors exceeded that from any other state except New York. An oft-told story featured author Opie Read visiting Fort Wayne, Indiana. Aware of the state's literary reputation, he invited any writer in the audience to stand up, at which point all but one person rose. When the visitor commented on the elderly man who remained seated he was told, "'Oh, no, he writes too. He's just deef [deaf] and didn't hear the question.'"

James Whitcomb Riley

James Whitcomb Riley was and remains a beloved poet of many Hoosiers, both young and old. This photo was taken in the front yard of his Indianapolis home in 1916.

The most popular of Indiana's Golden Age authors were the poet James Whitcomb Riley (1849–1916) and the novelist Booth Tarkington (1869–1946). Riley's poetry expressed longing for an idealized rural and small-town past. Generations of schoolchildren memorized "The Old Swimmin' Hole," "When the Frost Is on the Punkin," and "Little Orphant Annie." Heard in his lyrics, journalist Irvin Cobb wrote, were "the click of the mowing-machine in the wheat, the gurgle of the catbird in the paw-paw thicket, the ripple of the sunfish's fins in the creek." Riley's poems created

for Indiana the most popular expressions of pioneer values and Hoosier traditions of the time.

Tarkington's books, often set in a fictionalized Indianapolis, were almost as well-known as Riley's poetry. Tarkington won Pulitzer Prizes for two of his novels, *The Magnificent Ambersons* (1918) and *Alice Adams* (1921). Throughout these two novels Tarkington explores the social problems resulting from urban and industrial growth with a focus on class issues and threats to the traditional individualism and stability at the core of Hoosier values. In his novels, his beloved Indianapolis seems at times alien and cold, consumed by a zeal to build more factories and suburbs as it spreads outward under a pall of sooty smoke.

Less popular in Indiana than Riley and Tarkington was Theodore Dreiser (1871–1945). Although Dreiser, too, drew on his Indiana childhood, unlike the idealist's perspective of Riley and Tarkington, Dreiser wrote in a grimly realistic manner about poverty, corruption, and prostitution, reflecting what he had witnessed in Terre Haute and Evansville. His first masterpiece, *Sister Carrie* (1900), shocked many. To Riley, Dreiser's ultra realistic writing was "'feverish nasty stuff,'" with "'no right to exist.'" The reluctance of traditional Hoosiers to accept him as one of their own tells us as much about

WWI Propaganda Poster

This WWI propaganda poster, ca. 1914–18, demonstrates how it is easier to fight an enemy that is dehumanized—as is the bloody-fingered figure at the top of this image. Americans dehumanized the Germans by referring to them as brutish "Huns." However, their rhetoric also negatively affected German Americans, who suppressed their culture during this period to avoid prejudice against them.

Freedom of the Open Road

In the 1920s, prosperity and new technology opened a wide range of options for Hoosiers to spend their free time, such as taking road trips across America. This group from Indiana, including Willis and Isabelle Miller, traveled to Pike's Peak in Colorado in 1929.

Indiana culture as does their eager embrace of Riley and Tarkington.

Indiana's painters were part of this Golden Age too. They first earned national praise with an exhibition in Chicago in 1894 titled "Five Hoosier Painters," which showed the work of T. C. Steele, J. Ottis Adams, William Forsyth, Otto Stark, and Richard Gruelle. This Hoosier group mostly painted rural landscapes and had little interest in cities or factories. The best known was T. C. Steele. Steele eventually settled in rural Brown County, where a flourishing artists' colony developed before World War I. Golden Age paintings have remained very popular into the twenty-first century. The Indiana State Museum has a large collection as do other museums and galleries.

The Great War Threatens Democracy at Home, 1917–1918

In 1916 Indiana celebrated its first one hundred years as a state. Early the next year the United States declared war on Germany. Many Hoosiers were not sure at first that America should join the near world-

wide fight, but most supported the cause as their patriotic duty. Eventually, however, the Great War, later known as World War I, demonstrated that war can threaten democracy and civil liberties at home.

Many leaders thought Americans needed a big push to get behind the war effort, and so they began a propaganda campaign to persuade citizens to support America's war involvement. Some fierce propaganda posters and other media depicted Germans as barbarians and suppressed the state's vibrant German American culture. The vast majority of Indiana's German-language newspapers ceased publication. German street names and music disappeared. The center of German American culture in Indianapolis, *Das Deutsche Haus*, was renamed the Athenaeum. Beer became *verboten* (forbidden) because of its close German association.

Some zealous patriots targeted the teaching of the German language in schools. The foreign language was now, one state legislator proclaimed, "'the German poison that must of necessity corrupt the channels of patriotism in this land.'" German language instruction was not just frowned upon; it was against the law. The

Indiana General Assembly passed a ban with only one vote against it—that of an Irish American Catholic from South Bend.

Kurt Vonnegut (1922–2007), the Indianapolis-born author, stated later that his German American parents were ashamed of their heritage and "resolved to raise me without acquainting me with the language or the literature or the music or the oral family histories which my ancestors had loved. They volunteered to make me ignorant and rootless as proof of their patriotism." This led to what Vonnegut called a "dismantling and quiet burial of a culture." By the time Vonnegut served during World War II in Germany, Indiana's German culture had nearly disappeared. Not until the late twentieth century did Hoosiers begin to rediscover their German roots.

Patriotic duty required 100 percent "Americanism," a term widely used during the war and in the twenties. Senator James Watson told the 1917 meeting of the Indiana State Teachers Association that "there are no real German-Americans today; they all ought to be Americans." Indiana Governor James Goodrich claimed that "There can be no middle course in this war. There are just two kinds of people in America—patriots and traitors." All ethnic Hoosiers needed careful watching and should melt into the American pot. In Gary, where nearly half the population was foreign born, the Calumet Township Council of Defense worked to stamp out "disloyalty, sedition or treason." People could be and were arrested for speaking out against the war. The anti-war speeches of labor union organizer Eugene V. Debs earned him a ten-year prison sentence under the Espionage Act of 1917.

Storms Ahead

Wartime patriotism taught Hoosiers to fear differences and demand conformity. Ironically, this form of patriotism contradicted some of the state's long-held traditions of freedom. Thus, the Great War laid a base for the troubling twenties. Indiana had long been divided by ethnicity, race, religion, gender, and class. The decade of the twenties brought those divisions to the surface, particularly with the rise of the Ku Klux Klan.

Nevertheless, there were bursts of sunlight in the twenties. "Hoosier Hysteria" was born as basketball became one of Indiana's favorite pastimes; the automobile continued its rise in popularity; and the rhythms of jazz and ragtime came to symbolize new types of freedom.

8.1

A Klan State?

"I did not sell the Klan in Indiana on hatreds—that is not my way. I sold the Klan on Americanism, on reform."

— D. C. Stephenson, Grand Dragon of the Ku Klux Klan in Indiana, ca. 1924

Clarifying the Klan

The Ku Klux Klan (KKK) can be a confusing subject to study. That confusion stems largely from the fact that there have been multiple Klan groups in American history. The Klan of the 1920s was distinct from the other groups.

Nationwide, there have been two important Klan groups known especially for their violence, racism, and opposition to civil rights laws. The Klan first appeared in the South after the Civil War. Its members were often cloaked in white hoods and used violent means to deny former slaves their freedom and to end Reconstruction laws, which aimed to give African Americans equal standing with whites. This group did not exist in the North.

The most recent strain of the Klan emerged in the 1960s in resistance to the Civil Rights Movement and was characterized by bombings and murders. This newer version of the hate group had very little impact in Indiana as evidenced by a 1999 Klan rally at the Indiana State House. The rally attracted the media, five hundred police officers, fifty anti-Klan protestors, and a scant thirteen Klan members shouting "White Power" through a weak public address system.

KKK Parade

Members of the Ku Klux Klan parade in Anderson, Indiana, in 1922. According to the writing on the photograph, this was the largest crowd ever seen in Anderson to that date. Public KKK parades occurred in many Indiana towns during the 1920s, always with the display of the American flag as seen in this picture.

ANNOUNCING A TREMENDOUS

KU KLUX

KLAN CELEBRATION

- AT -

KOKOMO, INDIANA

Saturday, June 30, July 1, 2, 3 & 4

OTHER REALMS ARE INVITED TO PARTICIPATE

Greatest gathering of National and State Speakers ever assembled together before speaking on vital subjects of the conditions of our country.

Continuous program, best of band music and many surprise features.

MELFALFA PARK

FOUR MILES WEST OF KOKOMO. GO WEST ON SYCAMORE STREET PIKE THREE MILES (Look for Cross Road Marker.) TURN SOUTH ONE MILE TO WILDCAT CREEK BRIDGE.

Come on Saturday and Camp. Plenty of cold spring water. Toilet facilities for both men and women.

Bring your Drum Corps, Bands and Glee Clubs. Bring your bathing Suits. Swimming pool in operation FREE to everyone. Pool lighted at night. Plan now to charter a Car, a Bus or come as an Auto Caravan.

Ground well lighted at night for those arriving during the night.

Those intending to camp are invited to have their mail addressed to R. R. 1, Box 60, Kokomo, Indiana, and it will be delivered to the grounds daily.

Concession Stand in operation day and night. Don't bother taking lunch. Plenty of eats at the right price.

Come one and all!   This celebration open to public!

GENERAL ADMISSION 25c FOR ALL FIVE DAYS.   FREE PARKING AND CAMPING PRIVILEGES. (Under Twelve Years Admission Free)

FOR ADDITIONAL BILLS OR INFORMATION: ADDRESS R. R. NO. 1, BOX 60, KOKOMO, INDIANA

Klan Celebration Poster

This 1923 poster announces a five-day KKK celebration at Melfalfa (Malfalfa) Park in Kokomo, Indiana. Besides uniting members around its narrow ideas of who an American should be, the Ku Klux Klan of the 1920s served as a social organization. This celebration featured speeches, live music, swimming, and concession stands.

The KKK of the 1920s

Indiana's Klan of the 1920s was part of a new national movement of the Klan. However, this new strain of the movement was less stigmatized and less prone to flamboyant outbursts than either of the national movements that preceded or followed it. As across the country, the members of Indiana's 1920s-era Klan included hard-working, middle-class white people—ministers, mayors, shopkeepers, and factory workers. Klansmen came from cities, towns, and farms—more of them from northern and central Indiana than from the southern part of the state. One scholar who has analyzed membership lists estimates that approximately one-quarter or more of the state's native-born white men joined as did thousands of Hoosier women. Many Americans joined the Klan out of a sense of outrage and fear over what they saw as dangerous social forces in the 1920s—booze, sex, jazz, and declining family values. As elsewhere in the United States, Indiana's 1920s-era Klan was primarily an organization whose membership used fear and intimidation—and only occasional violence—as a way to beat down those social elements it considered a threat to white Protestant Americanism.

Symbols and Beliefs of the KKK

We do not believe in popery. History does not believe in it. Progress does not believe in it. Liberty does not believe in it. Free institutions do not believe in it. Democracy does not believe in it. The light of Christian truth does not believe in it.

— *Methodist newspaper* Western Christian Advocate, *February 1922*

Klan symbols in the 1920s were the cross and the American flag—symbols of their core values of Christianity and patriotism. The burning cross—long an emblem of Klan terror—symbolized Christ as the light of the world, purification by fire, and the beacon of truth. The Klan's white-robed members came from a variety of Protestant denominations. Their white robes and hooded masks represented the white race and the purity of Protestantism—as the Klan perceived it. The mask performed other functions, too. It concealed the identity of the person wearing it, thus reducing the significance of the individual in the community of Christian fellowship. The Klan's strong demonstration of religious belief was the foundation of its appeal to ordinary Hoosiers and to ordinary Americans throughout the country.

The Klan of the 1920s dedicated itself to fighting what members believed to be an erosion of spiritual and civic values threatening the state and the nation. For example, Klan members considered alcohol a major source of moral corruption and worked closely with the Anti-Saloon League to insist on enforcement of national prohibition, which began in 1920. The Klan also pushed for passage of the Wright Bone Dry law in 1925 that criminalized possession of empty bottles or kegs that had contained liquor. Even the odor of alcohol lingering in a container was evidence enough to be arrested. First-time violators received thirty-day jail sentences.

The Klan considered white, native-born Protestants such as themselves to be the only true Americans and stood firm against the spread of racial or ethnic diversity. One of their spokespersons claimed that "there are nations and races that can never by any process of education or assimilation become Americanized, and we have determined that the time shall come when there will be no place in America for people who cannot think in terms of Americanism." Klan members counted Catholics among the most dangerous of these groups. The Klan dug up centuries of anti-Catholic propaganda to justify their claim that the Catholic Church was a foreign religion and that its followers did what the Pope told them to do. The *Fiery Cross*, an Indianapolis Klan newspaper, printed allegations of immoral priests and Catholic conspirators trying to tear down Protestant America. One Protestant minister voiced a popular sentiment when stating that Catholics "cannot continue allegiance to the Pope of Rome and still be loyal to the institutions of America."

The 1920s-era Klan also singled out other groups as posing threats to white America, including immigrants, especially those coming from eastern and southern Europe, Jews, and—in the group's most obvious tie to its earlier and later incarnations—African

Americans. For the most part, the Klan used a combination of public propaganda and legislative pressure to suppress the groups they considered undesirable. To the delight of many Klan members, in 1924 the U.S. Congress passed a law severely restricting immigration. Meanwhile, the White Supremacy League and related citizen groups pushed for segregation in housing and public schools.

The Klan at Work

This is a free country and no masked g[a]ng of law breakers, whose leaders should be sent to the penitentiary for the crimes they are committing, with the sanction of the prosecutor one of their number, will be allowed to terrify free American citizens very much longer.

— Muncie [Indiana] Post–Democrat, *June 16, 1922*

There is a popular misconception that the Klan did all of its damage with a lynch rope. Yet outright violence was rarely the Klan's way in the 1920s. Instead, the organization relied on a combination of intimidation and persuasion. Intimidation took the form of burning a cross in someone's front yard or threatening to boycott a business whose proprietor refused to join the KKK or to buy ads in the *Fiery Cross*. The Klan newspaper also published the names of Catholic-owned businesses so that Protestants would not patronize them and urged the boycotting of Jewish-owned businesses. More aggressive Klan members resorted to vigilantism. Claiming that law enforcement was weak or corrupt, Klan enforcers stopped cars to search for alcohol or raided gambling and prostitution dens.

The Klan of the 1920s used persuasion as its main means of recruiting members. Protestant ministers were among the chief persuaders. Many Klan-related ministers would praise the Klan from the pulpit and gladly accept offerings from Klansmen who marched up the church aisle on Sunday mornings. Pamphlets and speeches helped spread the word, and movie theaters showed Klan films. Gennett Studios in Richmond, Indiana—site of early jazz recordings performed by black musicians—produced records from Klan sheet music.

The Klan also favored big public events, such as rallies and parades, where they sought to create a community of like-minded Americans. Many *klaverns*, or local Klan units, had their own bands that marched behind a car carrying an electrically lighted cross. One of the largest rallies in Indiana took place at Kokomo's Malfalfa Park on July 4, 1923. Thousands of white Protestants traveled long distances to the "Konklave in Kokomo." The day was festive. There was a picnic on the banks of Wildcat Creek, a parade, and a few performances of the hymn "Onward Christian Soldiers." The day also included two cross burnings.

Flexing Political Muscle

With its strength in numbers, the Klan inevitably moved into politics. Although Republicans tended to be more sympathetic to the Klan, many Democrats also had ties to the organization. The Klan was instrumental in electing candidates who reflected its ideals. The organization published information about each candidate's religion, stance on prohibition, and friendliness to the Klan. During the 1924 elections, Klan support ensured the election of many local and state officials, including that of Republican Ed Jackson as Indiana's governor. Jackson was a close friend of Indiana Grand Dragon David Curtis "D. C." Stephenson. After the new governor's inaugural speech, Stephenson joined Jackson and 150 leading Republicans for a gala banquet at which poet William Herschell recited his "Ain't God Good to Indiana" poem.

In 1925 the Indiana General Assembly had a Republican majority. This gave Indiana Klan leaders great hope for the passage of a long list of Klan-backed legislation that centered on Americanism and schools. One of the most publicized bills prohibited Catholic nuns from wearing "religious garb" while teaching in some schools. The bill failed to pass—as did all of the Klan's major proposals except for the bone dry prohibition law. Seeds of dissent were germinating. As some legislators spoke against Klan bills and in defense of religious or individual freedom, deep splits began to emerge within the Klan leadership.

Fiery Summons

Faithful and Esteemed Klansman: _____

A special meeting has been called of members and **worthy** former members of your organization to be held Thursday night, March 11, 1926, at the hour of 7:45 o'clock, in Indianapolis, Ind., at Tomlinson Hall.

I will be present upon this occasion to discuss with you certain conditions and circumstances now existing in your community and state. Events are moving which have a deep significance to you. In justice to the solemn oath you have taken you owe it to yourself, and to your family to be present at this meeting. "Learn the true facts."

If you fail to answer, by your presence, this summons (Providence alone preventing) you may never be permitted to cross the threshold of a Klavern again.

Can you be depended upon?

Faithfully yours,
In the Sacred Unfailing Bond,

W. Pee Smith

GRAND DRAGON,
REALM OF INDIANA

P. S. Present this summons to the Klexter of the Klavern upon admittance.

Fiery Summons

This "fiery summons" of 1926 calls KKK members together for a meeting at the time when the organization was in decline. The invitation aims to intimidate, stating that if a member does not respond he or she "may never be permitted to cross the threshold of a Klavern again."

D. C. Stephenson and the Decline of the Klan

Indiana has a political world. One D. C. Stephenson was the self-appointed monarch of this world for some time. . . . He boasted that his word was "law in Indiana."

— *W. H. Settle in the* Indianapolis News, *December 30, 1925*

Although Stephenson boasted to be the law in Indiana, his reign lasted for but a brief time. Born to sharecroppers, or tenant farmers, in Texas in 1891, Stephenson made his way to Indiana in 1920, lured by the prospect of a job. Soon after arriving, he joined the KKK in Evansville and swiftly rose through the organization's ranks. On July 4, 1923, he was inducted as Indiana's Grand Dragon (head of the state's Klan) at the Konklave in Kokomo. By the end of that year,

Indiana had one of the largest Klan memberships in the country.

Stephenson had many powerful associates in state government, including Governor Jackson. He had high hopes of using Klan contacts to shape state legislation. In fact, Stephenson was much more interested in the Klan to gain political power than because he shared its beliefs. He also had a lust for alcohol and attractive young women. His unbridled appetites, coupled with excessive pride and self-confidence, would bring about his fall.

In March 1925 Madge Oberholtzer, a young woman who met Stephenson at Jackson's inauguration, committed suicide by swallowing poison. Before she died, Oberholtzer offered deathbed testimony that Stephenson had sexually assaulted her on a Chicago-

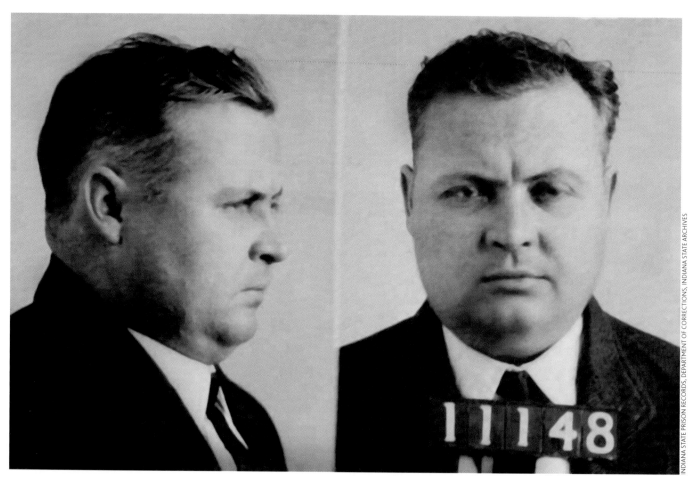

D. C. Stephenson

David Curtis Stephenson, leader of the Ku Klux Klan in Indiana, was arrested for sexually assaulting and contributing to the death of a young woman named Madge Oberholtzer. This mug shot was taken when he was imprisoned for murder in the second degree in 1926. His arrest led to the discovery of political scandals involving the Klan.

bound train. Stephenson was tried in Noblesville and convicted of second-degree murder. Other scandals soon came to light involving the Klan and high-ranking politicians, including Jackson.

The Klan lost its grip on Indiana as Republicans tried to distance themselves from the organization. Stephenson's conviction played a part in the group's downfall, as did corruption and turmoil within the organization. External forces were at work, too. Labor unions condemned the Klan. The Indiana Bar Association warned in 1923 that the group threatened to replace courts with "secret tribunals." Although many newspapers avoided criticizing the Klan, others took it to task. The *Fort Wayne Journal–Gazette* consistently spoke out against the Klan; and in 1928 the *Indianapolis Times* won a Pulitzer Prize for its Klan investigations.

Groups that were persecuted by the Klan most openly opposed it. Catholic and Jewish opposition were equally strong. In Indianapolis, Rabbi Morris Feuerlicht often spoke against the Klan, stating in one sermon, "'These white-robed men . . . should not be allowed to take the Bible away from us.'" A south side Indianapolis grocery store defiantly changed its name from the American Grocery Store to Shapiro's and placed Stars of David on its front. Black Hoosiers also challenged the Klan, notably in moving away from Jackson's Republican Party. Since the Civil War, African Americans had consistently voted for the Republican Party—known to many at the time as the party of Lincoln.

There is no single answer to the question of why Hoosiers or other Americans joined the Klan. Some were true believers in the group's moral crusade. Others joined because the Klan provided a sense of community and belonging. And, of course, some opportunistic politicians saw it as an avenue to power and influence. The Klan's rapid growth during the 1920s was also the result of poor political leadership that did not question the Klan's activities.

Not surprisingly, Hoosier voter turnout dropped in the 1920s. This may have resulted from disgust over the state's mediocre political leadership or from the confusion caused by the Klan's meddling in politics. By the end of the decade, Indiana had survived its most serious political crisis since the Civil War. The Klan was dead in Indiana. Yet, it's memory endures to the present. Thoughtful Hoosiers today can sense the dark blot on the fabric of the Roaring Twenties. Perhaps that awareness has inspired moderation and equity amidst the religious, ethnic, and racial diversity that exists in twenty-first century Indiana.

8.2

"Hoosier Hysteria": The Rise of Basketball in Indiana

"Welcome to Indiana basketball."

— *Coach Norman Dale in the 1986 movie* Hoosiers

While the Ku Klux Klan was dying out in Indiana, basketball was on the rise. Basketball was the perfect game for small-town Indiana. Only five kids needed to show up. A ball and a basket sufficed for equipment. Enthusiasm for the high school game reached massive proportions by the mid-twentieth century. At one point, the state boasted fifteen of the nation's sixteen largest high school gymnasiums. In these Hoosier cathedrals on cold Friday nights, fans created a warm community focused on the home team. "Basketball," wrote historian David Halberstam, "became critical in determining a town's identity."

Birth of a Tradition

"Basket Ball" was born in 1891, when James Naismith, a Canadian American physical education teacher at a Springfield, Massachusetts, YMCA, sought to develop an indoor athletic activity that could be played during New England's long winters. The game spread like a wild fire and was soon played in Indiana. By the early 1900s, basketball was wildly popular in many of the state's high schools. The Indiana High School Athletic Association (IHSAA) formed in 1903. By 1916, 450 schools had joined. The first Indiana high school state boys basketball tournament took place in 1911—the same year the Indianapolis 500 debuted—with Crawfordsville High School taking home the trophy.

Early Cinderella Teams

"Basketball really had its origin in Indiana, which remains the center of the sport."

— *James Naismith, inventor of basketball, ca. 1925*

The first eight Indiana boys state champion teams came from a three-county, thirty-mile radius in the west-central portion of the state: Crawfordsville, 1911; Lebanon, 1912, 1917, 1918; Wingate, 1913, 1914; Thorntown, 1915; and Lafayette Jefferson, 1916. Led by Coach Ernest "Griz" Wagner, Franklin's "Wonder Five" won three consecutive championships in 1920, 1921, and 1922. Both Wagner and Wonder Five star player, Robert "Fuzzy" Vandivier, were installed as charter members of the Indiana Basketball Hall of Fame in 1962.

Girls Basketball Team, 1914

The Muncie High School Girls Basketball Team poses for a team picture in 1914. After its introduction in 1891, basketball quickly caught on in Indiana high schools—for boys and girls.

Hot Dogs, Artesians, and Wooden

"The size of our gyms astounded people from other parts of the country. . . . Before I entered high school, Martinsville built a gym that seated 5,200 people. The whole town had only 4,800, but we always filled the gym."

— *Basketball legend John Wooden, ca. 1982*

After Franklin's reign, Frankfort's Hot Dogs and Martinsville's Artesians duked it out for boys hardwood supremacy from 1923 to 1929. Under Coach Everett Case the Hot Dogs swept eleven straight regional titles from 1921 to 1931, a record which still stands. In 1939 Coach Glenn Curtis and his Martinsville Artesians tied Case for a career record of four state championships.

During his long career at Martinsville, Curtis mentored many outstanding players, but John Wooden stood in a league of his own. The Artesians' star player in their state championship season of 1927, Wooden went on to play for Purdue University where he made All American three years running. After coaching stints at South Bend Central High School and Indiana State University, Wooden went to the University of California at Los Angeles (UCLA) in 1948. There he became one of the most revered coaches in sports history. During Wooden's twenty-seven years at UCLA, the Bruins had a record 88-game winning streak and won ten National College Athletic Association (NCAA) titles in twelve years. A member of the founding class of the Naismith Memorial Basketball Hall of Fame, Wooden, a soft-spoken man known as much for his wisdom about life as for his athletic brilliance, passed away in 2010, a few months before his one hundredth birthday. He had received practically every honor that can be bestowed upon a sports figure. In 2009 *Sporting News* named Wooden "Greatest Coach of All Time." Today, the gym at his alma mater, Martinsville High School, bears his name, and there is a street in Martinsville named John R. Wooden Drive.

Hoosier Basketball Mythology— Milan and Beyond

"Our guys had a quiet confidence about them. They knew they were good and that it was going to take a good team to beat them. Bigger schools have the opinion that they should beat the smaller schools."

— *Milan boys basketball coach Marvin Wood, ca. 1954*

The golden age of Indiana high school basketball culminated in the 1954 David-and-Goliath showdown between Milan High School and Muncie Central. Before 1953 few people in Indiana knew the location of Milan, a town so tiny it did not even appear on some maps. Just a year later, as the town's boys high school

COURTESY OF INDIANA BASKETBALL HALL OF FAME

Wingate High School Pennant

This pennant celebrates Wingate High School's title as basketball champion in 1913 and 1914.

John Wooden at Indiana State University, 1947

John Wooden, back row left, coached the Indiana State University basketball team for two seasons from 1946 to 1948. In 1948 the team competed in the National Association of Intercollegiate Basketball Tournament. This was the first year that African American players were allowed to play in the tournament.

team prepared to play mighty Muncie Central for the state championship, Hoosiers turned their eyes to the small town in southeastern Indiana. Even though Milan High School had only 162 students and none of its players was over six feet, two inches tall, Milan won the state championship in large part because of Bobby Plump's fifteen-foot jump shot in the final seconds of the game. Fans, even those born after 1954, include that game—and that shot—among the greatest events in basketball history.

In 1997 the IHSAA divided the state's high schools into four classes, determined by school enrollment size. Before that, all high school teams in Indiana—regardless of size—played in a single division. Everyone got an equal shot at winning. Milan, the smallest school ever to win the state championship within a single-class tournament, could not have played against a large school under the new rules. To this day, some lament the end to the possibility of another Milan-style miracle, arguing that the multiclass system has deflated the spirit of Hoosier high school basketball.

Thirty years after the Milan miracle, two Hoosiers in Hollywood brought it to the big screen. Director David Anspaugh and writer Angelo Pizzo met as students at Indiana University. Both grew up hearing about the Milan story. They filmed the movie *Hoosiers* on location in Indiana. It was a huge hit that received two Oscar nominations. Tourists swamped tiny Milan after the film's release. Basketball, explained Anspaugh, was incredibly important to towns in Indiana. "'It is a religion,'" Anspaugh said. "'It's how communities and schools define themselves.'"

1954 Milan Basketball Team
The Milan Indians celebrate their 1954 Indiana State Championship victory over Muncie Central High School.

Chuck Taylors

Chuck Taylor, who got his start playing basketball in Columbus, Indiana, became well-known as a promoter for Converse All Star shoes, also known as "Chuck Taylors."

IHSAA Boys Basketball State Champions, 1911–1954

1911 | *Crawfordsville* **24** | *Lebanon* **17**
1912 | *Lebanon* **51** | *Franklin* **11**
1913 | *Wingate* **15** | *South Bend Jesse* **14** | 5 OT
1914 | *Wingate* **36** | *Anderson* **8**
1915 | *Thorntown* **33** | *Montmorenci* **10**
1916 | *Lafayette* **27** | *Crawfordsville* **26** | OT
1917 | *Lebanon* **34** | *Gary* **26**
1918 | *Lebanon* **24** | *Anderson* **20** | OT
1919 | *Bloomington* **18** | *Lafayette Jefferson* **15**
1920 | *Franklin* **31** | *Lafayette Jefferson* **13**
1921 | *Franklin* **35** | *Anderson* **22**
1922 | *Franklin* **26** | *Terre Haute Garfield* **15**
1923 | *Vincennes* **27** | *Muncie* **18**
1924 | *Martinsville* **36** | *Frankfort* **30**
1925 | *Frankfort* **34** | *Kokomo* **20**
1926 | *Marion* **30** | *Martinsville* **23**
1927 | *Martinsville* **26** | *Muncie* **23**
1928 | *Muncie* **13** | *Martinsville* **12**
1929 | *Frankfort* **29** | *Indianapolis Technical* **23**
1930 | *Washington* **32** | *Muncie* **21**

1931 | *Muncie* **31** | *Greencastle* **23**
1932 | *New Castle* **24** | *Winamac* **17**
1933 | *Martinsville* **27** | *Greencastle* **24**
1934 | *Logansport* **26** | *Indianapolis Technical* **19**
1935 | *Anderson* **23** | *Jeffersonville* **17**
1936 | *Frankfort* **50** | *Fort Wayne Central* **24**
1937 | *Anderson* **33** | *Huntingburg* **23**
1938 | *Fort Wayne South Side* **34** | *Hammond* **32**
1939 | *Frankfort* **36** | *Franklin* **22**
1940 | *Hammond Technical* **33** | *Mitchell* **21**
1941 | *Washington* **39** | *Madison* **33**
1942 | *Washington* **24** | *Muncie Burris* **18**
1943 | *Fort Wayne Central* **45** | *Lebanon* **40**
1944 | *Evansville Bosse* **39** | *Kokomo* **35**
1945 | *Evansville Bosse* **46** | *South Bend Riley* **36**
1946 | *Anderson* **67** | *Fort Wayne Central* **53**
1947 | *Shelbyville* **68** | *Terre Haute Garfield* **58**
1948 | *Lafayette Jefferson* **54** | *Evansville Central* **42**
1949 | *Jasper* **62** | *Madison* **61**
1950 | *Madison* **67** | *Lafayette Jefferson* **44**
1951 | *Muncie Central* **60** | *Evansville Reitz* **58**
1952 | *Muncie Central* **68** | *Indianapolis Technical* **49**
1953 | *South Bend Central* **42** | *Terre Haute Gerstmeyer* **41**
1954 | *Milan* **32** | *Muncie Central* **30**

8.3

Risky Business: Bootleg Booze, Flappers, and French Lick

People throughout the country wanted jazz and liquor. People were restless.

— *Hoagy Carmichael,* The Stardust Road *(1983)*

Not Your Father's Decade

Young people set the mood in the 1920s. Hoosier songwriter Hoagy Carmichael spoke for his generation when he said that as a college student in Bloomington, Indiana, he realized that "there was a wide world out there. . . . Being young, we knew it couldn't bend and push us around the way it had our fathers." Sociologists Robert and Helen Merrell Lynd, studying Muncie, Indiana, in the 1920s, agreed: "No two generations of Americans," they wrote, "have ever faced each other across as wide a gap in their customary attitudes and behavior as have American parents and children since the World War."

While young people such as Carmichael reveled in new freedoms and pursued new avenues of pleasure, older folks and church-going citizens were anxious about what they saw as rapidly increasing immorality: bootleg alcohol, gambling, racy Hollywood films, rising hemlines, and jazz—music that became the soundtrack of the era.

Jazz was a free and uninhibited form of music that inspired new dances such as the Charleston, with its fast, provocative moves favored by young women with bobbed hair and short skirts, known as "flappers." Traditionally minded folks considered such expression an "unholy mingling of the civilized with the savage," partly since it derived from African American culture.

Life in the Fast Lane

Nine-tenths of our crimes an' calamities are made possible by th' automobile. It has unleashed all th' pent-up criminal tendencies o' th' ages. It's th' central figure in murders, hold-ups, burglaries, accidents, elopements, failures an' abscondments. It has well nigh jimmed th' American home.

— *Kin Hubbard, ca. 1924*

In the 1920s the popularity and increasing affordability of the automobile made it possible for young people to take off down the road to a jazz club or a secluded dating spot. Dark movie theaters were another popular destination. Sex was an effective marketing strategy for films of the day. A Crawfordsville newspaper advertised a film called *Single Wives* as a chance to see women "who sometimes listen when forbidden love calls." A film called *Wild Company* showed in Marion, Indiana, promising "wild ways and jazz days," where "parents are indifferent and children in search of thrills pick their own paths for play."

"Hoosier Hop"

Sheet music for the song "Hoosier Hop." The song was used in the 1929 film *It's a Great Life*, showing that the new styles of music and dancing had caught on in Indiana. As the lyrics go, "It's a hick step, but a slick step called the Hoosier Hop. It's the high school kids invented the thing, grown up folks caught onto the swing."

Despite the fact that Prohibition had outlawed alcohol since 1920, illegal booze flowed. Speakeasies (illegal bars) popped up from rural crossroads to major cities. With them came illegal gambling and prostitution, vices that flourished in neighborhoods such as Terre Haute's booming red light district. Sometimes law enforcement and government officials turned away or even joined in the action. Police often lacked patrol cars, radios, or other tools of effective law enforcement. This gave lawbreakers the advantage in their pursuits—whether it was running whiskey or holding up a bank.

Opulence and Decadence in Orange County

All Irish Patriots (sex or color no bar) are cordially invited to visit the annual ball of the sons of Erin, to be held on Tuesday night, March 17. Grand March at 8:30. . . . Ladies must not appear in green bloomers. Gentlemen must wear more than their complexion.

— Announcement of the Saint Patrick's Day Ball at West Baden Springs Hotel, March 1896

In the late nineteenth and early twentieth centuries, people with money for expensive indulgences often headed to spas and hotels located near mineral springs that were believed to have medicinal properties. Two of America's most luxurious spas were located just a mile from each other in rural Orange County, Indiana—French Lick Springs Hotel and West

Policemen with Still

After conducting a raid on a Wanamaker, Indiana, farmhouse, policemen pose next to the alcohol distillation equipment they recovered in 1920. Anyone making or selling alcohol was subject to punishment during Prohibition.

PLUTO WATER
Trade Mark Registered

Pluto Water Advertisement
Pluto Water was bottled in French Lick, Indiana, and sold across the country with its trademark devil logo. Thomas Taggart, the owner of the French Lick Springs Hotel, advertised the water as a cure for a multitude of ills.

FRENCH LICK SPRINGS HOTEL CO.
FRENCH LICK, INDIANA

49555

Baden Springs Hotel. Southern Indiana's inadequate roads ensured that most people traveled to French Lick by train. Wealthy Chicagoans took the Monon Railroad on tracks that stopped at the front entrance of the French Lick Springs Hotel. At the peak of French Lick's popularity, affluent visitors would take long leisurely vacations there. They might stay as long as a month, taking the train to the Kentucky Derby in Louisville and then back north to see the Indianapolis 500.

A spa had operated in French Lick since the 1840s, but it was Thomas Taggart, mayor of Indianapolis from 1895 to 1901 and Democratic Party bigwig, who made the French Lick Springs Hotel a destination for the rich and famous. In 1901 Taggart and three business partners—a brewery owner in Terre Haute, a quarry owner, and a president of the Monon Railroad—purchased the existing French Lick hotel and its grounds. Over the next several years they renovated and expanded the property, including bathhouses and a golf course, sparing no expense for the first-class facilities. Taggart masterminded a national marketing campaign for the Pluto Water that he pumped from nearby Pluto Spring. He claimed that the water was helpful for "'diseases of the stomach, intestines, liver, gall bladder and ducts, auto-intoxication (toxins in the system), intestinal indigestion, gout . . . diseases of the heart and blood vessels, diseases of the urinary system, diseases of the skin, and diseases of the nervous system.'"

Celebrities including Bing Crosby, William "Bud" Abbott and Lou Costello frequented French Lick Springs Hotel and the nearby West Baden Springs Hotel. The latter's ornate architecture and soaring dome earned it the nickname "The Eighth Wonder of the World." Taggart, who was chairman of the Democratic National Committee from 1904 to 1908, made his resort an unofficial Democratic Party headquarters during the 1920s. In 1931 Franklin D. Roosevelt rounded up support for his presidential nomination at a Democratic governors' meeting at French Lick.

Golf, celebrity sightings, and rejuvenating water were not the only attractions in Orange County. Alcohol, gambling, and prostitution flourished. Despite rumors to the contrary, there is no evidence that gangster Al Capone stayed there. Capone was a frequent visitor to the area, but legend has it that Taggart refused to let Capone hold his wedding reception at French Lick Springs Hotel. Despite its reputation, the hotel never officially functioned as a gambling hall, although Taggart's biographer writes that "it stretches the imagination to believe he was not connected in some way to the rampant gambling in the valley."

West Baden Springs Hotel

The interior of West Baden Springs Hotel after it was restored and reopened in 2007. When it originally opened in 1903, it had the largest unsupported dome in the world—a spectacle that drew in many visitors.

Architectural Rescue of the Century

French Lick Springs Hotel and West Baden Springs Hotel were the crown jewels of Hoosier architecture when they were built during the first years of the twentieth century. At the close of the century, after decades of changing hands, it appeared that both were destined for demolition. Many felt that they were too large and too far gone to be rescued. Who had the kind of money needed to restore them to their glory?

During the 1990s, the endangered historic hotels found a fairy godmother in the form of a Hoosier corporation with an interest in historic preservation. Bloomington-based Cook Group, a global manufacturer of medical devices, purchased both properties and spent millions of dollars to restore both to the grandeur they had known during Thomas Taggart's time. Cook Group founders and passionate architectural preservationists Bill and Gayle

Cook and their son Carl oversaw the project. French Lick Springs Hotel, now a resort, reopened in 2006, and West Baden Springs Hotel reopened in 2007.

Today, the French Lick Resort advertises "One Amazing Resort—Two Grand Hotels." Guests' jaws drop in amazement as they enter the palatial lobbies—not just because of the restored beauty of these spaces but because of the fact that they are in rural southern Indiana rather than in some European capital. Shuttle service operating between the French Lick Springs and West Baden Springs Hotels gives guests access to big-name entertainers, restaurants, spa treatments, horseback riding, golfing, and *legal* casino gambling. The hotels' restoration has also been an economic shot in the arm for Orange County, which had struggled in the years that followed the resorts' original heyday.

8.4

The Musical State of Indiana

"A common image of courting in nineteenth-century advertising literature was the woman seated at the piano, playing sentimental classics to her anxious male caller. Certainly, the minds of these young couples were on other things besides Chopin nocturnes, but the piano stood as a moral institution."

— *Rick Kennedy, historian, ca. 1999*

Hoosiers have enjoyed music since the pioneer days—singing and fiddling, harmonicas and even pianos. By 1900 church choirs and town bands were commonplace. In the 1920s one could still hear traditional country, gospel, and folk, but young adults could not ignore the new jazz music. Much of it was composed, played, and recorded right in Indiana.

From Ragtime to Jazz

Ragtime, a precursor to jazz that is characterized by its fast, cheerful quality and interesting, syncopated rhythms, made its debut in the late 1890s. Although it started in African American communities, both black and white composers and musicians embraced the new style. Published in Missouri in 1899, Scott Joplin's

"Maple Leaf Rag" is considered the first ragtime hit. Indianapolis also had a number of talented ragtime composers who gained national recognition, including two women, May Aufderheide and Julia Niebergall. Niebergall, a pianist and music teacher, published her "Hoosier Rag" in 1907. A year later Aufderheide's father, a loan broker, published her "Dusty Rag" and "Richmond Rag."

In 1917 a group from New Orleans called the Original Dixieland Jazz Band released their first recordings, which sold more than a million copies. For many jazz aficionados and historians, the release of these records marked the birth of the jazz era. A piano player named Hoagy Carmichael, then an Indiana high school student, was aware of the exciting new music and would soon find himself in the thick of it.

Unlike New Orleans, Indiana was not a "root source" for jazz. Instead, it was a crucible—a place where a hot new interpretation of the music developed—a popular style called "midwestern jazz." As residents of a crossroads, Hoosiers were accustomed to blending styles and cultures. In music, the state's Germans brought a passion for choral compositions; the Anglo-Saxons contributed folk melody and songs; and African Americans who came North brought syncopated rhythms and a bluesy tone—all essential to homemade Hoosier jazz.

Jingling Jazz Orchestra

The "Original Jingling Jazz Five Piece Orchestra" of Terre Haute, Indiana, ca. 1918. This band performed jazz and the swing music that grew out of it—two of the most popular musical genres of the 1920s to 1940s.

Hoagy Carmichael

The younger of the two men behind the piano, Hoagy Carmichael, plays with Hitch's Happy Harmonists in Gennett Studios in Richmond, Indiana, in 1925. This was the first time Carmichael was involved in recording his music.

Gennett Studios and Early Jazz Recordings

"I was nervous in anticipation of my first recording. The studio was a dreary looking Rube Goldberg place with lily-shaped horns sticking oddly from the walls. . . . The horns . . . looked spooky and I was pretty upset by the time we were ready to make test records."

— *Hoagy Carmichael, recalling his first Gennett recording session in 1925*

Gennett Studios in Richmond was a key agent in the national craze. Owned by the Starr Piano Company, a local company that supplied Hoosiers with pianos before the turn of the century, the recording studio was not much more than a small shed near the railroad tracks in the Whitewater River Gorge. But to this small building came some of the nation's best early jazz musicians to make 78 rpm record albums. At a time when music making and marketing were often racially segregated, Gennett accommodated white and black artists as well as integrated jazz groups. The studio might record a white Appalachian country band in the morning and a black jazz band in the afternoon. The young Hoosier pianist, Hoagy Carmichael, was among those who recorded at Gennett. Also, on April 6, 1923, Gennett recorded the Chicago-based Joe "King" Oliver's Creole Jazz Band, one of the premiere groups in early jazz, with a young Louis Armstrong on cornet. These discs are universally regarded as the first true masterpieces in jazz recording.

Music brought blacks and whites together in a segregated world where there were few opportunities for blacks and whites to interact in everyday life. Often these interactions occurred at the clubs and bars lining Indiana Avenue in Indianapolis. Additionally, the African American roots of ragtime and jazz meant that many white musicians, including Carmichael, learned from black musicians and composers such as Reggie DuValle, an Indianapolis ragtime pianist and band leader. Bloomington was also a music hotspot with the help of Carmichael, who formed some of his first bands while he attended Indiana University. It was in Bloomington that Carmichael composed "Washboard Blues," "Stardust," and other songs that have become classics in the American songbook.

The Great Depression hit the recording industry hard. Gennett Studios was one of its casualties. The music preserved on the label outlived the company, however. By the mid-1930s, Gennett discs were beginning to become collectors' items.

Heart and Soul

Hoagy Carmichael wrote "Heart and Soul" in 1938, and it remains one of his most famous compositions. It was featured in the 1948 film *A Song Is Born*, played by Larry Clinton's Orchestra, pictured on the cover of this sheet music.

Indiana Avenue, the Hoosier Harlem

Its soundtrack, if it could be heard today, would be the music that spilled out into the streets on summer nights in the days before air-conditioning, the doors propped open, the Avenue alive and a town unto itself.

— *David Brent Johnson, jazz historian, 2007*

Although most Hoosiers today associate Indiana Avenue with Indianapolis's early jazz scene, the first black-owned businesses opened on the block in the 1860s. By the early 1900s the street had become the center of Indianapolis's African American community. On Indiana Avenue in 1927, millionaire businesswoman Madam C. J. Walker opened her magnificent Walker Building, which included a 1,500-seat theater and other shops and offices. On opening night, DuValle played to a sold-out house; the Walker Theater was thus christened one of the city's premiere jazz venues. Brothers Denver and Sea Ferguson owned other popular clubs on the Avenue, most notably the Cotton Club at Vermont and West Streets, where one outstanding night in the 1930s jazz greats Louis Armstrong and Fats Waller appeared together. Some of the jazz joints were not classy places—quite the contrary. Clubs such as the Hole-in-the-Wall and the Blackstone were reputed to be dangerous places where only the bravest "insiders" dared venture. Legend has it the notorious gangster John Dillinger was so scared by his visit to the Blackstone that he quickly left.

At its peak in the 1930s, Indiana Avenue was home to more than twenty-five jazz clubs. Its character resembled New York's Harlem, where well-to-do whites came to listen to top black entertainers. According to jazz historian Duncan Schiedt, "It was not a place where white people would congregate, but people who were interested in the music went there and nobody gave them any trouble."

Crispus Attucks High School, founded as an all-black school near Indiana Avenue in 1927, not only dominated state high school basketball—winning the 1955 and 1956 state championships—it also nurtured talented young jazz musicians. A haven of African American scholarship and achievement, the school's outstanding music teachers tutored students such as

Indiana Avenue Jazz Club Featuring Willis B. Dyer

Indiana Avenue was the place to hear jazz in Indianapolis. Willis Dyer, in the back on the electric organ, and Buddy Parker, in the front on the saxophone, were captured performing in a club on the avenue by photographer Emmett Brown sometime in the 1940s or 1950s.

cellist-composer David Baker, trombonist J. J. Johnson, guitarist Wes Montgomery, and many others. Out of school, the young musicians also earned their reputations by playing on Indiana Avenue. As Baker recalls, "'At that time, a black was expected to play religious music, R & B or jazz. I can remember auditioning for the Indianapolis Symphony Orchestra and being told, in no uncertain terms, that even though my audition was the best, there was no chance that I'd become a member.'"

Indiana Avenue continued to thrive into the 1950s. By the 1980s, however, much of the avenue was run down, a victim of economic forces and cultural change. Middle-class blacks had moved to the suburbs. Highway construction and the expansion of Indiana University–Purdue University, Indianapolis (IUPUI) resulted in the razing of the buildings where Indiana jazz made history. Today, only the street's crown jewel, the Madame Walker Theater, reminds passersby of the street's heyday.

David Baker

David Baker conducts an ensemble at Indiana University's Musical Arts Center in Bloomington. Baker grew up in Indianapolis and earned his jazz education firsthand by playing in jam sessions in clubs along Indiana Avenue as a high school student. As of 2014 Baker was distinguished professor of music and chair emeritus, Department of Jazz Studies, at the Indiana University Jacobs School of Music.

Selected Bibliography

Baker, Kelly J. *Gospel According to the Klan: The KKK's Appeal to Protestant America, 1915–1930.* Lawrence: University of Kansas Press, 2011.

Blee, Kathleen M. *Women of the Klan: Racism and Gender in the 1920s.* Berkeley: University of California Press, 1991.

Bodenhamer, David J., and Robert G. Barrows. *The Encyclopedia of Indianapolis.* Bloomington: Indiana University Press, 1994.

Bunting, Christina R. "Mineral Springs: The French Lick Springs Hotel in Orange County, Indiana." *The Hoosier Genealogist: Connections* 52, no. 2 (Fall/Winter 2012): 42–46.

Carmichael, Hoagy. *The Stardust Road.* Bloomington: Indiana University Press, 1983.

Carmichael, Hoagy, with Stephen Longstreet. *Sometimes I Wonder: The Story of Hoagy Carmichael.* New York: Farrar, Strauss, and Giroux, 1965.

Crocker, Ruth Hutchinson. *Social Work and Social Order: The Settlement Movement in Two Industrial Cities, 1889–1930.* Urbana: University of Illinois Press, 1992.

Crowe, Jason. "The Cradle of Basketball." *Indiana Basketball History Magazine* (Summer 1995), http://www.tctc .com/~gmm/cradle.htm.

Endelman, Judith E. *The Jewish Community of Indianapolis, 1849 to the Present.* Bloomington: Indiana University Press, 1984.

Fadely, James Philip. *Thomas Taggart: Public Servant, Political Boss, 1856–1929.* Indianapolis: Indiana Historical Society, 1997.

Guffey, Greg. *The Greatest Basketball Story Ever Told: The Milan Miracle.* Bloomington: Indiana University Press, 1993.

Halberstam, David. *Everything They Had: Sports Writing from David Halberstam.* New York: Hyperion Books, 2008.

Hoover, Dwight W. "To Be a Jew in Middletown: A Muncie Oral History Project." *Indiana Magazine of History* 81, no. 2 (June 1985): 131–58.

"Hotel History." French Lick Springs Hotel, http://www.frenchlick .com/aboutus/history/flsh.

"IHSAA Basketball State Champions." Indiana High School Athletic Association, http://www.ihsaa.org/Sports/Boys/Basketball /StateChampions/tabid/124/Default.aspx.

Kennedy, Rick. *Jelly Roll, Bix, and Hoagy: Gennett Studios and the Birth of Recorded Jazz.* Bloomington: Indiana University Press, 1999.

Lantzer, Jason S. *"Prohibition Is Here to Stay": The Reverend Edward S. Schumaker and the Dry Crusade in America.* Notre Dame, IN: University of Notre Dame Press, 2009.

Lutholtz, M. William. *Grand Dragon: D. C. Stephenson and the Ku Klux Klan in Indiana.* West Lafayette: Purdue University, 1991.

Lynd, Robert S., and Helen Merrell Lynd. *Middletown in Transition: A Study in Cultural Conflicts.* New York: Harcourt, Brace and World, 1937.

Madison, James H. *Hoosiers: A New History of Indiana.* Bloomington: Indiana University Press; Indianapolis: Indiana Historical Society Press, 2014.

———. *Indiana through Tradition and Change: A History of the Hoosier State and Its People, 1920–1945.* The History of Indiana 5. Indianapolis: Indiana Historical Society, 1982.

———. *The Indiana Way.* Bloomington: Indiana University Press, 1986.

———. *A Lynching in the Heartland: Race and Memory in America.* New York: St. Martin's–Palgrave, 2001.

McMahon, John R. "Our Jazz-Spotted Middle West." *Ladies Home Journal* (February 1922): 38.

Moore, Leonard J. *Citizen Klansmen: The Ku Klux Klan in Indiana, 1921–1928.* Chapel Hill: University of North Carolina Press, 1991.

———. "Indiana and the Klan: A Review Essay." *Indiana Magazine of History* 88, no. 2 (June 1992): 132–37.

Musgrave, Paul. "'A Primitive Method of Enforcing the Law': Vigilantism as a Response to Bank Crimes in Indiana, 1925–1933." *Indiana Magazine of History* 102, no. 3 (September 2006): 190–95.

O'Malley, John W. "The Story of the West Baden Springs Hotel." *Indiana Magazine of History* 54, no. 4 (December 1958): 365–80.

Peckham, Howard H. *Indiana: A Bicentennial History.* New York: W. W. Norton, 1978.

Pegram, Thomas R. *One Hundred Percent American: The Rebirth and Decline of the Ku Klux Klan in the 1920s.* Chicago: Ivan R. Dee, 2011.

Phillips, Clifton J. *Indiana in Transition: The Emergence of an Industrial Commonwealth, 1880–1920.* The History of Indiana 4. Indianapolis: Indiana Historical Bureau and Indiana Historical Society, 1968.

Rains, Rob, and Hellen Carpenter. *James Naismith: The Man Who Invented Basketball.* Philadelphia: Temple University Press, 2009.

Ramsey, Paul J. "The War against German-American Culture: The Removal of German-Language Instruction from the Indianapolis Schools, 1917–1919." *Indiana Magazine of History* 98, no. 4 (December 2002): 285–303.

Restoring the Legend: The French Lick Springs Hotel. DVD. Produced by Ron Prickel and Gino Brancolini. Bloomington, IN: WTIU Public Television, 2007. Indiana University, http://www .indiana.edu/~radiotv/wtiu/frenchlick/.

Safianow, Allen. "'You Can't Burn History': Getting Right with the Klan in Noblesville, Indiana." *Indiana Magazine of History* 100, no. 2 (June 2004): 109–54.

Schiedt, Duncan. *The Jazz State of Indiana*. Pittsboro, IN: Duncan P. Shiedt, 1977; Reprint, Indianapolis: Indiana Historical Society, 1999.

"The Shirt Tail Parade." *Muncie Post-Democrat,* June 16, 1922. Ball State University Libraries Digital Media Repository, http://libx.bsu.edu/cdm/singleitem/collection/PostDemNews/id/985.

Smith, Ron F. "The Klan's Retribution Against an Indiana Editor: A Reconsideration." *Indiana Magazine of History* 106, no. 4 (December 2010): 381–400.

Sudhalter, Richard M. *Stardust Melody: The Life and Music of Hoagy Carmichael*. New York: Oxford University Press, in association with the Indiana Historical Society, 2002.

Taborn, Karen Faye, and Traditional Arts Indiana. *Indiana Avenue and Beyond: A History and Heritage Reflecting a Community of Jazz in Indianapolis*. Wordpress blog, http://jazzindiana avenue.wordpress.com/introduction/.

Thornbrough, Emma Lou. *Indiana Blacks in the Twentieth Century*. Bloomington: Indiana University Press, 2000.

Van Allen, Elizabeth J. *James Whitcomb Riley: A Life*. Bloomington: Indiana University Press, 1999.

Vonnegut, Kurt. *Palm Sunday: An Autobiographical Collage*. New York: Dell Publishing, 1984.

Wade, Wyn Craig. *The Fiery Cross: The Ku Klux Klan in America*. New York: Simon and Schuster, 1987.

Walsh, Justin E. *The Centennial History of the Indiana General Assembly, 1816–1978*. Indianapolis: Select Committee on the Centennial History of the Indiana General Assembly in cooperation with the Indiana Historical Bureau, 1987.

Williams, Bob. *Hoosier Hysteria: Indiana High School Basketball*. South Bend, Icarus Press, 1982.

Williams, Pat. *How to Be Like Coach Wooden: Life Lessons from Basketball's Greatest Leader*. Deerfield Beach, FL: Health Communications, 2006.

Wolff, Alexander. "Class Struggle." *Sports Illustrated,* December 2, 2002. SI Vault: Your Link to Sports History, http://sports illustrated.cnn.com/vault/article/magazine/MAG1027660/2/index.htm.

Yeats, Norris W. *The American Humorist: Conscience of the Twentieth Century*. Ames, IA: Iowa State University Press, 1964.

Essential Questions

1   Why were the last decades of the nineteenth century and the first years of the twentieth century considered to be a Golden Age of art and literature in Indiana? How do the works of authors such as James Whitcomb Riley and Booth Tarkington and artist T. C. Steele reflect nostalgia for an earlier time?

2   Why did basketball become so popular in Indiana?

3   Name at least three activities and/or trends that young people participated in during the "Roaring Twenties" that older people found troubling.

4   How did the popularity of the automobile help to promote these "morally questionable" activities?

5   How did "Hoosier jazz" combine different cultural and musical traditions?

6   How did Gennett Studios in Richmond, Indiana, contribute to the popularity of jazz music? What was remarkable about Gennett Studios?

7   What was Indiana Avenue like in the 1920s through the 1950s? What factors led to the decline of Indiana Avenue as the center of Indianapolis's African American community?

8   How did the 1920s incarnation of the Ku Klux Klan differ from the original southern incarnation of the organization and the nationwide 1960s version of the KKK? What made the 1920s Klan attractive to many Hoosiers and other Americans?*

9   What factors led to the decline of the 1920s KKK in Indiana?*

   See student activities related to this question.

Activity: The Ku Klux Klan of the 1920s

Introduction: While the 1920s was a time of great economic prosperity in Indiana and nationwide, it was also an era in which many people clung to a nostalgic American identity, one that was generally defined quite narrowly. As industrialization led to urbanization and immigrants flocked to Indiana cities in search of jobs and new opportunities, some Hoosiers—specifically some white, American-born Protestants—felt threatened by these newcomers whose traditions, religions, and cultures were unlike their own.

▶ Re-read the section of chapter eight that discusses the rise and fall of Indiana's 1920s Ku Klux Klan. Keep in mind that the Klan of the 1920s differs from versions of the group after the Civil War and in the 1960s. The Klan that formed in the South following the Civil War used violence to try to deny freedom to former slaves and to oppose Reconstruction. The most recent nationwide incarnation of the Klan was born in the 1960s in reaction to the Civil Rights Movement and also used violent methods as an expression of the racism of its members. While this group remains active in Indiana, it has had relatively little impact in the state.

▶ Read the following excerpt from the 1924 Ku Klux Klan pamphlet, *Why You Should Become a Klansman: Of Interest to White, Protestant, Native-Born Americans Who Want to Keep America American.* This publication illuminates the ways in which the 1920s Klan differs from earlier and later versions. After reading the excerpt from the pamphlet, answer the questions below.

In its influence and its teachings, and its principles, the Knights of the Ku Klux Klan seeks to generate and impart a spirit of loyalty to America, of consecration to her ideals, of fealty to her institutions, of support to her government, of obedience to her laws, and of unselfish devotion to her interests.

1 Define the following words:

   A Loyalty

   B Consecration

   C Fealty

   D Support

   E Obedience

   F Devotion

2 Do these terms have positive or negative connotations?

3 The pamphlet claims that it is the goal of the Klan to promote these feelings and/or actions in America. As such, do you think the Klan of the 1920s was considered by its members to be a patriotic organization?

4 Based on this description of the purpose of the Ku Klux Klan, do you think Klan supporters looked upon non-members in a positive or negative light? Explain your answer.

▶ The 1924 Klan pamphlet also claimed that the KKK was necessary to keep America 100 percent American:

The Jews are organized to protect Jewish interests; the Roman Catholics are organized to further papal interests; the Negroes are organized to advance the interests of that race; and in various parts of America, various racial and alien-national groups are organized for the furtherance of their particular interests, and the spread of their peculiar ideals among our own American people. These racial and religious groups exercise the rights of freedom of assembly, free speech, and free press. The Knights of the Ku Klux Klan believes that White, Native-born Protestant Americans should be protected in their own exercise of these fundamental American rights, and especially in their right to insist that America shall be made American through the

promulgation *of American principles, the* dissemination *of American ideals, the creation of* wholesome American sentiment, *the preservation of American institutions, and through all of those* means *that will make for a nobler, purer, and more prosperous America.*

1 According to this excerpt, what groups were endangering the "American-ness" of America? Why?

2 Define the following terms:

   A Promulgation

   B Dissemination

3 What might the phrase "wholesome American sentiment" mean?

4 What other "means"—or methods—might the last sentence refer to when it states that "Protestant Americans should be protected . . . in their right to insist that America shall be made more American through . . . all of those means that will make for a nobler, purer, and more prosperous America?" In other words, what may the Klan have been willing to do to achieve its goals?

▶ From 1915 through the 1920s the Ku Klux Klan existed in states throughout the United States. In 1922 W. C. Witcher of Texas wrote an exposé of the Klan, which he believed to be a corrupt organization that duped its supporters. In *The Unveiling of the Ku Klux Klan*, Witcher addresses the Klan's supposed goal of promoting American ideals and its doctrine of 100 percent Americanism. Witcher writes:

We know that the Klan has repeatedly stated through its chief representatives that it stands for "Law and order, the Constitution of the United States" to "Aid the officers in the enforcement of law, etc." All of which we know to be ABSOLUTELY FALSE, but these high-sounding phrases have especially appealed to a large and respectable class of people, for the reason that the majority of our citizenship respect law and order, and quite naturally, they would be easily induced *to contribute both their time and money toward the accomplishment of these ideals.*

1 Why does Witcher write that the stated motive of the Klan would be appealing to "a large and respectable class of people?"

2 What does the word *induce* mean? Does it have a positive or negative connotation? What did Witcher believe the Klan had induced people to do?

▶ In regard to the notion of 100 percent Americanism, Witcher writes:

It is surprising to know that [this philosophy] has succeeded, in a large degree, in sowing the poisonous seed of class antagonism, religious intolerance and race hatred throughout the breadth and width of our land. . . . The Constitution knows neither Catholic, Jew, Methodist, Baptist, Presbyterian, Quaker, Shaker, nor any other kind of religion. For the simple reason that a belief in or rejection of, any and all religions neither qualifies, nor disqualifies a man for the acceptance or rejection of the Constitution. Therefore this doctrine of "100 per cent Americanism" is the product of either an ignorant, or a very mean, depraved mind—a mind raging and seething with the spirit of persecution—tyranny and intolerance, and this is the kind of mind which is at the FOUNDATION of the Ku Klux Klan.

1 What, then, would Witcher say was the true motive of the Klan of the 1920s?

2 According to Witcher, what is the ultimate result of the Klan philosophy of 100 percent Americanism?

3 Is the philosophy of 100 percent Americanism rooted in the Constitution?

4 Witcher implies that the 100 percent Americanism doctrine that is the foundation of the KKK is in itself un-American. Explain Witcher's reasoning.

Today, Witcher's argument seems obvious, but in the 1920s many Americans joined the Klan as an act of patriotism. They failed to see the contradiction that the organization claimed to defend American ideals—such as liberty, democracy, freedom of speech, freedom of religion, and so forth—by persecuting those who were unlike themselves in appearance, religious ideals, or social customs.

▶ In language, an oxymoron is a figure of speech that pairs two contradictory words or ideas, for example "living dead." "Unconstitutional patriots" is an oxymoron that Witcher would say applies to the Klan of the 1920s. Write a poem titled "Unconstitutional Patriots" in which you reflect upon the contradictions of the Klan of the 1920s. You may choose any format or type of poem, but be sure to incorporate at least three poetic devices, such as figurative language (for example, similes, metaphors, hyperbole, or understatements), imagery, irony, or satire.

Activity References

Ku Klux Klan. *Why You Should Become a Klansman: Of Interest to White, Protestant, Native-Born Americans Who Want to Keep America American.* N.p.: Knights of the Ku Klux Klan, 1924.

Witcher, W. C. *The Unveiling of the Ku Klux Klan.* Fort Worth, TX: W. C. Witcher, 1922.

9

The Great Depression and World War II

"In our generation, we knew how hard it was to come by things and make money last.... [I]t was something that stayed with me because I realized how quickly it could all be taken away."

— *Betty Gehrke, Whiting, Indiana*

Hoosiers of the generation that grew up during the 1930s never forgot the worst economic depression in American history. There had been hard times before, all the way back to pioneer days. But the Great Depression of the 1930s was something different—for Indiana and for the country. Then the worst war in human history erupted in Europe and once again the United States joined in the fighting.

The Great Depression

The depression that followed the prosperity of the 1920s was deeper and lasted longer than any other economic downturn in Indiana history. Many Hoosiers lost their jobs and could not find work. Widespread unemployment spread across all types of jobs and workers—skilled and unskilled, white and blue collar. The economic decline caused banks to close and couples to postpone marriage and starting families. Some people went hungry; lucky were the families who had their own homegrown and canned food. Most people rarely bought new clothing; many altered and mended feed sacks to wear. One White County woman later recalled, "We had to do a lot of patching to make the boy's overall[s] last." So troubling were the times

that in Fort Wayne, where five thousand families were on relief by early 1933, a lawyer feared that "the time is not far distant when we are going to be confronted with riots and violence." A wealthy businessman in Muncie later stated, "It seemed for a while that everything might collapse, many of us bought a great deal of canned food, and stored it in our cellars, fearing a possible siege."

Women, African Americans, Appalachian migrants, and Mexican Americans were among the hardest hit in the depression. To save jobs for men, women were often told to stop working. African Americans were generally the last people to be hired and the first to be fired. In 1940, after economic recovery began, 38 percent of the African Americans in Fort Wayne were still unemployed. At this time only 11 percent of Fort Wayne's white population was unemployed.

Newcomers from the Appalachian south suffered special discrimination. White and black southerners had flocked to Indiana's factories in the prosperous 1920s. By the 1930s there were around sixty thousand southerners living in Indianapolis, about half of them black and half white. A cruel witticism made the

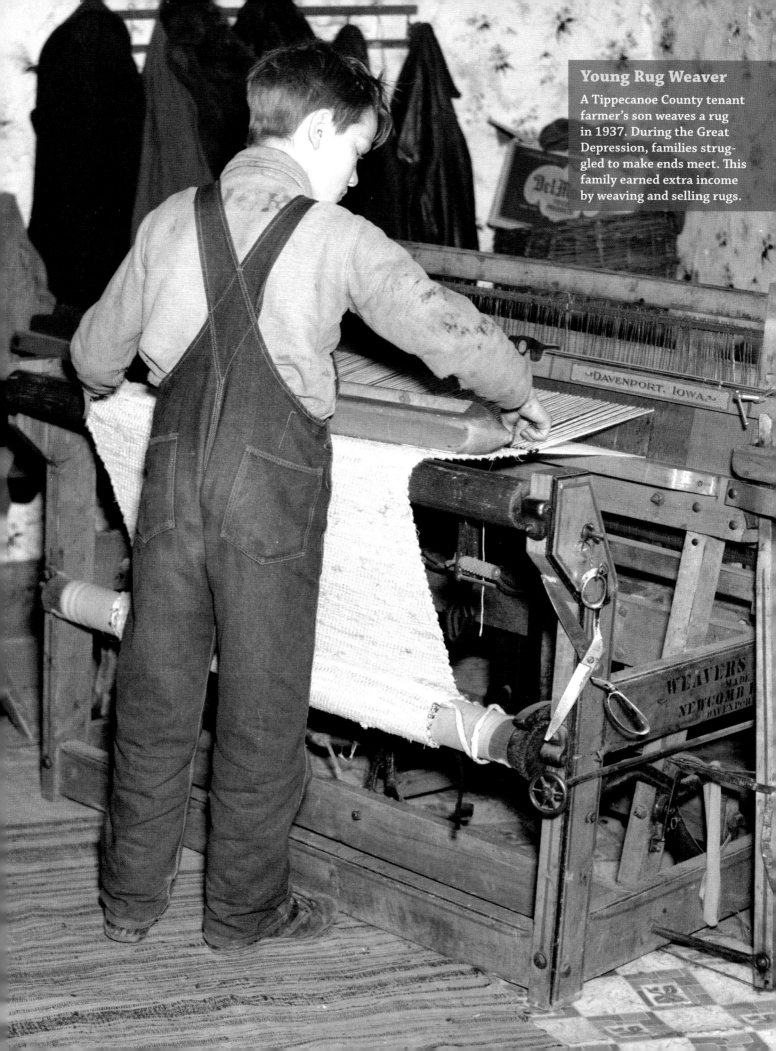

Young Rug Weaver
A Tippecanoe County tenant farmer's son weaves a rug in 1937. During the Great Depression, families struggled to make ends meet. This family earned extra income by weaving and selling rugs.

rounds among native Hoosiers who thought the immigrants were taking their jobs: "Have you heard there are only forty-five states left in the Union? Kentucky and Tennessee have gone to Indiana, and Indiana has gone to hell." Some of these newcomers had come seeking agricultural work, often seasonal labor in the state's tomato fields and canneries. Johnson County, for example, had more than one hundred canneries before the depression. A 1936 report claimed that the Kentucky pioneers from a century earlier "were of a much higher type than the recent ones." Sterilization was even discussed for those judged least fit.

There were unwelcome newcomers from Mexico, too. Mexican immigrants settled in Lake County as railroad and steel mill workers. Some were brought in by the mill owners to break the union strikes in 1919, an action that led many whites to resent Mexican immigrants. Thirty-five percent of Inland Steel's East Chicago workforce was Mexican in the 1920s, making it one of the nation's largest employers of Mexican immigrants.

As the depression deepened, steel production declined and many jobs were lost. Mexicans were hit harder than other steelworkers. As a result, many Mexican immigrants and U.S. citizens of Mexican descent decided to move back to Mexico. Those who wanted to go but were unable to afford the trip were helped by various aid agencies. This was the start of a repatriation movement. In 1932, when the depression was at its worst, pressure was put on Mexicans to move back to Mexico. For instance, the depression-era financial assistance administered by township trustees was given sparingly to Mexicans—especially if they refused repatriation. The American Legion, the North Township Trustee's Office, and the East Chicago Manufacturers Association all cooperated to fund repatriation. In total, counting the Mexicans who left voluntarily and those who were coerced, more than a thousand people—nearly half of Lake County's pre-depression Mexican population—boarded the repatriation trains and moved south of the Rio Grande River.

Hard times also brought out the best in Hoosiers. Families and neighbors shared food, helped bring in the corn harvest, and took care of the sick. Jobless young people moved back with parents and grandparents. Local charities stepped up their aid to the hungry and homeless. As the depression cut deeper, traditional forms of relief were not enough. The bread lines got longer and the soup kitchens more crowded.

A New Deal Comes to Indiana

In 1923 Indiana Governor Warren McCray told the general assembly, "What the people of Indiana want is a season of government economy and a period of legislative inaction and rest." Ten years later, at the depth of the Great Depression, newly elected Governor Paul V. McNutt called on Hoosiers to "prove that government may be a great instrument of human progress."

Hoosiers had always been wary of government power. They had never liked paying taxes or being told what to do. While they had sometimes wanted government to help, as it had in removing Indians or building canals, they mostly clung to traditions of low taxes and small government.

The massive storm of the Great Depression challenged Indiana's traditions as had nothing before. Hoosiers began to think that government needed to step in and step up. Consequently, voters put more liberal Democrats in power in the 1932 elections. New government programs in the state and nation offered relief, recovery, and reform. It was a New Deal for the country and Indiana as politicians sought to increase employment and provide for the hungry. President Franklin Delano Roosevelt's "alphabet soup" agencies, such as the Works Progress Administration (WPA), Civilian Conservation Corps (CCC), Federal Art Project (FAP), and others helped Indiana and the rest of the nation begin to recover. But then came war.

World War II

In December 1941 the Japanese attacked the U.S. fleet of ships at Pearl Harbor in Hawaii. Not long after, the United States officially entered World War II. The world had never experienced anything like World War II. Brutal, global, and total, this war reached deeply into Indiana, affecting every aspect of Hoosier life.

Bread Line

In this 1930s photograph, people of all ages wait in line to receive food from the Salvation Army in Terre Haute. Widespread unemployment caused by the Great Depression left many people unable to provide for themselves and their families. Charities offered food to many of these struggling families during the Great Depression.

Hoosiers were not eager to join in the troubles of other nations. They remembered the costs of the Great War, now known as World War I. But with the Japanese attack on Pearl Harbor they rushed to the battlefields and turned their factories and fields toward the war effort. This new war required the economy to marshal all its resources to manufacture maximum numbers of planes, tanks, army uniforms, food, and medicine. Indiana was an integral part in "the arsenal of democracy," and so the daily lives of most Hoosiers on the home front were altered.

World War II, though tragic in the number of lives lost, brought about the defeat of the Axis nations—Germany, Italy, and Japan. It also ended the Great Depression and began the longest period of sustained economic prosperity in Indiana and American history.

Hoosiers who experienced the Great Depression and World War II would never forget. These two massive storms shook the foundations of Indiana's traditions, profoundly shaping a generation and affecting the lives of the children and grandchildren to come.

FREED to join the fight for freedom

Each regularly employed laundry worker releases 7 housewives for voluntary war service

WWII Poster

This poster from 1942 promoted the war effort at home by emphasizing that soldiers were not the only ones needed for service. Women also participated in the war effort in large numbers doing many of the jobs soldiers had to leave behind. In turn, their housework was sometimes taken over by others in the household or by paid help, such as laundry workers.

YOUR JOB HERE IS

Vital to Victory

9.1

Governor Paul V. NcNutt and the "Little New Deal"

The change in government, for which we have prepared, is here. It carries with it tremendous responsibilities and the possibility of far-reaching consequences.

— *Indiana Governor Paul V. McNutt, Inaugural Address, January 9, 1933*

Not Hoosier Politics as Usual

Never in Indiana's history had two decades been so different. The prosperity of the 1920s ended with the stock market crash on October 29, 1929, making the 1930s a struggle from the start. From the steel mills of Gary to shipyards in Jeffersonville business ground to a halt, leaving thousands of Hoosiers without jobs. As unemployment lines grew longer, many questioned Indiana's tradition of small government.

Indiana's governors had traditionally been caretakers who waited for the legislature to set an agenda. This was not the case with Paul V. McNutt, who became governor in the Democratic landslide election of 1932. In his inaugural address, McNutt laid out "immediate tasks" to relieve the suffering state. The first was to provide food, clothing, and shelter for the destitute, followed by the necessity of lowering the cost of government, reducing and redistributing the burden of taxation, and maintaining an adequate system of public education.

Paul V. McNutt—From Small-Town Hoosier to Statesman

Paul Vories McNutt was born in Franklin, Indiana, on July 19, 1891, to county prosecutor John C. McNutt and Ruth (Prosser) McNutt. Two years later, the McNutt family moved to Indianapolis where John became librarian of the Indiana State Supreme Court. When Paul was seven, the family moved to Martinsville, where his father established his own law office.

McNutt idolized his father and as a young boy spent hours with him in the law library. The younger McNutt attended Indiana University where he proved an excellent student and became a good friend of classmate Wendell L. Willkie, who was later his political rival.

After graduating from IU, McNutt attended Harvard University Law School. He returned to Martinsville after receiving his law degree in 1916 to practice law with his father. A year later, McNutt accepted an assistant professorship at Indiana University Law School. However, World War I soon diverted him.

McNutt enlisted in the army in November 1917 and attained the rank of major in the field artillery. While stationed in San Antonio, Texas, he met Kathleen Timolat, who became his wife. When he returned to civilian life, McNutt remained interested in military affairs, especially the American Legion.

After his military service, McNutt returned to teaching law at IU. In 1925, at the age of thirty-four, he became the youngest dean in the school's history. While serving as dean, McNutt began his political career. In 1928 he was elected national commander of the American Legion. Subsequently, a group of his supporters encouraged him to run for governor. At this point, he considered his chances were too low. Four years later, however, McNutt felt the time was right, and in 1932 he won the governorship. In his single term, McNutt proved himself a powerful leader, ushering in sweeping change at the height of the Great Depression.

McNutt's "Little New Deal"

McNutt promised immediate action—and he delivered. The only other governor in Indiana history to wield as much power as McNutt had been Oliver P. Morton, governor from 1861–67. Instead of waiting for the legislature to send him its agenda, McNutt and his advisors got to work drafting bills and pushing them through the general assembly. Helping Hoosiers was McNutt's top priority. He began working on relief through his "Little New Deal" two months before Franklin D. Roosevelt became president and created the federal New Deal program that he had mentioned

Governor McNutt and President Roosevelt

Governor Paul V. McNutt, second on left, and President Franklin D. Roosevelt, to the right, ca. 1933–37. McNutt supported Roosevelt's New Deal policies and implemented them in Indiana as well as initiating reforms of his own.

during his presidential campaign—an idea that McNutt supported. McNutt's program resulted in the formation of the Indiana Department of Public Welfare, which centralized relief at the state level. Before the advent of the Department of Public Welfare, relief had been provided by townships, which had proven inadequate in the early 1930s.

McNutt also embraced the "alphabet soup" of federal New Deal programs, including Social Security and the Works Progress Administration (WPA), which put people back to work on public infrastructure projects, such as highways and reforestation, and employed out-of-work writers, historians, artists, and others for tasks in their fields. At its peak, the WPA employed 99,000 people in Indiana and spent a total of $302,000,000. The results transformed the state by adding 24,000 miles of road, 3,000 bridges, 361 parks, 78 schools, and many other resources that would benefit Hoosiers for decades to come.

McNutt Takes on Taxes and State Government

Taxes were always a hot potato for Hoosier politicians—each one trying to avoid the issue as much as possible—but McNutt grabbed the issue with his bare hands and did not let go. He was determined to reform the state's tax system. Before 1933 when Governor McNutt introduced the Gross Income Tax, much of Indiana's income had been from property taxes. Because there were more people than property holders, this meant that the tax base—the people who paid taxes—was very small. This tax system overburdened the property owners and ignored most potential income from other citizens. The Gross Income Tax, however, taxed everyone who had an income from salaries, wages, and commissions. It also included a pre-cursor to what is now a sales tax. Retailers such as clothing stores had to pay a tax on each sale. Property taxes

Ouabache Lodge

This lodge in Oubache State Park, in Bluffton, Indiana, was built by members of the Civilian Conservation Corps (CCC) during the 1930s. Many state parks in Indiana benefitted from the labor of the CCC.

were lowered. Indiana was able to balance its budget in 1933 and to increase state aid to struggling public schools.

McNutt also reorganized state government to be more effective and efficient. Both Democrats and Republicans had long complained about the state's bureaucratic disorder and inefficiency. More than one hundred departments and agencies existed in a patchwork quilt of uncertain authority and procedures. McNutt's Executive Reorganization Act of 1933 placed them in eight new departments, each with a clearly defined purpose: executive, state, audit and control, treasury, law, education, public works, and commerce and industry. The reorganization strengthened the governor's power over state bureaucracy, which many believed was essential to efficient management.

June 18, 1935

Mrs. Lee K. Amsden

Mrs. Lee K. Amsden, Chai[r]
Shelby County Women's De[mocratic Club]
Eagles Hall, East Frankl[in]
Shelbyville, Indiana

Dear Mrs. Amsden:

I wish that it were po[ssible]
picnic supper on June [...]

Since I am prevented [...]
remind you that our p[...]
alarms in order to co[...]
concern they are atte[...]
interests by branding [...]
sensible suggestions [...]
to communize the nat[...]
whether they hail fr[...]
radicalism will be [...]

The activities of t[...]
designated as "The [...]
but I prefer a mor[...]

The use of the te[...]
that "subsidy" is [...]
culated to return [...]
the government.

We are prone to [...]
associated with [...]
best repute.

But it achieves [...]
benefit of man[...]
we are pleased [...]
as a benign in[...]

The first obligation of government is to protect the humanity which it serves. To make certain the complete performance of this obligation the President of the United States has proposed a program which includes three great objectives:

1. The security of livelihood through the better use of the national resources of the land in which we live.

2. The security against the major hazards and vicissitudes of life.

3. The security of decent homes.

If our people are to be served instead of starved in a land of potential plenty, it is the first duty and welcome privilege of state governments to lend every possible support to the proposal. All units of government must and will act and work together in order to assure success. Humanity will be saved as well as subsidized.

With kindest regards and every good wish for a most successful meeting, I am

Very cordially yours,

Paul V. McNutt

PVMcN R

Sent Special

Governor McNutt Letter

Governor Paul V. McNutt wrote a two-page letter to Mrs. Lee K. Amsden, chairwoman of the Shelby County Women's Democratic Club, on June 18, 1935. In the letter McNutt explains his beliefs regarding subsidies and the role of government, stating that he prefers the title "A Subsidy to Humanity" to "The New Deal," because it is more descriptive. He goes on to state that the government's primary obligation is "to protect the humanity it serves."

Governor Paul V. McNutt

This portrait of Paul V. McNutt was painted by noted Hoosier artist Wayman Adams in 1933.

McNutt's Critics

Not everyone was in favor of McNutt's changes. Some feared that the relief programs would "contravene the spirit of Anglo-Saxon traditions, encourage laziness, and create a class of permanent dependents" or "bring about a state of communistic or socialist government." Congressman Charles Halleck, a conservative Republican, criticized McNutt for his "wild orgy of spending," stating that it was making Indiana's government "into a Santa Claus." Some Democrats worried that the federal government's programs would weaken states' rights. These Democrats were also concerned that McNutt's centralization program might end local government by township trustees.

McNutt did not always win the approval of labor. Although his policies strongly supported the workers, he declared martial law—in which the military replaces local government—in eleven counties during a violent coal mining strike in 1935 and forced the resignation of a union leader. Socialist leader Norman Thomas called him a "Hoosier Hitler" for his intervention in labor disputes.

Another McNutt initiative, the Hoosier Democratic Club (also known as the Two Percent Club), raised hackles in both parties. McNutt required Democratic state and local employees to pay two percent of their salaries to the club to fund Democratic Party campaigns. It was rumored that to refuse joining the Two Percent Club meant giving up one's job. The Two Percent Club carried with it the whiff of corruption through patronage—appointing people to government offices out of favoritism. This haunted McNutt for the rest of his political career. Republicans were sharply critical—until they won the governor's office and then began their own version of the Two Percent Club.

In 1936, having gained national attention for his accomplishments in Indiana as well as for his movie star good looks, McNutt hoped to make a run for the White House. Appointed by FDR in 1937, McNutt served for two years as high commissioner of the Philippines as he harbored hopes of running for president in 1940.

FDR's decision to seek a third term in 1940 ended McNutt's presidential aspirations, but he continued in public service. From 1939 to 1945 he was administrator of the Federal Security Agency, which later became the Department of Health, Education, and Welfare. During the war, he acted as chairman of the War Manpower Commission. After the war McNutt returned to his post as high commissioner to the Philippines and helped the Philippine Commonwealth negotiate for its independence. For his final government posting he became the first United States ambassador to the new Philippine Republic.

After retiring from public life in 1947, McNutt established residency in New York City where he had a law practice, but he remained a partner in his father's old law firm in Martinsville. In 1955 he died at age 63 after a brief illness. Tributes poured in from around the globe, but perhaps the most meaningful was the eulogy delivered by Indiana University President Herman B Wells, another legendary Hoosier. At McNutt's graveside service at Arlington National Cemetery, Wells stated, "As it is with mountains, so it is with men. Some dominate their scene even though they walk with giants. Such a man was Paul Vories McNutt."

Today, the Paul V. McNutt Quadrangle, a residence complex comprised of a half dozen five-story buildings at IU in Bloomington, bears his name and features a bust of him in the front foyer. The campus home to around 1,350 undergraduates, McNutt quad is one of the largest student residences among the Big Ten universities.

9.2

New Deal Projects in Indiana

*Government is competent when all who compose
it work as trustees for the whole people.*

— *Franklin Delano Roosevelt, second presidential
Inaugural Address, January 20, 1937*

President Franklin Delano Roosevelt responded
to the Great Depression by creating major federal programs designed to put unemployed Americans to work,
modernize the nation's infrastructure, and revive the
economy. For Hoosiers hit hard by the depression, one
of the FDR administration's most visible initiatives
was the Works Progress Administration (WPA), which
provided jobs for the unemployed.

The WPA began to operate in Indiana in July 1935.
By October, nearly 75,000 Hoosiers were on its employment rolls. Between 1935 and 1940, the percentage of Indiana residents working on WPA projects was
considerably higher than the national average. The
majority of Hoosiers working for the WPA built infrastructure such as roads, bridges, and sewers. Others
worked on public buildings and recreational facilities.
Nearly every Indiana community enjoyed some physical evidence of the program. The WPA also hired artists
and writers to document and create tributes to Hoosier
culture that the general public could enjoy and are still
enjoying today.

Indiana: A Guide to the Hoosier State

The cover of *Indiana: A Guide to the Hoosier State*, written by Hoosiers employed in the Federal Writers' Project and published by Oxford University Press in 1941

Indiana: A Guide to the Hoosier State

*Every Hoosier believes that Indiana has made a great con-
tribution to culture in the United States, and that the story
of this peculiarly distinctive State is worthy of the closest
scrutiny by all Americans.*

— *Ralph N. Tirey, "Foreword" to* Indiana: A Guide to the
Hoosier State *(1941)*

One white collar WPA program was the Federal
Writers' Project, which employed writers in each
state to produce a comprehensive book on that state's
unique culture and history. These volumes, produced
between 1935 and 1943, became part of the American
Guide Series. Hundreds of Hoosiers from all walks
of life worked on the book—historians, sociologists,
novelists, librarians, naturalists, geographers, photog-
raphers, college and university presidents, and public
administrators. In 1939 oversight of the Guide Series

shifted from the federal government to the states. Indiana State Teachers College, now Indiana State University in Terre Haute, sponsored *Indiana: A Guide to the Hoosier State*, which first appeared in 1941.

Indiana: A Guide to the Hoosier State offers a window through which to view Indiana in the 1930s. It remains an invaluable primary source for today's historians, teachers, students, and the general public. The original edition was about 550 pages long and included dozens of historic and then-contemporary images, as well as a state map. In Part One, "Indiana's Background," the editors provide succinct summaries of general topics, including Indiana's natural setting and archaeology, Indian tribes, history, agriculture, industry and labor, education, media, folklore, and the arts. Part Two covers fourteen "principal cities"—Gary, Hammond, East Chicago, Whiting, Corydon, Evansville, Fort Wayne, Indianapolis, Muncie, New Albany, New Harmony, South Bend, Terre Haute, and Vincennes. Part Three contains twenty driving tours that cover sites of interest across the entire state.

Interviews with Former Slaves

"I am 110 years old; my birth is recorded in the slave book. I have good health, fairly good eyesight, and a good memory, all of which I say is because of my love for God."

> — *Rosaline Rogers, Indianapolis resident, December 29, 1937*

The WPA Federal Writers' Project saved a remarkable piece of history when fieldworkers interviewed former slaves. The freed slaves who told their stories in the Indiana interviews had been held in slavery in any of eleven other states. While some of the former slaves interviewed had gone on to successful lives in Indiana as ministers or teachers and one as a doctor, many ex-slaves lived in poverty. Writers' Project interviewers spoke with sixty-two former slaves in Indiana between 1936 and 1939; the interview transcripts are located with other Indiana Federal Writers' Project files in the collections of the Cunningham Memorial Library at Indiana State University, and many are published in a recent book by Ronald L. Baker.

LIBRARY OF CONGRESS, PRINTS AND PHOTOGRAPHS DIVISION, LC-USZ62-125149

Former Slave Mary Crane

When this photo was taken, Mary Crane was 82 years old and living in Mitchell, Indiana. She was born into slavery and was one of many former slaves interviewed as part of the WPA Federal Writers' Project between 1936 and 1939.

New Deal Recreational Landmarks and State Parks

"Our parks and preserves are not mere picnicking places. They are rich storehouses of memories and reveries. They are guides and counsels to the weary and faltering in spirit. They are bearers of wonderful tales to him who will listen; a solace to the aged and an inspiration to the young."

> — *Richard Lieber, director of the Department of Conservation, 1928*

Hoosiers love their state parks, which had their origins in Indiana's centennial celebration in 1916. There were twelve state parks by 1933, and in the following decades, the state continued to add new parks to its state park system. In 1930 total state park attendance was nearly half a million people.

A decade later attendance had more than doubled. In the years since, generations have enjoyed the park improvements and recreational facilities created by the New Deal. The parks as we know them today owe a great deal to the Civilian Conservation Corps (CCC), a program that put unemployed young men to work building recreational structures such as cabins, picnic tables, shelters, saddle barns, hiking trails, band shells, and swimming pools at state parks and other public recreational sites. CCC camps, supported by Governor

Civilian Conservation Corps

These photographs depict life at segregated Civilian Conservation Corps (CCC) camps in Worthington and Corydon, Indiana, and come from photo albums of former CCC workers. Young men struggling to find jobs came from across the country to build infrastructure throughout Indiana, often in natural areas such as the Harrison County State Forest. Some could also gain an education and receive high school diplomas if they had not yet graduated. CCC workers constructed the camps they lived in, as well as roads, bridges, and park structures.

Paul V. McNutt and the state's Democratic legislature, emerged in Indiana shortly after Roosevelt instituted the program in 1933.

Indiana's first CCC camp was located in Morgan–Monroe State Forest. Camps soon sprang up in Spring Mill, Lincoln, Turkey Run, McCormick's Creek, and Indiana Dunes State Parks. Each camp had approximately two hundred male workers living in racially segregated accommodations. The workers used native materials such as timber and split rock to build handsome, solid structures, many of which are still in use today. Among the finest are Lower Shelter at Brown County State Park, Pokagon's CCC Shelter, and the saddle barn at Clifty Falls.

CCC projects included protecting and restoring natural resources. Workers planted thousands of native trees, mostly black locust and white pine, to reforest parks such as Pokagon and Shakamak. New dams and spillways aided in flood control and created new bodies of water, especially welcome in southern Indiana where natural lakes were rare.

No new Indiana state parks were created during the New Deal era, but two Recreation Demonstration Areas (RDAs), at Winamac and Versailles, became state parks soon after. The New Deal created RDAs to show the recreational value of land unsuitable for farming. For example, the Winamac area in Pulaski County was mostly marshy floodplain, and Versailles in Ripley County was primarily stony hills and wetlands. The areas became Tippecanoe River and Versailles State Parks, respectively.

During the New Deal, the state's Department of Conservation educated Hoosiers about responsible stewardship of natural resources and the conscientious enjoyment of state parks. In 1934 the department published the first issue of *Outdoor Indiana*. The magazine proved very popular; it was still in print in 2014 and even had its own Facebook page.

Murals of Indiana

Colonel Lieber's quick understanding of my desire to represent a social progression made it possible for me to transfer my original historical plan from the United States as a whole to the State of Indiana, the context of whose history is symbolical of the entire country.

— Thomas Hart Benton, "A Dream Fulfilled"
in Indiana: A Hoosier History (1933)

Starting in 1934 and 1935, respectively, the Section of Painting and Sculpture (a division of the U.S. Treasury renamed the Section of Fine Arts in

PHOTO BY DAVID TURK, INDIANA HISTORICAL SOCIETY

Suburban Street

The mural *Suburban Street* by New Deal artist Alan Tompkins, graces the walls of the post office in Broad Ripple, Indiana. Tompkins wrote that the mural depicted "the atmosphere of mutual trust and friendliness, of peace and security, that is the essence of life in a democracy" when he finished it in 1942.

Benton Mural

Thomas Hart Benton painted this mural, *Parks, the Circus, the Klan, the Press*, for Indiana's exhibit at the 1933 Century of Progress Exposition in Chicago. Some have objected to depicting the Klan with their burning cross and American flag, but Benton's panel actually condemns the Klan and celebrates, in the foreground, a white nurse tending to an African American child and the press, which played a role in the Klan's downfall.

1938) and the Federal Art Project (FAP) put to work hundreds of artists who applied their talents to beautifying public buildings. Many public buildings, especially post offices in Indiana, contain beautiful murals created by these programs. These remarkable murals depict scenes from Indiana history and Hoosiers engaged in daily activities. Attica's post office mural, *Trek of the Covered Wagons to Indiana* by Reva Jackman, shows pioneers seeking their new home. *Gas City in Boom Days*, painted on the wall of that town's post office by William A. Dolwick in 1939, illustrates a prosperous time during the natural gas boom of the 1890s. In *Indiana Farm—Sunday Afternoon*, painted by Alan Tompkins in 1938 and mounted on the walls of the North Manchester post office, a Hoosier family relaxes outside on their day of rest.

One of the New Deal era public mural projects stirred major controversy—Thomas Hart Benton's Indiana Murals. Not directly part of the FAP, the murals were commissioned by Richard Lieber, director of Indiana's Department of Conservation, for the state's exhibit at the 1933 Century of Progress Exposition in Chicago. Lieber granted Missouri-born Benton com-plete artistic control for his ambitious plan to depict "The Social History of Indiana" from "the Savage Indians to the present days of our machine culture"—with one exception. Lieber questioned Benton's inclusion of a Ku Klux Klan rally in a panel titled "Parks, the Circus, the Klan, the Press," which illustrates scenes of Hoosier life in the 1920s. Benton insisted that the Klan's rise and fall was significant and needed to be included. His wishes prevailed. Controversy over the "KKK mural" continues to this day.

In 1938 Governor M. Clifford Townsend presented Benton's Indiana murals as a gift to Indiana University after IU President Herman B Wells expressed an interest in them. Today, they grace the walls of three buildings on the Bloomington campus and are seen daily by the people they represent—the men, women, and children of Indiana.

Many New Deal era works of art have been restored, but sadly others have not. In towns and cities throughout the state, Hoosiers should be on the lookout for amazing work of 1930s public art the next time they go to buy stamps or mail a package.

9.3

World War II: Hoosiers on the Home Front

"America became very patriotic, everyone pitching in to get the job done so there would be no more, 'too little and too late,' supplies like there had been for months."

— *Lovilla (Horne) Greene, Indianapolis, Lukas–Harold plant employee during World War II, reminiscing ca. 1991*

No bombs fell on Indiana. At first the violence of World War II was far removed from the state. But in the end, almost every Hoosier had friends and relatives in uniform. No generation had experienced such enormous change in such a short time since the Civil War. Hoosiers waited anxiously for letters and read about the war in newspapers, particularly reports from Hoosier correspondent Ernie Pyle. For the people left on the home front, these letters and newspaper reports were constant reminders that victory over Germany and Japan would require more than soldiers fighting in foxholes, fighter planes, tanks, and battleships. On the home front they were fighting an economic war, and the decisive battle was one of production. America's ability to produce everything from weaponry to food would decide who won the war, and Indiana was on the front lines of that battle.

Hoosiers Working for Victory

No one in Evansville on 7 December 1941 could have anticipated the degree to which the war would alter the way they existed.

> — *Darrel E. Bigham, "The Evansville Economy and the Second World War,"* Traces of Indiana and Midwestern History *(Fall 1991)*

The industries and companies that contributed most to the war were at the center of Indiana's economy even before the war. Factories switched from producing for peacetime to producing the necessities of war. The automobile industry, for example, manufactured everything from trucks and other military vehicles to shell casings and electrical equipment for tanks, planes, and ships. The growing industrial cities received most of the war supply contracts. Indianapolis, South Bend, Gary, Hammond, Fort Wayne, and Evansville led the list.

Shipbuilding in Evansville

During the first three months of 1942, Evansville secured several huge War Department contracts for the national defense effort. The city's inland location on a major waterway—the Ohio River—made it ideal for large-scale war production. In early January Chrysler began operating under an ordnance works, a service of the army tasked with making military supplies, and announced that it would hire five thousand workers to assemble airplane wings and tail surfaces. February brought an announcement by the Navy Department that a forty-acre site on the city's west side would be cleared for the building of a shipyard for producing landing craft. Then in March, the Republic Aviation Company released news that it would build a massive aircraft factory on the city's north side to build P-47 Thunderbolts to be used as fighter planes and bomber escorts.

Production boomed. Chrysler was busy cranking out plane parts and ammunition. Its huge ordnance works produced more than three billion rounds of .45 caliber ammunition, 96 percent of what was used in the war. In February 1942 site preparation for the Evansville Shipyard began. Shipbuilders at the yard began building the first landing ship and tank (LST) in June. The largest inland shipyard in the nation, Evansville Shipyard produced around 170 LSTs and 31 smaller craft. The Republic factory broke ground in April 1942, and the first P-47 Thunderbolt rolled off the line in September. By the war's end, the factory had built approximately 6,000 Thunderbolts.

The war brought Evansville an economic reversal of fortune. By 1944 Vanderburgh County had received nearly $580 million in war defense contracts, the highest of any southern Indiana county and fourth highest in the state. Employment went from 18,000 in 1940 to approximately 60,000 by midwar. By the war's end, about 75 percent of Evansville's factories were involved in war production.

Do with less— so they'll have enough!

Rationing Poster

World War II greatly affected Hoosiers on the home front, as this poster from 1943 shows. In order to save resources for soldiers, the government rationed how much food people could buy as well as rationing gasoline, rubber, and shoes. Hoosiers adapted by carpooling, planting "victory gardens," and in other ways. However, some also bought gasoline or meat on the black market, defying the government rationing system.

RATIONING GIVES YOU YOUR FAIR SHARE

Evansville LST

A crowd gathers to celebrate a newly built landing ship and tank (LST) waiting to be launched in the Evansville Shipyard on September 30, 1943.

War production also brought some long-term growth to Evansville. For instance, International Harvester bought the Republic plant; the factory that had turned out thousands of Thunderbolts began to manufacture refrigerators after the war. However, the end of the war also brought some returns to the status quo. After the war most women left their factory jobs and went back to work in their homes, some more willingly than others. Racial tension and segregation remained. Labor and management, which had been on good terms during the war, were again at each other's throats. In addition, unexpectedly on January 26, 1946, the largest fire in the city's history destroyed the Evansville Shipyard.

The Calumet Region Gears Up for War

World War II also turned around the economy of the Calumet Region. The lean depression years were gone. Jobs were plentiful, with the mills operating three shifts a day, seven days a week, to meet the needs of defense production. The Region's industrial might played a major role in the Allied victory. Led by U. S. Steel's Gary Works and Inland Steel's Indiana Harbor Works in East Chicago, steel was used to build ships, tanks, trucks, jeeps, bombs, ammunition, and even mess kits.

Standard Oil refineries in Whiting stepped up production to provide the government with millions of gallons of high octane aviation fuel, diesel fuel, and gasoline for military planes and vehicles. Home front industries developed a great demand for lubricants and grease to keep their overworked machines running smoothly.

Industries in Hammond met the government's demand for other items. American-Maize Company turned forty thousand bushels of corn into sugars each day. The W. B. Conkey Company supplied essential

Women Workers

In this photograph, women are making turbine blades for military planes in 1944. During World War II, women took on new jobs in factories such as this one in Kokomo, Indiana.

printed materials such as manuals for pilots and tank operators. Another Hammond company made army and navy pennants.

Work Place Inequality— A Home Front Battle Continues

Round-the-clock production meant a need for more workers. The iconic image of Rosie the Riveter represents the women workers who flooded into the factories during wartime. But the war did not bring gender equality. Many women took a "man's job" at lower pay than the man who had done the work before the war. After Victory Day in Europe, known as V-E Day, women's jobs vanished almost as quickly as they had appeared. Factories replaced women with men, many of them returning veterans.

Wartime necessity also resulted in unprecedented hiring of Mexican American and African American workers, but they generally had the lowest-paying and least desirable jobs. Many black workers commuted from Gary to the Kingsbury Ordnance Works in La Porte County, one of the nation's largest shell-loading plants, for difficult and dangerous work. Kingsbury managers designated jobs as male or female and white or black, with separate assembly lines for African American workers. Racial tensions appeared in several plants. Some unions shut out black workers. A bill to lessen discrimination in defense employment met strong opposition in Indiana's General Assembly.

In a war for freedom, African American Hoosiers continued to experience segregated jobs, housing, and schools. This was a bitter pill to swallow for black veterans returning home after fighting for their country. Fed up with inequality, many became part of what would later be called the Civil Rights Movement.

World War II: Myth vs. Reality

"You know—we've had to imagine the war here, and we have imagined that it was being fought by aging men like ourselves. We had forgotten that wars were fought by babies. When I saw those freshly shaved faces, it was a shock. 'My God, my God'—I said to myself, 'It's the Children's Crusade.'"

> — *Kurt Vonnegut, dialogue in* Slaughterhouse-Five *(1969)*

Benjamin Franklin said there never was a good war or a bad peace. Yet, many considered World War II a "good war," for reasons that are complex and provoke animated discussion. Hoosier novelist Kurt Vonnegut was an American POW in Germany and survived the devastating bombing of Dresden. He fictionalized part of his traumatic war experience in *Slaughterhouse-Five*, arguably one of the greatest war novels ever written. Vonnegut would probably agree with Franklin and have a colorful (and likely unprintable) comment if he heard someone call World War II "good." Good or bad, the war certainly never ended for Vonnegut and his generation, who marked segments of their lives as "before the war" and "after the war."

In 1945 Hoosiers were thinking about jobs, homes, babies, going to college on the GI Bill, and the possibility of another depression. Little did they know, they were living at the beginning of America's longest period of economic growth. Few imagined that they would come to be called the Greatest Generation for having lived through and survived the Great Depression and World War II.

Kurt Vonnegut Jr.

Kurt Vonnegut Jr. served in World War II, where his experiences as a prisoner of war in Dresden, Germany, profoundly influenced him and provided the basis for his novel *Slaughterhouse-Five*.

9.4

Eli Lilly and Company: A Hoosier Family Business Goes Global

"My whole existence has been rather humdrum, and I can't imagine who on earth would want to read even the best possible sketching of my life."

— *Eli Lilly to C. W. Hackensmith, April 21, 1972*

Eli Lilly and Company, the phenomenally successful Indianapolis pharmaceutical company, has produced medicines that have saved millions of lives since Colonel Eli Lilly, a Civil War veteran and chemist, founded it in 1876. Successful from the start, the company's innovation, productivity, and impact exploded during the 1920s and continued after World War II. Today Eli Lilly and Company is one of the world's largest drug manufacturers.

Eli Lilly (1885–1977), the Colonel's grandson, was key in transforming a family business into a global corporation. To the casual observer, Lilly was a typically modest Hoosier who once called his existence "humdrum." His unassuming manner belied the intelligence and vision that made him one of Indiana's greatest business leaders.

A Remarkable Leader for Remarkable Times

Born on April 1, 1885, Lilly grew up in Indianapolis near his paternal grandparents. His family and his Indiana roots were extremely important to him throughout his life. After graduating from Shortridge High School, Lilly earned a degree in pharmaceutical chemistry from the Philadelphia College of Pharmacy, as had his father, Josiah K. Lilly. In 1907 he returned to Indianapolis and joined his family's business on McCarty Street. He once said that he never thought of doing anything else.

Lilly had worked at Eli Lilly and Company since he was ten years old. As a young man out of college, qualified and eager for a challenge, he headed the new Economic Department. His task was to increase

efficiency and production. To accomplish this, Lilly embraced research and new technologies. He even designed a bottle-filling machine that saved the company $7,500 in its first year of implementation. He also educated his workers to be mindful of wasteful practices. By 1917 the McCarty Street complex had four new buildings, one housing the largest capsule factory in the world, which was capable of producing 2.5 million capsules per day.

Mass-Producing a Miracle Drug

In 1922 the Indianapolis pharmaceutical company acquired an exclusive license to produce and sell insulin in the United States. The drug's Canadian inventors had difficulty mass producing the medicine, which had proven to be a virtual miracle treatment for diabetes, a deadly disease that previously had no effective

Eli Lilly
Eli Lilly speaks at an event, ca. 1960s.

Lilly Straight-Line Production

This photograph shows Eli Lilly and Company's straight-line production method in 1923. With this new assembly-line process, Lilly increased output and profits.

treatment. Led by brilliant British chemist George Henry Alexander Clowes, whom Lilly had hired as director of biochemical research, Eli Lilly and Company began to produce insulin in large quantities. It was a win-win situation for the company and for diabetics. By late 1923 nearly half of the company's profits came from insulin sales, with nearly 25,000 Americans taking the drug.

Insulin's success encouraged Lilly to expand the company's research capabilities by working with academic researchers around the globe. In the 1920s the company introduced many important new products including Amytal (the first American barbiturate/sedative), Merthiolate (an antiseptic/germicide), ephedrine (for asthma and allergies), and liver extract (for anemia). The company continued to grow, and Eli Lilly took over as president in 1932.

More, Better, Faster— Supplying the War Effort

Like many other businesses, Eli Lilly and Company supported the war effort during World War II. The war increased the need for the company's products, especially typhus and flu vaccines and Merthiolate.

There was also a huge demand for blood plasma and penicillin. Even with a shortage of trained personnel, the company managed to ramp up production of those products essential for treating war casualties. A year after Pearl Harbor, it manufactured ten thousand packages of blood plasma a week. By the war's end, Eli Lilly and Company had supplied nearly twenty percent of the United States' total plasma production. The company earned no profit from the blood because Lilly believed it would be wrong to make money on blood that individuals donated. Mass producing penicillin, an antibiotic discovered in 1928 and not produced or used on a large scale until the war, proved very challenging, but it was worth the effort, given the drug's life-saving capabilities. The penicillin produced in 1943 was grown in thousands of milk bottles using a painstaking surface culture method. A year later, due to research breakthroughs, the company made the drug in eight 1,000-gallon tanks.

The post-war years brought prosperity to Eli Lilly and Company. It expanded again in order to keep up with demand, building a new plant and shipping department on Kentucky Avenue. By 1948 the company was a global corporation with employees in thirty-five countries. That year, Lilly stepped down as president of the company and passed the title over to his brother, Josiah K. Lilly Jr., who held the position for five years. Gradually, the company shifted away from family management but continued to play an immense role in central Indiana.

The Legacy of Eli Lilly

There is nothing so pathetic as the person who keeps his nose so close to the grindstone that when the time comes to adopt an easier mode of life, he has no other interests.

— *Eli Lilly, "The President's Column,"* SuperVision, *company newsletter, November 1946*

Eli Lilly masterfully guided his family's business from the first decade of the twentieth century to the middle of the century. But his legacy extends far beyond building an innovative Hoosier corporation with a reputation for treating its employees well. Lilly passionately pursued his interests in Indiana history and giving back to his native state.

Lilly discovered an interest in archaeology in the 1930s and soon employed an aspiring Hoosier archaeologist named Glenn Black to study and map Indiana's archaeological sites. When Black died in 1964, Lilly encouraged and financially backed the publication of his nearly finished research on the Angel Mounds site. He also established the Glenn A. Black Laboratory of Archaeology at Indiana University in Bloomington to which he donated his extensive archaeology collection and library.

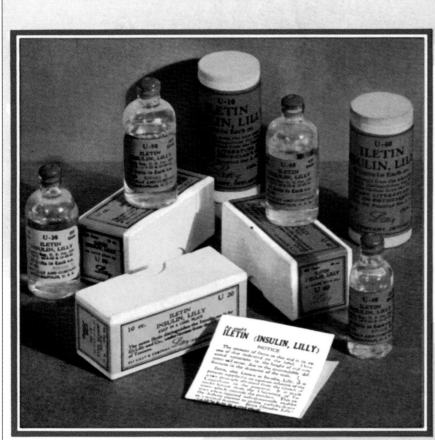

ILETIN
INSULIN, LILLY
was the
**First Insulin
Commercially Available In
The United States**

Lilly Insulin Ad

This advertisement for insulin, ca. 1930, showcases that Eli Lilly and Company was the first commercial producer of insulin in the United States, which it marketed under the brand name Iletin. This treatment for diabetes, which Lilly began producing in the 1920s, earned the company widespread recognition and large profits.

Lilly's other strong interest was preserving Indiana's historical sites. In 1934 he purchased the 1823 home of Indian trader William Conner and rescued it from ruin. Along with restoring the Conner house, Lilly wanted to re-create pioneer Indiana on the adjacent property. His vision and money made possible the experiences enjoyed today at Conner Prairie Interactive History Park.

Conner Prairie was Lilly's largest historic preservation project, but he had many others, including William Henry Harrison's Vincennes home, various projects in the historic river town of Madison, and the Waiting Station at Crown Hill Cemetery and Lockerbie Square in Indianapolis. All the while he became an active leader and financial contributor to the Indiana Historical Society. Today, the endowment income from his gifts helps continue the historical society's work. As the state's major archive of non-governmental records the IHS collects, preserves, interprets, and shares the history of Indiana and the Old Northwest.

Giving Back to Indiana

Like his grandfather and father, Eli Lilly believed in charitable giving, and he gave generously to causes he believed in, such as archaeology and history. In 1937 Lilly joined with his father and brother to form the Lilly Endowment to support good work, especially in religion, education, and community development. For example, the Lilly Endowment supplied most of the funding for the Glenn Black Laboratory's handsome building.

Today, in keeping with the founders' wishes to give back to the city and state that were so good to them, about seventy percent of the Lilly Endowment's funds go to Indianapolis and Indiana non-profit organizations, including community foundations in each county in the state. As of January 2014, the Lilly Endowment ranked sixth on the list of top U.S. foundations, with assets exceeding more than $7 billion.

Selected Bibliography

Arnold, Eleanor, ed. *Buggies and Bad Times*. Indiana: Indiana Extension Homemakers Association, 1985.

Baker, Ronald L. *Homeless, Friendless, and Penniless: The WPA Interviews with Former Slaves*. Bloomington: Indiana University Press, 2000.

Berry, Chad. *Southern Migrants, Northern Exiles*. Urbana: University of Illinois Press, 2000.

Blakey, George T. "Battling the Great Depression on Stage in Indiana." *Indiana Magazine of History* 90, no. 1 (March 1994): 1–25.

Bodnar, John. *Our Towns: Remembering Community in Indiana*. Indianapolis: Indiana Historical Society, 2001.

Carlisle, John C. *A Simple and Vital Design: The Story of the Indiana Post Office Murals*. Indianapolis: Indiana Historical Society, 1995.

"CCC Brief History." Civilian Conservation Corps Legacy, http://www.ccclegacy.org/CCC_Brief_History.html.

Chambers, David Laurance, and Thomas Hart Benton. *Indiana: A Hoosier History*. Indianapolis: Bobbs–Merrill, 1933.

"Federal Art Programs." GSA: U.S. General Services Administration, http://www.gsa.gov/portal/content/101818.

"'For the Duration': Memories of the Hoosier Home Front." *Traces of Indiana and Midwestern History* 3, no. 4 (Fall 1991): 8–21.

Foster, Kathleen A., Nanette Esseck Brewer, and Margaret Contompasis. *Thomas Hart Benton and the Indiana Murals*. Bloomington: Indiana University Press in cooperation with the Indiana University Art Museum, 2000.

Fuller, Robert L. "Mr. Halleck's New Deal: Congressman Charles Halleck and the Limits to Reform." *Indiana Magazine of History* 103, no. 1 (March 2007): 66–92.

Greiff, Glory-June. *People, Parks, and Perceptions: A History and Appreciation of Indiana State Parks*. Trafford Publishing, 2009.

———. "The WPA in Indiana." In *Indiana History: A Book of Readings*, edited by Ralph D. Gray. Bloomington: Indiana University Press, 1994.

Kotlowski, Dean J. *Paul V. McNutt and the Age of FDR*. Bloomington: Indiana University Press, 2014.

Indiana Gross Income Tax Division, Department of Treasury. "The Indiana Gross Income Tax Passes in Review." *Gross Income Tax and Store License Digest* (August, September, October 1938).

Indiana Writers' Project/Program Collection Introduction. Cunningham Memorial Library, Indiana State University, http://library.indstate.edu/about/units/rbsc/iwpp/intro.html.

Lilly Endowment, Inc. http://www.lillyendowment.org/theendowment.html.

Lynd, Robert S., and Helen Merrell Lynd. *Middletown in Transition: A Study in Cultural Conflicts*. New York: Harcourt, Brace and World, 1937.

Madison, James H. *Eli Lilly: A Life, 1885–1977*. Indianapolis: Indiana Historical Society Press, 2006.

———. *Hoosiers: A New History of Indiana*. Bloomington: Indiana University Press; Indianapolis: Indiana Historical Society Press, 2014.

———. *Indiana through Tradition and Change: A History of the Hoosier State and Its People, 1920–1945*. The History of Indiana 5. Indianapolis: Indiana Historical Society, 1982.

Mangione, Jerre. *The Dream and the Deal: The Federal Writers' Project, 1935–1943*. Syracuse, NY: Syracuse University Press, 1996.

Manuscript Division, Library of Congress, and Prints and Photographs Division, Library of Congress. "Born in Slavery: Slave Narratives from the Federal Writers' Project, 1936–1938." American Memory, Library of Congress, http://memory.loc.gov/ammem/snhtml/snhome.html.

McCray, Warren T. "Message of Governor Warren T. McCray to the 73d Biennial Session of the Indiana General Assembly at the Capitol in Indianapolis, Thursday, January 4, 1923." In *Message of [the] Governor to . . . [the] General Assembly*. Serial, 1873–1939. Available on Google Books.

McNutt, Paul. *Inaugural Address of Governor Paul V. McNutt of Indiana*. Indianapolis: Wm. B. Burford Printing, 1933.

McShane, Stephen G. "Boom! The World War II Home Front in the Calumet Region." *Traces of Indiana and Midwestern History* 3, no. 4 (Fall 1991): 22–25.

Morgan, Iwan. "Fort Wayne and the Great Depression: The Early Years, 1929–1933." *Indiana Magazine of History* 80, no. 2 (June 1984): 122–45.

Obermiller, Phillip J., Thomas E. Wagner, and E. Bruce Tucker, eds. *Appalachian Odyssey: Historical Perspectives on the Great Migration*. Westport, CT: Praeger Publishers, 2000.

Rosales, Francisco Arturo, and Daniel T. Simon. "Mexican Immigrant Experience in the Urban Midwest: East Chicago, Indiana, 1919–1945." *Indiana Magazine of History* 77, no. 4 (December 1981): 333–57.

Ruegamer, Lana. *A History of the Indiana Historical Society, 1830–1980*. Indianapolis: Indiana Historical Society, 1980.

Sample, Bradford. "A Truly Midwestern City: Indianapolis on the Eve of the Great Depression." *Indiana Magazine of History* 97, no. 2 (June 2001): 129–47.

Thornbrough, Emma Lou. *Indiana Blacks in the Twentieth Century*. Bloomington: Indiana University Press, 2000.

Turk, Katherine. "'A Fair Chance To Do My Part of Work': Black Women, War Work, and Rights Claims at the Kingsbury Ordnance Plant." *Indiana Magazine of History* 108, no. 3 (September 2012): 209–44.

Vonnegut, Kurt. *Slaughterhouse-Five, or, The Children's Crusade: A Duty-Dance with Death*. New York: Dial Press, 1969.

Walsh, Justin E. *The Centennial History of the Indiana General Assembly, 1816–1978*. Indianapolis: Indiana Historical Bureau, 1987.

Writers' Program of the Works Projects Administration in the State of Indiana. *Indiana: A Guide to the Hoosier State*. American Guide Series. New York: Oxford University Press, 1941.

Essential Questions

1 How did the Great Depression affect Hoosier families?*

2 What "Little New Deal" programs did Paul McNutt enact as governor? Describe how these programs were intended to provide emergency help for unemployed Hoosiers in need.

3 What was the goal of the 1933 gross income tax?

4 How and why did Governor McNutt reorganize the state government?

5 What criticisms did McNutt's opponents offer of him?

6 What projects did the Works Progress Administration (WPA) undertake in Indiana between 1935 and 1940? What were/are some products of these projects?

7 How did the Civilian Conservation Corps (CCC) leave a lasting impression on Indiana's landscape?*

8 Describe the experiences of African Americans and Mexican Americans during the Great Depression and World War II and compare their experiences to those of white native Hoosiers.

9 How did Indiana businesses aid the World War II effort to make the home front the "arsenal of democracy"?

10 How did World War II transform the lives of many Hoosier women? What happened to them following the war?

11 How did the production of insulin propel Eli Lilly and Company to international success in the pharmaceutical industry?

12 What role did Eli Lilly and Company play in the war effort?

See student activities related to this question.

Activity 1: Unemployed in Bloomington

Introduction: Prior to the Great Depression, economic aid programs were organized at the local level. However, the stock market crash of 1929 brought on circumstances so severe that local aid could not fill the need. The desperation of the situation is evidenced in a letter written in February 1931 by a Mrs. Jess Beyers of Bloomington, Indiana, to Thomas W. Rogers, chairman of the Bloomington Citizens Committee on Unemployment Relief. The committee was a local agency that sought work for those in need and held fund drives, appealing to those still able to help. A brochure for this committee states, "This community is being called upon to aid in relieving the distress existing among a number of our own citizens due to prolonged unemployment." (Citizens Committee on Unemployment Relief Records)

In her letter, Beyers points out that the aid her family receives through this committee does not bridge the gap caused by chronic unemployment and leaves her family helpless to buy food or fuel for heat. Ultimately, the State of Indiana and the federal government stepped in to help families like that of Mrs. Beyers. In 1935 President Franklin D. Roosevelt signed the Social Security Act, establishing federal old age insurance (that is, Social Security), welfare, and unemployment insurance programs. A year later, Indiana established a Department of Public Welfare as part of Governor Paul V. McNutt's "Little New Deal" programs.

▶ Read the following excerpt from the February 1931 letter from Mrs. Jess Beyers to Mr. Thomas W. Rogers:

I know there is some people in the world that follows beging [begging] for a living but that [is] not me, Now here I set this afternoon with two sick children and ½ bucket of coal and nothing to eat. I can buy $1.00 worth of coal and one dollar worth of groceries and that will last maby [maybe] until Thursday. I feel like it is up to you to see to things like this as you are one at the head of the unemployment releaf [relief] work, you know as well as I do that this town does about the lease [least] of any town close around for there [their] unemployed. Terre Haute payes [pays] there [their] men

$10.00 for three days a week and many other places the same. You know a family of nine can't live on $7.00 a week and our new trustee things [thinks] 9 people aught [ought] to live on $1.50 for two weeks.

▶ With your classmates, divide the class into three groups:

- One group should budget $0.75 for a week's worth of groceries and coal

- The second group should budget for $7.00 a week

- The third group should budget for $10.00 a week.

▶ Use the prices on the chart below that lists the average retail price of many common foods for the years 1928–36 (Retail Prices of Food; Retail Prices and Cost of Living).

▶ Now answer the following questions based on your budgeting experience:

1 Was it difficult to create your budget? Why or why not?

2 Do you believe that the supplies of food and heating fuel you can purchase with $0.75 would be enough to last a family of nine for one week? What about with $7.00 or $10.00? Explain your answer.

3 How much more money do you estimate it would take to realistically sustain a family of nine for a period of one week?

4 How do you think situations like that of Mrs. Beyers in Bloomington affected the push to create federal aid programs such as the unemployment insurance provision of the Social Security Act of 1935?

Expenses, 1928–36

Grocery Item	Price/unit	Grocery Item	Price/unit
Wheat flour	3.3¢/pound	Cabbage	3.6¢/pound
Wheat cereal	24.9¢/28 oz. package	Onions	4.5¢/pound
Corn flakes	9.0¢/8 oz. package	Potatoes	2.2¢/pound
Chuck roast	22.5¢/pound	Canned beans with pork	8.1¢/16 oz. can
Pork chops	28.3¢/pound	Canned corn	12¢/no. 2 can
Roasting chickens	32.1¢/pound	Peas	12.8¢/no. 2 can
Butter	34.6¢/pound	Tomatoes	10.5¢/no. 2 can
Cheese	28.1¢/pound	Coffee	31.6¢/pound
Milk, fresh delivered	10.1¢/quart	Tea	85.4¢/pound
Milk, evaporated	8.2¢/14 ½ oz. can	Lard, pure	11.8¢/pound
Eggs	26.9¢/dozen	Vegetable shortening	25.5¢/pound
Bananas	8.7¢/pound	Oleomargarine	20.1¢/pound
Oranges	37.8¢/dozen	Sugar, granulated	5.8¢/pound

Energy Item	Price/unit		
Coal	$1.00/week ("Average Retail Prices of Coal Per Ton of 2,000 Pounds")		

Activity 2: The Civilian Conservation Corps in Indiana

Introduction: President Roosevelt championed a host of New Deal programs that were designed to provide aid for those hit hard by the depression. Some of these programs, such as the Civilian Conservation Corps (CCC), provided employment for out-of-work young men. CCC workers built recreational structures at state parks and completed projects protecting and restoring natural resources. The fruits of CCC labor remain today in the form of park structures, such as shelters, cabins, dams, and spillways, passages for surplus water from dams. CCC workers also planted trees to reforest land. Planting trees helped to prevent erosion, in which the rich top soil is washed away by wind and rain.

CCC camps were located at more than fifty places around Indiana, including the Morgan-Monroe State Forest and Spring Mill, Lincoln, Turkey Run, McCormick's Creek, and Indiana Dunes State Parks. The camps were segregated, each with approximately two hundred workers living in separate accommodations according to their race.

The Indiana Historical Society collections contain the letters of W. E. Mayo, an African American member of the CCC, to Ruth Greathouse in Indianapolis. Mayo began his time in the CCC at Camp Knox in Kentucky and was later stationed at the CCC camp near Cromwell, Indiana. He mostly performed office work, scheduling workers and administering projects, so he does not write much about the physical work itself. However, his letters offer a glimpse into daily camp life. For example, in his letter of April 4, 1935, to Greathouse, Mayo describes one of his CCC projects: "I went out with a group of leaders today and planted some trees as a part of a National Conservation Program. We had a lot of fun and planted 850 trees in two and one-half hours." (Ruth Greathouse Collection)

▶ A national group called CCC Legacy maintains a list of all the CCC Camps in each state. Visit the group's website, http://www.ccclegacy.org/CCC_Camp_Lists .html, to view a list of Indiana's camps.

1 Using Google Maps or other mapping software, mark the locations of Indiana's camps on a map of the state.

2 On this same map, mark the locations of state parks and state forests.

▶ Answer the questions below based on your map:

1 What camps were located at the site of a state park or forest?

2 What do you notice about the locations of other camps?

3 Identify the presence of natural resources such as trees, rivers, lakes, or wetlands near the camps. Label these natural resources on your map.

▶ Study the four CCC photos in Section 9.2. These photos were taken at the Indiana CCC camps at Worthington and Corydon, Indiana. The images depict daily life and labor at the camps. Select a photo and imagine camp life from the perspective of one of the young men pictured or who you imagine resides at the camp. Compose a letter home from this young man's point of view. Consider the following questions to help guide your writing:

1 What kind of work do you do at or around the camp? How does the work make you feel physically and mentally?

2 What are some of the sights, sounds, and smells you experience at camp?

3 Would you rather be working at the camp or be back at home? Explain.

4 What, if any, do you see as the long-term impacts of your work?

5 What activities do you engage in when you are not at work?

Activity References

Citizens Committee on Unemployment Relief Records, 1930–1973, M 1031. Indiana Historical Society.

Ruth Greathouse Collection, M622. Indiana Historical Society.

United States Department of Labor, Bureau of Labor Statistics. *Retail Prices and Cost of Living: June 1932.* Washington DC: U.S. Government Printing Office, 1932, http://babel.hathitrust.org/cgi/pt?id=mdp.39015073250121 ;view=1up;seq=29.

United States Department of Labor, Bureau of Labor Statistics. *Retail Prices of Food, 1923–36.* Bulletin No. 635. Washington DC: U.S. Government Printing Office, 1938, http://fraser.stlouisfed.org/docs/publications/bls/193710 _bls_635retailpr.pdf.

10

Economic Change Blows through the Hoosier State

"There are still plenty of things for us to produce. But mass production with low skills—that's doomed."

— *Ball State University economist Patrick Barkey, 2006*

Hoosiers in 1945 surely looked back over the previous decade and a half with a sense of relief. The depression and the war were over. But they must have wondered what the future held. Would a war with the Soviet Union soon follow the war with the Axis nations? Would the economic depression return, along with soup lines and patched clothing?

A Booming Economy

No one in 1945 could have imagined that the years from World War II to the end of the 1960s would be the longest period of sustained economic prosperity in American history. Indiana would be at the center of a steep ride up.

During this twenty-five-year period the state's factories of all kinds clanked and purred, producing the goods that fueled growth. Massive quantities of steel shipped out of the Calumet Region to build cars in Kokomo, refrigerators in Evansville, diesel engines in Columbus, and heavy-duty trucks in Fort Wayne. Workers at Conn and Selmer created band instruments in Elkhart, and RCA workers built television sets in Bloomington.

Indiana soil produced record crop yields. With new equipment, chemicals, and techniques, Hoosier farmers planted to the fence rows. As farms grew larger, agriculture moved toward the kinds of mass production methods that characterized manufacturing.

A New Affluence

The economic boom of the post-World War II years meant material prosperity for most Hoosiers. Washing machines, televisions, and two-car garages became part of the middle-class dream. Brightly-lit stores ringed county courthouse squares, offering an array of goods and services that would have awed nineteenth-century pioneers. In larger towns and cities multi-story department stores became cathedrals of consumerism. Shoppers at L. S. Ayres & Company in downtown Indianapolis could find furniture, shoes, typewriters, and mink coats, plus a tearoom where ladies in white gloves could have lunch.

Babies were part of the driving force of the new prosperity. Born in massive numbers between 1946 and 1964, they needed more of everything, from diapers to bigger houses. Plus, more parents were saving

Hudson Family Farms

Fertilizing corn on Hudson Farms, owned by fourth- and fifth-generation grain farmers near Crawfordsville, Indiana. Farming methods continue to evolve while agriculture remains an important part of Indiana's economy. Modern farms rely on new science and technology to increase their size and yields.

for their children's college educations than ever before. The loud and insistent voices of this boomer generation were the soundtrack of the era. (And boomer voices remain loud as they retire during the first third of the twenty-first century.)

The baby boomers also pushed Indiana toward reform in education. It was not just the need for more classrooms, teachers, and desks; it was the very nature of learning and how schools were organized that moved education toward the top of the Hoosier agenda, where it has stayed well into the twenty-first century.

Globalization and the Winds of Change

Many Hoosiers came to believe that the economy of the mid-twentieth century would last forever. Many believed that there would always be good-paying, lifetime jobs down at the factory. Consequently, many people were unprepared for the changes and challenges that stemmed from an increasingly global economy in the 1970s and after. Globalization was perplexing.

In some ways, though, Indiana had always been part of a global economy. After all, eighteenth-century French traders on the Wabash sent their furs across the Atlantic to European markets, and pioneer farmers shipped their pork down the Ohio River and on to New Orleans and foreign markets. But the late twentieth century brought new and deeper connections to the world economy. T-shirts, toys, and even basketballs manufactured in other parts of the world began to appear in Indiana stores, challenging American-made goods. Indiana jobs moved overseas or south to Mexico.

The most obvious sign of globalization came in the volatile price of gasoline. The oil embargo of 1973–74, when Arab nations banned trade of petroleum with the United States, created long lines at gas stations and highlighted American dependence on Middle Eastern petroleum. This glimpse of the global economy was a subject of endless talk for Hoosiers and a fact many found difficult to digest.

Talk also centered on new competition in the auto industry, first from Germany and then Japan. When, in 1989 the first Japanese-owned auto plant (Subaru–Isuzu) appeared in a cornfield near Lafayette, there was a growing realization that the world was changing.

Shopping in Columbus

Driving became a way of life in the mid-twentieth century. Fewer and fewer people walked or used public transportation to finish their errands as seen in this Columbus, Indiana, photo. Outside the strip mall of stores, including Kroger, a camera shop, and a bakery, the parking lot is filled with cars.

Boomer Classroom

The Baby Boom and school consolidation led to full classrooms, such as this first and second grade classroom in a Monroe Township Consolidated School in Kosciusko County, ca. 1959–60.

Chevys and Fords might not always rule the roost.

Increasing factory automation and other productivity gains meant fewer workers were needed. By the late 1980s U. S. Steel's Gary Works was producing more steel with far fewer workers, which Gary's mayor, Thomas Barnes, stated was "'a great success story for the company.'" But, he added, "'It ha[s] been a painful experience for us. The fact is, a business that once employed 21,000 people now employs about 7,500, and that number is probably never going to go any higher.'"

The kinds of high paying, low-skill jobs that were abundant in the 1950s became scarcer by the end of the century. Hoosiers wondered how to prepare for the new economy. What kinds of education and training would qualify a high school student for a good twenty-first century job? Industry had shifted so that a high

school dropout had little chance of finding a job in a modern auto factory.

During the era of postwar prosperity there was impressive expansion of the middle class. A rising tide did, indeed, lift most boats. But there were always Hoosiers outside the sphere of affluence, people left behind, who struggled to feed and house their families. As good jobs declined, the middle class shrank as the gap between rich and poor widened.

Such massive changes in the Indiana economy at the turn of the twenty-first century made a very different world from that known by the generation of the Great Depression and World War II. Today's generations face new questions not just in jobs but in education, health care, social welfare, environmental responsibility, and politics.

Subaru Plant

Inside the Subaru of Indiana Automotive plant near Lafayette, cars go through the body shop before moving on to be painted. The Subaru plant is one example of how Indiana fits into a global economy.

10.1

Car Culture and Suburbanization

See the USA, in your Chevrolet;
America is asking you to call.

— *Chevrolet advertisement jingle, 1949*

In the years following World War II, cars drove their way straight to the middle of Hoosiers' lives. Indiana's auto plants roared with life twenty-four hours a day as they struggled to keep up with the postwar demand. With profits soaring for the Big Three (General Motors, Chrysler, and Ford), the United Auto Workers (UAW) union negotiated higher wages, better pension plans, and health care for its members. In Anderson, Marion, and other auto industry towns, jobs were abundant. Workers moved into the middle-class income brackets, enjoying the pleasures of new suburban houses and paid vacations, and for some, luxury items, such as boats, and college educations for their children. Just as car production was fueling Indiana's postwar economy, the product itself was changing the landscape and the way Hoosiers lived.

Road Rage

Roads were all the rage. Hoosiers couldn't get enough of them. Thanks to generous federal subsidies provided by the Interstate Defense Highway Act of 1956, highways spread across the state and through its cities. Indianapolis, already considering itself the Crossroads of America, was blessed with seven interstate highway spokes, eventually joined by one highway, I-465, connecting the spokes like a wheel and surrounding the inner city and its outlying areas. This interstate system expanded the path of the old railway line that had ringed the inner city in the late 1800s.

In Indiana and across America middle-class white families left the older city neighborhoods near early rail lines in favor of new suburbs built close to the new interstates. Their migration, sometimes called "white flight" in reference to its racially specific nature, left

downtowns blighted and practically empty. Urban neighborhoods grew increasingly poor with a greater percentage of minority groups living in them.

With suburban expansion and increased highway mileage, public transportation declined—even in larger cities such as Indianapolis, where the last electric streetcar on rails stopped running in 1953. New construction was auto-centric. Hoosiers could conduct their business and pursue their pleasures from behind the wheel. Columbus attracted famed architect Harry Weese to design a bank in which the drive-up window was "the key element"—everything else stemmed from it. Among the first of the state's many malls, Glendale in Indianapolis opened for business in 1958. Others soon followed, their acres of parking lots pulling shoppers from former retail districts and faraway Main Streets. Drive-in hamburger stands and movie theaters, strip malls, and gas stations popped up in the ample spaces opened for development by new roads to suburbia. Many Hoosiers took to the roads for their vacations in recreational vehicles (RVs), most of which were made in Elkhart, an older industrial city that acquired new fame as the "RV Capital of the World."

Baby Boomers Take the Wheel

For a state that benefited directly from increasing automobile use, Indiana's future seemed bright. The Baby Boomers—a generation of children born between 1946 and 1964—came of age alongside a new generation of powerful wheels such as Mustangs and GTOs with V-8 engines that propelled their passengers down suburban streets and around town squares. Hot cars were coveted items for teenage baby boomers.

Cruising became a common activity for teens who had no particular place to go but wanted to be out in a car with other teens. But, while cruising was enjoyable, making a beeline to a special destination was better. Like the 1920s generation, young people drove to the places where they could have the most fun and hear popular music. On September 3, 1964, for example, thousands of young Hoosiers converged on the Indiana State Fairgrounds to hear one of the decade's most popular groups, The Beatles. Just getting there was tricky as fair officials barricaded streets, re-routed traffic, and called in emergency and security personnel to handle the crush.

On a more ordinary Friday or Saturday night, teens might head to a favorite drive-in restaurant to grab a burger and meet friends. A. R. McComb's Wigwam Drive-in, built next to the State Fairgrounds in 1932, rebuilt and renamed the Tee Pee in 1939, became a beloved Indiana landmark until its demolition in 1988. A&W Drive-ins offered a kiddy mug—manufactured by the Indiana Glass Company in Dunkirk, Indiana—for the siblings in the back seat. Drive-ins declined in the 1970s as fast food chains (including Indiana-based Burger Chef, a long-time

rival of McDonald's and Burger King) offered quicker, cheaper food in a paper bag from a drive-up window. Today, drive-ins are quaint relics and few remain.

Only later, as they approached middle age, would members of the Baby Boom generation question the auto-dependent world that their parents had built and they had bought into. Constant road construction brought with it increased traffic congestion and air pollution. Interstate highways cut through older urban neighborhoods, cutting off downtowns from intercity residential areas and creating eyesores such as the mass of interstate interchanges known as the "spaghetti bowl" in downtown Indianapolis. Farms and private land were sliced and diced to make way for new

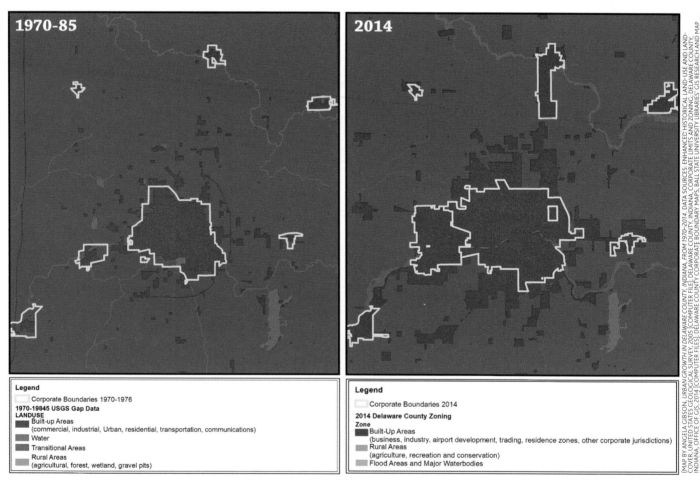

1970-85

2014

Legend
☐ Corporate Boundaries 1970-1976
1970-19845 USGS Gap Data
LANDUSE
■ Built-up Areas
  (commercial, industrial, Urban, residential, transportation, communications)
■ Water
■ Transitional Areas
■ Rural Areas
  (agricultural, forest, wetland, gravel pits)

Legend
☐ Corporate Boundaries 2014
2014 Delaware County Zoning
Zone
■ Built-Up Areas
  (business, industry, airport development, trading, residence zones, other corporate jurisdictions)
■ Rural Areas
  (agriculture, recreation and conservation)
■ Flood Areas and Major Waterbodies

Urban and Suburban Growth in Muncie, Delaware County, 1970–2014

Between 1970 and 2014, Muncie grew in size as residents moved away from the town center, fueling the creation of suburbs. This map shows Muncie's outward expansion. This suburbanization movement is found to an even greater extent around other Indiana cities such as Fort Wayne and Indianapolis. Movement to the suburbs developed along with interstate highways and strip malls.

Tee Pee Drive-in Restaurant

A popular hangout for teenagers, the Tee Pee Drive-in in Indianapolis served up hamburgers, French fries, and shakes. Servers brought the food directly to the car, where people could sit and eat as this 1957 photograph shows.

interstate paths, including the controversial extension of I-69 from Indianapolis south to Evansville. Downtowns, courthouse squares, and eventually some older shopping centers died slow deaths as customers clogged the big discount department stores and fast food chains that continued to cluster near interstate ramps. The suburbs of Marion, Lake, Hamilton, Allen, Vanderburgh, and other populous counties could offer safe streets, good schools, and green lawns, but they could also be sprawling, traffic-clogged enclaves of blandness and boredom. On a Sunday afternoon in the twenty-first century, nostalgic Boomers sometimes hop in their cars and head for the city centers—now often rejuvenated with preserved architecture and new cultural and retail opportunities.

James Dean—Hoosier Car Lover, Cultural Icon

"Jimmy wanted speed. He wanted his body to hurtle across over the ground, the faster the better. Jimmy was a straightaway driver. His track was the shortest distance between here and there."

— *Ken Miles, auto mechanic who raced with James Dean*

In the flat fields that flank Interstate 69 between Muncie and Fort Wayne, billboards announce that "You are Now Entering James Dean Country." The signs typically feature the image of the handsome young Hoosier that everyone recognizes, even though he's been dead for almost sixty years.

Dean was a typical Hoosier teen who was fascinated by speed and anything with a powerful engine. Growing up on a farm just outside the small town of

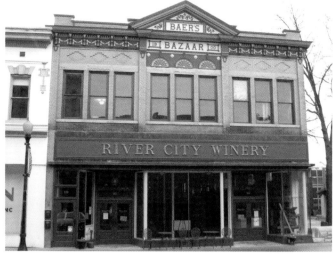

New Albany Storefront Before and After

Suburbanization and a changing economy led to the deterioration of many inner cities and main streets. However, in recent years growing historic preservation and revitalization efforts have created new life in old places. In New Albany in 2009, the River City Winery opened in the newly restored Baer's Bazaar building, which dates from 1900. The restoration helped spark other preservation projects in this Indiana river town.

Fairmount, he played basketball and rode his motorcycle—fast. When people complained about his reckless driving, Dean once said, "I've got to go places in a hurry. There just isn't time."

Professionally, Dean did go places in a hurry. After graduating from Fairmount High School in 1949, he went to Los Angeles, where he briefly attended college before dropping out to pursue acting full time. At warp speed, Dean attained superstardom, though he didn't live to know it.

"Terminal God"

"James Dean was Hollywood's Terminal God," wrote Dean biographer David Dalton many years later. "He arrived at a time when the movie industry desperately needed a new star." Dean starred in just three movies, but they ensured his admission to the Hollywood Pantheon: *East of Eden* (1955), *Rebel without a Cause* (1955), and *Giant* (1956). *Rebel*, with its climactic scene involving a fatal car crash, became the emblematic film of the young generation.

Off-screen, Dean, who had once dreamed of racing in the Indianapolis 500, did some racing in Hollywood. While shooting *Giant*, he purchased a silver Porsche 550 Spyder, a seductive car on the European and

American racetracks. On September 30, 1955, before the release of his second and third films, he was driving the Porsche across flat southern California farmland not unlike the countryside around Fairmount. A college student, oblivious of the low silver sports car flying toward him, turned into Dean's path. Hollywood's newest star was dead at the age of twenty-four. In Indiana, the reaction to Dean's death was low-key as this headline attests, "Fairmount Man Dies in Traffic Accident in West."

James Dean

Like many Hoosiers, actor James Dean loved to drive. He is pictured here on September 30, 1955, with his new Porsche Spyder prior to the drive that ultimately took his life.

10.2

Educating Hoosiers: The Evolution of Indiana Public Schools

It shall be the duty of the General Assembly to encourage, by all suitable means, moral, intellectual, scientific, and agricultural improvement; and to provide, by law, for a general and uniform system of Common Schools, wherein tuition shall be without charge, and equally open to all.

— 1851 Indiana Constitution, Article VIII, Section 1

No area of state government responsibility has changed more significantly than education. Indiana's 1816 constitution declared high-minded intentions regarding public education but lacked the power to deliver. Laws giving life to these intentions evolved only gradually. Circumstances for the pioneers and their children required them to clear land, work farms, and build roads; they never implemented a progressive system as outlined in the constitution.

Indiana's 1851 Constitution reiterated the commitment to provide a free and equal system of public education, but throughout the nineteenth century education was primarily a local responsibility over which the state had little control. Town and/or township governments ran public schools. A group of teachers

and citizens founded the Indiana State Teachers Association (ISTA) on Christmas Day 1854 out of concern for the state of education in Indiana, which had fewer children attending school than any other non-slave-holding state. The state subsequently mandated some changes, such as the compulsory school law of 1897, but city and township governments still paid the bills, hired the teachers, and set the agendas.

The School Reorganization Act

By the late 1950s disparity, or gaps, in the quality of education between urban and rural schools was more apparent; city schools offered wider curricula, better educated teachers, modern school buildings, and extracurricular activities such as band, theater, and sports teams. In 1959, after decades of debate, the general assembly passed one of the most significant pieces of legislation in twentieth-century Indiana: the School Corporation Reorganization Act—generally known as the school consolidation bill.

The 1959 law consolidated, or combined, small township schools into large consolidated schools. By 1968 the number of school corporations had dropped from 939 to 382, and more than 90 percent of Indiana students attended school in consolidated districts run by professional administrators. Greater efficiency and more uniform standards often lessened identification

ALLEN COUNTY PUBLIC LIBRARY'S COMMUNITY ALBUM, FORT WAYNE, INDIANA

Old Rural Schoolhouse

As township schools consolidated and larger regional schools took their place, the old school buildings got left behind. Rural schools, such as Oak Grove in Noble County, built in 1898 and photographed in 1973 surrounded by a corn field, remained a part of the landscape as a reminder of a very different era of schooling.

A Consolidated Indiana High School

South Dearborn High School in Aurora, Indiana, opened its doors in fall 1978. One of many new consolidated schools in the state, South Dearborn combined the populations of three township schools.

with a school, which lessened community pride. Old basketball trophies seemed out of place in a glass case in a new consolidated school known as "North Central" or "Eastern."

The State Steps In

As state control over schools increased so did state financing. During the Great Depression, a state gross income tax accounted for 30 percent of the revenue for schools, with the rest coming from local taxes. The state provided about one-third of the school funds until 1973 when a property tax freeze reversed the proportions. By the early twenty-first century, the state was providing three-fourths of education funding.

Recent governors have put education at the top of their list of priorities. During the 1980s Governor Robert Orr pushed hard for his A+ education package, which included increasing the school year from 175 to 180 days and implementing Indiana Statewide Testing for Educational Progress (ISTEP). Governor Frank O'Bannon put all-day kindergarten at the top of his agenda, although the legislature did not pass a law supporting all-day kindergarten until spring 2012 during Mitch Daniels's administration. Governor Daniels also pressed to offer parents and children more choices by championing charter schools and school vouchers.

By the early twenty-first century, Indiana had created one of the nation's more equitable school-spending systems, with less disparity between richer and poorer school districts than most states. Critics continued to argue, however, that the state did not spend as much on education as it should or could since it spent less than the national average on public education except in the area of higher education. Achievement gaps still remained, with students in wealthier communities scoring higher on standardized tests than students in inner-city schools or in many rural communities.

Well-schooled?

"Faith in education has been a dominant feature of our society since the beginning of the republic — a faith so strong that through private philanthropy and public taxation a school system has been built unparalleled elsewhere in the world."

— *Herman B Wells, president of Indiana University, December 1, 1938*

After World War II, state leaders focused simultaneously on K–12 education and higher education. Many of Indiana's private colleges continued to thrive, and the state universities grew rapidly. Indiana University under the leadership of Herman B Wells and Purdue University under Frederick L. Hovde established themselves nationally and internationally as outstanding institutions. The state universities created regional campuses and attracted adult learners around the state.

On the other hand, Indiana was slow in creating community colleges, in part because state universities resisted competition. Also, many Hoosiers believed adult education was not necessary; some believed there would always be well-paying assembly line jobs. There was also the general fear of added taxpayer expense for community colleges.

In 1963 Indiana took a step toward broader adult educational opportunities with the creation of Indiana Vocational Technical College, known as Ivy Tech or Ivy Tech Community College. As the economy changed, Ivy Tech expanded rapidly, with campuses sprouting up across the state. Confronted with fewer job opportunities in traditional manufacturing and in the auto industry, Hoosiers recognized the need for more training and education in the areas of higher-skilled manufacturing and technology, health care, service industries, and other developing fields of employment.

Educating for the Future

The burden of Indiana's educational future rests, therefore, it would seem, upon this fact: The schools can only be improved through the elevation of teachers as a body.

— *Indiana University professor of pedagogy Richard G. Boone,* Indiana School Journal, *1887*

Teachers have always been central to Indiana's educational system. As in any field, some teachers were better than others—some earned immense respect and long-lasting gratitude from former students while others were only minimally educated themselves. In 1854 ISTA pushed for better pay, better working conditions, and job security. More than one hundred years later, in 1973, Governor Otis R. Bowen signed into law a bill that allowed teachers to bargain collectively rather than as individuals with their respective school boards for their salaries, wages, hours, and benefits. This put more power than ever before into ISTA's hands.

Government leaders and educators continued to face the question of how to better prepare Hoosier students to work in a swiftly evolving global economy.

Comprehensive Plan for School Corporations in Allen County

This plan from 1962 spells out why Allen County needed to consolidate its schools. Allen County schools had been in the process of consolidating throughout the 1950s, but nine townships still operated their own schools in the early 1960s. Planners wanted to ensure that disparities between schools lessened and that resources were effectively allocated. They planned for school corporations to have a minimum of one thousand students for greater efficiency and to reorganize corporations so that the assessed tax valuation per student would be more equal.

CHAPTER II

Need for Reorganization

The need for reorganization of the Allen County School Corporations has been in evidence for a number of years. There are four school corporations that do not operate schools for all twelve of the grades. Experience has indicated that it is not practical to operate any school corporation with less than 1000 resident pupils in average daily attendance. Of the fifteen school corporations in Allen County, only three meet this recommended minimum. The number of pupils in average daily attendance varies from 110 (in Scipio Township) to 24,137 (in the Fort Wayne Community Schools).

All of the high schools in Allen County are giving instructions in forty or more units. All but two of the elementary schools have at least one teacher for each grade. The school buildings in Allen County are, on the average, in "good" condition. Only five of the 57 buildings which were rated received a "poor" rating while 16 received an excellent rating. The remainder were rated either "good" or "fair".

The overall pupil-to-teacher ratio in Allen County is approximately 18 to one.

A prime reason for the reorganization of the school corporations within Allen County is the difference in tax rates and in tax valuation per pupil in average daily attendance. The 1960 school tax rates in Allen County varied from a high of $3.62 per $100.00 assessed valuation to a low of $1.23 per $100.00 assessed valuation. The average tax rate for the entire county is approximately $2.42 per $100.00 assessed valuation. Table XXIV shows the details of the tax rates for each township in the county compared with the tax rates for the year 1950. The table also shows the percentage of increase in tax rates for a ten-year period.

The average assessed valuation per resident pupil in average daily attendance is approximately $13,379.00. The highest is $23,459.00 (Pleasant Township) and the lowest is $6,834.00 (Lafayette Township). Table XXV gives the details of these assessed valuations for each school corporation.

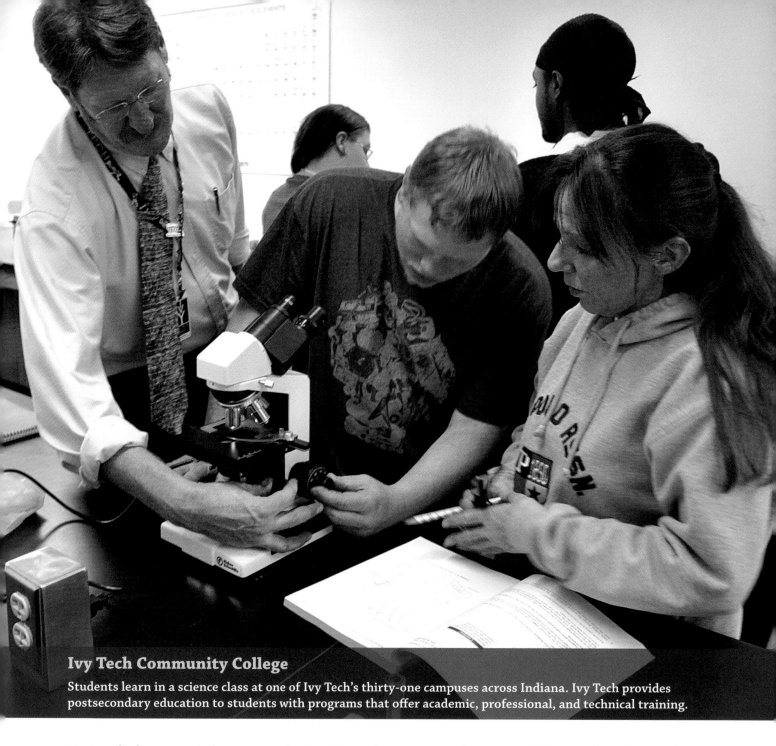

Ivy Tech Community College

Students learn in a science class at one of Ivy Tech's thirty-one campuses across Indiana. Ivy Tech provides postsecondary education to students with programs that offer academic, professional, and technical training.

During the late twentieth century, schools enhanced curricula with interactive media. Limited funds and rapidly-changing technologies made the "digital divide"—students who had access to new technology and those who did not—an ongoing challenge. State initiatives such as Indiana's 21st Century Scholars Program encourage at-risk students to stay in school and apply themselves. Launched in 1990, the program prepares low-income Hoosiers for college and grants students who take the Scholar Pledge a scholarship to help pay for their college education. In addition, state universities and colleges partner with high schools to offer programs for high school students that introduce them to higher education and enhanced future possibilities for their lives.

10.3

Farming Advances and Adaptations

Nothing is more erroneous than to think of agriculture as a declining industry. American agriculture is an expanding industry in every important respect except one—the number of people required to run our farms.

— Earl L. Butz, Dean of Agriculture,
Purdue University, 1962

After 1945 Hoosier farmers had to change how they farmed or fail. Even with their fortuitous location in the great American corn belt, the modern economy demanded more than ever before. Purdue University was at the forefront of agricultural research and helped Indiana farmers make the transition.

Many farmers sold their land and took factory jobs in the cities. Those who stayed—and succeeded—bought as much acreage as they could afford. Farms, like factories, were moving toward mass production and high-volume output as they connected to processors and retailers in a complex and massive food supply chain. New agricultural technology was in large part responsible for the transformation of small farms giving way to large farms. Tractors had replaced horses completely by the 1950s. Harvesting the corn also became mechanized with farmers using corn pickers and self-propelled combines that shucked the corn, instead of spending long hours completing the task by hand. In the 1930s scientists came up with hybrid corn seed that increased yields and quality. There were also advances in commercial fertilizers, herbicides, and insecticides.

What farmers grew was also changing in the middle of the twentieth century. Whereas farmers once produced a variety of crops and livestock, they began to move toward growing only one or two crops; most often those crops were corn and soybeans. Over the last century, Indiana has generally ranked as one of the top five corn and soybean producers in the United States.

By the late twentieth century, a rural "businessman" running a farm thought and acted much like his city cousin. Using large amounts of capital, wealth in the form of money and assets, as well as science, and technology, the Hoosier farm increasingly assumed the characteristics of any other business.

Farm consolidation

As the number of Indiana farms decreased, their individual size tended to grow. Instead of thousands of farms of one hundred acres or so, there were fewer farms with more than double the acreage and many with more than one thousand acres. In 1962 Earl L. Butz, Dean of Agriculture at Purdue who would serve as Secretary of Agriculture under Presidents Richard Nixon and Gerald Ford, refuted claims that fewer farms indicated agriculture was a declining industry. Butz reported that of the 68 million people employed in America at the time, about 26 million worked in some facet of agriculture. Even though there was a smaller share of the population directly involved in farming, the agricultural industries of processing and distribution employed millions of workers. Whereas in the mid-nineteenth century a farm worker could provide food and clothing for himself and three others, his 1960s counterpart fed and clothed himself and twenty-seven others.

The consolidation trend also applied to livestock farming. The majority of livestock, such as hogs, cattle, and chickens, were now being raised by large-scale, industrial facilities that produced for a few large corporations instead of on small family farms. Hoosier farmers also began to shift toward industrial production practices for eggs, milk, and other dairy products. By the twenty-first century places such as Midwest Poultry Services, in North Manchester, Indiana, kept six million laying hens; Fair Oaks Farms, near Merrillville, housed thirty thousand milking cows; and Leesburg's Maple Leaf Farms raised almost half of the ducks in the United States. Wooden barns, chicken coops, and pig pens were rapidly becoming quaint artifacts of an earlier time and of little use to modern Hoosier farmers.

Agribusiness, Science, and Technology

"We have a population that's headed toward nine billion by 2050, depending on which number and year you look at. The ability to feed all those people is going to become more and more of a challenge."

— *Susanne Wasson, Dow AgroSciences executive, 2012*

Science and technology played a major role in agricultural development in the late twentieth century. Universities used state and federal government grants to develop and disseminate new discoveries and methods. Indiana agribusiness companies, such as Dow AgroSciences, Elanco, and Beck's Hybrids, researched animal and grain production in laboratories and in the fields. Farmers became businessmen using computers and connecting their machinery to global positioning satellites. They learned to watch harvest numbers all over the world, from Asia to South America. Consequently, farmers became aware of the global economy before most Hoosiers.

The new technologies generally increased the state's agricultural production. Food was more plentiful and cheaper than ever before. However, by the early twenty-first century, there was growing concern about some methods of food production. Critics were skeptical of biotechnology, genetically-modified seeds, chemical fertilizers, and pesticides. Some were alarmed by reports of contamination and animal cruelty in meat producing industries. A general anxiety began to grow about the harmfulness of food additives and ingredients such as corn syrup in soft drinks and in many other foods. Some felt there must be a better way.

Organic Backlash—Back to Basics

"I swear when you talk to farmers today, you see a lot of the same passions my granddad would have seen. . . . They're people who believe in taking care of the earth and their neighbors."

— *Dr. Jay Akridge, dean of the College of Agriculture, Purdue University, 2012*

During the early twenty-first century, some American farmers began embracing more sustainable agriculture, using earlier farming practices such as crop rotation and fertilizing with manure. Adding to the push back against the dominance of corporate agribusinesses, some consumers began to prefer organic and locally-grown foods. In Indiana, to meet the growing demand, Hoosier small-farm entrepreneurs started producing a broad range of local and organic foods, including maple sugar, wine grapes, popcorn, honey, goat cheeses, mint, and bison meat. By the second decade of the twenty-first century, hundreds of local food producers dotted every part of Indiana. Open

Maple Leaf Farms

Maple Leaf Farms, a family-owned company based in Leesburg, Indiana, leads North America in duck production. Like many modern poultry companies, it works with a number of independent family farms to grow and care for its ducks. Its business has expanded and become more efficient over the years due to strategic business choices and new technologies.

air farmers markets became popular venues for local producers of fruits, vegetables, flowers, meats, and eggs. Organic dairy producers include Traders Point Creamery, northwest of Indianapolis; Gunthorp Farms in LaGrange, which sells pasture-fed pork and poultry to some of the nation's finest restaurants; and Fischer Farms, which raises high quality beef on an all-vegetarian diet outside of Jasper.

Working alongside local food producers are Hoosier restaurateurs who are committed to preparing and serving locally grown and raised food in traditional and healthy ways. Such restaurants are part of a broader trend in growing and eating habits across the United States called the Slow Food Movement. For example,

Chef Daniel Orr, who has cooked in fine Manhattan and Caribbean restaurants, returned to his Hoosier roots and opened FARMbloomington, a restaurant that serves food made from local ingredients in season. Orr states, "'When I think of Midwestern food, I think of my grandmother's kitchen—country cooking of the early 1900s. I go back and I look at some of those old cookbooks . . . and see what people were doing then and kind of add my own twist.'" The efforts of chefs such as Orr and other Slow Food restaurant owners are rewarded by Americans, who are generally more aware of what they eat because of the foodie phenomenon inspired by TV cooking shows and celebrity chefs.

Farmers Planting Hybrid Corn

Men pour a bag of hybrid corn seeds into a planter in this photo from Purdue University. Hoosier Jim Holbert was a leader in developing hybrid corn seed, which is bred to be disease resistant and to produce higher yields.

Indiana's Local and Global Food Economies

Since Native Americans and the first European settlers established roots in Indiana's fertile soil the state has had a farming tradition. With some of the top chefs in the country wanting products labeled "Made in Indiana," Hoosier agriculture has experienced a renaissance that includes the grassroots food producers as well as Indiana-based corporate brands with a global reach. The coexistence of the local and global in the state's food scene has been a win-win for both. Large purveyors are exploring new avenues of sustainability, while grassroots producers are finding new ways to expand their markets.

PHOTOS BY KRISTIN HESS, COURTESY OF INDIANA HUMANITIES, FROM DAVID HOPPE AND KRISTIN HESS, *FOOD FOR THOUGHT: AN INDIANA HARVEST* (2012)

Chef Daniel Orr

Chef Daniel Orr operates FARM-bloomington restaurant in Bloomington, Indiana, where he incorporates local and seasonal meat and produce into his dishes. Regarding ingredients Orr comments, "Being a great chef is 90 percent being a good shopper and 10 percent not messing up what you bought."

Jeff Hawkins, Sustainable Farmer

Jeff Hawkins, a pastor and farmer on Hawkins Family Farm in North Manchester, Indiana, is especially interested in the concept of health in agriculture and religion. Hawkins believes sustainability comes from having a polyculture on his farm, meaning there are multiple animals and crops that support one another.

10.4

RCA: A Tale of "Creative Destruction"

"A lot of people have built their dreams and their houses and their families working for that company."

— *Bill Breeden, trucker for RCA, 1997*

Boom Times in Bloomington

In February 1940 the people of Bloomington received great news: the Radio Corporation of America (RCA) had purchased one of the old factory buildings belonging to the Showers Brothers Furniture Company and was bringing hundreds of good-paying jobs to town. The *Bloomington Evening World* called it "one of the greatest forward advances in the history of the city." Bloomington's gain was a loss for Camden, New Jersey, since the company would largely abandon its East Coast operation. RCA's move was a classic example of what economists and business leaders call "creative destruction"—the movement of capital (wealth in the form of money and assets) to locations that produce greater profit. It provides us with a good model of the changing face of industry in many Indiana towns and cities during the decades that followed World War II.

Since the Great Depression, rural southern Indiana counties such as Monroe, where Bloomington is located, had been desperate for jobs. Monroe County's main industries, furniture making and limestone production, had been hit hard by the depression and had never fully recovered. Unlike Camden workers, the Bloomington workforce was mostly not unionized and was willing to work for lower wages. Bloomington also had a large population of what RCA deemed "high-class feminine labor"—young women with high school educations. RCA hired many workers from this pool,

paying its new women employees between 17.5 and 19.5 cents per hour, or $7.00 to $7.80 for a 40-hour work week, which was the highest pay rate for women workers in the county. Most of the women worked on assembly lines doing tedious jobs, such as crimping and soldering wires for radios, which required great manual dexterity.

By 1942 RCA employed 1,200 workers in Bloomington. Bursting with pride over the city's newfound prosperity, local government officials altered their stationery to read: "'Bloomington, in the Heart of the Famous Oolitic Stone Belt, is the Home of Indiana University, the world's Largest Furniture Factory and RCA Manufacturing Company.'"

Television Arrives

"A new art and a new industry, which eventually will provide entertainment and information for millions and new employment for large numbers of men and women, are here."

— *RCA founder David Sarnoff at the 1939 World's Fair*

RCA had conducted television research since the 1930s. World War II delayed the company's ability to get its new product into the marketplace, but America's post-war prosperity meant millions of potential customers for the device. In September 1949 the first televisions rolled off the assembly line in Bloomington. Color followed black and white and soon billboards on the outskirts of town proclaimed that travelers were entering the "'Color Television Capital of the World.'"

By 1960, RCA had relocated even its non-manufacturing divisions as well as its administration and marketing headquarters from Camden to Indianapolis. A year later the company employed more than 12,000 Hoosiers, having opened plants in Marion and Monticello.

Hoosier Workers Want More

"There was full employment, people didn't value a job. You'd have . . . songs like 'Take Your Job and Stick It [Take This Job and Shove it].'"

— *Ed Riedweg, Bloomington RCA plant manager, 1994*

While the first generation of RCA workers in Bloomington willingly worked for low wages, subsequent waves of workers demanded more. As in Camden, Hoosier RCA workers compiled a list of complaints. In 1950 workers staged a brief strike for wage increases, vacation and holiday pay, as well as for the right to choose their own insurance company. It was settled quickly, but the seeds of discontent and dissent were germinating. During the 1960s workers were unhappy with a variety of issues ranging from the speed of assembly lines to unequal pay scales for men and women.

Strikes became more frequent in the mid-1960s. RCA's threats to relocate had little impact on workers who had grown accustomed to plentiful jobs. Then, in 1968, the company announced the layoffs of more than 2,000 workers. It would be the first of many downsizings. Following the layoff, RCA management began to move lower-skilled production jobs from Bloomington to Ciudad Juarez, Mexico, where they found an abundance of non-union workers willing to work for lower pay. Creative destruction, which had helped bring jobs to Indiana, was beginning to take them away.

RCA Color TV

It may not have a large screen or high definition, but this RCA CT-100 console television was state-of-the-art in 1954! These televisions, RCA's first color televisions on the market, were manufactured in Bloomington, Indiana.

RCA Assembly Line

In this photograph, assembly line workers manufacture television sets at the RCA Victor Television Factory in Bloomington during the 1950s. The first color television set was produced here in 1954.

The Long Good-Bye

"The uncertainty of the future and the uncertainty of whether RCA will even keep producing in Bloomington or not has changed the worker from a secure, proud person to an uncertain, unruly, stubborn [one]."

— *Bloomington RCA worker, 1994*

Between April 1975 and July 1982, RCA eliminated 3,500 more positions in Bloomington. One Bloomington worker commented that rather than laying everybody off at once, "they just sort of snuck it out one line at a time." Historian Jefferson Cowie, whose work has highlighted the RCA story, points out that Bloomington workers were more fortunate than many other electronics workers in the nation because the company continued production in the United States longer than many of its competitors.

In 1994, even as RCA was downsizing its Hoosier workforce, the company purchased the naming rights to the Hoosier Dome in Indianapolis for $10 million. The ten-year-old, nearly 58,000-seat stadium was the home of the Indianapolis Colts football team. In February 1997, RCA announced that the Bloomington plant would close permanently the following year. Eleven hundred workers in the town, along with an additional 420 in Indianapolis, would lose their jobs. Despite the shocking news, employees showed up for work the next day, a Friday, and surpassed their daily production quota. Nelda Stuppy, a thirty-one-year RCA veteran, stated that they were "from the old school," explaining, "We're paid for a day's work and that's what we've always done. We all went in, started doing our jobs and did it well." On their last day in April 1998, Bloomington workers, with classic Hoosier stoicism, exited the plant singing, "Auld Lang Syne" and "Happy Trails to You."

Jesse Jackson in Job March

Anderson, Indiana, suffered extremely high unemployment in the 1980s due to layoffs in the auto industry. Thousands of residents and community leaders joined prominent national activist Reverend Jesse Jackson, second from left, in the "March for Jobs, Justice, and Peace" in 1983 to protest government inaction on unemployment.

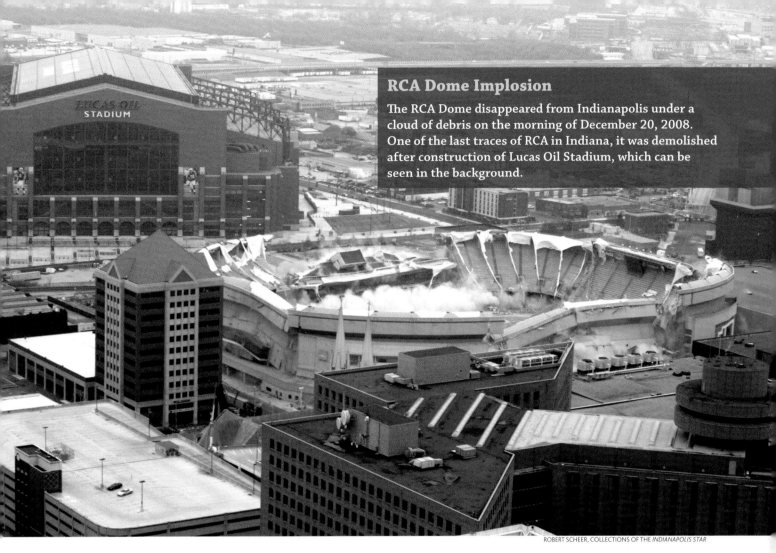

RCA Dome Implosion

The RCA Dome disappeared from Indianapolis under a cloud of debris on the morning of December 20, 2008. One of the last traces of RCA in Indiana, it was demolished after construction of Lucas Oil Stadium, which can be seen in the background.

Going Out with a Bang

The final shutdown of RCA in Indiana was part of a widespread trend of moving factories abroad. In the late twentieth and early twenty-first centuries, other electronics companies, including General Electric and Westinghouse, opted to pull up stakes in Indiana and head for the border or across the sea. Heavy industries, such as Kokomo's Continental Steel or Muncie's Borg-Warner, an auto parts manufacturing plant, were similarly affected by the rise of global competition and new technologies. In most places, the well-paying, steady jobs that were lost were not replaced. Some workers opted for early retirements or buyouts but many employees decided to go back to school in order to acquire new skills. Others found work at some of the new foreign-owned auto plants that sprang up in Lafayette, Greensburg, and Princeton—Subaru, Honda, and Toyota, respectively—while many tried to make ends meet by working several low-paying jobs. Today, empty factories dot Indiana and similar midwestern states, standing as painful reminders of a prosperous era that was creatively destroyed.

Indianapolis's RCA Dome—that symbol of downtown's revival and of RCA's commitment to its Indiana base—was imploded by a Baltimore-based company called Controlled Demolition at 9:35 a.m. on December 20, 2008. *USA Today* reported, "It took about 20 seconds and 875 explosive devices to reduce a landmark of the Indianapolis skyline to a broken pile of rubble." Not obliterated in the demolition was the $75 million debt still owed by the City of Indianapolis for the dome's construction in 1984. Hoosiers were now left to find new and sustainable ways of bringing good jobs and reliable business partners back to a state that had, for more than a century, invested heavily in its industrial future.

Selected Bibliography

1851 constitution, http://www.in.gov/history/2473.htm.

21st Century Scholars Indiana, http://www.in.gov/21stcenturyscholars/2524.htm.

"A Brief History of U.S. Unemployment." Business, *Washington Post*, http://www.washingtonpost.com/wp-srv/special/business/us-unemployment-rate-history/.

Bodenhamer, David J., and Robert G. Barrows. *The Encyclopedia of Indianapolis*. Bloomington: Indiana University Press, 1994.

Boone. R[ichard] G. "Indiana Teachers' Reading Circle." *Indiana School Journal* 32 (May 1887): 270–78. Available on Google Books.

Butz, Earl L. "Agriculture—An Industry in Evolution." In *Indiana: A Self Appraisal,* edited by Donald F. Carmony. Bloomington: Indiana University Press, 1966, 55–64.

———. "'Don't Downgrade Agriculture': Portion of Talk by Dr. Earl Butz, Dean of Agriculture, Purdue University, Taken from *Arizona Cattlelog*." University of Arizona, http://arizona.openrepository.com/arizona/bitstream/10150/299169/1/pa-14-02-16.pdf.

Capshew, James H. *Herman B Wells: The Promise of the American University*. Bloomington: Indiana University Press; Indianapolis: Indiana Historical Society Press, 2012.

Carnevale, Anthony P., and Nicole Smith. "The Midwest Challenge: Matching Jobs with Education in the Post-Recession Economy." Lake Superior State University, https://www.lssu.edu/ir/documents/midwest-challenge.pdf.

"City Still Owes $75 Million on Soon-to-Be Demolished RCA Dome." *South Bend Tribune*, October 29, 2006, http://articles.southbendtribune.com/2006-10-29/news/26976513_1_rca-dome-lucas-oil-stadium-debt.

"Corporate Tax Rate History." Indiana Department of Revenue, IN.gov, http://www.in.gov/dor/3470.htm.

Cowie, Jefferson. *Capital Moves: RCA's 70-Year Quest for Cheap Labor*. Ithaca and London: Cornell University Press, 1999.

Gehring, Wes D. *James Dean: Rebel with a Cause*. Indianapolis: Indiana Historical Society Press, 2005.

———. "The Last Ride: The Death of James Dean." *Traces of Indiana and Midwestern History* 17 no. 2 (Spring 2005): 36–47.

Hadley, David J. "Indiana: Interest Groups in a Changing Party Environment." In *Interest Group Politics in the Midwestern States,* edited by Ronald J. Hrebenar and Clive S. Thomas. Ames: Iowa State University Press, 1993.

Harris, Betty. "'I Want to Hold Your Hand': The Beatles at the Indiana State Fair." *Traces of Indiana and Midwestern History* 14, no. 4 (Fall 2002): 24–35.

Hoppe, David, and Kristin Hess. *Food for Thought: An Indiana Harvest*. Indianapolis: Indiana Humanities, 2012.

Hudson, John C. *Making the Corn Belt: A Geographical History of Middle-Western Agriculture*. Bloomington: Indiana University Press, 1994.

"Indiana Bank Is Automobile Oriented." *Architectural Record* (January 1964): 118.

"Indiana Glass Company." Historic Businesses, Indiana Historical Society, http://www.indianahistory.org/our-services/books-publications/hbr/indiana-glass.pdf.

Indiana State Teachers Association. *Advancing the Cause of Education: A History of the Indiana State Teachers Association, 1854–2004*. West Lafayette: Purdue University Press, 2004.

Longworth, Richard C. *Caught in the Middle: America's Heartland in the Age of Globalism*. New York: Bloomsbury, 2008.

Madison, James H. *Hoosiers: A New History of Indiana*. Bloomington: Indiana University Press; Indianapolis: Indiana Historical Society Press, 2014.

———. *The Indiana Way: A State History*. Bloomington and Indianapolis: Indiana University Press and Indiana Historical Society, 1986.

———. "John D. Rockefeller's General Education Board and the Rural School Problem in the Midwest, 1900–1930." *History of Education Quarterly* 24 (Summer 1984): 181–99.

———. "Old Times and New Times in Bloomington." In *Bloomington Past and Present*, edited by Will Counts, James H. Madison, and Scott Russell Sanders. Bloomington: Indiana University Press, 2002, 29–33.

Marcus, Morton J. "Taxing Hoosiers." *InContext* 4, no. 6 (November–December 2003), Indiana Business Research Center at Indiana University's Kelley School of Business, http://www.incontext.indiana.edu/2003/nov-dec03/government.asp.

McCarthy, Martha, and Ran Zhang. "The Uncertain Promise of Free Public Schooling." In *The History of Indiana Law*, edited by David J. Bodenhamer and Randall T. Shepard. Athens: Ohio University Press, 2006.

McCleery, Bill. "Home to Colts and Final Fours, RCA Dome Imploded." *USA TODAY*, December 20, 2008, http://usatoday30.usatoday.com/sports/football/nfl/colts/2008-12-20-rca-dome_N.htm?csp=34.

Metz, George W., and Penny Poplin Gosetti. "Indiana Higher Education: The Hoosier Commitment to Localism and Vocationalism." *Community College Journal of Research and Practice* 23 (1999): 43–59.

Michael, Robert S., Terry E. Spradlin, and Fatima R. Carson. "Changes in Indiana School Funding." *Education Policy Brief* 7, no. 2 (Summer 2009). CEEP: Center for Evaluation & Education Policy, http://ceep.indiana.edu/projects/PDF/PB_V7N2_Summer_2009_EPB.pdf.

Michna, Mary Ann. "Entering James Dean Country." *Traces of Indiana and Midwestern History* 17, no. 2 (Spring 2005): 30–35.

Nordin, Dennis Sven, and Roy Vernon Scott. *From Prairie Farmer to Entrepreneur: The Transformation of Midwestern Agriculture*. Bloomington: Indiana University Press, 2005.

O'Hara, S. Paul. *Gary: The Most American of All American Cities*. Bloomington: Indiana University Press, 2011.

Powell, Michael, and Monica Davey. "The Indiana Exception? Yes, But...." *New York Times*, June 23, 2011, http://www.nytimes.com/2011/06/23/us/23indiana.html?pagewanted=all&_r=0.

Sirico, Robert A. "Creative Destruction and the Pruning Shears: Choosing between Withering on the Vine and Fruitful New Growth." *American Spectator*, July 3, 2012, http://spectator.org/articles/35296/creative-destruction-and-pruning-shears.

Slow Food USA, http://www.slowfoodusa.org/about-us.

Stokes, Kyle. "Why Education Technology May Have to Wait for the Mainstream," October 18, 2011. State Impact Indiana: A Reporting Project of WFIU and WTIU, with support from IPBS, http://indianapublicmedia.org/stateimpact/2011/10/18/why-education-technology-may-have-to-wait-for-the-mainstream/.

Working America, "The 'Right to Work' Editorial that Renews Our Faith in Modern Journalism." *Daily KOS*, January 8, 2014, http://www.dailykos.com/story/2014/01/08/1268033/-The-Right-to-Work-Editorial-That-Renews-Our-Faith-in-Modern-Journalism#.

Essential Questions

1 In what ways did Indiana become "auto-centric" in the post-World War II era?

2 How did the construction of interstate highways change the Indiana landscape and lead to urban blight?

3 Name some positive and negative impacts of the 1959 School Reorganization Act.

4 How did school financing change in the 1970s?

5 Name at least two ways in which farming changed in the post-World War II era.

6 How have these changes affected farmers?

7 What is the "Slow Food Movement"?

8 What is "creative destruction"? Name one example of this process in Indiana.

9 Why did some industries, such as the Radio Corporation of America (RCA) and automobile-related industries find Indiana a hospitable place to do business?*

10 What caused RCA and other industries, such as those associated with automobile manufacturing, to begin downsizing their Indiana workforce and eventually leave Indiana?*

11 Define "globalization." How has it affected the Indiana economy?*

See student activities related to this question.

Activity: Economic Policy and its Effect on the Lives of Hoosier Workers

Introduction: Section 10.4 details the story of RCA's role in the Indiana economy. In 1940 when RCA first relocated a factory to Bloomington from Camden, New Jersey, Hoosier laborers were willing to work for less than their counterparts in Camden had been. Furthermore, state government created an environment hospitable to RCA and other corporations through a low corporate tax rate and a right-to-work law that enabled corporations to hire non-union workers. This enabled RCA to make a higher profit (money earned after paying expenses) than it did in Camden.

However, as the Hoosier workforce unionized and began to make demands of the corporation, Indiana seemed less of an ideal location for its factories and headquarters. Strikes in the 1950s and 1960s were generally focused on raising compensation and highlighted tensions between the corporation and its workforce. Eventually, these tensions resulted in RCA downsizing its Hoosier workforce beginning with a loss of 2,000 jobs in 1968. The company slowly moved production to Ciudad Juarez, Mexico, where it found many non-union workers willing to work for lower wages.

In February 1997 RCA announced that it would pull out of Bloomington, permanently closing the plant there and laying off 1,100 Bloomington and 420 Indianapolis workers. In April 1998 the factory shut its doors for good and left Bloomington reeling from the loss of jobs.

The story of the "creative destruction" Indiana experienced as a result of RCA leaving the state is not unique. It has been repeated in other industries, namely auto-related industries and the steel industry.

▶ With a partner or as a class discussion, consider the following questions:

1 RCA found Indiana an attractive environment in which to do business in part because of Indiana's right-to-work law. Define "right-to-work law." When was Indiana's first right-to-work law passed? When was it repealed, or revoked? How does a right-to-work law affect, positively or negatively, corporations and workers?

2 Why would a low corporate tax rate in Indiana be advantageous in attracting industry to the state? What might be some downsides of low corporate tax rates?

3 Using the RCA example, summarize how state laws and government economic policy can play a role in promoting economic prosperity.

4 As labor unions gained ground in Indiana, the state's economic policy became more supportive of workers and less advantageous for corporations. What improvements do you suppose Hoosier workers experienced as a result of this shift in policy? Consider the following issues in your answer:

• Wages

• Benefits—such as vacation pay and insurance

• Working conditions—environment, such as noise and danger levels

• Purchasing power—the costs of goods and services in relation to wage amounts

▶ Examine the photo of Jesse Jackson at a job march in Anderson in 1983 in Section 10.4. Auto-related industries also grew up in or relocated to Indiana due to economic policies that favored corporations in the post-World War II era. The workers in these industries also unionized and enjoyed high salaries and good benefits gained through union action. However, this photo reveals some long-term consequences of economic policies that bring significant benefits to labor.

1 Notice that one of the marchers is holding a sign stating, "America Works When Americans Are Working." What does this sign tell you about what happened to Anderson's auto industry jobs?

2 Article 4 of the Indiana State Constitution grants the legislature the right to pass laws; and Article 10 gives the state government the right to levy taxes. Given your understanding of the "creative destruction" Indiana experienced with RCA and auto-related industries, what do you think the role of state government should be in shaping economic policy? Who should the state economic policy benefit—corporations, individual workers, the state, others? All of the above?

3 Define "globalization" as it relates to economics. Do you think Indiana has benefitted from globalization or not? Explain your answer.

So far we have discussed economic policy at the state level, but federal economic policy has also affected the Hoosier workforce. In the 1990s the United States negotiated free trade agreements such as the North American Free Trade Agreement (NAFTA). NAFTA reduced or eliminated tariffs, or taxes, paid on goods imported into the countries that signed the agreement. In many cases, this made foreign-made goods less expensive than American-made goods. Before NAFTA, the United States charged taxes on many imported foreign goods. At the same time, the wages paid in these foreign countries were lower than the wages paid in America. The tax raised the cost of foreign goods so that it was about the same or higher than the cost of American-made goods. By eliminating or reducing the taxes, NAFTA made the foreign goods cheaper than the American goods. This had two results for American workers. They paid less for foreign-made goods than they had previously. However, it also resulted in American jobs being outsourced, or moved, to countries with cheaper labor costs.

As you have read, this happened with RCA, which outsourced jobs to Ciudad Juarez, Mexico. Auto and steel industry jobs also fell victim to outsourcing. Communities that were once dependent on those industries found that the rise in unemployment caused by deindustrialization and outsourcing often reduced standards of living and caused social problems such as higher occurrences of divorce, suicide, and domestic violence. (*Industrial Location*, 140)

Despite the results of outsourcing on communities that lose industries, many economists think that outsourcing is good in the long run because they consider outsourcing a form of trade. In 2005 Timothy Taylor, managing editor of the *Journal of Economic Perspectives*, stated, "'Eras of expanding global trade, like recent decades, have generally been times of economic growth. Periods of contracting trade have often involved recession or worse.'" ("Outsourcing Jobs to Other Countries")

Taylor's latter observation proved true in the ensuing global recession that began in December 2007, when trade also decreased. (*State of Working America*, 11–12) Many economists also point out that outsourcing makes up only a small part of the overall economy and that other countries outsource jobs (mainly service jobs, such as financial services) to the United States, offsetting some job losses. In addition, economists state that outsourcing lowers prices for the American consumer. Even if outsourcing brings challenges in the short term, in the long run it can be seen as a positive process. ("Outsourcing Jobs to Other Countries")

▶ Imagine that you are one of the protesters in the photo of Jesse Jackson at the job march in Anderson. You are about to lose your job to outsourcing. How would you react to the reasoning that outsourcing is positive for the economy? What evidence can you give that outsourcing hurts the economy? Consider the following issues in your answer:

- The effect of outsourcing on the purchasing power of those who lose their jobs

- The effect that competing with lower-wage overseas workers may have on wages in America

- The effect of outsourcing on the balance of trade— the monetary difference between a country's imports and exports (that is, does the United States buy more products from other countries or does it sell more products to them?)

▶ What actions, if any, do you think government (local, state, and/or federal) should take to encourage businesses to use American labor and to prevent jobs from going overseas? Write a letter to the editor of your local newspaper arguing your point of view.

Alternate Activities

1 Hold a class debate in which some students argue against outsourcing from the point of view of an affected worker and some argue for it from a corporate point of view.

2 In 2012 the Indiana General Assembly passed a new right-to-work law. Discuss arguments for and against the law, including speculating whether or not the law would help protect Hoosier jobs from outsourcing. Then, hold a mock election in which students cast a vote for or against the law. Tally the votes to see if the law would have passed if voted on only by the students in the class.

Activity References

Harrington, J. W., and Barney Warf. *Industrial Location: Principles, Practice, and Policy*. London: Routledge, 1995.

Mishel, Lawrence, Josh Bivens, Elise Gould, and Heidi Shierholz. *The State of Working America*, 12th ed. Ithaca, NY: Cornell University Press, 2012. Economic Policy Institute, http://stateofworkingamerica.org/subjectsoverview/?reader.

"Outsourcing Jobs to Other Countries: Is Globalization a Threat to the American Worker?" *Bill of Rights in Action*, 21, no. 3 (Summer 2005). Constitutional Rights Foundation, http://www.crf-usa.org/bill-of-rights-in-action/bria-21-3-c-outsourcing-jobs-to-other-countries-is-globalization-a-threat-to-american-workers.html.

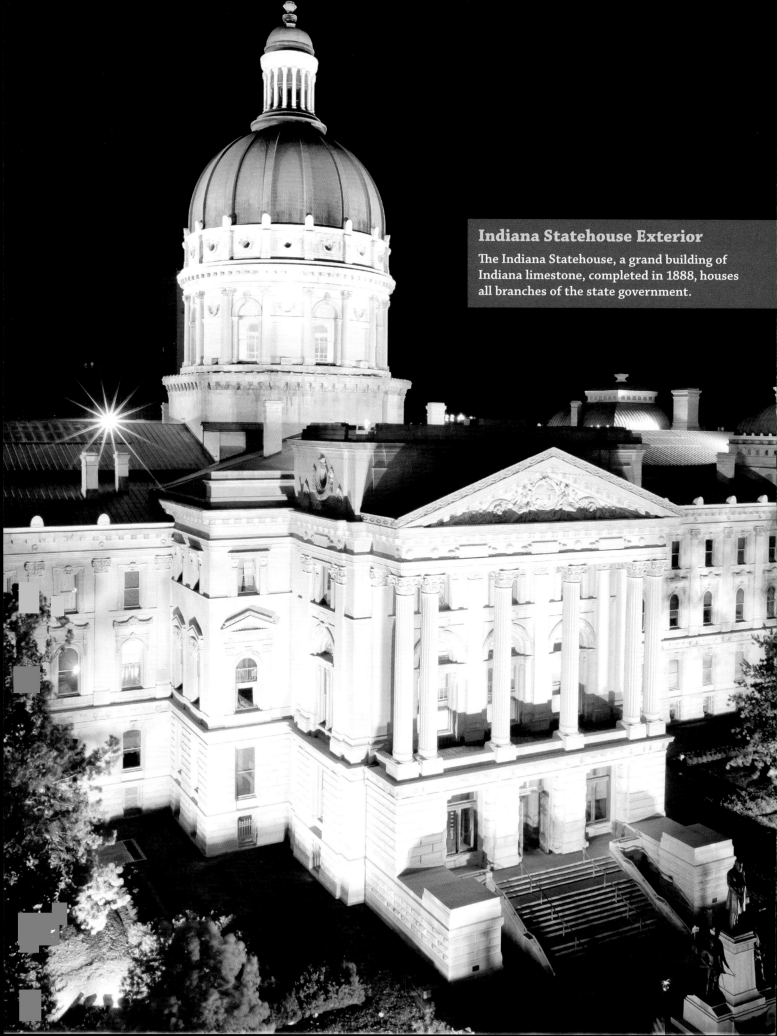

Indiana Statehouse Exterior

The Indiana Statehouse, a grand building of Indiana limestone, completed in 1888, houses all branches of the state government.

11

Justice, Equality, and Democracy for All Hoosiers

All men are born equally free and independent, and have certain natural, inherent, and unalienable rights.

— *Indiana State Constitution of 1816*

From the start, our nation and state claimed the highest ideals of equality and justice for all. The pioneers who wrote Indiana's first constitution in 1816 asserted boldly that "all men are born equally free" and that "all power is inherent in the people." They believed that such principles were essential to true democracy.

Writing such lofty words was easier than the reality of building and maintaining everyday democracy. Some Hoosiers allowed their own selfish interests or narrow prejudices to stand in the way of justice for all. Many men struggled to believe that women were worthy of full equality. Many whites thought blacks, Asians, and Hispanics were inferior. There were always Hoosier dissenters, people who lived outside the mainstream, who did not share the majority's beliefs in religion, politics, sexuality, and other contentious issues.

African American Hoosiers and Civil Rights

As Indiana became a state, the white majority in Indiana insisted that African Americans were second-class citizens. The 1816 constitution denied black Hoosiers the right to vote. Two years later the state legislature denied them the right to testify in courts and also prohibited marriages between white and black Hoosiers—a law that remained on the books until 1965. Such restrictions worsened in the decades before the Civil War, culminating in the addition of Article XIII to the 1851 constitution, prohibiting African Americans from moving into the state.

The Civil War (1861–65) and the period following, called Reconstruction (1865–77), produced important steps toward equal rights. Most notable was the Fourteenth Amendment to the U.S. Constitution, which guaranteed equal protection under the law, and the Fifteenth Amendment, which promised the right to vote to all men, black or white.

One of Indiana's major steps toward equality was the Civil Rights Law of 1885. As so-called Jim Crow laws were being passed in many states, relegating blacks to second-class status, Indiana's law promised that all Hoosiers could eat in any restaurant, sit in any theater, ride any streetcar, or rent any hotel room "regardless of color or race." The law was seldom enforced, however. In fact, Jim Crow discrimination became commonplace in late-nineteenth-century Indiana and lasted into the mid-twentieth country. As late as the 1950s, for example, some Indiana hotels still refused a room to a black traveler.

Segregation at Riverside Park

At Indianapolis's Riverside Amusement Park in 1962, these young people point to a sign that says "Patronage Whites Only Solicited," meaning the park only wanted white customers' business. Legal segregation also barred African Americans from hotels, restaurants, and education facilities into the mid-twentieth century, but implicit forms of segregation continued long afterward, often visible in housing patterns.

Especially troubling was discrimination in education. Some communities created separate schools for black children. Notable were Crispus Attucks High School, which opened in 1927 in Indianapolis; Lincoln High School, which opened in 1928 in Evansville; and Roosevelt High School, which opened in 1930 in Gary. All three are examples of schools built to keep black students out of white schools.

Housing patterns also developed along racial lines. Larger towns tended to divide into black neighborhoods and white neighborhoods. Some neighborhoods incorporated racial covenants in property deeds, making it impossible for African Americans to buy homes in certain areas. For example, deeds for one Bloomington neighborhood in 1927 stipulated that "the ownership and occupancy of lots or buildings in this sub-division are forever restricted to members of the pure white race."

There were always Hoosiers who challenged segregation and discrimination. The National Association for the Advancement of Colored People (NAACP) began its long fight in the early twentieth century. In Terre Haute, Indianapolis, Evansville, Gary, and elsewhere, NAACP branches worked with African American lawyers to bring suits in court against businesses and organizations accused of racial discrimination.

Black attorneys such as Robert Lee Brokenburr and Robert Lee Bailey in Indianapolis were determined and courageous opponents of Jim Crow. Such lawyers argued for the rule of law to remind whites of America's ideals of justice and equality.

Ordinary people also played major roles in bringing about change. Black veterans returned home from service in World War II believing they had earned full rights as Americans that had previously been denied them. Sadly, they were once again subject to racism at almost every turn. In the next two decades these veterans, joined by other Hoosiers, became the foot soldiers in the fight against discrimination which, by the 1960s, became the Civil Rights Movement.

Women and Equality

Nineteenth-century women never had rights equal to men. Many women came to believe that the right to vote was the most important step toward real citizenship. In the early twentieth century they shifted from "ladylike" protest—that is less public and more quiet—toward more assertive talk and action—such as protest marches in the street—in their long battle for suffrage. Finally, the Indiana legislature in 1920 ratified the Nineteenth Amendment to the federal constitution, guaranteeing a woman's right to vote. In 1921 the women's suffrage amendment was added to the Indiana State Constitution and ratified by voters at a special election. Hoosier women had the right to vote in local, state, and national elections.

The ballot box did not bring all the changes suffragists had hoped for, however. Many Hoosiers continued to expect women to defer to men. Jobs were still designated as men's work or as women's work. Salaries and wages were generally lower for women even if they were doing the same job as a man. Women could generally become secretaries, teachers, or nurses. Few were doctors, lawyers, or heads of business. Traditionalists thought women should stop working outside the home when they married. Although a number of jobs for women opened up during World War II, the gains were mostly temporary since women were expected to give up those jobs when soldiers returned home. It was not until the Women's Rights Movement of the 1970s that gender equality really took center stage.

Hoosier Differences

Hoosier pioneers prided themselves on their commitment to individual freedom. Many claimed they could do as they pleased so long as they did not harm others. Such freedom was the heartbeat of democracy. However, individual freedom did not always square with majority rule. The idea of majority rule was widely accepted. But what if the rule of the majority conflicted with the rights

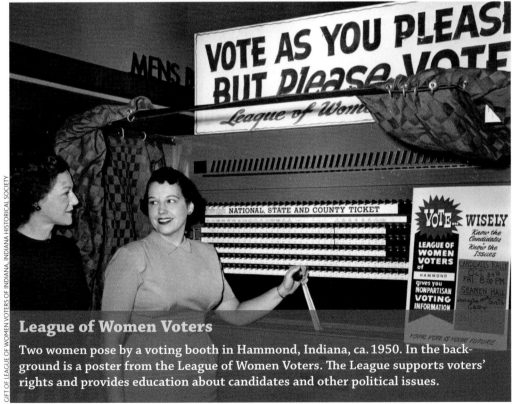

League of Women Voters

Two women pose by a voting booth in Hammond, Indiana, ca. 1950. In the background is a poster from the League of Women Voters. The League supports voters' rights and provides education about candidates and other political issues.

GIFT OF LEAGUE OF WOMEN VOTERS OF INDIANA, INDIANA HISTORICAL SOCIETY

During the late twentieth and early twenty-first centuries, some Hoosiers raised issues of separation of church and state, objecting to prayers in public schools or to Christian crosses on government spaces.

Sex was another difficult subject for many Hoosiers. Indiana University Professor Alfred Kinsey's research on human sexuality revealed many varieties of sexual behavior, including homosexuality. While many Hoosiers supported his work, many others thought Kinsey should be fired. Twentieth-century advocates of birth control education faced strong opposition. Today, there is strong opposition for abortion—some Hoosiers draw lines limiting when and how a woman can have an abortion; while others are against any

Alfred Kinsey

Alfred Kinsey conducts a sample interview in this photograph from 1953. Kinsey's interviews with a wide range of Americans led to his ground-breaking publications on human sexuality.

or wishes of a minority that wanted to live differently from the majority? Here was a central tension in Indiana and American democracy.

All sorts of individuals and groups found themselves in the minority. Often their different views and actions deeply troubled the majority. Standing outside the Indiana mainstream, for example, were the utopians at New Harmony in the early nineteenth century (see chapter 3). In the early twentieth century there were religious freethinkers—men and women who opposed organized religion. One freethinker also advocated a vegetarian diet, cold showers, and nudism.

abortions, as in cases of rape or when a mother's life is endangered.

Indiana's democracy has been fraught with tensions surrounding such issues as majority rule, individual rights, and minority freedoms. Differences over race, gender, religion, sexuality, and personal beliefs rumble through the state's history. Yesterday and today Hoosiers face tough questions about the meaning of democracy, not just in school textbooks, but in everyday issues concerning justice, equality, and freedom. These issues are often at the heart of legislative discussions and election battles—in Indiana and in America.

11.1

Robert Kennedy and the 1968 Indiana Primary

"Indiana is a terribly important state. If we can win in Indiana, we can win in every other state, and win when we go to convention in August."

— *Robert F. Kennedy on the steps of the Indiana Statehouse, March 28, 1968*

The Indiana Challenge

Of the three candidates in Indiana's 1968 Democratic presidential primary, Robert F. Kennedy seemed to face the greatest disadvantage. Kennedy entered the contest late, after his opponents had already gained a leg up. Roger D. Branigin, Indiana's popular governor, ran as a stand-in for President Lyndon B. Johnson and then, after Johnson withdrew from the race, Branigin remained. Many believed he did so in support of Vice President Hubert H. Humphrey. Minnesota Senator Eugene McCarthy had almost defeated Johnson in the New Hampshire primary earlier that spring and was popular with young voters because of his stance against American involvement in Vietnam.

All three primary candidates faced another huge challenge: Hoosiers. Kennedy's adviser, John Bartlow Martin, who was from Indianapolis, warned his candidate that Hoosiers were "skeptical, hard to move, with a 'show me' attitude." Kennedy's domestic policies, which championed the poor and disadvantaged, white and African American alike, were hard to sell to many Indiana voters, who remained focused on the virtues of hard work and limited government.

While not a southern state, Indiana was slow to implement and embrace its laws promoting racial equality. In the 1964 Democratic presidential primary, Alabama's pro-segregation governor, George Wallace, had done surprisingly well in the state, particularly in the northern industrial cities. Nonetheless, Hoosiers of all races advocated for civil rights. In the 1960s,

lunch counter sit-ins and other non-violent protests were bringing Martin Luther King Jr.'s dream of equality very slowly to Indiana.

April 4, 1968

"If I can win here in Indiana, I could go on to win the Democratic presidential nomination and turn this country around with your help."

— *Robert F. Kennedy, to a crowd in South Bend, April 4, 1968*

Kennedy's first day of campaigning in Indiana was a busy one. Like his brother, President John F. Kennedy, before him, he was particularly popular with Catholic voters, and he chose to stop first in South Bend, where a crowd of about five thousand gathered to hear him speak in the geodesic-domed Stepan Center at the University of Notre Dame. After squeezing in a visit to a home for the elderly, he traveled to Muncie, where he addressed an estimated crowd of twelve thousand at Ball State University's Men's Gym. The day was scheduled to end with two stops in Indianapolis, first at the

Primary Election Cartoon

This cartoon from the 1968 primary campaign season in the *Indianapolis Star* depicts Robert Kennedy (middle) and Eugene McCarthy (left) as unwelcome guests in the state as they try to charm a disturbed Mrs. Indiana. Governor Roger Branigin looks on disapprovingly from the right.

Robert F. Kennedy

A few days before the May 1968 primary election, Robert F. Kennedy made a campaign stop in Indianapolis where he reached out to African American audiences who comprised some of his main supporters. A month earlier, he had inspired many in the city with his speech given in response to Martin Luther King Jr.'s assassination.

opening of "Indiana Kennedy for President" headquarters at 36 Washington Street, and then at a rally at the Broadway Christian Center at 17th and Broadway, in the city's predominantly African American near north side.

It was around the time Kennedy addressed the crowd at Ball State that one of the nation's great tragedies took place: Martin Luther King Jr. was shot in Memphis, Tennessee. Kennedy heard the news while heading to Delaware County Airport for his flight to Indianapolis; when he reached Indianapolis's airport, he learned that King had died. The day's meticulous planning became instantly irrelevant. Concerned for the candidate's safety because of the possibility of riots erupting, Indianapolis Mayor Richard G. Lugar, the police, and other city officials urged Kennedy to cancel his Broadway Christian Center appearance. When Kennedy decided to follow through, they told him that he would proceed at his own risk.

Kennedy's Speech: Breaking the News and Defusing the Bomb

Kennedy canceled his visit to the downtown campaign headquarters and went directly to Broadway Christian Center. There, a large, primarily African American crowd awaited him. His staff had no idea how he would handle the situation. Kennedy's speechwriters had provided him with a few suggestions for what to say, but standing on the back of a flatbed truck he discarded any prepared remarks and instead looked directly into the upturned faces before him. Those near the front appeared eager with anticipation. Others on the periphery of the crowd were becoming agitated; some had heard the dreadful news.

Kennedy dispensed with the usual opening formalities, telling the crowd directly, "I have bad news for you, for all of our fellow citizens and people who love peace all over the world, and that is that Martin Luther King was shot and killed tonight." The screams and

Robert F. Kennedy's Speech in Indianapolis, April 4, 1968

Ladies and gentlemen, I'm only going to talk to you just for a minute or so this evening, because I have some very sad news for all of you. Could you lower those signs, please? I have some very sad news for all of you, and, I think, sad news for all of our fellow citizens, and people who love peace all over the world; and that is that Martin Luther King was shot and was killed tonight in Memphis, Tennessee.

Martin Luther King dedicated his life to love and to justice between fellow human beings. He died in the cause of that effort.

In this difficult day, in this difficult time for the United States, it's perhaps well to ask what kind of nation we are and what direction we want to move in. For those of you who are black—considering the evidence evidently is that there were white people who were responsible— you can be filled with bitterness, and with hatred, and a desire for revenge.

We can move in that direction as a country, in greater polarization—black people amongst blacks, and whites amongst whites, filled with hatred toward one another. Or we can make an effort, as Martin Luther King did, to understand, and to comprehend, and replace that violence, that stain of bloodshed that has spread across our land, with an effort to understand, compassion and love.

For those of you who are black and are tempted to fill with—be filled with hatred and mistrust of the injustice of such an act, against all white people, I would only say that I can also feel in my own heart the same kind of feeling. I had a member of my family killed, but he was killed by a white man.

But we have to make an effort in the United States. We have to make an effort to understand, to get beyond, or go beyond these rather difficult times. My favorite poem, my—my favorite poet was Aeschylus. And he once wrote:

Even in our sleep, pain which
cannot forget
falls drop by drop upon the heart,
until, in our own despair,
against our will,
comes wisdom
through the awful grace of God.

What we need in the United States is not division; what we need in the United States is not hatred; what we need in the United States is not violence and lawlessness, but is love, and wisdom, and compassion toward one another, and a feeling of justice toward those who still suffer within our country, whether they be white or whether they be black.

So I ask you tonight to return home, to say a prayer for the family of Martin Luther King—yeah, it's true—but more importantly to say a prayer for our own country, which all of us love—a prayer for understanding and that compassion of which I spoke.

We can do well in this country. We will have difficult times. We've had difficult times in the past, but we—and we will have difficult times in the future. It is not the end of violence; it is not the end of lawlessness; and it's not the end of disorder.

But the majority of white people and the vast majority of black people in this country want to live together, want to improve the quality of our life, and want justice for all human beings that abide in our land.

And let's dedicate ourselves to what the Greeks wrote so many years ago: to tame the savageness of man and make a gentle life in this world. Let us dedicate ourselves to that, and say a prayer for our country and for our people. Thank you very much.

A Landmark for Peace

Dr. Martin Luther King Jr. Park at 17th and Broadway, just north of downtown Indianapolis, is a typical city park in many ways, with a playground, basketball goals, and picnic tables. But it also includes an evocative sculpture commemorating Robert F. Kennedy's speech at that site shortly after King's assassination on April 4, 1968—a historical moment that left powerful memories for those who experienced it. The sculpture by Hoosier artist Greg Perry, *A Landmark for Peace*, commemorates the Civil Rights work of Martin Luther King Jr. and Robert F. Kennedy.

In *A Landmark for Peace*, figures on two panels face each other with outstretched arms. One of the figures is King, and the other is Kennedy. The figures are immobile metal rather than flesh-and-blood men; they can never touch. And yet, the statue brilliantly symbolizes their yearning to realize their shared dream of racial harmony.

wailing were heard blocks away. Mary Evans, a white high school student who was in the crowd, feared for her life. Later she remembered thinking, "Oh, my God, I'm going to be killed." The situation was a potential powder keg.

During Kennedy's speech, which lasted only around six minutes, he spoke from his heart and connected with his audience—most of them filled with shock, grief, and rage. Kennedy had not spoken publicly of his brother John's assassination since 1963, but he chose to do so at this moment. He reminded the crowd that he understood how they felt—that a member of his own family had also been killed by an assassin's bullet. Kennedy, who had found comfort in the words of ancient Greek poets and playwrights after John's death, quoted Aeschylus from memory: "'Even in our sleep, pain which cannot forget / falls drop by drop upon the heart / until, in our own despair, / against our will, / comes wisdom through the awful grace of God.'"

Soothed by Kennedy's words, the crowd dispersed peacefully. Later, some who were present described the experience in religious terms. Mary Evans remembered feeling as if Kennedy had "laid his hands upon the audience" and healed them, deflating the anger that coursed through the packed throng. Although other American cities, such as Washington, DC, Chicago, Illinois, and Baltimore, Maryland, erupted in riots that night, Indianapolis's streets remained quiet.

Connecting with Hoosiers

"There was some fellow from Massachusetts that was here the other day that called it 'Indian-er.' That was my younger brother Teddy. He looks like me. But I call it Indiana-uh! And we're going to elect a President of the United States that knows how to pronounce the name of this state!"

— *Robert F. Kennedy, speaking in Gary, April 1968*

With Indiana primary voting just a month away, Kennedy and McCarthy attended Martin Luther King's funeral and then resumed their campaigns. While a confident Branigin worked his Hoosier connections, Kennedy rolled up his sleeves and learned what made Hoosiers tick. On his campaign visits to Indiana following King's assassination, he followed John Bartlow Martin's advice and spoke of Hoosier legends such as Abraham Lincoln and James Whitcomb Riley. He also visited the George Rogers Clark Memorial and Grouseland, William Henry Harrison's home in Vincennes. Kennedy even chartered a train, dubbed the Wabash Cannonball, to take him on an old-fashioned political tour of Indiana's small towns and cities. Before visiting a town, Kennedy relied on Martin's background briefings about key places along the route, telling him what to expect. In his stump speeches, Kennedy spoke less about new social programs and concentrated on practical issues that mattered to Hoosiers.

In the campaign's last month, McCarthy's Indiana team began to lose steam. Plagued by financial problems and disorganization, the Minnesotan's campaign lost the edge it had enjoyed before Kennedy entered the race. Kennedy began to attract some of the young Hoosier voters—a demographic that was one of McCarthy's strongest supporters. In the end, the Kennedy campaign viewed Branigin as the larger threat to winning Indiana in the primary.

Hoosiers Decide

"He came across as authentic, direct, and straightforward—a person in whom people could have confidence. And that's what, I think, brought Indiana around."

> — *John Douglas, aide to Kennedy for Indiana Campaign, June 1969*

On May 6, the day before Hoosiers went to the polls, Kennedy made his final push through northwest Indiana. Riding in his Gary motorcade were two local heroes, Gary Mayor Richard G. Hatcher, the state's first African American mayor, and Tony Zale, the middleweight-champion boxer known as "The Man of Steel." Members of Kennedy's family traveled the state on Election Day to reinforce his message and show family solidarity, a value important to Hoosiers. Kennedy himself felt he had forged a bond with people in Indiana. The day before the election he said, "The people here are not so neurotic and hypocritical as in Washington or New York. They're more direct."

Kennedy's well-organized grassroots campaign mobilized block captains in Indianapolis, South Bend, and Evansville to reach out to Hoosier voters. Shortly before the election, one of his aides reported, "We could have the public support of over 10,000 teachers." Kennedy's team lacked the name of a single prominent business leader, but in the end that did not matter. When the votes were tallied, Kennedy had won 42.3 percent of the 776,000 votes cast. Governor Branigin finished second with 30.7 percent, and McCarthy came in third at 27 percent. Kennedy won nine of Indiana's eleven congressional districts and captured fifty-six of the state's sixty-three delegates to the Democratic National Convention. His team left Indiana in high spirits, convinced of his viability as a national candidate and ready to move on to the Nebraska primary.

Robert Kennedy was never to run in the 1968 general election, though. He was assassinated—only two months after King—on June 5, 1968, in Los Angeles, after winning the California primary. His death left the Democratic Party in disarray. It did not recover in time for the general election in November. Vice President Hubert Humphrey secured the party nomination, but Republican Richard Nixon won the presidential election.

Civil Rights Poster

In this poster, ca. 1965, the Gary Freedom Movement urged a boycott against businesses that opposed Civil Rights legislation in Gary, Indiana. The Gary Freedom Movement was one of many groups in Indiana that actively demonstrated for Civil Rights.

11.2

The Struggle for School Desegregation in Indiana

The trustee or trustees of such township, town, or city may organize the colored children into separate schools . . . having all the rights, privileges, and advantages of all other schools . . . Provided, That in case there may not be provided separate schools for the colored children, then such colored children shall be allowed to attend the public schools with white children.

— Indiana law regarding schools and schoolhouses, Article VII, Section 4496, March 5, 1877

Into the twentieth century, African Americans accounted for less than 5 percent of the state's population. For many Hoosiers, racial equality was not a priority. As in so many states, education often highlighted for Hoosiers the continuing disparities of opportunity that awaited black and white Americans long after the end of slavery.

As African Americans moved from the South to Indiana in the 1920s, white leaders, many affiliated with the Ku Klux Klan, insisted on building segregated high schools. As late as World War II, although school segregation was common in northern states, Indiana was one of the few states that legally allowed it. Then, in 1949—five years ahead of the U.S. Supreme Court desegregation decision in *Brown v. Board of Education*— the Indiana General Assembly passed the Indiana School Desegregation Act. While the law represented an obvious step forward for equal rights in the state, legislators chose not to impose any penalty on school corporations that failed to desegregate. Therefore, many Indiana schools remained racially segregated long after 1949. But a growing national movement for civil rights would soon push for an end to the "separate but equal" philosophy that existed in education and other institutions.

Crispus Attucks Evens the Score

Membership in the Association shall be open beginning August 15, 1942, to all public, private, parochial, colored and institutional high schools of the state offering and maintaining three or four years of high school work provided they meet the requirements of the Association and also subscribe to its rules and regulations.

— Handbook of the Indiana High School Athletic Association, December 20, 1941

One of the most visible symbols of segregation was the Indiana high school basketball court. Teams at all-black Roosevelt High School in Gary, Lincoln High School in Evansville, and Crispus Attucks High School in Indianapolis played quite well, but the Indiana High School Athletic Association (IHSAA) refused to allow them to enter the annual state tournament until World War II.

Named for the legendary African American patriot who was shot by British troops in the 1770 Boston Massacre, Crispus Attucks High School opened in 1927 as Indianapolis's first all-black high school—thus reserving all other Indianapolis high schools for white students. While the new school became a source of great neighborhood pride, its size was inadequate from day one. The school had a capacity of 1,000, but more than 1,300 students enrolled the first year, and the number climbed in subsequent years.

One of the many places where Attucks proved itself far more than adequate was on the basketball court. According to one sportswriter, "From 1950 to 1957, the Crispus Attucks Tigers were the most invincible team this basketball-crazed state had seen." In spite of their talents, Attucks's players and students were the objects of curiosity, prejudice, and racial threats as they traveled around the city and state. A former Crispus Attucks student recalled, "It was like we were from outer space. I mean, I would hear their comments to each other: 'Look at that one, he's really black. And that one, she's as light as my mother's coffee.' Some just gawked open mouthed. But, hell, I was sort of surprised that they weren't chewing on a piece of straw."

September 28, 1948

THE NEGRO TAXPAYERS AND CITIZENS POSITION ON THE
INDIANAPOLIS PUBLIC SCHOOL SYSTEM AND BLUE PRINT OF INTEGRATION

By
HENRY J. RICHARDSON, JR., ATTORNEY

The Negro taxpayers and citizens will not be placated and will not be compromised by wishful thinking, the scare of displaced teachers or the old adage of "the time is not ripe." We, of school district #43, are definite that the present school policy is a waste of more than one hundred thousand dollars per year ($100,000.00) and is illegal and detrimental to-wit:

I   A. The present school pattern of discrimination based solely on race is

        1. Unchristian
        2. Undemocratic
        3. Increases race tensions because of misunderstanding
        4. Equally detrimental to white and Negro pupils.

II   Present school Board Policy is unnecessary waste of taxpayers money on a duel school system, when maintenance and additional building are direly needed.

III   The present School Board Policy of segregation and discrimination based on race fails to provide equal educational facilities for Negro pupils as compared with those of white pupils, and attempts to stigmatize them as inferior.

    A. Children in this district who formerly attended P S #42 <u>out of their district</u>, were arbitrarily shifted to P S #87, still <u>out of their district</u>, when P S #43 <u>in their district</u> could have accommodated them equally as well if not better.

    B. Segregation and discrimination of children based on race are vexing, hazardous and work an undue hardship on Negro children - for example:

      a. When 1 B's go to school half days, parents must go for them - a distance of more than 2 miles or the children must wait until 3:00 P.M. when the regular bus returns for them.

      b. The bus has no definite schedule. (During the three weeks of this school year, the bus has arrived at Bernard Street on Rockwood from 7:45 to 8:15). In inclement weather, children are exposed unduly to rain and cold. Bus drivers

-1-

Desegregation Position Paper

African American attorney Henry J. Richardson pushed for a school desegregation law and served as a spokesman for civil rights. Wanting to send his children to an Indianapolis school in his neighborhood that was designated for white students, he wrote this 1948 position paper, outlining the discrimination and extra expenses caused by segregated schools.

Coached by Ray Crowe, the Crispus Attucks team won six regional championships, four semi-state championships, back-to-back state titles between 1950 and 1957, and the state championship in 1959 under Coach Bill Garrett. In 1955, led by future National Basketball Association (NBA) legend and Hall of Famer Oscar Robertson, the Tigers beat Gary's Roosevelt High School, 97–74, and became the nation's first all-black basketball team to win a state championship. Not only did Attucks win the state championship the following year, defeating Lafayette Jefferson High School, 79–57, the team also was the first in Indiana high school history to be undefeated for an entire season.

Despite their remarkable achievement, the Tigers did not receive statewide acclaim as did Milan, the tiny, white rural high school that won the championship in 1954 and inspired the 1986 film *Hoosiers*. Robertson remembered: "When Milan won the state championship they got a ride around all the squares in Indy—all through downtown. But when it was an all-black school . . . city officials thought that all these black people would terrorize the city. 'We can't have them congregating around our Circle monument,' they probably said. 'We will take them back to their neighborhood.' And the police escorted us there."

Sports historians, players, and true basketball fans give credit where credit is due. Bobby Plump, the Milan guard who made the championship-winning shot in 1954, had this to say about the Crispus Attucks Tigers: "What they were able to accomplish is as significant as anything that's ever been done in this state's illustrious basketball history. There's nothing that I can say, there's nothing you will hear, there's nothing you can write that can possibly get to the depth of what they had to go through to accomplish everything they did." The team's wins also brought some positive changes to race relations in Indianapolis, as they gained the support of whites in the community who began to cheer on the Crispus Attucks team in the championships.

Busing and Other Would-be Solutions

Even with new civil rights laws and basketball victories, school segregation continued due, in large part, to strong racial divisions between white and black neighborhoods and school transfers. Whites would transfer out of schools with large black populations; and blacks would transfer out of schools where blacks were a small minority. It soon became clear in Indiana and many other states that neither state law nor the 1954 Supreme Court decision in *Brown v. Board of Education* would produce integrated schools.

INDIANAPOLIS RECORDER COLLECTION, INDIANA HISTORICAL SOCIETY

Oscar Robertson

Oscar Robertson cuts down the net after winning the 1955 Indiana State High School Basketball championship with Indianapolis's Crispus Attucks Tigers. Roberston went on to a successful career with the NBA and was inducted into the Basketball Hall of Fame, although he remained unhappy about the racism he faced both on and off the court.

Crispus Attucks Basketball Team Wins State Championship!

The Crispus Attucks Basketball Team members celebrate their state championship win in 1956 on the court of Butler University's Fieldhouse and in a police-escorted ride from the field-house to their neighborhood.

However, several of Indiana's northern cities had integrated their schools by the early 1950s. Black migrants from the South made up a large percentage of the total population in Gary during the first half of the twentieth century. Like most school systems in Indiana, Gary's school system was segregated prior to 1947. By that year, however, Gary's civic and school leaders had forged a way to work toward ending school segregation by redrawing school districts and through new policies, such as not allowing students to transfer out of their neighborhood school district. East Chicago, Elkhart, and other northern cities followed Gary's lead. By the 1950s Indianapolis and Evansville were among the few large American cities outside of the South with segregated school systems, despite the anti-segregation act Indiana passed in 1949.

Indianapolis presented one of the hardest challenges to desegregation. Historian Richard B. Pierce of Notre Dame University commented that the city of Indianapolis "fought school desegregation with a ferocity rarely matched by any other northern city." Some saw the 1969 creation of Unigov, which consolidated many of Indianapolis's and Marion County's governmental functions—with the exception of schools—as a means of maintaining white suburban schools. In a 1971 ruling for a suit put forth by the NAACP and initiated by the U.S. Department of Justice, federal judge S. Hugh Dillin wrote that the Indianapolis School Board, "through the years, has consistently employed policies and practices causing and maintaining racial segregation." Dillin ordered desegregation of Indianapolis schools in a plan that included busing black

INDIANAPOLIS RECORDER COLLECTION, INDIANA HISTORICAL SOCIETY

IPS Picket

Protestors from the Congress of Racial Equality march outside of Indianapolis School #17, ca. 1960. They called for better integration and the redistricting of Indianapolis schools, many of which were segregated because of housing patterns.

students to Marion County suburban schools. Heated controversy ensued, but in 1973 the first buses began carrying black students to schools away from their inner-city neighborhoods. No white students were bused the other way.

Few people were happy with the results. Many black parents were upset over the loss of their neighborhood schools and the fact that only their children were to be bused far away from their homes. Neither did they accept the idea that white schools were better for their children. On the other side, many white parents and their children were angered to have black students forced upon them. Some white suburbanites moved to more remote suburbs, while, at the same time, Indianapolis Public Schools in downtown Indianapolis experienced a decreasing enrollment.

Although even in the 1990s controversy still clouded Indianapolis's busing situation, integration was starting very slowly. By the second decade of the twenty-first century, Indianapolis's suburban neighborhoods were becoming integrated—perhaps as an outcome of the forced busing of a couple of generations of black children to white suburban schools.

"By Littles"

Wells adroitly walked the tightrope between relentless pressure from blacks to be fully included in the life of IU and demands by whites that Negroes be kept away from them. He did this balancing act for fifteen years before university dormitories were fully desegregated in 1952, three years before I arrived on campus.

— *Janet Cheatham Bell,* The Time and Place That Gave Me Life *(2007)*

Abraham Lincoln used the phrase "by littles" to describe his education. The phrase could also apply to the long, slow journey to school desegregation in In-

COLLECTIONS OF THE CALUMET REGIONAL ARCHIVES, INDIANA UNIVERSITY, NORTHWEST

Mayor Richard Hatcher with Robert F. Kennedy
Richard Hatcher, Mayor of Gary, on the left, supported Robert Kennedy, middle, during Kennedy's campaign for the presidential nomination in 1968.

diana. Some pushed hard to achieve it; others pushed back with equal force. As a result, progress came in small increments over a long period of time, but it did come—thanks to victories by people, black and white, who bucked the status quo and refused to quit.

The struggle was not unique to the public schools. Recalling her arrival at Indiana University in 1955, Indianapolis native Janet Cheatham Bell thought that "the *racial* climate in Bloomington felt more threatening than in Indianapolis." Although African American students were allowed to study at IU during the early twentieth century, dormitories and the student union were segregated. IU President Herman B Wells garnered praise for desegregating the campus in the 1940s and 1950s. Nevertheless, in the year that Bell arrived, only 350 of the university's 12,000 students were black.

As with high schools, basketball played a role in bringing racial equality to universities. Shelbyville's Bill Garrett broke the color barrier on IU's basketball court in 1947. The first African American to play Big Ten college basketball, Garrett became one of the greatest players IU ever had. Garrett went on to be the third black player drafted by the NBA. A year after he graduated there were six African Americans on Big Ten college basketball teams.

"The Times They Are A-Changin'"

Gary, a leader in school integration, achieved another distinction in 1967 when it became one of the nation's first two major cities (alongside Cleveland, Ohio) to elect an African American mayor. Mayor Richard Hatcher was a young attorney who had attended Indiana University in the 1950s and had gone on to a successful career in the Lake County Prosecutor's Office and the Gary City Council. Some observers saw his victory as a win not only for civil rights but for good government in a city whose corrupt politics had several years earlier been under intense scrutiny from a Justice Department headed by Attorney General Robert F. Kennedy. Hatcher prioritized building more moderate income housing, severely lacking in Gary, and providing more job training for the city's unemployed and underemployed. A year after his election, Hatcher was riding through the streets of Gary with Kennedy, now a candidate for the presidency who would win the Indiana primary thanks in part to the help he received from civil rights advocates in Lake County and elsewhere. Hoosiers, known for clinging to their traditions, were ready for change.

May Wright Sewall

As one of Indiana's leading suffragists May Wright Sewall, pictured here ca. 1890, championed women's rights and education at home and nationally.

11.3

Equal Rights for Hoosier Women

Much has been said about the need of the ballot to protect the industrial interests of men, but is it not as ungallant as it is illogical that they should have the ballot for their protection while women, pressed by the same necessities, should be denied it?

— *May Wright Sewall, National [Women's] Suffrage Convention, February 1886*

Hoosier suffragist and educator May Wright Sewall (1844–1920) dedicated her life to creating opportunities for women and championing their equal rights. She died in July 1920, less than one month before the ratification of the Nineteenth Amendment to the U.S. Constitution gave women the right to vote.

Since the 1850s, some female and male Hoosiers had, like Sewall, joined in the national movement to secure equal rights for women. New Harmony's Robert Dale Owen made a valiant effort to include a provision in Indiana's 1851 Constitution giving married women the right to own property in their own names, rather than in their husbands' names. However, most of the other delegates voted down the idea.

Sewall acted upon her theories of women's rights in her Girls' Classical School in Indianapolis, which opened in 1882. She instituted a curriculum equal to that of a boys' school that her husband directed and advocated for physical education and wearing less restrictive clothing. At the same time Sewall became a leader in the suffragist movement, eventually speaking before international audiences of suffrage advocates.

Suffragists fought for the vote and also for other rights. Unequal property rights remained encoded in law during the nineteenth century, despite the efforts of many women to change the law and some gains from legislation in 1879 and 1881. In 1896 the Indiana Supreme Court held that a "valid marriage made the husband and wife one person in law. The legal existence of the woman was suspended, or merged in that of the husband. . . . The husband, by virtue of the marriage, was entitled to all the personal property . . . of his wife, which, when reduced to possession, became his absolute property, and was also entitled to the exclusive possession, use, and control of her real estate during their joint lives."

The Equal Rights Amendment (ERA)

Equality of rights under the law shall not be denied or abridged by the United States or by any state on account of sex.

— *ERA, Proposed Twentieth Amendment to the United States Constitution, 1943 revision*

New Jersey-born suffragist Alice Paul drafted the original Equal Rights Amendment (ERA) in 1923 only three years after the Nineteenth Amendment passed.

COLLECTIONS OF THE INDIANA HISTORICAL SOCIETY

NOW Rally

Members of the National Organization for Women (NOW) demonstrate in Indianapolis, ca. 1970. NOW was founded in 1966 in Washington, DC, to promote gender equality in employment, education, and politics. Four years later, Indiana's first NOW chapter was established in Muncie.

AP PHOTO; COURTESY OF ALLEN COUNTY PUBLIC LIBRARY'S COMMUNITY ALBUM, FORT WAYNE, INDIANA

Birch Bayh with Lobbyists

In 1978 Indiana Senator Birch Bayh met with Hoosiers who shared his strong support for the Equal Rights Amendment. A year earlier Indiana had been the last state to ratify the ERA. Three more states needed to ratify the amendment before 1979 for it to become part of the U.S. Constitution. These supporters lobbied politicians in Washington, DC, to extend the ratification deadline to 1982. Even with the extension, however, Indiana remained the last state to ratify the ERA. Supporters continue to introduce the bill into Congress every year.

Button in favor of the Equal Rights Amendment, ca. 1977

The proposed Twentieth Amendment came before the U.S. Congress each session from 1923 to 1970—without success.

The persistent drive to pass the ERA reflected the changing times in which Americans lived during the twentieth century. The Civil Rights Movement, which picked up steam after the end of World War II, raised Americans' awareness of what democracy meant—not just in relation to skin color but also in other areas, such as gender equality. Judges and legislators faced growing calls to address questions about equality for women, who faced discrimination in education, the workplace, sports, and other areas. An increasingly well-organized women's rights movement developed

in the 1960s and 1970s alongside the Civil Rights and Anti-Vietnam War Movements. Yet the issues associated with gender rights conjured up uniquely powerful emotions on both sides.

The ERA enjoyed broad political support nationally, uniting public figures as diverse as Democratic First Lady Eleanor Roosevelt and Republican President Dwight D. Eisenhower. In Indiana most Democrats and some Republicans in the general assembly supported the ERA. The state's chapters of the League of Women Voters, the National Organization for Women, the Indiana Women's Caucus, and others worked at a grassroots level to pass the ERA in the state. Indiana Senator Birch Bayh led the Senate fight for the amendment in 1972. That year Congress approved the amendment, which then passed to the states for ratification.

The amendment's opponents acted with equal fervor. Senator Joan Gubbins of Indianapolis was one of the most outspoken among them. At the University of Alabama on November 13, 1975, Gubbins stated, "What the 'women's libbers' desire is not to free women but to take away their choices in life." She and her supporters believed that the ERA not only violated states' rights, but would force all school-children to use the same public restrooms, draft women into combat, erode the family, lead to legalized abortion, and advance the agenda of "homosexual and socialist organizations." Another legislator, Charles E. Bosma, claimed that the ERA "would deal a severe blow to the time-honored relationship between husbands and wives."

ERA advocates dismissed the claims of those opposed to the ERA as scare tactics and asked why constitutional rights should apply only to men. The battle seemed as if it had come to its conclusion in 1977 when Indiana became the thirty-fifth state to ratify the ERA. The pro-ERA victory proved to be temporary, though. Indiana was the last state to approve the measure. Since the bill failed to pass in the thirty-eight states necessary to ratify it, it failed.

To ERA proponents, the amendment remains "unfinished business." While it continues to be introduced annually into Congress, it is still not part of the U.S. Constitution.

Leveling the Playing Field

"We are all familiar with the stereotype of women as pretty things who go to college to find a husband, go on to graduate school because they want a more interesting husband, and finally marry, have children, and never work again. The desire of many schools not to waste a 'man's place' on a woman stems from such stereotyped notions. But the facts absolutely contradict these myths about the 'weaker sex' and it is time to change our operating assumptions."

    — Indiana Senator Birch Bayh, speaking of Title IX to the U.S. Senate, February 28, 1972

Despite the fate of the ERA, many changes in late-twentieth-century America did move women toward equality before the law. Hoosier women who had helped win World War II by keeping the factories of Gary and Evansville at full production levels did not easily return to their kitchens when the men came home. In the 1970s laws and court decisions helped to ensure their daughters the right to work where they wanted and to be paid as much as their male co-workers. In 1977, for instance, the Indiana Supreme Court ruled it unconstitutional for the Indiana State Teachers' Retirement Fund to pay retired male teachers $15 a month more than female retirees, when both had contributed equal amounts of money to the fund.

As women became an ever more active presence in the workplace, their daughters gained equal rights in the gym and on the playing field. Again, Hoosier Senator Birch Bayh was a trailblazer. On the heels of the ERA, Bayh authored Title IX of the Education Amendment of 1972, which guaranteed young women a previously unimaginable level of access to education and athletics. Title IX states: "No person in the United States shall, on the basis of sex, be excluded from participation in, be denied the benefits of, or be subjected to discrimination under any education program or activity receiving Federal financial assistance." Unlike the ERA, which was a proposed *constitutional amendment*, Title IX was a proposed *law*. With very little fuss President Richard M. Nixon signed the bill into law on June 23, 1972. With Title IX, Bayh laid the legal groundwork for a revolution in women's rights.

In keeping with Title IX, the Indiana High School Athletic Association (IHSAA) added the first woman to its executive staff. A year later the IHSAA officially endorsed girls' sports. Empowered by improved funding and higher visibility, girls attained their own "Miss Basketball" Award alongside the long-lived boys' "Mr. Basketball" Award, and girls' teams built up dynasties that made their way into the record books alongside their male counterparts. By 2014, for example, Fort Wayne's Bishop Luers High School girls' basketball team had appeared in an unmatched nine state basketball finals, and Muncie Burris's girls' volleyball team had won twenty-two state championships.

The women's movement succeeded in reshaping life in Indiana because of the persistence of its leaders and because of Hoosiers' willingness to accept gradual

Girls' Basketball Game

In 1972 Title IX of the Education Amendment removed barriers for women in sports, paving the way for today's female athletes. Here the girls' basketball teams from Mooresville and Plainfield go head-to-head in the consolation game that determines third place at the 2009 City Securities Girls' Hall of Fame Classic.

and sensible change. Gender inequalities still remain, such as pay gaps and "glass ceilings," or limits on how high women are allowed to achieve in their careers. Nevertheless, more women have entered law, medicine, and other professions, including politics. In 2013 women comprised 21 percent of the Indiana state legislature, just below the national average of 24.2 percent. Although more work remains to attain gender equality, the Indiana of the early twenty-first century is a long way from the world that May Wright Sewall and her students knew in Indianapolis in the 1880s.

11.4

The Messy Business of Democracy

*"I don't know why Hoosiers have such
a high tolerance for political mischief."*

— *Indiana Director of Common Cause,
Julia Vaughn, ca. 2005*

The drafters of Indiana's 1851 constitution stated that the purpose of government was to ensure "that justice be established, public order maintained, and liberty perpetuated." Subsequent generations of Hoosiers have found that carrying out those goals can be both noble and frustrating. Indiana's political party organizations first appeared in the pioneer era and were in flux until the Civil War. A two-party system firmed up in the late nineteenth century, flourished into the mid-twentieth century, then went through fundamental transformations by the century's end. According to a 1983 *Congressional Quarterly* survey of all fifty states, "The salient feature of Indiana politics is fierce partisanship, more pronounced here than almost anywhere else in the country."

Into the second decade of the twenty-first century, Indiana's government continued to function under the constitution of 1851. The governor remained a relatively weak executive whose veto could be overturned by a simple majority of the legislature. Unlike the chief executives of most other states, Indiana's was not given a line-item veto, allowing him or her to veto certain parts of a bill. A constitutional amendment approved in 1972 permitted governors to serve two consecutive terms; previously they were restricted to one term. The general assembly's power also increased. Under a constitutional amendment ratified in 1970, the assembly shifted from holding sessions every other year to annual sessions. What started as a part-time citizens' assembly has become a more professional entity. With its increased workload, the legislature has acquired salary increases and more support staff.

Redistricting

In the late twentieth and early twenty-first centuries, the legislative reform that attracted the most attention was redistricting. The state constitution required that the general assembly redraw legislative districts every six years to ensure a roughly even number of citizens in each district. Legislators redrew the districts in 1921, but not in subsequent years. This resulted in underrepresentation for the urban areas, which were growing in population, and overrepresentation for the rural areas. Republicans, who depended on rural votes more than Democrats, were especially reluctant to redistrict.

In 1962 the U.S. Supreme Court determined in the landmark case *Baker v. Carr*, which was based on redistricting practices in Tennessee, that legislatures

Indiana House of Representatives

Members of the 1975 session of the Indiana House of Representatives and principle officers and staff members are pictured here in their chamber.

COLLECTIONS OF THE INDIANA STATE ARCHIVES

Form 95

Certificate Number.........................

Certificate of Employment
As A Lobbyist

———

This certificate of employment as Legislative........AGENT..

is issued to............WILLIARD B. RANSOM.., a representative

of.......NATIONAL ASSOCIATION FOR ADVANCEMENT OF COLORED PEOPLE..........on the application

of.......INDIANAPOLIS, INDIANA..., who has filed the

prescribed statement and paid the prescribed fee.

            Pursuant to "An act regulating lobbying; requiring the registration
of legislative counsel and agents and regulating their activity; and
prohibiting improper and corrupt lobbying."
            Approved, February 4, 1915.

The period of employment covered by this certificate is.........86th SESSION OF LEGISLATURE......

....and the subject matter is........EDUCATION: CIVIL RIGHTS:.....

EMPLOYMENT LABOR: PUBLIC WELFARE: CHILD WELFARE:...

....

....

....

           CHARLES F. FLEMING
Now, therefore, I, ~~Thomas E. Bath~~, Secretary of State of the State of Indiana, by virtue of the

powers vested in me, do hereby issue this certificate, subject, however, to all the provisions and penal-

ties provided by the act as aforesaid.

        IN TESTIMONY WHEREOF, I have hereunto set my hand

        and affixed the seal of the State of Indiana, at Indianapolis,

        this.....8th.....day of.....February....................., 19...49

                            Secretary of State.

Lobbyist Certificate

Willard B. Ransom graduated from Crispus Attucks High School in Indianapolis in 1932. By 1946 he was a lobbyist, representing the National Association for the Advancement of Colored People (NAACP) to the Indiana General Assembly. In this position, he helped to pass major civil rights legislation in the state over several decades. Besides this political action, he took on civil rights cases as an attorney in Indianapolis, managed the Madam C. J. Walker Manufacturing Company, and served five terms as chairman of the Indiana branch of the NAACP.

must redistrict regularly and fairly. Indiana complied by redistricting more regularly. This made more room for urban legislators, often including more women and more African Americans. Redistricting also became a partisan issue, with the majority party using sophisticated means to draw boundaries that worked in its favor, called gerrymandering. By the end of the century cleverly gerrymandered districts often left a strong majority candidate with little pressure from the opposition to compromise with the other party.

Special Interest Groups and Lobbyists

In addition to gerrymandering, fulfilling the promise of the constitution has been further complicated by the increasingly common practice of interest groups lobbying legislators for particular causes. By the 1960s there were a handful of powerful interest groups in the state among other less influential groups. Included among the more powerful groups were the Indiana AFL-CIO (American Federation of Labor and Congress of Industrial Organizations) and the Indiana State Teachers Association, which were very influential with Democratic legislators. The Indiana State Chamber of Commerce and the Indiana Farm Bureau held a lot of sway with Republican legislators. By the end of the twentieth century, lobbyists were spending $20 million annually to enlist legislators' help to further their interest group's agenda. Labor unions gained strength and then declined as the state shifted away from its mid-twentieth-century manufacturing base. Other

Voter Registration Campaign

People register to vote in Marion County in 1963 at a registration campaign organized by the All Citizens Voter Registration Committee, the Indianapolis Social Action Council, and the NAACP. The groups collaborated in order to register 35,000 African Americans in Indianapolis.

The Statehouse

The first statehouse in Indianapolis, built in the 1830s, looked like the Parthenon with a dome on top of it. By the late 1860s it was deteriorating; after the ceiling of the Representative Hall caved in, Hoosiers decided it was time to consider building a new, sturdier statehouse. The process was long and involved planning, budgeting, and a modest tax increase. Finally, in 1888 the Indiana General Assembly held its first meeting in the new magnificent Neo-Classical Revival building—a popular style for public buildings at the end of the nineteenth and early twentieth centuries. The new statehouse cost $2 million.

The building where Hoosiers conduct their lawmaking could rival many palaces for its size and fine craftsmanship. Built in the shape of a cross, the four-story Indiana limestone structure features a stunning stained-glass inner dome that soars more than one hundred feet above the marble floor. Pillars of polished marble, eighty-one doors carved from white oak, and statues that stand for the ideals of democracy can be seen throughout the building.

The work of the three branches of Indiana's

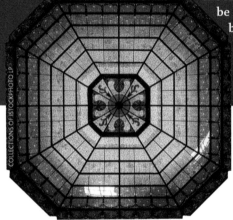

The magnificent stained-glass enclosed dome in the Indiana Statehouse rises more than one hundred feet above the floor.

government is carried out inside the statehouse. Modeled on the federal government system, Indiana's branches are: the executive (governor), the legislative (general assembly), and the judicial (supreme court). The Governor's Office is on the main floor just south of the main entrance; this is where the governor reviews 100–300 legislative bills every year. The 150-member Indiana General Assembly, commonly called the legislature, has two houses—the House of Representatives and the Senate. The 100-member House of Representatives occupies the third and fourth floors in the east wing. The 50-member Senate occupies the third and fourth floors above the west entrance. Members of the House of Representatives serve two-year terms; senators hold office for four years. The Indiana Supreme Court resides on the third floor of the north wing. Here five to eight justices, elected to ten-year terms, interpret the Constitution of Indiana as it relates to various court cases or laws passed by the state legislature.

Although the statehouse is a grand building in which intricate matters are debated, one basic fact looms even higher than its magnificent dome: Hoosiers elect the legislators who work there. It is the people's house.

Voting vs. Political Apathy

A person must meet the following requirements to be a registered voter in Indiana: (1) be a citizen of the United States; (2) be at least eighteen (18) years of age on the day of the next general or municipal election; (3) live in a precinct continuously for at least thirty (30) days before the next election; and 4) not currently be in prison following conviction of a crime.

— *"Voter Qualifications,"* 2012 Indiana Voter Registration Guidebook

lobbying groups grew stronger, advocating proposals regarding education, health care, gambling, real estate, and abortion.

In the opening decades of the twenty-first century, most legislators depended on campaign contributions from special interest groups. They claimed that the money had no influence on the way they voted, but critics adamantly disputed these claims. Indiana ranked near the bottom among states known for effective campaign finance laws, but Hoosiers generally avoided the corruption scandals that sent legislators to jail in other states.

Over two centuries, Indiana's government may have changed greatly, but Hoosiers still hold to many of the same traditions. They tend to be wary of government involvement in their everyday lives, just as the Hoosier pioneers had been. Hoosiers continue to be concerned over the government's power to tax and to restrict freedom. Some complain about government, but fail to vote or otherwise engage in their democratic rights and responsibilities as citizens.

The ornate interior of the Indiana Statehouse has undergone various renovations to modernize fixtures and meet the government's needs. Nevertheless, its beautiful brass chandeliers, marble columns, and wood paneling remain largely unchanged.

By the late twentieth century, many Hoosiers decided to opt out of voting. The state's election turnout percentage dropped below the national average. An increasing number of voters began going to the polls only when they wanted to vote on a particular issue. Many Hoosiers became independent voters, who did not vote on party lines, while others were only weakly affiliated with a party. A 2011 survey revealed that "nearly 45 percent of Hoosiers . . . do not discuss politics at all." This can be attributed to a number of factors, including voter apathy—a lack of interest in or indifference to politics. Hoosiers may also avoid discussing politics because it is a very contentious topic.

Some Hoosiers have felt thwarted when they have tried to vote or register to vote. The state's 2005 voter ID law, which required voters to show government-issued photo identification, was among the strictest in the nation. While the law's defenders state that it minimizes the possibility of election fraud, critics argue that it unjustifiably burdens the old, the poor, and minority groups who may not have access to transportation, a driver's license, or alternate forms of identification. In 2008, only weeks before the Indiana primary election, the U.S. Supreme Court upheld Indiana's voter identification law as constitutional, ruling that the state had a "valid interest" in both improving election procedures and deterring fraud.

Fortunately, in the twenty-first century Hoosiers are returning to the poll booth. One 2007 study revealed that the overall state voter turnout increased by around two percentage points after the photo ID law passed, and that there had, in fact, been an increased turnout in counties with a greater percentage of minorities or families in poverty. Senator Richard G. Lugar, the former Indianapolis mayor who represented Indiana in the U.S. Senate for more than three decades, admitted that sometimes "government doesn't work very well" and that those involved in it must work harder to invigorate young people's interest in politics.

Selected Bibliography

1851 constitution, http://www.in.gov/history/2473.htm.

2012 Indiana Voter Registration Guidebook. Indianapolis: Indiana Election Division. http://www.in.gov/sos/elections/files/2012_Voter_Registration_Guidebook_12_6_11_version__2_.pdf.

Aamidor, Abe. "Who Was Chuck Taylor: The Man and the Shoe." *Traces of Indiana and Midwestern History* 19, no. 3 (Summer 2007): 4–15.

Anthony, Susan B., and Ida Husted Harper, eds. *History of Woman Suffrage.* Vol . 4. Indianapolis: Hollenbeck Press, 1902. http://www.gutenberg.org/files/29870/29870-h/29870-h.htm.

"Appellate Courts: Indiana Supreme Court." Courts.IN.gov, http://www.in.gov/judiciary/2668.htm.

Bell, Janet Cheatham. *The Time and Place that Gave Me Life.* Bloomington: Indiana University Press, 2007.

Bodenhamer, David J., and Robert G. Barrows. *The Encyclopedia of Indianapolis.* Bloomington: Indiana University Press, 1994.

Bodenhamer, David J., and Randall T. Shepard, eds. *The History of Indiana Law.* Athens: Ohio University Press, 2006.

Boomhower, Ray E. *Fighting for Equality: A Life of May Wright Sewall.* Indianapolis: IHS Press, 2007.

———. *Robert F. Kennedy and the 1968 Indiana Primary.* Bloomington: Indiana University Press, 2008.

Carmony, Donald F., and Josephine M. Elliott. "New Harmony, Indiana: Robert Owen's Seedbed for Utopia." *Indiana Magazine of History* 76, no. 3 (September 1980): 161–261.

Cruikshank, Kate. "Birch Bayh Biography." Indiana University-Bloomington Libraries, http://www.libraries.iub.edu/index.php?pageId=8621.

Daugherity, Brian J., and Charles C. Bolton. *With All Deliberate Speed: Implementing Brown v. Board of Education.* Fayetteville: University of Arkansas Press, 2008. Project Muse, http://muse.jhu.edu/books/9781610754675/.

Douglas, John. Recorded interview with Larry J. Hackman, June 16, 1969. John F. Kennedy Library Oral History Program, http://archive2.jfklibrary.org/RFKOH/Douglas,%20John%20W/RFKOH-JWD-01/RFKOH-JWD-01-TR.pdf.

"The Equal Rights Amendment: Unfinished Business for the Constitution," http://www.equalrightsamendment.org.

Graham, Tom, and Rachel Graham Cody. *Getting Open: The Unknown Story of Bill Garrett and the Integration of College Basketball.* New York: Atria Books, 2006.

Gray, Virginia, Russell L. Hanson, and Thad Kousser, eds. *Politics in the American States: A Comparative Analysis.* 10th ed., Los Angeles: Sage Publications, 2013.

Higdon, Hal. "Indiana: A Test for Bobby Kennedy." *New York Times,* May 5, 1968.

Hinkle, Sara E. "Herman B Wells: Champion for Racial Equality at Indiana University." *Journal of the Indiana University Student Personnel Association* (2001): 10–31. Indiana University Bloomington School of Education Portal, http://portal.education.indiana.edu/Portals/32/Herman.pdf.

"How Indiana Compares to the Rest of the Nation: Indiana Civic Health Index, 2011," September 14, 2011. National Conference on Citizenship, http://ncoc.net/How-Indiana-Compares-to-the-Rest-of-the-Nation-INCHI.

Indiana Department of Commerce. *A Walk through the Indiana State Capitol: The State House, 1888 to Present.* Indianapolis, IN, n.d.

Indiana High School Athletic Association, http://www.ihsaa.org/.

The Indiana High School Athletic Association: Thirty-Ninth Annual Handbook. Indianapolis: Indiana High School Athletic Association Board of Control, 1942.

"Indiana Senator Says ERA Takes Away Women's Choices in Life." *Florence Times–Tri Cities Daily,* November 13, 1975. http://news.google.com/newspapers?nid=1842&dat=19751113&id=2yAsAAAAIBAJ&sjid=BZ4FAAAAIBAJ&pg=935,2527624.

"Indiana Statehouse." National Park Service, http://www.nps.gov/nr/travel/indianapolis/indianastatehouse.htm.

Kempker, Erin M. "Coalition and Control: Hoosier Feminists and the Equal Rights Amendment." *Frontiers: A Journal of Women Studies* 34, no. 2 (2013): 52–82. Project Muse, http://muse.jhu.edu/login?auth=0&type=summary&url=/journals/frontiers/v034/34.2.kempker.html.

Kettleborough, Charles, ed. *Constitution Making in Indiana. Vol. I: 1780–1851.* Indianapolis: Indiana Historical Commission, 1916.

Madison, James H. *Hoosiers: A New History of Indiana.* Bloomington: Indiana University Press; Indianapolis: Indiana Historical Society Press, 2014.

Martin, John Bartlow. Undated memo from Martin to Robert F. Kennedy, Theodore Sorenson, and the Indiana Schedulers, Writers, and Television Men. John Bartlow Martin Papers, MSS57844, Library of Congress.

McCammon, Holly J. "'Out of the Parlors and into the Streets': The Changing Tactical Repertoire of the U.S. Women's Suffrage Movements." *Social Forces* 81, no. 3 (March 2003): 787–818. Project Muse, https://muse.jhu.edu/login?auth=0&type=summary&url=/journals/social_forces/v081/81.3mccammon.html.

McDowell, James L. *The Emperor's New Clothes? Legislative Reform in Indiana.* Terre Haute: Indiana State University, 1976.

Miller, Holly, "Virginia Dill McCarthy Awaits Presidential Nod for District Attorney Post." *Anderson Sunday Herald,* June 5, 1977. Available on NewspaperArchive.com.

Milyo, Jeffrey. "The Effects of Photographic Identification on Voter Turnout in Indiana: A County-Level Analysis." MA thesis, University of Missouri–Columbia Institute of Public Policy, 2007. MOspace, https://mospace.umsystem.edu /xmlui/handle/10355/2549.

Moore, Wilma L., "Everyday People: The Golden Era of Crispus Attucks High School Basketball." *Traces of Indiana and Midwestern History* 21, no. 3 (Summer 2009): 30–32.

Morgan, Iwan W. "Latecomers to the Industrial City: African Americans, Jobs, and Housing in Fort Wayne, Indiana, 1940–1960," *Indiana Magazine of History* 95, no. 1 (March 1999): 31–57.

Newfield, Jack. *Robert Kennedy: A Memoir.* E. P. Dutton, 1969.

The Northeastern Reporter: Containing all the Current Decisions of the Supreme Courts of Massachusetts, Ohio, Illinois, Indiana, Appellate Courts of Indiana, and the Court of Appeals of New York. Vol. 44. St. Paul: West Publishing, 1896. Available on Google Books.

"Photo ID Law." IN.gov, http://www.in.gov/sos/elections /2401.htm.

Pierce, Richard B. *Polite Protest: The Political Economy of Race in Indianapolis, 1920–1970.* Bloomington: Indiana University Press, 2005.

Poinsett, Alan. *Black Power Gary Style: The Making of Mayor Richard Gordon Hatcher.* Chicago: Johnson Publishing, 1970.

Reese, William J., ed. *Hoosier Schools Past and Present.* Bloomington: Indiana University Press, 1998.

Roberts, Randy. *"But They Can't Beat Us": Oscar Robertson and the Crispus Attucks Tigers.* Indianapolis: Indiana Historical Society, 1999.

Scroggins, Eloise E. "Organizing on Their Own Terms: Women and the Equal Rights Amendment in Indiana." MA thesis, Indiana University-Indianapolis, 2003.

Shanahan, Eileen. "Equal Rights Amendment Is Approved by Congress." *New York Times,* March 23, 1972. Proquest Historical Newspapers, http://www.nytimes.com/learning /general/onthisday/big/0322.html.

Stout, David. "Supreme Court Upholds Voter Identification Law in Indiana," *New York Times*, April 29, 2008, http://www .nytimes.com/2008/04/29/washington/28cnd-scotus.html ?_r=0.

Thornbrough, Emma. *Indiana Blacks in the Twentieth Century.* Bloomington: Indiana University Press, 2000.

Thornton, William Wheeler. *The Municipal Law of Indiana, including the General School Law, General Election Law, Tax Law, and All Other Statutes of the State Appertaining to Cities and Towns, with Notes of Decisions and a Complete List of Forms.* Cincinnati: W. H. Anderson and Co., 1891.

Title IX, Education Amendments of 1972. United States Department of Labor, Office of the Assistant Secretary for Administration and Management, http://www.dol.gov /oasam/regs/statutes/titleix.htm.

United States Congress. *Congressional Record: Proceedings and Debates of the Congress.* Vol. 118, no. 4. Washington, DC: U.S. Government Printing Office, 1972.

United States of America v. *Board of School Commissioners of the City of Indianapolis, Indiana, et al.*, 332 F. Supp, 655 (1971), District Court, S.D. Indiana. Court Listener, https://www .courtlistener.com/insd/9jWR/united-states-v-board-of -sch-comrs-indianapolis-in/.

Walsh, Justin E. *The Centennial History of the Indiana General Assembly, 1816–1978.* Indianapolis: Indiana Historical Bureau, 1987.

Whitcover, Jules. *85 Days: The Last Campaign of Robert Kennedy.* New York: Quill, 1988.

Whitson, Brian. "Q&A with [Davison M.] Douglas: Northern Segregation." *News,* December 13, 2005. College of William and Mary, Office of University Relations, http://web.wm.edu /news/archive/index.php?id=5438.

"Women in State Legislatures: 2013 Legislative Session." National Conference of State Legislatures, http://www.ncsl.org /legislators-staff/legislators/womens-legislative-network /women-in-state-legislatures-for-2013.aspx.

Essential Questions

1 Why was Indiana slow to embrace and implement laws promoting racial equality? Give an example of the struggle to secure civil rights for African-American Hoosiers.*

2 How did Robert F. Kennedy help to diffuse tension in Indiana the night of the assassination of Dr. Martin Luther King Jr.?

3 How was Robert F. Kennedy able to win the 1968 Democratic primary election in Indiana?

4 Why were the 1949 Indiana School Desegregation Act and the 1954 *Brown v. Board of Education* U.S. Supreme Court decision unsuccessful in producing integrated schools in Indiana?*

5 What solution to school segregation did Judge S. Hugh Dillin put forth in a 1972 decision against the Indianapolis School Board? How successful was his plan and why?

6 What is the Equal Rights Amendment? When was it first proposed to the U.S. Congress?*

7 For what reasons did some people oppose the ERA?*

8 When did Indiana ratify the ERA? Did it then become an amendment to the U.S. Constitution? Why or why not?*

9 What did Title IX of the Education Amendment of 1972 do? What Hoosier politician championed this provision?

10 What is redistricting and why is it necessary?

11 What is gerrymandering; who uses it; and why?

12 How do lobbyists participate in the political process?*

13 Why was the 2005 Indiana Voter ID law controversial?

14 As a citizen, what responsibilities do you have to be involved in the political process?

See student activities related to this question.

Hoosiers and the Promise of America

Chapter 11 focuses on the struggles to make the promise of democracy a reality for all Hoosiers. In particular, we read about female Hoosiers and African Americans' struggles to secure civil rights and equal protection under the law. The following Activities provide insight into the challenges these groups faced as they attempted and continue to attempt to secure the full benefits of democracy.

Activity 1: The Equal Rights Amendment

Introduction: The photograph of the NOW rally in Indianapolis in Section 11.3 was taken around 1970 as a chapter of the National Organization for Women (NOW) rallied in Indianapolis in support of equality for women and to combat discrimination against women. The organization supported passage of the Equal Rights Amendment, which was originally drafted in 1923 by Alice Paul.

▶ The text of the proposed amendment reads as follows:

Section 1: *Equality of rights under the law shall not be denied or abridged by the United States or by any state on account of sex.*

Section 2: *The Congress shall have the power to enforce, by appropriate legislation, the provision of this article.*

Section 3: *This amendment shall take effect two years after the date of ratification.*

1 Restate the first section of the proposed amendment in everyday language.

2 When this photograph was taken, approximately fifty years had passed since the ERA was first proposed. However, it had not yet been ratified by enough states to pass. How are the women in the photo exercising their rights as U.S. citizens by promoting the passage of the ERA?

3 In what other ways might these NOW members have exercised their rights as citizens to promote Indiana's ratification of the ERA?

4 Where in the U.S. Constitution are the rights of citizens stated and guaranteed?

► In 1977 Indiana became the thirty-fifth state to ratify the ERA. A proposed amendment must be ratified by thirty-eight states to be added to the U.S. Constitution. To date, no additional states have ratified the amendment, and advocates continue to fight for its passage.

1 Based on your opinion of the status of equal rights for women in America, do you think that the Equal Rights Amendment is necessary today? Why or why not?

2 Imagine that you are rallying for or against the ERA. What would your protest sign say? Design a protest sign advocating for your position.

Activity 2: The National Association for the Advancement of Colored People (NAACP)

Introduction: The NAACP was founded in 1909 and pursues the following mission:

The mission of the National Association for the Advancement of Colored People is to ensure the political, educational, social, and economic equality of rights of all persons and to eliminate race-based discrimination.

The NAACP uses the avenues provided by the democratic process to achieve its mission. Its members advocate for legislation that protects the civil rights of African Americans; and they also work within the justice system to make sure that African Americans receive equal protection under the law.

► Willard B. Ransom was very active in the Civil Rights movement in Indianapolis. Ransom graduated from Crispus Attucks High School in 1932, Talladaga College in 1936, and Harvard Law School in 1939. He began practicing law the same year he graduated from Harvard. Ransom became active in the Indiana state chapter of the NAACP and ultimately served as the state chair of the organization for five terms. Ransom fought for civil rights for black Hoosiers in a number

of ways, from representing them in court to lobbying legislators to organizing protests. Examine Ransom's Lobbyist certificate in 11.4 and discuss answers for the following questions with your class:

1 Look up the definition of the term "lobbyist." What does a lobbyist do?

2 On behalf of what organization was Ransom lobbying?

3 How might Ransom have been particularly well-suited to work with the NAACP?

4 What subject matters does the certificate list as being of concern to Ransom?

5 What rights, guaranteed by the U.S. Constitution allow lobbyists to try to influence lawmakers?

► The NAACP and other groups also work among the citizenry at large. They hold voter registration drives to help African Americans and other minority groups, the elderly, and the poor exercise their right to vote. The NAACP also initiates legal suits when voting rights are denied to minorities. Examine the photograph titled "Voter Registration Campaign" and, with your class, discuss the following questions:

1 Explain how the right to vote can also be seen as a responsibility.

2 All Americans are indebted to the struggles of our forebears that have resulted in us having the right to vote. Whether that privilege was gained as a result of the American Revolution; the Fifteenth Amendment to the U.S. Constitution, which gave African American men the right to vote; the Nineteenth Amendment, which gave women the right to vote; or the Voting Rights Act of 1965, which prohibits voting discrimination, we are only able to reap the promise of democracy through the sacrifice of others. How might you express your appreciation for those sacrifices?

Activity 3: Democracy and the Issue of Same-Sex Marriage

Introduction: Many would say that the struggle for equal rights and equal protections for all is far from over. One controversial issue today is that of gay marriage. A resolution was under consideration by the Indiana legislature in 2014 proposing an amendment to the Indiana State Constitution that would read:

Only marriage between one man and one woman shall be valid or recognized as a marriage in Indiana.

▶ With your class, consider the following questions about the proposed amendment to the Indiana State Constitution as they relate to the context of this chapter:

1 Using the historical examples discussed in this chapter, make an argument about whether or not a ban on same sex marriage would infringe upon civil rights guaranteed by the Indiana and U.S. constitutions.

2 Should the struggle for gay marriage be considered on par with previous struggles for equal rights, such as the Women's Movement and the Civil Rights Movement? Explain your reasoning.

3 Should this issue be determined by the state legislature or should it come to the electorate for a popular vote? Defend your position.

4 How can you use your rights as a citizen to promote your view?

Activity References

"The Equal Rights Amendment: Unfinished Business for the Constitution," http://www.equalrightsamendment.org.

House Joint Resolution 3, Indiana General Assembly, 2014 Session, http://iga.in.gov/legislative/2014/resolutions /house/joint/3#.

"Our Mission." NAACP, http://www.naacp.org/pages /our-mission.

CONCLUSION
Hoosiers in Our Time

We are living in the swiftest moving and most restless time the world has known.

— *Booth Tarkington,* The World Does Move *(1928)*

The problem with Tarkington's statement above is that nearly every generation has believed it was living in the "swiftest moving and most restless time the world has known." The stories in this book are often unsettling and full of rapid change, from the Battle of Tippecanoe to labor unions to woman's suffrage to Crispus Attucks basketball. Everything changes. And that's what makes history so interesting. Even if we can't always see it, change is all around us.

For example, few Hoosiers today eat the way pioneers did: hunting game, harvesting corn, and cooking in front of an open fireplace. Our meals today include bagels, tuna, avocados, and dozens of other foods that were unknown when Indiana became a state in 1816. And yet, traditions of the past endure, even in food. Pork tenderloin sandwiches remain a Hoosier favorite, especially in the many small-town cafés where the fried, breaded pork extends far beyond the bun. Likewise, chicken and noodles, biscuits and gravy, persimmon pudding, and sugar cream pie remain favorites of many in the state.

There have always been Hoosiers who eagerly sought change: pioneers clearing forests to create farmland, women claiming the right to vote, inventors tinkering with horseless carriages, education reformers consolidating schools, African Americans seeking a hotel room in a segregated town, scientists looking for the next big cure for an ominous disease. Every generation has had innovators pushing to knock down the boundaries. Madam C. J. Walker pushed against restrictions of race and gender. Eugene V. Debs questioned Americans' beliefs about capitalism and the social classes it engenders. Alfred Kinsey pioneered scientific research on sexuality.

Hoosiers have resisted change, too. During the 1980s some Hoosiers found it difficult to allow Ryan White, a teenager diagnosed with AIDS, to stay in school despite his doctors' assurances that he posed no risk to his classmates. In the late twentieth and early twenty-first centuries some waited for the return of 1950s-type factory jobs instead of training for new technologies. Some lamented rule changes in high school sports that made another Milan basketball miracle impossible. Some hesitated to accept new minority groups such as Hispanics and Muslims, relegating these immigrants to the sidelines of Hoosier life. "We

Canoe Trip

Families enjoy a canoe trip along the Blue River in O'Bannon Woods State Park in southern Indiana. Efforts to preserve the state's natural spaces have led to the creation of state parks, nature preserves, and fish and wildlife areas. From a source of sustenance to a source of enjoyment for Hoosiers, Indiana's natural resources continue to shape its history as they are shaped by its people.

Aerial View of Wabash, Indiana

At one time, residents of the town of Wabash depended on the Wabash River for transportation. Later roads, canals, and railroads connected it to other places. Today, major highways pass near the town. The landscape has also changed as the town and surrounding farms expanded.

were peripheral," Muslim Mohja Kahf stated in 2007, describing the experience of growing up in Indiana.

Many Hoosiers were long reluctant to restrict smoking in public places or to mandate healthier school cafeteria menus because of deep attachments to individual freedom. Hoosiers were hesitant also to employ government power to regulate pollution of water, air, and soil—even as emissions from burning coal to make electricity caused growing environmental concerns.

An early environmental step forward came with creation in 1916 of one of the nation's best state park systems. A century later new efforts to protect natural places included the creation of Goose Pond Fish and Wildlife Area in Greene County, one of the na-

tion's finest wetlands. The Bicentennial Nature Trust has provided permanent protection for thousands of acres of land. The Indiana Nature Conservancy, the Indiana Department of Natural Resources, and many individuals and groups have helped Hoosiers rise to a new awareness of land and water. Pioneer traditions of using up and throwing away seem less and less reasonable, and so Hoosiers are searching for sustainability in energy sources and in their environment.

Hoosiers have responded to change in many positive ways. Their cornfields have produced some of the greatest harvests on Earth, while their manufacturers have been among the world's most productive. Their basketball teams are legendary. Hoosiers have also responded at times in less positive ways. Some fought against the creation of public schools in favor of local control; some argued that white men were the only people who should be able to vote; and some saw the Ku Klux Klan as a much-needed Christian reform movement.

Hoosiers before our time made hard choices in a world of swift change. In this way earlier generations were no different from ours. To see the fullness of their lives, to imagine that they lived in full color, with blue skies and dark tornadoes and with sounds and smells all around them—this is the challenge and wonder of glimpsing the past. For instance, we might even imagine that teenagers before our time had sexual urges—because they really were not much different than we are today.

Except in a few museums, pioneer log cabins and spinning wheels have faded away. So, too, did canals and interurbans. James Whitcomb Riley's poetry eventually seemed less relevant to many, as did T. C. Steele's landscape paintings, and the state song, "On the Banks of the Wabash." Such landmarks of the past persist in tradition, but they cannot stop the winds of change.

Indiana has a rich past, always changing, always mixing with traditions. Hoosiers are blessed to be able to listen to voices that came before our day and to live in dialogues of past, present, and future. Indiana's history is part of the American story—a story that Hoosiers can claim as their own.

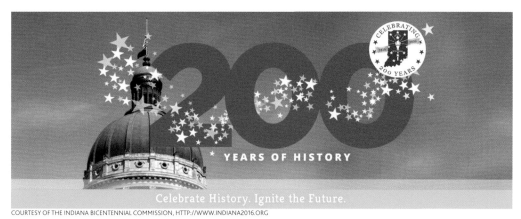

COURTESY OF THE INDIANA BICENTENNIAL COMMISSION, HTTP://WWW.INDIANA2016.ORG

Indiana Bicentennial Logo

This logo commemorates the two-hundredth anniversary of the State of Indiana in 2016. A time of celebration, the bicentennial is also a time for Hoosiers to reflect on their past and to look forward to an always changing future.

GLOSSARY

Agrarian: A social system or state with farming as its economic and cultural foundation.

Aide-de-camp: An assistant to a higher ranking officer in the military.

Aqueduct: A structure that is capable of carrying a large volume of running water, sometimes used to carry a canal over a river or hollow.

Arsenal: A place where weapons are stored.

Austerity: An extreme economic practice that reduces government spending.

Cede: To give up or transfer ownership of something, such as land, generally by treaty.

Confederation: An alliance between groups in which each party promises to support the others.

Confluence: A place where two rivers or streams come together.

Contravene: To go against or oppose something.

Culvert: A drain or pipe that redirects water under roads or railroads.

Embargo: A government's order prohibiting the shipment of goods to specific places, such as the Arab oil embargo of 1973–74, in which Arab oil suppliers cut off shipments to the United States.

Enclave: An area largely inhabited by people of similar ethnic, social, and/or cultural backgrounds within a larger area of people of a different background, for example, an ethnic section of an American city, such as Chinatown in San Francisco, California.

Endowment: The part of an institution's income that is invested and restricted so that only the interest on the money may be spent and not the principal, or initial investment.

Exodus: A mass emigration.

Federalism: A government organization in which power is distributed between the federal, or central, government and the states.

Flatboat: A flat-bottomed boat with square ends that is generally used in shallow waters to transport bulky cargo.

Global economy: Worldwide economic activity between countries.

Globalization: The spread of increasing connectivity between the nations of the world, especially regarding the economy.

Gratis: Free or without charge.

Hod carriers: Laborers who carry supplies, such as bricks or plaster, to construction workers.

Homogeneity: When a majority of the residents of a state or region share the same ethnic, racial, and religious backgrounds.

Hydrophobia: A fear of water that is often symptomatic of rabies.

Jigger: A unit of measure for mixing drinks that holds one to two ounces of liquid.

Keelboat: A shallow riverboat that is generally rowed or towed in order to transport cargo, especially when traveling upriver.

Labor union: Organizations formed by employees to collectively negotiate their pay, hours, and benefits with a company or institution's owners or managers.

Lock: An enclosure in a canal with gates at either end used to raise or lower boats as they pass through each level.

Lynching: To hang a person by mob action without legal authority.

Magnate: A person who has great influence and power in a specific economic field, such as steel or oil production.

Monopoly: Exclusive control by one or a few owners of a good or service in a particular area that results in a higher price than if the supplier was in competition with another company.

Ordnance: A branch of the army tasked with acquiring, distributing, and storing military supplies.

Popery: A derogatory term for Roman Catholicism derived from the fact that the Pope heads the church.

Preliterate: A society that does not use writing to record its history and stories.

Racially restrictive covenant: A contractual agreement in a neighborhood that makes it impossible for certain ethnic groups to buy houses within it.

Reconnaissance: Exploring and reporting on enemy territory for the military.

River-centric: A society that lives and travels along rivers.

Salient: A prominent or most notable feature of something.

Sedition: An act or speech that encourages people to rebel against a legal authority.

Sharecropper: A farmer who does not own land but who is a tenant given credit to buy seeds, tools, and housing and who receives a share of the value of the harvested produce.

Soldering: Melting a metal or metallic alloy to join two metallic surfaces.

Spillway: A passage for surplus water from a dam or mill.

Status quo: A Latin term used to indicate what the current situation or condition is.

Stenographer: A person who transcribes what was said, for instance, in a courtroom, often using shorthand.

Stump speech: A speech given by a political candidate on the campaign trail.

Symposium: A formal meeting in which experts discuss a topic.

Syncopated: In music, a rhythm in which the accent falls on the weaker beat in a measure.

Tenement: An apartment building, usually in a city, that only meets the minimum standards of cleanliness, safety, and comfort.

Unglaciated: A region, such as the southern portion of Indiana, that has not been covered by a glacier.

Vigilantism: The methods used by vigilantes, who are people that take the law into their own hands to stop crime and are often characterized by militancy and/or bigotry.

Zealous: Characteristic of someone who believes passionately in a cause.

INDEX

Cobb, Irvin S., 141, 198

Coffin, Catharine White, 91–92

Coffin, Levi, 91–93; house museum, 93

Cold Storage Law (1911), 181

Colfax, Schuyler, 77, 85, 168

Colonization, 85, 94

Columbus, 212, 260, *262*, 265

Committee on Mental Defectives, 181

Common Cause, 311

Compromise of 1850, pp. 86, 94

Congress of Racial Equality, 303

Conn Company, 260

Conner, Elizabeth Chapman, 51

Conner, James, 49

Conner, John, 49

Conner, Margaret, 49

Conner, Richard, 49

Conner, William, 21, 31, *49–52*, 254; house, *50*

Conner Prairie Interactive History Park, 50, 52, 254

Connersville, 70, 114, 154

"Constitution Elm," *44*

Continental Steel, 281

Converse All Star shoes, 212

Cook, Bill, 218

Cook, Carl, 218

Cook, Gayle, 218

Cook Group, 218

Copperheads, 89

Cord, Errett Lobban, 154

Corn, 5, 10, 60, 216, 273, *275*

Corydon, 43, 44, 89, 241, 242

Costello, Lou, 217

Cotton Club, 221

Court of Common Pleas, 41

Cowie, Jefferson, 280

Cox, Jacob, 49

Crane, Mary, *241*

Crater, Battle of the (Petersburg, VA), 99, 100, 101, 102

Crawfordsville, 59, 72, 104, 105, 122, 214, 261; high school, 208

Crawfordsville Oak Hill Cemetery, 104

"Creative destruction," 277, 278

Crispus Attucks High School, 221, 290, 312; basketball team, *302*

Crosby, Bing, 217

Crossroads of America, 9, 265

Crowe, Ray, 301

Crown Hill Cemetery, 176, 254

Crownland Cemetery, 52

Cunningham Memorial Library, 241

Curtis, Glenn, 209

D. H. Burnham and Company, 122

Dalton, Davis, 268

Daniels, Mitch, 270

Danville, 122

Darby, William, 21

Das Deutsche Haus. See Athenaeum

Daughters of the American Revolution (DAR), 176, 177

Davis, Jefferson, 95

Deaf Man's Village, *17–18*, 19, 20

Dean, James, *267–68*

DeBaptiste, George, 90

Debs, Eugene V., 132, 134–35, 200; foundation, 135

Declaration of Independence, 45, 75, 172

Delaware County Airport, 294

Delaware Indians, 9, 10, 11, 14, 17, 20, 40, 47, 49, 50

Delco Remy, 154

Democratic National Committee, 217, 297

Democratic Party, 76, 87, 88, 89, 94, 97, 104, 167, 168, 169, 171, 175, 185, 204, 217, 231, 234, 237, 239, 243, 293, 297, 308, 311, 313

Dennis, Philip, 33

Denny, Ebenezer, 40

DePauw University, 183

Dependent and Disability Pension Act (1890), 175

Desegregation, 299–305

Diabetes, 251–52, 253

Diamond Chain Company, *135*

Dillin, S. Hugh, 303

Dillinger, John, 221

Dimmick, Mary Lord. *See* Harrison, Mary Lord Dimmick

Discrimination, 289–91

Diseases: flu, 12; measles, 7; milk sickness, 62; scarlet fever, 189; smallpox, 7, 12; tuberculosis, 189

Dixie Flyer, *156*

Dolwick, William A., 245

Dorsey, Azel, 63

Douglas, Jesse C., 25

Douglas, John, 297

Douglass, Frederick, 86, 92

Dow AgroSciences, 274

Dreiser, Theodore, 1, 198

Dresser, Paul, 123

Drive-ins, 266, *267*

Dru, Pierre le, 16

Drug Sample Law (1907), 181

Dublin, 78

Dubois County, 144

Dunkirk, 266

"Dusty Rag" (song), 219

DuValle, Reggie, 221

Dyer, Willis B., *222*

Dylan, Bob, 154

Earlham College, 254

East Chicago, 118, 131, 146, 149, 158, 231, 241, 303

East Chicago Manufacturers Association, 231

East of Eden, 268

Eddy, Catherine. *See* Beveridge, Catherine Eddy

Education, 71–74, 77, 149, 262, 269–72, 299–305, 307; Amendment of 1972, pp. 309, 310; classroom, *263*

Eisenhower, Dwight D., 308

Elanco, 273

Electoral College, 48, 167, 175

Eleventh Indiana Infantry Regiment, 104

Eli Lilly and Company, 50, 129, 251–53; production line, *252*

Elkhart, 105, 265, 303

Elston, Susan. *See* Wallace, Susan Elston

Emancipation Proclamation, 89, 98

Emerson School, *160*

Greensboro, 103

Greensburg, 281

Greenville, Treaty of, 11, 12

Grigsby, Aaron, 64

Grigsby, Sarah Lincoln, 64

Grouseland, 16, 46, 47, 297

Gruelle, Richard, 199

Gubbins, Joan, 309

Guide Lamp, 154, 156

Gunthorp Farms, 275

Halberstam, David, 208

Halleck, Charles, 239

Hamilton, Henry, 36–37, 38

Hamilton, Tom, 22

Hamilton County, 50, 51, 52, 59, 267

Hammond, 158, 241, 246, 248, 291

Hanford, Ben, *135*

Hanks, Nancy. *See* Lincoln, Nancy Hanks

Hardee Hat, *106*

Harding, Warren G., 159

Harmar, Josiah, 40

Harmonists, 73

Harpers Ferry (VA), 87

Harrison, Anna Symmes, 46, 48

Harrison, Benjamin (father of William Henry), 45

Harrison, Benjamin (grandson of William Henry), 48, *166*, 168, *172*, 175–76; election day, *174*; home, *173*

Harrison, Caroline Scott, 172, 175, *176–77*

Harrison, Elizabeth, 176

Harrison, Mary, 172

Harrison, Mary Lord Dimmick, 176

Harrison, Russell, 172

Harrison, William Henry, 15, 16, 33, 35, 43, 44, *45*–48, 49, 166, 167, 172, 175, 254, 297

Harrison County, 41; state forest, 242

Harroun, Ray, 152, 155

Hartford City, 3

Harvey, Sarah, 1

Hatcher, Richard G., 297, *304*, 305

Hawkins, Jeff, *276*

Hawkins Family Farm, 276

Haynes, Elwood, 152, 153

Haynes Automobile Company, 152

Haynes–Apperson Company, 152

Health reform, 178–82

"Heart and Soul" (sheet music), *221*

Hemingray Glass Company, 134

Hendricks, Thomas A., 168

Hendricks County, 88

Hennepin, Louis, 9

Henry, Patrick, 38

Henry County, 78, 103

Herschell, William, 171, 204

Hiatt, Fred B., 122

Hine, Lewis, 134

Holbert, Jim, 275

Hole-in-the-Wall (club), 221

Holliday, Samuel, 32

Holmes–Shake Bill (1927), 181

Honda, 281

"Hoosher's Nest, The" (poem), 1

Hoosier Cabinet, *130*

Hoosier Democratic Club (Two Percent Club), 239

Hoosier Dome, 280, *281*

"Hoosier Hitler," 239

"Hoosier Hop" (sheet music), *214*

Hoosier Hysteria, 200, 208–13

Hoosier Manufacturing Company, 129, 130

"Hoosier Rag" (song), 219

Hoosier Store, *2*

Hoosiers, 211, 301

Hoosier's Nest, The (painting), *61*

Housing reform, 188–89, 191

Hovde, Frederick L., 270

Hovey, Alvin P., 183

Howard County, 152

Hubbard, Kin, 154, 214

Hudson Farms, *261*

Huggart Settlement, 59

Humphrey, Hubert H., 293, 297

Huntington, 68, 160

Hurty, Ann Irene, 179

Hurty, Ethel Johnstone, 179

Hurty, John Newell, *178*–79, 181–82

Hurty, Josiah, 179

Hydrophobia Law (1911), 181

Ice Age, 5

Iglehart, Asa, 188

Iletin, 253

Immigrants: 131, 133, 141–51, 203; Canadian, 142; Chinese, 181; Croatian, 146; eastern European, 181; German, 61, 87, 89, 141, 142, 144, 145, 146, 147, 198, 199–200; Greek, 142, 159; Hungarian, 146, 147; Irish, 61, 68, 141, 142, 144, 146; Italians, 142; Jewish, 133; Lithuanian, 146; Mexican, 159, 160, *161*, 181, 229, 231, 249, 322; Muslim, 322; Polish, 142, 146, 159; Russian, 147; Slovakian, 146

Indentured servants, 41, 44, 46

Indian Removal Act, 21

"Indiana" (poem), vii

Indiana: A Guide to the Hoosier State, 240–41

Indiana: A Hoosier History, 243

Indiana Asbury University, 183

Indiana Avenue, 221–22

Indiana Bar Association, 207

Indiana Basketball Hall of Fame, 208, 301

Indiana Bicentennial Logo, *325*

Indiana Capitol. *See* Indiana Statehouse

Indiana Colonization Society, 85

Indiana Conference of Charities and Correction, 189

Indiana Constitution (1816), 35, 44, 61, 71, 72, 75, 85, 269, 289; convention, 44

Indiana Constitution (1851), 61, 70, 74, 75–78, 291, 307, 311; Article VIII, 269; Article XIII, 85, 94, 289; convention, 75–76, 94

Indiana Corn Growers Association, 124

Indiana Department of Conservation, 241, 243, 245

Indiana Department of Natural Resources, 324

Indiana Department of Public Welfare, 235

Indiana Department of Statistics, 132

Indiana Dunes State Park, 243

Indiana Farm Bureau, 124, 313

Indiana Farm—Sunday Afternoon (mural), 245